COLD WAR

Jeremy Isaacs and Taylor Downing

COLD

WAR

AN ILLUSTRATED HISTORY, 1945–1991

LITTLE, BROWN AND COMPANY Boston New York Toronto London

First Edition

LIBRARY OF CONGRESS CATALOGING-IN-PUBLICATION DATA

Isaacs, Jeremy.
    Cold War: an illustrated history, 1945–1991/Jeremy Isaacs and Taylor Downing.
      p.   cm.
    ISBN 0-316-43953-3
    1. Cold War. 2. World politics — 1945– I. Downing, Taylor II. Title.
D843.I77 1998
909.82'5 — dc21   97-48724

10 9 8 7 6 5 4 3 2 1

Q-HAW

Book design by Julia Sedykh

Published simultaneously in Canada by Little, Brown & Company (Canada) Limited
Printed in the United States of America

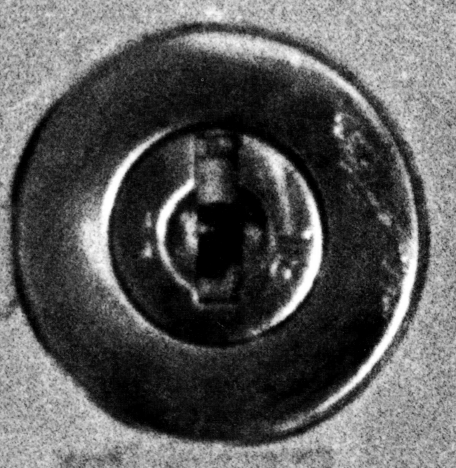

WAR

PEACE

For colleagues-in-arms

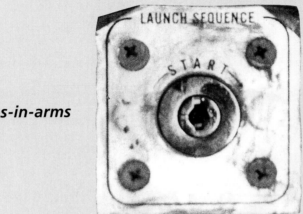

Contents

PHASE 1   PHASE 2   PHASE 3   PHASE 4

This book tells the central story of our times. It is aimed at the reader with an interest in contemporary history and in the series of events that shaped the second half of the twentieth century: the confrontation — military, economic, ideological — between two great power blocs, the United States and the Soviet Union, that began at the close of the Second World War and ended with the dissolution of the USSR. Where possible, each chapter begins roughly at the time the previous chapter ends; the story has a beginning, a middle, and an ending.

The United States and the Soviet Union were major protagonists, but almost every nation in the world was affected in some way, as were all who lived through those years. The book follows the Cold War's impact on every continent, on Asia, the Middle East, Africa, and the Americas. It describes not just a geopolitical conflict but everyday changes that occurred, or failed to occur, in Soviet and in American society in that period. We show not only how key strategic decisions were made, but their impact on ordinary lives, West and East. The Cold War was more than an arms race. It touched many aspects of life — ideology and science, culture and sport. It influenced the images we saw, the songs we sang, and the very language we used for nearly half a century. It helped fix the standard of living in East and West.

In the book we recount in detail crises — in Berlin, Budapest, Havana, Prague, and Saigon — that brought us, more than once, to the brink of nuclear war. Each side had the capacity to destroy the other, and every living thing on the planet. At crisis after crisis parents worried their families might not live to see another day. Yet, as the story ends, humanity has survived.

This book had its origins in a television series, also called *Cold War,* commissioned by Ted Turner of CNN fame, now vice chairman of Time Warner Inc. In August 1994, in St. Petersburg, Russia, during the Goodwill Games, Ted Turner told his staff they should mark the end of the Cold War by telling its story. In November 1994, Pat Mitchell, then president of Turner Original Productions, invited Jeremy Isaacs to undertake the project. After a visit to Atlanta, Isaacs assembled historians, journalists, and television documentary makers to discuss and define how the subject could be made into television. Turner commissioned us to go ahead.

This book owes more than we can say to everyone involved in making the television series. First of all, we thank Ted Turner, who not only envisaged the documentary but — what is rare these days — ensured we had the budget to implement his vision. We hope we have done justice to it. We thank also Pat Mitchell, now president of CNN Productions, Time Inc. Television, an inspiring guide throughout. In particular we warmly acknowledge the role of Martin Smith, series producer, whose commitment and professionalism brought the work in on time and on budget. Martin Smith is that rare bird, an unassuming leader. But his contribution made all else possible.

For the television documentary five hundred interviews were conducted with eyewitnesses and participants; their testimony has informed this book. These included world leaders Castro, Gorbachev, Bush; those who served them, McNamara, Westmoreland, Kissinger, Shevardnadze; and men and women of every continent whose lives were affected, for good and ill, by the Cold War. For use on screen, 8,500 film stories were researched in the world's archives. Whether tracking witnesses or trawling archives, the researchers played a vital role in the documentary, and, with writers and producers for each episode, made our scope in writing ampler.

We have benefited enormously from the comments of three principal historical advisers to the series: John Lewis Gaddis, Robert Lovett Professor of Military and Naval History at Yale University, New Haven, Connecticut; Lawrence Freedman, head of the Department of War Studies at King's College, London; and Vladislav Zubok, National Security Archive, Washington, DC. Each scrutinized every frame and read every syllable of the text of the series. John Gaddis has, in addition, most kindly found time to read this book in manuscript.

We have found invaluable the bulletins published by the Woodrow Wilson International Center for Scholars, Washington, DC, produced by the Cold War International History Project, first under James G. Hershberg — an early inspiration — and now Christian Ostermann. The bulletins present crucial documents of Cold War history, extracted from the archives of the East, translated and published in the West. They contain the latest available knowledge on a range of Cold War issues. Their work continues.

Thomas Blanton, Vlad Zubok, and Bill Burr, at the National Security Archive, provided fact-filled briefing books from their extensive database which we found extremely useful, and stimulating comment besides. Alexander Tchoubarian, at the Moscow Institute for Universal History, gave the series helpful guidance. In every case, the spirit in which advice was given was generous and encouraging.

Jerome Kuehl made many detailed criticisms (not always followed) and contributed some additional matter, in particular an essay on literature in the Cold War. Philip French, distinguished film critic of the *Observer,* London, contributed an essay on Cold War movies. We are grateful to both. And we thank Isobel Hinshelwood, paragon of fact-checkers, for keeping us, and our text, in due order.

We thank Bill Phillips, editor in chief at Little, Brown in New York, for wise words; and, in London, Sally Gaminara, publishing director of Bantam Press, and Ursula Mackenzie, hardcover publisher at Transworld Publishing, for guidance and support. Picture researchers Celia Dearing and Sheila Corr, of Transworld, found the illustrations that bring to the book a dimension that image and interview gave the television series. In the Boston offices of Little, Brown, Julia Sedykh, design manager, laid out these pages to eye-catching effect, and Peggy Leith Anderson, developmental editor, pulled all together in the end. We salute them.

Walton Rawls, in Atlanta, has edited our text with skill and patience. Gratefully, we acknowledge his crucial contribution. Any errors are our own.

Federal Express, who shipped pages expeditiously back and forth between Atlanta, Boston, New York, and London, should not go unrecognized. We thank Charles Walker at Peters, Fraser, Dunlop for guarding our interest.

Gillian Widdicombe and Anne Fleming have put up with long hours of our absence at word processor and text. We hope they think it was worth it.

JEREMY ISAACS
TAYLOR DOWNING
London, April 1998

Torgau, 1945

Comrades-in-arms. Soviet soldiers had fought their way westward into Hitler's Reich; American and Allied soldiers had fought eastward. They finally met at Torgau on the Elbe on 25 April. The first joyous meetings were followed, two days later, by a repeat performance for the cameras. Hitler had brought the United States and Soviet Union face to face in the heart of Europe.

Comrades
1917–1945

6 June 1944. Allied troops land in Normandy, opening a long-awaited second front in Europe, where since 1941 the Russians had been fighting Hitler alone. Of all the Germans who saw combat, two-thirds of them fought on the Eastern Front.

April 1945

The noose was tightening around Berlin, the capital of Hitler's so-called Thousand Year Reich. For three ferocious years the Red Army had advanced on that city like a steamroller crushing everything in its path. The Soviets had fought their way fifteen hundred miles from Stalingrad to Berlin and now were prepared for the final assault. From the beaches of Normandy, American and British armies had battled across northern Europe, also reaching the heart of Hitler's Reich. The war in Europe was near its end.

The Wehrmacht was disintegrating. Most German soldiers wanted to surrender to the Americans — fearing the revenge Russian soldiers might take for German atrocities in the Soviet Union. German civilians, too, welcomed the Americans. The men of the Sixty-ninth Division, US First Army, had advanced 180 miles in seven days in their race across central Germany. When they reached the Mulde River, about fifteen miles east of Leipzig, they halted to await orders. The question everyone asked was, "Where are the Russians?"

On 25 April, American patrols were ordered forward to reconnoitre up to the Elbe River. These veteran troopers were not eager to take any more risks; they'd got this far and wanted to survive the war. At about 11:30 that morning one patrol made contact with Red Army units near Strehla on the Elbe. Firing green flares, to signal "friends," the patrol crossed a pontoon bridge to the other side, where soldiers of both armies hugged and kissed. In vodka they toasted Stalin first, then Truman, then Churchill. Someone produced a concertina and started to play. Among the Russian soldiers were women, both snipers and officers, who danced with the Americans. The young Americans and Russians solemnly swore an oath; they would do everything in their power to extend peace and friendship between their two nations.

On 27 April advance units of the US Army and the Red Army met again on the Elbe, this time in the bigger town of Torgau. Photographers from both sides were present to capture this moment of happiness and unity between the youth of the two nations, comrades-in-arms. Who present could have imagined then that their two countries would spend the next half century icily staring at each other across the no-man's-land of the Cold War?

Twilight of the Tsars

In the nineteenth century tsarist Russia had sought to expand through Poland into Central Europe and into the Levant; it sought access through the Dardanelles to the Mediterranean. On its southern borders, Russia probed at Persia and, through the annexation of large stretches of Central Asia, extended its empire almost to the borders of India.

Asiatic Russia, a vast landmass of frozen snow and tundra, reached to the Pacific and Bering Strait. Across it, some forty miles away, Alaska was discovered in 1741 by a Russian expedition that brought back the otter skins that launched numerous fur trade settlements in the Aleutians and along North America's Pacific coast. When American pioneers, moving steadily west, reached California, they found Russians as far south as Fort Ross, sixty miles north of San Francisco. In 1867 Secretary of State William Seward was able to buy Alaska from the tsar when fur profits seriously declined. No significant conflict marred relations between these two powerful neighbours, who occupied so much of the world's landmass. Russia was confined within its borders, and the United States did not look beyond its own hemisphere. Neither was yet a world power. But each would be, and in 1917 their geopolitical relationship would become envenomed by ideology.

In March 1917, after three years of enduring the enormous strain of fielding a huge, and flagging, army in the First World War, the Russian people rose up against the absolutist dynasty that had ruled them for three centuries and forced Tsar Nicholas II to abdicate, installing a provisional government in his place. Social upheaval swept Russia. A growing band of radical socialist revolutionaries, known as Bolsheviks, had spent years exploiting the discontents of workers and peasants. Their leader, Vladimir Ilyich Lenin, a brilliant theorist and strategist, directed their efforts during periodic exiles through his inflammatory writings. On the night of 6 November 1917 (24 October by the Old Style calendar — hence the term October Revolution) a number of Lenin's Bolshevik supporters took control of the Winter Palace, the seat of the provisional government, and seized power. Lenin proclaimed: "We shall now proceed to the construction of the socialist order." He and the other ideologists of this revolution were convinced that history was on their side, that capitalism was on the brink of collapse, and that progress towards world revolution was inevitable.

Few expected the Bolshevik regime to survive; it still had to deal with all the social, economic, and political problems its predecessor had faced. To concentrate on internal issues, the revolutionary government abandoned the European war effort in late November and signed a peace treaty with Germany in March 1918, despite onerous terms and a massive loss of territory. The own-

They were still using horse-drawn wagons, cavalry pieces, horse-drawn artillery. . . . We couldn't imagine how they could have advanced against the might of the Germans with such primitive weaponry. . . . The soldiers were on horseback. It was like the medieval times meeting the American times.

— Pfc. Jim Kane,
on meeting the Russians at the Elbe River, April 1945

ership of land that had been seized by Russian peasants was legitimized, private trade was forbidden, and all industry was nationalized. Central planning was instituted. A secret police force, the Cheka, was formed to ensure total obedience to the new regime; Lenin's government would be as authoritarian as that of the tsars — a "proletarian dictatorship." In protest, various nationalists and counter-revolutionaries known as "White" Russians led an armed uprising against the Bolsheviks, who organized a "Red" army under Leon Trotsky. A bitter civil war between Whites and Reds erupted.

The Western powers looked with horror at the Bolshevik Revolution. Winston Churchill, British secretary of state for war, wrote that "civilisation is being completely extinguished over gigantic areas, while Bolsheviks hop and caper like troops of ferocious baboons." Although socialist ideas had been circulating for decades, Russia was the first state to attempt implementing Marxist doctrine, and the Allies felt obliged to intervene. Fourteen thousand British troops were sent to northern Russia to support anti-Bolshevik armies. French, Japanese, Canadian, and US soldiers intervened elsewhere. The Polish army invaded the Ukraine and seized Kiev. Churchill spoke of building up a defeated Germany in order to fight communism. He summarized his policy: "Kill the Bolshie. Kiss the Hun."

But the Allied intervention, never on a massive scale, failed to stop the Bolsheviks. Peasants and workers rallied behind the Red flag to expel the foreign invaders and to claim the revolution's promise of peace, land, and bread. The civil war in Russia ended, the Union of Soviet Socialist Republics (USSR) was established, and the Bolsheviks renamed themselves the Russian Communist Party.

Tiflis Railway Station, January 1920. Refugees fleeing the Bolshevik advance also included soldiers, "White" Russian counter-revolutionaries.

Lenin

Lenin, founder of the Russian Communist Party and leader of the Bolshevik Revolution, was born Vladimir Ilyich Ulyanov in 1870 in Simbirsk, a provincial city on the Volga. His father was a teacher and provincial director of elementary education, who instilled in his son a deep commitment to bettering the lives of ordinary Russians. Lenin was expelled in his first year at the University of Kazan for taking part in a radical demonstration, but later, as an external student, received an honours degree in law from the University of St. Petersburg.

He discovered the works of Karl Marx when he was nineteen and believed that in these writings he could find the key to Russia's future development: the country would move from its current feudalism directly to communism without passing, as Marx predicated, through a capitalistic stage. Tough-minded revolutionaries would ensure that the Russians could actually shortcut history.

In a series of books and pamphlets, Lenin, a prolific writer, outlined his faith in the ability of dedicated conspirators like himself to bring about first socialism and then its final stage, communism. The First World War gave him his opportunity to test this. The collapse of Russian imperial authority made a Bolshevik coup possible. Lenin, who took personal control of the revolution, became head of the new government.

Lenin was directly responsible for the broad outlines of the new Union of Soviet Socialist Republics. His socialist principles were meant to ensure decent education, free health care, common ownership of land, and fairness for all under the tough guidance of the Bolsheviks. In practice, however, the "dictatorship of the proletariat" created an intolerant, monolithic, one-party system, and a political terror far worse than that experienced under the tsars.

A series of strokes killed Lenin in 1924, at the age of fifty-three.

American troops march into Vladivostok in 1920. Fearing that Bolshevism would spread beyond Russia, the Western powers intervened to crush the new Communist state at birth. They failed.

President Woodrow Wilson, and the United States, offered the world an alternative to communism. Wilson initially had kept the United States officially neutral in the Great War that divided the nations of Europe from 1914, but proclaiming to Congress in April 1917 that the "world must be made safe for democracy," he finally took the United States into the war on the side of the British, French, and Russians. Following the defeat of Germany, at the Versailles Peace Conference, he put forward a programme of Fourteen Points dedicated to removing the causes of injustice and to eradicating war. His stated goals were self-determination, open markets, and collective security. Free trade was the guarantee of national wealth and individual freedom; a League of Nations would be founded to guarantee political independence and territorial integrity. Wilson wanted to project good, healthy, liberal American values into the heart of world politics.

The century would be left to witness the rivalry between these opposing ideologies: Lenin's state communism and Wilson's liberal, free-enterprise capitalism. But the two nations that championed these rival ideals effectively withdrew from Europe after the First World War. The US Senate, swayed by a tradition of isolationism, failed to ratify the Versailles Treaty or the Covenant of the League of Nations. In 1920 Warren G. Harding, who had campaigned for a "return to normalcy," was elected president in a landslide victory. Washington retired from active participation in European affairs, while Lenin and his successors turned inwards, to consolidate their control over Soviet life.

The Man of Steel

In the Soviet Union, Lenin's death in 1924 was followed by several years of internal power struggle. Ultimately, Josef Vissarionovich Dzhugashvili, who

Stalin

The man who became the supreme Soviet leader after the death of Lenin was born in 1879, the son of a poor shoemaker from the village of Gori in the Caucasus. Josef Vissarionovich Dzhugashvili's mother had hoped that he would become a priest, but his formal education ended with expulsion from the nearby Tiflis Orthodox theological seminary. A clandestine trades union organizer for the Bolsheviks, he was frequently arrested and exiled to Siberia, but always escaped. In 1912 he adopted the name Stalin, and that year Lenin appointed him to the Bolshevik Central Committee, but he played an exceedingly modest role in

the 1917 October Revolution. He used his organizational ability and elephantine memory to make himself indispensable to the party, and in 1922 he was made general secretary of the Communist Party, which gave him control over party records and political appointments. Lenin later changed his mind about Stalin, arguing that he was too crude to exercise the "tremendous power" that he would acquire, but it was too late. Challenged during the 1920s, Stalin played off rivals against each other, and he remained general secretary for the rest of his life.

Stalin used his pre-eminent position in the USSR to force industrialization

and collectivize agriculture, which led to an astonishing growth rate for the country but also to a disastrous famine in the Ukraine in the early 1930s. His paranoia and ruthless will to crush potential enemies brought about the great purges of the 1930s, in which millions died, and millions more were sent to forced labour camps.

Stalin directed the Soviet effort against Nazism during the Second World War, and although 27 million of his fellow countrymen lost their lives, the nation emerged as a superpower. With the war over, the purges began again, but when he died in 1953, millions mourned.

assumed the name Stalin, "man of steel," emerged as Lenin's successor. Shrewd, pragmatic, and hard-willed, Stalin was a brilliant administrator. By 1929 he had crushed his opponents and was undisputed master of the Soviet Union. Although he did not give up the concept of world revolution, Stalin placed greater emphasis on achieving "socialism in one country." He sought first and foremost to build a strong, secure Soviet state.

In little more than ten years, from a country based on a rural, peasant economy, Stalin forged an advanced industrial nation. Output doubled. New cities grew up across the Soviet Union, especially in the mineral-rich wastes of Asiatic Russia, east of the Urals. There was, however, an immense cost to achieving all this in so short a time: total state control from the centre meant the loss of all regional or national rights; a bureaucratic tyranny demanded complete and unquestioning obedience. There was suffering on a huge scale, as workers, without adequate food, clothes, and housing, were forced to meet ever more demanding production targets. The Soviet Union retreated from world affairs into the heart of its own totalitarian darkness.

To the outside world, the Soviet Union was a closed book, but the ideals it proclaimed won the support and loyalty of some activists in the West who hated the inequalities and injustices they saw in their own societies. They were unaware of the brutal murder of millions of peasants who opposed collectivization, or the results of terrible famine in the early 1930s. They believed communism was a just system, and that it would prevail throughout the world.

In 1929 the Wall Street stock market crashed, triggering a crisis in capitalism that plunged Western economies into the Great Depression. Factories closed from lack of product demand. Unemployment figures soared in the United States from 3 million to 12 million, in Germany from 2 million to 6

BELOW RIGHT: *The new Soviet state seized the farms of kulaks, peasants who owned land, and turned the properties over to collective ownership. Here kulaks are seen being deported from their village.*

million. Trade between nations nose-dived, wages dropped, the gap between rich and poor became extreme. Food queues appeared everywhere. The left believed that capitalism, as the Soviets predicted, was crumbling, and that it deserved to.

In the United States, Franklin Delano Roosevelt, elected president in 1932, pledged a "new deal for the American people." Increased federal spending, recovery programmes for farming and industry, and action to relieve poverty slowly helped the US economy revive.

Elected president in 1932, for the first of four terms, Franklin D. Roosevelt (ABOVE RIGHT) brought new hope and confidence to Americans impoverished by the Great Depression. ABOVE: Queueing up for government relief; not everyone shared in the "world's highest standard of living."

Roosevelt rethought the American position on the Soviet Union, and in 1933 the United States offered diplomatic recognition to the USSR, the last major power to do so. Among the first officials sent to the new US Embassy in Moscow was a young career diplomat, George F. Kennan. He saw the Soviet Union "as unalterably opposed to our traditional system." He pondered the ideological divide and concluded, "There can be no possible middle ground or compromise between the two. . . . The two systems cannot even exist in the same world unless an economic cordon is put around one or the other of them."

In 1936 Stalin staged a series of show trials of old Bolsheviks, who were forced to denounce themselves and confess to impossibly monstrous crimes. In a great purge two-thirds of the Communist Party leaders were shot or arrested. In 1937 the terror extended into almost every walk of life. Artists and writers, scientists and doctors, were executed or imprisoned. Top generals in the army were purged, and one in three of the entire officer corps were arrested. Millions of ordinary peasants and workers were also denounced as "enemies of the people." A knock on the door in the night, exile to a forced labour camp, a bullet in the back of the head, became the hallmarks of Stalin's rule. George Kennan, gazing out of his office window above Red Square, thought to himself that he was looking out over "one of the bloodiest spots in the world." Stalin sent between 17 million and 22 million of his own countrymen to their deaths

Cold War

during the 1930s, including those who starved or died of maltreatment in the labour camps of Siberia — nearly three times the number of victims that would be claimed by Hitler's Holocaust.

A New Chancellor, a New Alliance

The Great Depression had put the liberal democracies of Western Europe under intense pressure. In Britain a national coalition was formed to deal with the deep economic crisis. In France there were strikes and demonstra-

RENDEZVOUS

tions. In Germany, with unemployment running at 6 million and politics radicalized by harsh conditions, the fragile fabric of Germany's first republic, founded at Weimar following the war, disintegrated altogether. Forced to comply with the vindictive terms of the Versailles Treaty, which, among other things, required the bankrupt country to fund huge war reparations, Germany could no longer function with a parliamentary government. In January 1933 Adolf Hitler, leader of the Nazis, the National Socialist German Workers Party, the largest elected party in the Reichstag, was appointed chancellor. Hitler vowed to destroy international communism and to create a living space for the German people in the east — particularly in the vast territories relinquished to Poland under terms of the Versailles Treaty. He preached a savage anti-Semitic racism; world Jewry was the enemy. The new chancellor abolished all other political parties and arrested Communist leaders. Hitler's Nazi state, like Stalin's Soviet Russia, was propped up by an elaborate system of terror. For leftists in the United States, to oppose Nazism would justify their support for Stalin's communism. When, in 1936, General Francisco Franco led a rightist rebellion against the Spanish Republic, idealistic Americans and others joined Communists and Communist sympathizers in volunteering for the Abraham Lincoln Brigade, to fight fascism alongside the Republican Loyalists in the Spanish Civil War.

Hitler reasserted German power, intending to avenge the humiliations

ABOVE LEFT: *Adolf Hitler in 1933, the year he became chancellor of Germany. An avowed enemy of communism, Hitler shocked the world in August 1939 by signing a nonaggression pact with Stalin.*
ABOVE: *British cartoonist David Low shows the dictators meeting over the corpse of Poland, which they invaded and divided in September 1939.*

brought on by the Versailles Treaty, to colonize Eastern Europe, and to destroy world communism. The British and French decided to appease Hitler rather than resist him, and stood passively by as he reoccupied the Rhineland, demilitarized under Versailles provisions, annexed Austria, and then seized Czechoslovakia. In the summer of 1939 Hitler's demands in Poland pointed towards yet another crisis. Alarmed, the British and French governments now took a stand and signed a treaty of alliance with the Poles.

It was too late, for in a move that astonished the world, the two ideo-

German forces invading the Soviet Union in June 1941 appeared unstoppable. Unprepared, the Red Army was overrun. But Russia's men and women dug in, held on, and came back to win a crushing victory on the Eastern Front.

logical opposites, Nazi Germany and Communist Russia, announced a non-aggression pact in August 1939. Secretly, Stalin and Hitler agreed to carve up Poland. With his eastern flank thus secure, Hitler was now free to make his move. Within days, on 1 September 1939, his army crossed into Poland. Britain and France, respecting their treaty with Poland, declared war on Germany; Hitler had hoped they would acquiesce as they had when he invaded Czechoslovakia the previous year. On 17 September, Stalin attacked Poland from the east. The Poles held out bravely for two more weeks. Nazi Germany and the Soviet Union then partitioned the country; Poland ceased to exist. Stalin's buffer against a hostile Germany had gone also.

Roosevelt kept the United States out of the war to begin with. But when Hitler defeated and occupied France, Roosevelt firmly lined up with Winston Churchill, the new British prime minister. The United States began to finance Britain's war effort while that nation hung on against an expected invasion. But no invasion came. Instead on 22 June 1941, Hitler's armies turned eastward and invaded the Soviet Union. Operation Barbarossa was to change the face of history and make allies out of enemies. Churchill, a committed anti-Communist, now welcomed Soviet Russia as a partner in the war to defeat Nazi Germany. He justified the volte-face by saying he "would work with the devil if it would help defeat Hitler."

During the 1930s Japanese militarism had been on the march in Asia, looking for new markets and guaranteed sources of raw materials. Japan occupied Manchuria in 1931, and from 1937 fought a long, cruel, bloody war of conquest in China. Hundreds of thousands of Chinese civilians were massacred. Seeking to spread its economic influence over what it called the Greater East Asia Co-Prosperity Sphere, Japan stirred protests from the United States over infringements of American property rights in East Asia. On 7 December 1941 the Japanese made a ruthless pre-emptive strike against the US Pacific

BELOW LEFT: *Russian civilians return to homes devastated by the German invasion.* BELOW: *Thousands of German prisoners, taken at Stalingrad in 1943, file across the snow to prison camps.*

Fleet at anchor in Pearl Harbor. President Roosevelt, stunned, spoke of it as "a date which will live in infamy." Japanese troops then attacked British positions throughout the Far East. Within days, for reasons that have never been clear, Adolf Hitler declared war on the United States, bringing the most powerful nation in the world into the war against him in Europe. If Germany lost, as now it must, the United States and the Soviet Union would meet in the heart of Europe.

Following the German invasion of June 1941, Stalin, with dictatorial power, steadily transformed the Soviet Union into a vast fighting machine. Hitler's armies advanced to within sight of Moscow — officers reported seeing the towers of the Kremlin through their binoculars — but with the freezing Russian winter setting in, the Germans were forced to withdraw. They never threatened Moscow again. A siege of Russia's second city, Leningrad, lasted nearly two and a half years; one out of three civilians perished there. But at the battle of Stalingrad the tide of war began to turn. After fierce fighting, street by street, ruin by ruin, the German Sixth Army was encircled in November 1942, and surrendered three months later. Now the Soviets went on the offensive. From that point on, the tanks of the Red Army rolled relentlessly westward.

The Allied Powers began to plan for the future. Roosevelt was determined

This 1943 poster reminds us that in the Second World War the United States and USSR fought on the same side.

that the wartime co-operation with the Soviet Union would form the basis for the postwar world. Plans for a United Nations Organization were developed; it would consist of a consultative General Assembly, where internationalist ideals would reign, and an executive Security Council, which would have the power to act.

Stalin sought postwar security for the Soviet Union. The country had suffered dreadful destruction during the Nazi invasion, the third invasion from the west in less than a hundred and fifty years. But Stalin had no concept of collective security; for him, security came through eliminating opponents. Stalin would protect the Soviet Union by exerting his control over world communism.

The Big Three Meet

The Big Three wartime leaders met together for the first time at Tehran towards the end of November 1943. Military issues dominated the discussions. Stalin believed, rightly, that the USSR was bearing the brunt of the war and repeated his demands that the Allies open a second front in northern Europe. Churchill and Roosevelt assured him that such an invasion was planned for the spring of 1944. The Russians agreed to launch a major offensive on their eastern front at the same time. There was general agreement to divide Germany at the end of the war, and the future of Poland and of Eastern Europe was discussed. At one dinner Churchill asked Stalin about his postwar territorial ambitions. "There is no need to speak at the present time about any Soviet desires," Stalin replied. "But when the time comes we will speak."

All three leaders believed they had made progress at Tehran. Churchill felt he could get along with Stalin, and began to refer to him as "Uncle Joe." What the Western leaders did not know was that their rooms at Tehran were bugged and that every morning Stalin went through a transcript of their conversations. He would leave nothing to chance.

In line with the Tehran agreements, on 6 June 1944, D-day, 150,000 Allied soldiers clambered ashore onto the beaches of Normandy. Behind them 3 million more soldiers, sailors, and airmen supported the largest amphibious operation in history. American, British, and Canadian troops began their advance to the Rhine and the heart of Germany. Also in June, as agreed, 6 million men of the Red Army launched their offensive on a broad front from Leningrad to the Ukraine.

As the Red Army advanced westward it paused only once, near Warsaw. When the Russians approached, the free Polish resistance rose up and took control of the Polish capital, ready to proclaim an independent Poland. The Soviet troops unexpectedly waited at the Vistula River, and allowed the Nazis to return and crush the Poles. Churchill pleaded with Stalin to intervene; the Soviet leader said his armies needed time to regroup. The Allies asked that their planes be allowed to use Soviet airfields to supply the Poles. Again, Stalin refused. For sixty-three days, armed only with rifles and small arms, the Poles held out. Finally, the Nazis, in an orgy of slaughter, put down the rising. Two hundred thousand Poles were killed, nine out of ten of them civilians. The Germans reduced the city to rubble. Stalin had permitted the flower

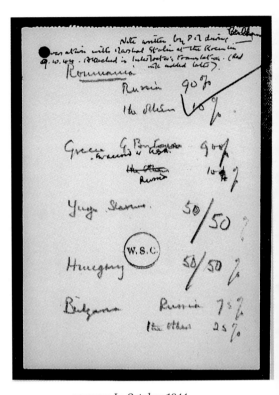

ABOVE: *In October 1944, during a talk with Stalin at the Kremlin, Churchill sketched out postwar spheres of influence, which Stalin approved with a tick mark.* OPPOSITE: *Yalta in the Crimea. The Big Three, Churchill, Stalin, and Roosevelt (who had only weeks to live), met in February 1945 to decide the shape of the postwar world.*

of the free Polish resistance to be massacred, so that he could hand Poland over to his own stooges. Hopes for genuine democracy in Eastern Europe after the war were destroyed in the ruins of Warsaw.

Churchill flew to Moscow in October 1944 and, in one late-night meeting, he and Stalin talked frankly about the shape of postwar Europe. Churchill produced a piece of paper on which he had outlined postwar spheres of influ-

ence. Romania, he suggested, should be 90 per cent Russian and 10 per cent British; Greece should be 90 per cent British-American and 10 per cent Russian; Yugoslavia and Hungary would be 50-50 and Bulgaria 75 per cent to Russia and 25 per cent to the others. Stalin studied the list and made a large tick mark on it. There was then a long pause. Churchill recalled later that he said: "Might it not be thought rather cynical if it seemed we had disposed of these issues, so fateful to millions of people, in such an offhand manner? Let us burn the paper." "No," Stalin replied, "you keep it."

In February 1945 the Big Three met again, this time at the old Livadia summer palace of the tsars at Yalta in the Crimea. Roosevelt, ailing, was tired from his journey, and Churchill was exhausted by the relentless pressure of war. But the sun shone and the end of the war was in sight. The Yalta Conference represented the high-water mark of Allied wartime collaboration. To the relief of the West, Stalin agreed to enter the war against Japan within three months of the end of fighting in Europe. But Yalta was also the beginning of the postwar world; the divisions between East and West became apparent.

Stalin was apprehensive that the new United Nations might be controlled by the United States and Britain, and that the Soviet Union would be outnumbered there. It was agreed that two or three Soviet republics would be

Might it not be thought rather cynical if it seemed we had disposed of these issues, so fateful to millions of people, in such an offhand manner?

— Winston Churchill, to Joseph Stalin, October 1944

Berlin 1945

A Soviet tank and a Russian photographer win German smiles at the Brandenburg Gate in defeated Berlin. The Soviet Union, devastated by Hitler's invasion, was ready to claim the spoils of war.

admitted as members and that each of the great powers should have a veto over resolutions of the Security Council. There was a dispute about the shape and governance of postwar Poland. The British wanted to install the pro-Western government that was in exile in London; the Soviets wanted the rival pro-Soviet government that had been set up in Lublin, in southeast Poland. Churchill explained that Britain had gone to war so "that Poland should be free and sovereign" and that this was a matter of "honour" for Britain. Stalin

A surprise choice as FDR's running mate in 1944, Harry S. Truman was catapulted into the presidency on Roosevelt's death. Truman, shown here being sworn in on 13 April 1945, gave the West determined leadership, and the Soviet Union a hard time.

argued that for the Soviet Union it was rather a question of "security"; the USSR had twice in the last thirty years been attacked through the "Polish corridor." In the end the Allies largely gave in to Stalin's insistence. The Allies agreed that the Soviet-Polish border should move west, and, in compensation to Poland, that the Polish-German border should also shift westward. Stalin formally agreed to free and fair elections in Poland, and he signed a somewhat fuzzy Declaration on Liberated Europe that pledged support for reconstruction based on free elections. Drained by long argument the West, for now, took Stalin at his word.

It was agreed to divide Germany into four zones of occupation: Soviet, American, British, and French. The Soviets insisted on taking massive reparations from Germany, partly as compensation for the vast destruction caused by the Nazis, partly to punish the Germans, partly as a symbol of victor's rights. Britain and the United States were opposed to reparations; they had caused havoc after the First World War and could now hinder Germany from recovering following the Second. Eventually, they did agree to them, and Roosevelt compromised on a figure of $20 billion, to be paid in goods and equipment over a period of years.

The Red flag is raised over the Reichstag in Berlin, 2 May 1945. The Soviets got there first, taking terrible casualties along the way. The city became a focus of Cold War tensions.

Yalta revealed cracks in the Grand Alliance. Only the common objective of defeating Hitler had kept it together; that and personal trust, such as it was, among the three leaders. After Yalta the relationship between Roosevelt and Stalin would be the key to co-operation. With victory in sight, on Thursday, 12 April 1945, having defused another dispute with Stalin, the president drafted a cable to Churchill: "I would minimize the general Soviet problem." Later that day he collapsed, and within a few hours he was dead.

A New President

As the constitution provided, the vice president, Harry S. Truman, immediately succeeded to the presidency of the United States. "I feel like I've been struck by a bolt of lightning," he told a colleague. "Boys," he said to a group of reporters, "if you ever pray, pray for me now." Despite his failing health, Roosevelt had kept Truman pitifully ill informed. There had been only two private meetings between the president and his vice president since Truman's election five months earlier. Although as a US senator he had played a major role in organizing the nation's war effort, chairing a vital Senate committee, Harry Truman was largely ignorant of foreign affairs and was now thrown into a crash course. Truman's tendency was to see things in clearly defined, black-and-white terms. He lacked the patience to weigh up subtleties of argument, freely admitting that he was "not up on all details." From what his advisers told him when he assumed the presidency, it seemed to Truman that the Soviet Union was behaving like a bully in Europe and should be told to mend its ways. Less than two weeks after taking office, Truman met with Soviet foreign minister Vyacheslav Molotov at the White House. The president proceeded to give Molotov a thorough dressing-down over Soviet behaviour in Eastern Europe, where the Communist takeover was well on its way. "I have never been talked to like that in my life," said Molotov furiously. "Carry out

The Potsdam Conference started with Stalin, Churchill, and Truman at the table. But halfway through, Churchill was voted out of office in Britain and replaced by Clement Attlee. Truman, like Attlee, was new to international conferences; this was his first.

A Word with Stalin

Victory over Hitler brought Russia back into the heart of Europe, with a vengeance. Averell Harriman, US ambassador to Moscow and one of those who helped bring Truman up to speed on foreign affairs, later recalled approaching Stalin at the Potsdam Conference and saying: "Marshal, this must be a great satisfaction to you after all the trials that you've been through and the tragedy you've been through, to be here in Berlin." Stalin looked at Harriman and replied: "Tsar Alexander got to Paris."

The Manhattan Project

As early as 1907 Albert Einstein reasoned that atoms, the basic unit of all matter, were held together by forces that if released could produce enormous amounts of energy. For thirty years scientists agreed that the ability to harness this energy lay far into the future. But just before the Second World War, German scientists succeeded in splitting the atom for the first time. Most Western scientists remained sceptical about the potential until they read the Maud Report in July 1941, in which a group of British scientists argued that it was possible to construct "an effective uranium bomb," containing twenty-five pounds of active material, that would detonate an explosion equivalent to 1,800 tons of TNT. James B. Conant, chemist, president of Harvard University, and senior scientific adviser to the US government, urged the president to make a major push. The result was the top secret Manhattan Project, a collaborative venture among the United States, Britain, and Canada, with research carried out in the safety of the United States.

In September 1942, General Leslie R. Groves was put in charge of the project on behalf of the US Army, and shortly thereafter he directed J. Robert Oppenheimer to set up a laboratory where the bomb would be designed and built. The site for the laboratory was Los Alamos, New Mexico. Fearing, wrongly as it turned out, that the Germans were themselves developing an atom bomb, Allied scientists raced to be the first to harness the energy of the atom in the process of fission. To obtain the necessary fissionable material, four different techniques were pursued: gaseous diffusion at Oak Ridge, Tennessee; chemical separation of plutonium at Hanford, Washington; electromagnetic research on the isotope uranium-235 at Berkeley, California; and plutonium breeding at Chicago, where the first nuclear reactor was built in December 1942. In time, a total of thirty-seven research sites, employing 120,000 people, would grapple with the scientific challenges of harnessing the power of the atom in a workable bomb. Washington devoted $2 billion to this work.

Although surrounded by secrecy, the Manhattan Project was infiltrated by Soviet agents from the very beginning. Klaus Fuchs, a brilliant refugee German physicist, started working on the bomb in England and later joined the team in Los Alamos. Fuchs was a Communist. He kept the Soviets informed of all developments in the project. In June 1945, a month before the first test, he handed to his contact, Harry Gold, documents that included a full description of the plutonium bomb, the type of core, a description of the tamper, the principles of the calculations behind the bomb, and a sketch of the bomb and its components with all the dimensions included.

On 16 July 1945, at Alamogordo, in the New Mexico desert, the first experimental atom bomb was tested in an operation code-named Trinity. One of the scientists present wrote: "Suddenly, there was an enormous flash of light, the brightest light I have ever seen or that I think anyone has ever seen. . . . Finally it was over, diminishing, and we looked toward the place where the bomb had been; there was an enormous ball of fire which grew and grew, and it rolled as it grew. . . . A new thing had just been born; a new control; a new understanding of man, which man had acquired over nature."

The Trinity test was a complete success. The war would be over in less than a month.

Robert Oppenheimer and General Leslie Groves (TOP), photographed on the site of a nuclear test explosion. The bomb was made in Oak Ridge, Tennessee, at the Clinton Engineer Works (BOTTOM).

Truman's note on the back of a photograph of himself and Stalin at Potsdam.

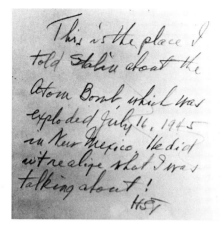

This is the place I told Stalin about the Atom Bomb, which was exploded July 16, 1945 in New Mexico. He did not realize what I was talking about!

HST

Truman decided to surprise us at Potsdam. . . . He took Stalin and me aside and — looking secretive — informed us they had a secret weapon of a wholly new type, an extraordinary weapon. . . . It's difficult to say what he was thinking, but it seemed to me he wanted to throw us into consternation. Stalin, however, reacted to this quite calmly, and Truman decided he hadn't understood. The words "atomic bomb" hadn't been spoken, but we immediately guessed what was meant.

— Vyacheslav Molotov, on Potsdam Conference, July 1945

your agreements," responded Truman, "and you won't get talked to like that." The Soviets now understood that the era of wartime collaboration was over. Washington officials realized that the new president would steer a course different from that of his predecessor.

Final victory over Nazi Germany was to come shortly after. From his underground bunker, Hitler ordered that every Berlin street should be fought over and every building defended "to the last man and the last bullet." Three hundred thousand Russian soldiers were killed in the battle of Berlin. On 30 April, Hitler committed suicide. On 7 May, the German High Command signed a document of unconditional surrender. Europe and America celebrated. The citizens of Berlin feared reprisals or even massacre by the Soviet soldiers. But the massacre never came. What did occur was looting and rape. Latest research suggests that as many as 2 million German women were raped by Soviet soldiers in the months following the end of the war. Stalin dismissed complaints. He said that having fought bravely for four years, "the boys deserve their fun."

In mid-July, in the ruins of the Berlin suburbs, at Cecilienhof Palace in Potsdam, the Allied leaders gathered for their last wartime conference. Truman was accompanied by James F. Byrnes, his new secretary of state, sworn in just three days before they set sail for Europe. One of Truman's principal objectives was to nail down the Soviet agreement to enter the war against Japan. Stalin reiterated his pledge, as given at Yalta, on the first day. "Could go home now," Truman whispered to Byrnes.

Agreement was swiftly reached on the occupation of Germany by the three victorious powers, along with the French. The military commanders would administer the defeated country in four separate zones. A Council of Foreign Ministers would resolve disputes among the victors. But there was still disagreement over the precise new borders of Poland, which were to advance westward to the Neisse River, and over reparations. Germany was to be treated as a single unit for economic purposes. But the US position was to insist that Germany must be able to pay for its imports before it could make any reparations. "If you want milk, you have to feed the cow." The Soviets argued that their people had suffered much from the Nazi invasion; they couldn't see why the "Wall Street bankers" had to be paid first.

A New Weapon

On 16 July 1945, the eve of the Potsdam Conference, the first atom bomb was successfully tested. The explosion was reported to be "brighter than a thousand suns." In Potsdam, Truman was informed right away of its success. Five days later he was told that the bomb had proved to be far more destructive than expected, and that it would soon be ready for combat use. Truman was delighted with the news. "He was a changed man," Churchill noted. News of the bomb transformed the American position. The US military had been planning for an invasion of Japan, to take place some time between November 1945 and March 1946. Nearly 2 million men would be involved, and General George C. Marshall, the army chief of staff, feared that casualties would be extremely high. On Iwo Jima and Okinawa, Japanese soldiers had fought to the bitter end, many choosing suicide over surrender. The United States had hoped that the Soviet Union's entry into the war would encourage the Japanese to sue for peace. But now that the Americans had the atom bomb they hoped the war would end before the Soviets became too embroiled in it, or involved in the occupation of Japan. Truman and Byrnes now tried to end the conference as quickly as possible. Following the afternoon session of 24 July, Truman walked across the room to Stalin and, in an offhand way, told him that the United States now had a big new weapon. Stalin, who knew about the bomb through spies, replied equally casually, "Good, I hope the

BELOW: *"Little Boy," the first atom bomb to be used in warfare, was 28 inches in diameter, 10 feet long, and weighed 9,000 pounds. Dropped on Hiroshima, 6 August 1945, by the B-29 Enola Gay, it killed some 100,000 people.* RIGHT: *The pilot of the bomber, Colonel Paul W. Tibbets, is shown, at centre, with his ground crew.*

United States will use it." Truman and Byrnes thought that Stalin had not understood. In fact, Stalin knew precisely what was at stake. Within days, he had ordered Molotov to speed up the Soviet bomb project.

The Potsdam Conference was held up for a few days while Churchill returned to Britain for the results of a general election. He discovered that he had been defeated in a landslide by the Labour Party. The conference resumed on 28 July with two new members, Clement Attlee as British prime minister and Ernest Bevin as foreign secretary. Byrnes decided to "do a little horse trading" to bring the conference to a rapid conclusion. On reparations, he suggested that each country take them from its own zone of occupation. Germany would no longer be treated as a single economic unit. If the USSR would accept this compromise — which meant the Soviets would have no access to the mining and industrial riches of the Ruhr Valley — then the West would approve the new Polish boundaries. This deal was done. A cobbled-together agreement on the satellites left Italy in the Western sphere of influence, and Romania, Bulgaria, and Hungary in that of the Soviet Union. Potsdam ended with such issues as the nature of the regimes to be installed in Eastern Europe unclear. But the rival powers had assented to the division of Europe.

Truman lost no time in using the atom bomb, hoping to prevent the huge American casualties an invasion of Japan was expected to bring. He was also aware of the immense strength the bomb would give the United States, especially in relations with the Soviets, if they should prove troublesome. The initial Japanese response to a call for unconditional surrender was unclear. On 5 August the first bomb was assembled and ready to go. On the following day, a B-29 Superfortress, *Enola Gay*, left its base in the Marianas for Japan.

At eight o'clock, on a bright, clear morning, a lone bomber appeared high in the skies over the city of Hiroshima. The plane was seen to drop something in a parachute and turn to depart. That something was an atom bomb, which exploded at 1,800 feet with the force of 13,000 tons of TNT. The heat from the explosion was so intense that it melted roof tiles, charred telegraph poles, and incinerated human beings so completely that nothing remained of them except light shapes on scorched pavements and walls where their bodies had momentarily blocked the severe heat. Two and a half miles away, bare skin was burned. After the heat came the blast, sweeping outward with the force of a 500-mile-an-hour wind. The heat and the blast destroyed the city within minutes. Perhaps 100,000 civilians were killed immediately. Thousands more would die of radiation poisoning over the next few months and years.

On 8 August, Stalin declared war on Japan. The Red Army advanced into Manchuria and then a few days later into Korea. As the Japanese cabinet discussed peace on 9 August, a second atomic bomb of a different type, a plutonium implosion bomb, was detonated over Nagasaki, with minimal strategic excuse. Nagasaki also was destroyed. On 10 August the emperor of Japan announced his intention to surrender. Terms were agreed on 14 August. The Second World War had ended. The atomic age had begun. For fifty years a divided world would live under the shadow of the mushroom cloud.

LEFT: *The mushroom cloud that arose from the atomic explosion over Hiroshima.* ABOVE: *The bomb's effects on the city. Destruction on this scale had never been so easily achieved. Death by radiation lingered on.*

An old woman trudges past
what is left of home. Warsaw,
with Berlin and Dresden, was
one of Europe's most devastated
cities at the war's end.

Iron Curtain
1945–1947

Senior girls clear rubble from a Berlin school destroyed during the war. One-fifth of the schools in the city were completely demolished by wartime bombing.

Bitter Aftermath of Victory

At the end of the war the victorious Soviet Union controlled the largest army the world had ever known. But the mother country lay ravaged; nearly one-third of its former wealth had been destroyed — 32,000 factories were in ruin, 65,000 kilometres of railway track were now useless. No one can say how many of its people died in this war, but estimates are that at least 27 million Soviet citizens lost their lives in defeating Nazism. Of the country's townships, 1,710 were destroyed; of its villages and hamlets, 70,000 were burned to the ground; of its collective farms, 100,000 were laid waste.

Most of Europe also lay devastated at war's end, and even Britain, neither invaded nor occupied, was severely impoverished. From Normandy to the Ukraine vast land areas had been destroyed by aerial bombs as well as by savage ground fighting. There were hundreds of thousands of flattened homes, demolished factories, and farms gone fallow. In addition the war had displaced millions of people who now had to be resettled — somewhere. In countries that were occupied by the Nazis, like France, the Netherlands, and Norway, there were numerous scores to be settled, particularly with collaborators. For most there was simply a sense of relief at having survived. From the depths of Poland, and elsewhere, intelligence emerged of the most dreadful and appalling acts of genocide in human history. Even those numbed by five and a half years of brutal war were horrified by the stark facts of the Holocaust — the extermination of 6 million Jews, more than a million Gypsies, and thousands of homosexuals.

The United States, by contrast, ended the war as the greatest industrial power in history, with an economy that had more than doubled during the war — from a gross national product of $90 billion in 1939 to one of $212 billion in 1945. Gone were the years of economic stagnation in the Great Depression. When it was fully directed towards the war effort, America's industrial capacity — "the arsenal of victory" — proved to be awesome. Cargo ships were built in three days flat, giant bombers were assembled in a few hours, and trucks and jeeps rolled off the assembly line every few minutes. There was full employment.

America was a global power, with its economy ready to expand into markets on every continent. During the war much of the world had built up a dollar debt to the United States, and many ex-allies now looked to America for financial relief. Britain negotiated a loan of $3.75 billion (on terms thought very unfriendly), and even the Soviet Union discussed with Washington the possibility of a $6 billion loan for desperately needed reconstruction. In 1944, at the Bretton Woods Conference on the postwar global economy, the dollar had been established as the world's principal trading currency. The pound was relegated to second place, and despite British hopes, sterling would never return to a position of international ascendancy. Everywhere there was a "dollar gap," since countries that had suffered greatly in the war were unable to produce the exports necessary to earn hard currency for purchasing sorely needed imports. The dollar was the only currency freely convertible throughout the world, so many nations hoped for loans and assistance from the United States. And, as the only power possessing the atom bomb, America seemed to have both the military and the economic muscle to play the key role in determining the future shape of the world.

The Soviet Union also basked in the glory of victory, since everywhere there was immense respect for the Red Army. From years of titanic struggle

In the Second World War women flexed their muscles to boost production. The number of women in heavy manufacturing increased nearly fivefold. At the war's end, reluctantly, they made way for the men.

Bring the Boys Back Home

With the fighting ended in both Europe and Asia (American losses totalled 292,000 men), the American military was obsessed with one objective: bring the boys back home — as soon as possible. In 1945 there were 12 million Americans under arms in different parts of the world; two years later that figure would be reduced to 1.5 million. This too meant upheaval. Soldiers returned to wives they sometimes hardly knew and to children they had never seen, and countless "GI brides" crossed an ocean to an unknown continent to start a new life. In the civilian sector, women like "Rosie the Riveter," who had experienced new freedoms in taking war jobs, were now thrown out of work and reluctantly returned to hearth and home.

against the Wehrmacht, the Soviets were widely regarded as having borne the brunt of destroying Nazism, and "Uncle Joe" Stalin had become a popular figure in Europe and in the United States. All across Europe sizable elements of the population were seriously considering the virtues of communism, for few wanted a return to the failed capitalism of the prewar era. In France the Communists were associated with the Maquis, resistance fighters during Nazi occupation. In Italy the Communists had led the struggle of the Partigiani, the partisans, against fascism, and now possessed a heroic aura. In Britain the Labour Party, committed to a planned economy and the nationalization of key industries, had successfully ousted wartime leader Winston Churchill from office. Many Europeans thought that having won the war, Stalin could now win the peace.

Inside the USSR, some experienced diplomats, like Maxim Litvinov and Ivan Maisky, advised Stalin to play along with the Western Allies and exploit the wartime popularity of the Soviet Union. But Stalin was of a suspicious nature, always fearful of outside influences. He cited what happened in 1825 when Russian officers, the Decembrists, staying on in Europe after the defeat of Napoleon, picked up Western ideas and, on the death of Tsar Alexander I, tried to prevent the succession of Nicholas I. Stalin and his right-hand man, Foreign Minister Vyacheslav Molotov, decided to keep the Soviet Union closed to those potentially tainted with foreign ways. Many former prisoners of war, instead of being welcomed as heroes on their return, were arrested and imprisoned. Unknown numbers of returning soldiers — hundreds of thousands of men — were sent to labour camps, for the Soviet economy had long relied upon slave labour. In June 1945 Averell Harriman, US ambassador in Moscow, reported to the State Department: "The Embassy knows of only a sin-

BELOW: *Wives and girlfriends in Moscow welcome Soviet soldiers returning from war. Millions never came back. But although the USSR was exhausted, the Red Army remained the largest fighting force in the world.* BELOW RIGHT: *The annual May Day Parade, Red Square, Moscow.*

gle instance in which a repatriated prisoner has returned to his home and family in Moscow. . . . Repatriates are met at ports of entry by police guard and marched off . . . to unknown destinations. Trainloads of repatriates are passing through Moscow and continuing east, the passengers being held incommunicado." By 1946 Lavrenti Beria, chief of the secret police, had imprisoned between 7 million and 12 million Soviet men and women in the labour camps known collectively as the Gulag. For those who had earlier suffered the humiliation of surrender in battle and the trauma of imprisonment by the Nazis, there were new horrors ahead — a daily struggle to survive without adequate food or shelter, often in settlements above the Arctic Circle.

ABOVE: *Survivors of a "death march" from Lodz, Poland, to Berlin. Displaced by war, millions trekked halfway across Europe, trying to get home, looking for relatives.* ABOVE RIGHT: *A woman searches the ruins of her home in Stalingrad for her past. The Soviet Union was laid waste by the Nazi invasion; villages, towns, and cities were destroyed.*

Setting Up a Buffer

The Soviet Union had suffered appalling devastation from German invasion. Stalin had one foreign policy objective that overrode everything else: to build a buffer zone along his country's western border. He wanted to ensure that Russia would never be invaded from Europe again — as it had been three times in the last century and a half. As territories were liberated by the Red Army, Stalin had instructed his henchmen to set up friendly, pro-Soviet regimes. However, in many regions Communists were still in the minority. In Hungary, for instance, even under the eyes of the Soviet military, the Communists took only 17 per cent of the vote in November 1945. Polish Communists did not dare risk an election until January 1947. Only in Czechoslovakia, in elections held in May 1946, did the Communists receive as much as 38 per cent of the vote. Communist ministers then participated in the democratically elected government under President Eduard Beneš, who had revived a free Czechoslovakia after six years of Nazi rule. He was not to last for long.

Throughout Eastern Europe, Stalin's tactics were the same. Communist exiles who had spent the war in Moscow subsequently returned to their homelands totally committed to the generalissimo and to the Soviet Union. There, they agreed initially to participate in coalition governments with social democrats and similar parties, like the right-wing Smallholders Party in Hungary and the country-based Polish Peasant Party. But Stalin insisted on

Hordes of displaced persons, and their meagre belongings, overload a train preparing to pull out of Anhalter Station.

Berlin, 1945

having Communists appointed to the key ministries of economic planning, justice, and the interior. This ensured that control of the police and internal security was in the hands of his accomplices. Across Eastern Europe key members of the non-Communist parties began to disappear, kidnapped in the dead of night. Slowly the Communists worked at eliminating the opposition, edging each satellite country towards their goal of one-party Communist rule, under Soviet hegemony.

In Poland, where a third of the national wealth had been destroyed and one in five Poles had been killed, everyone who was left seemed to be on the move. Millions of displaced persons were desperately trying to find their families again and return to their homes. Trains crawled slowly westward, packed with refugees and the survivors of Hitler's extermination camps. Trains also clogged the rails heading east, piled with booty and machinery from German factories seized by the Red Army. The Allies had agreed at the Potsdam Conference that the Soviet Union would annex parts of what had been eastern Poland and that Poland's western border would shift westward to the Oder and Neisse rivers. To make room for the displaced Poles, about 6 million Germans were uprooted, often brutally, and driven out of Pomerania, Silesia, and East Prussia, from homes some families had lived in for generations. Many Germans from western Poland were resettled in the British zone of Germany. Today this process would be called "ethnic cleansing," but it was then known as "population transfer." The Allies willingly took part.

Of the twenty-five members of the provisional Polish government, sixteen were Communists with Soviet support. Wladyslaw Gomulka, secretary of the Polish Workers Party (the Communists), led the drive against both Stanislaw Mikolajczyk, leader of the Peasant Party, and a non-Communist alliance supported by the West. The vast problems of reconstruction were overshadowed by the internal struggle for power, and the Communists freely used terror tactics to get their way. Meetings of the Peasant Party were broken up by mobs, and party members were arrested, kidnapped, and murdered. By the time full elections came about in January 1947, thousands of activists were already in prison, so the Communists were able to claim 80 per cent of the votes. In what had been agreed to be Stalin's sphere of influence, the West could do nothing to prevent the inexorable, formal imposition of Communist rule.

Stalin's tactics in Eastern Europe, as well as in zones of influence and occupation, risked confrontation with the West, but this was a risk Stalin seemed willing to take. In the latter months of 1945, he saw Romania and Bulgaria follow Poland in establishing pro-Soviet governments. In December of that year Russian intervention appeared to be spreading beyond Eastern Europe when pro-Soviet forces seized control in northern Iran and declared a new independent nation of Azerbaijan. In that same month the USSR also ordered troops to gather along the Turkish border.

James F. Byrnes, the US secretary of state, attempted to soften the USSR's hard line at a foreign ministers conference in Moscow in December 1945. Insisting that the Soviets broaden the base of the Bulgarian and Romanian

Ruins of the Warsaw Ghetto, 1948. Fierce fighting in 1944, followed by postwar demolition, left barely a wall standing. Extraordinarily, a Roman Catholic Church is almost undamaged in the distance.

James F. Byrnes

governments, Byrnes urged them to introduce non-Communist members. When Molotov gave way, Byrnes agreed to recognize the new pro-Soviet governments. This led to outrage at the State Department, where one diplomat wrote of using "fig leaves of diplomatic procedure to hide the nakedness of Stalinist dictatorship." President Truman, calling Byrnes into the Oval Office, firmly warned him about Soviet expansionism and later claimed this as "the point of departure of our policy." Less than six months after the end of the war, Washington had begun to see its wartime ally as a potential enemy.

Descent of the Iron Curtain

The situation went from bad to worse in February 1946 with a speech by Stalin on the eve of elections to the Supreme Soviet. In it Stalin took an uncompromising Marxist-Leninist line, claiming that capitalism made war inevitable: "The development of world capitalism proceeds not in the path of smooth and even progress but through crisis and the catastrophes of war."

To Stalin's audience this merely repeated familiar prophesies, but in Washington the speech caused great alarm. *Time* magazine said that it was "the most warlike pronouncement uttered by any top-rank statesman since V-J Day." Paul Nitze, a policy adviser in the State Department, pronounced the speech akin to a "delayed declaration of war against the United States." Other officials were confused by Stalin's attitude and sought clarification on Soviet

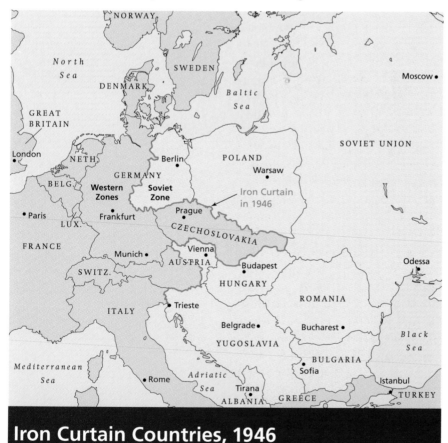

Iron Curtain Countries, 1946

The development of world capitalism proceeds not in the path of smooth and even progress but through crisis and the catastrophes of war.

— Joseph Stalin,
February 1946

thinking. The State Department cabled the US Embassy in Moscow for a background study of Stalin's foreign policy, and the request landed on the desk of George Kennan, who composed an eight-thousand-word response. The text of his cable to Washington has gone down in history as "the Long Telegram." It was to have a profound effect on the development of American thinking about the Soviet Union and the evolution of what later became known as the policy of containment.

Kennan was the State Department's Soviet expert and had first gone to Moscow in 1933, representing US interests even before Washington had formally recognized the Soviet government. In many ways he was an unlikely diplomat. Subject to extreme mood changes, he usually was determined to press his own point of view rather than listen to others. But, deeply immersed in Russia and its culture, he recognized how profoundly the Russian past influenced present-day thinking among Communist leaders. The Long Telegram predicted nothing less than a lengthy, life-and-death struggle between democracy and communism. Kennan described in detail the tsars' historic fear of outside influence, to which was now added the fanaticism of Communist ideology; the Soviet rulers "found justification for their instinctive fear of the outside world, for the dictatorship without which they did not know how to rule, for cruelties they did not dare not to inflict, [and] for sacrifices they felt bound to demand." The telegram included the prediction that "we have here a political force committed fanatically to the belief that with the US there can be no permanent modus vivendi, that it is desirable and necessary that the internal harmony of our society be disrupted, our traditional way of life be destroyed, the international authority of our state be broken, if Soviet power is to be secure."

The Long Telegram electrified Washington. All senior officers of the State Department were sent a copy, and hundreds of other copies were distributed throughout the Washington establishment. A few weeks later Kennan's warnings would seem to have been borne out when the Kremlin refused to withdraw its troops from northern Iran, threatening oil supplies to the West. At this point, the crisis worsening, Winston Churchill, now ousted from office, travelled with President Truman to his home state of Missouri. In an address at Westminster College in the small midwestern town of Fulton, on 5 March 1946, Churchill articulated in public what was being said privately in Washington: "From Stettin in the Baltic to Trieste in the Adriatic, an iron curtain has descended across the continent."

But American public opinion was not yet ready for this interpretation of Soviet ambitions, containing as it did such a strong attack on a wartime ally. Churchill's speech was thought at the time to be too extreme, and most of the press denounced it. Even Truman, who had known beforehand of its content, had to say he had not; when pressed for a reaction at the time, he declined to comment.

In Moscow, Churchill's dramatic speech confirmed Stalin's suspicions of the West's hostility towards the Soviet Union. In an interview with foreign correspondents, Stalin decried Churchill's charge that Europe was divided by an

The first page of Kennan's Long Telegram, nineteen pages in all, from Moscow in February 1946. The telegram helped to mould US policy towards the Soviet Union in the early Cold War years.

> *From Stettin in the Baltic to Trieste in the Adriatic, an iron curtain has descended across the continent.*
>
> — Winston Churchill,
> 5 March 1946

"Churchill and His Predecessors." Following the Fulton speech, Hitler and Goebbels look approvingly at a warmongering Churchill in a Soviet cartoon in the magazine Krokodil. *The flags read: "Iron Curtain Over Europe" and "Anglo-Saxons Should Rule the World."*

ideological Iron Curtain as warmongering, as a call to arms against the Soviet Union. *Pravda* called Churchill a racist, and even compared him to Hitler — a theme that Soviet cartoonists eagerly took up. The old wartime alliance was splitting at the seams.

Time to Get Tough

As the political temperature rose, the consensus in Washington came round to a realization that the West would have to stand up to the Soviet Union. Truman's mother passed him a message via a cousin: "Tell Harry to be good, be honest, and behave himself, but I think it is now time for him to get tough with someone." Byrnes was criticized for failing to take a harder line with the Soviets and risked losing support. But at a meeting of senior officials at the State Department he declared, "We're going to take a stand." In March the opportunity offered itself in Iran.

Iran shared a thousand-mile border with the Soviet Union, and there was a history of tensions along that line. Since early in the century Britain had dominated what used to be called Persia. That country's oil supplies had generated huge profits for British Petroleum (BP) and for the British government, which controlled the concessions to exploit the reserves. In 1941, to prevent the oil fields from falling into the hands of Germany, the Russians and the British had jointly occupied Iran. The old shah was forced to abdicate in favour of his son, Mohammed Reza Pahlavi, who was less pro-German and more friendly to the Allies. An agreement was then drawn up stipulating that both the British and Soviet armies would withdraw after the war. However, when the departure date came up in early March 1946, only the British withdrew. The Soviet troops remained, "pending examination of the situation." An American consul reported large-scale troop movements, and Washington was gripped with a sense that here was a critical issue. Not wanting to be presented with another Soviet fait accompli, Truman warned Ambassador Harriman: "The Russians are refusing to take their troops out — as they agreed to do in their treaty with the British — and this may lead to war." America would now act.

Byrnes decided to reprove the Soviet Union publicly before the United Nations, providing the newly created international forum with its first full-scale crisis. The American case was presented to the Security Council by Byrnes himself: "There are forty nations not represented here. They look to us to give each one of them the assurance that the doors of the Security Council are open to them to present a grievance when they say that grievance threatens national security." He warned that unless the UN took a tough line, it "will die in its infancy of inefficiency and ineffectiveness." The Soviet representative, Andrei Gromyko, tried to get a postponement of the debate; failing in that, he ceremoniously walked out of the Security Council — the first of many Soviet walkouts during the Cold War.

Stalin, however, had never wished to risk military confrontation with the West over Iran, and after a few weeks of negotiations with the Iranians, he withdrew his troops. As quickly as the Iranian crisis had flared up, it was over.

Andrei Gromyko

Fulton, 1946

5 March. Harry Truman and Winston Churchill ride through Fulton, Missouri, in Truman's home state, on their way to Westminster College, where Churchill would deliver his "Iron Curtain" speech. His words of warning rang out around the world.

But it foreshadowed the pattern of crisis behaviour to come: the Soviet Union wished to seize every opportunity to test Western resolve, but would stop short of direct military engagement when the other side refused to back down; America, for its part, felt the need to draw a line on the map, and to rally forces in support of that line. And there were other considerations; in the case of Iran, the question of oil. By the end of the war, the United States needed to find new sources of oil to replace its own dwindling reserves. President Roosevelt had courted the princes of Saudi Arabia, and the whole Middle East had fast become a region of prime strategic importance to the United States. Throughout the war, the American presence in the Iranian oil industry grew, and Truman and Byrnes were determined to maintain that growth. Even though the Iranian crisis did not develop into full-scale conflict, it did help to further the rift between East and West.

The Problem of Germany

The major area of disagreement and confrontation throughout the rest of 1946 and 1947 would remain Europe. And at the heart of Europe was the problem of a defeated Germany, divided by agreement of the victors into four zones of military occupation. The British, French, and American zones, in the west of Germany, included the great iron and steel plants of the Ruhr and most of that nation's industrial heartland. The Soviet zone, in the east, was mostly agricultural. Soviet policy towards Germany was to extract as much as possible in reparations, as a way of making up for massive losses endured in the Nazi invasion. At Potsdam the Allies had endorsed this policy. They even agreed to dismantle industrial plants in the Ruhr for the Soviets to cart away. A plan was put forward to reduce German industry to 70 per cent of its pre-war level and to eliminate some industries completely: the manufacture of synthetic oil, petrol, and rubber, for instance. Stalin was determined to prevent the revival of a strong, aggressive Germany, backed by the United States, which might once again threaten the Soviet Union.

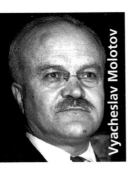

Vyacheslav Molotov

On 25 April 1946 the Council of Foreign Ministers convened at the Luxembourg Palace in Paris for preliminary discussions of a peace settlement, and its meetings lasted for two months. Secretary Byrnes came under more pressure to "get tough," and for much of the time he was accompanied by the Senate Foreign Relations Committee chairman, Senator Arthur Vandenberg of Michigan, a Republican. In Paris, Vandenberg said, "I am more than ever convinced that communism is on the march on a world-wide scale, which only America can stop." The Soviets wanted the four-power agreements already negotiated at Yalta and Potsdam to be the basis for any settlement, but one sticking point followed another: the question of peace treaties with Austria and Italy; reparations from Italy; the position of Trieste; the demilitarization of Germany.

During this long round of diplomacy, Molotov, the Soviet representative, became known in the Western press as "Mr. No." It suited Western interests for public opinion to perceive the Russian position in negative terms; it helped America claim the moral high ground in the debate that followed. Byrnes

I am more than ever convinced that communism is on the march on a worldwide scale, which only America can stop.

— Sen. Arthur Vandenberg, 25 April 1946

repeatedly asked his aides whether the Russian position was "based on a desire for security or expansion," and the answers he got always emphasized expansion. Now it is clear that the Soviets' sense of their own weakness, carefully concealed, was what determined their actions. In Eastern Europe, Stalin would risk confrontation with the West to secure a buffer zone against Germany. Elsewhere he would broadly respect the agreements reached at Yalta and Potsdam and would avoid direct confrontation. Although in his speeches he paid lip service to the old Marxist ideals of world revolution, including a belief in the ultimate victory of communism over capitalism, there is no hard evidence that Stalin ever realistically thought about invading the West. Despite the strength of the Red Army, Stalin knew that technologically he was still weaker than his opponents. And in these immediate postwar

ABOVE: Dresden, devastated by Allied bombing in February 1945. ABOVE RIGHT: German soldiers, captured on the Eastern Front, return to Berlin. Wherever one looked in postwar Europe, there was dejection, suffering, and ruin.

years, America had the atom bomb and the Soviet Union did not.

The Soviets were determined to keep Germany weak. So too were the French, whose armies were defeated in 1940 by Hitler's blitzkrieg, and who then suffered four years of occupation, the third invasion of their territory by Germany in less than a century. The fact that these major diplomatic negotiations took place in Paris, and that France was now one of the Big Four, was a boost to French national pride, but the French were no less hard-line than the Soviets in wanting to keep Germany down and to seize its industries as reparations.

On the last night of the Council of Foreign Ministers meeting, Byrnes and Molotov had dinner together. For once the mood was fairly cordial, and Byrnes decided to take advantage of the opportunity. He asked Molotov, "Why then don't you tell me what is really in your heart and mind on the subject of Germany?" Molotov replied that the Soviet Union simply wanted what it had asked for at Yalta: $10 billion in reparations, and participation with the United States, Britain, and France in four-power control over the industries of the Ruhr. Byrnes later reflected that, whatever else the Soviets and their propaganda might say, "the statement made by Molotov that night represents the real desires of the Soviet High Command."

During the summer of 1946 America took a new view of the central issue concerning Germany. Byrnes and his advisers now came to the conclusion that there could be no industrial recovery in Europe until the German economy had itself begun to recover. At a speech in Stuttgart on 6 September 1946, Byrnes announced: "It is not in the interests of the German people, or in the interests of world peace, that Germany should become a pawn or a partner in the military struggle for power between the East and the West." He went on to say: "The American people want to return the government of Germany to the people of Germany. The American people want to help the German people to win their way back to an honorable place among the free and peace-loving nations of the world." Byrnes even suggested that Germany's new eastern frontier with Poland, which the Poles thought vital to their security, might be unfair and subject to change in the future.

This critically important speech marked the final breakup of the old wartime alliance. American policy in Europe over the next couple of years would be driven by the need to build up Germany, to provide an effective buffer against what was believed to be the threat of Soviet expansion. The Soviet Union persisted in creating its own buffer zone against Germany. And although both sides continued publicly to call for re-unification of Germany under four-power control, it became slowly more clear that everyone's interests were served by keeping Germany divided — at least in the short run.

Secretary of State James F. Byrnes, speaking in Stuttgart on 6 September 1946, announces that the United States wishes to see a rehabilitated Germany. The speech, coming so soon after the war, caused tremors in Poland and the Soviet Union.

The Paris Peace Conference

At the end of July 1946 twenty-one nations gathered in Paris for a peace conference intended to resolve outstanding issues from the war. Just before the conference opened, the United States detonated two atom bombs at Bikini Atoll in the Pacific, perhaps to remind the Kremlin of its atomic weapons monopoly. It was not an auspicious prelude to a peace conference.

The Paris peace conference was modelled on the Versailles conference, which had redrawn the map of Europe after the First World War. But the spirit of co-operation between the victorious powers was so poor that the conference achieved little of substance. Harold Nicolson, a British veteran of Versailles, who was in Paris to report for the BBC, said, "It is a public performance, not a serious discussion." Ernest Bevin, British foreign secretary, is reported to have told Nicolson, "Believe me, 'arold, our trouble is that the Russians are frightened and the Yanks bomb-minded."

After hundreds of hours in session, the peace conference adjourned on 15 October, leaving final agreement on all remaining issues to be reached by the Council of Foreign Ministers. The Big Four were to meet again and again over the following months, but the strains of the developing Cold War prevented finalization of any comprehensive postwar treaty. As if to signal this failure, Britain and the United States agreed to unify their two zones in Germany as of 1 January 1947 in a new federation to be called, bizarrely, Bizonia. This was the first step towards acceptance of the division of Germany.

Throughout 1946 tension between the United States and the Soviet Union grew. In July, Truman asked his special counsel, Clark Clifford, to compile a

Between 1946 and 1948, the United States would detonate twenty-three nuclear devices at Bikini Atoll in the Marshall Islands. This atomic blast in 1946 sent up a column of water 5,000 feet high and 2,000 feet across at its base.

Bikini Atoll, 1946

list of agreements the Soviets had broken or were not living up to. Instead Clifford and his assistant, George Elsey, reviewed every aspect of postwar Soviet behaviour and American-Soviet relations. The two aides spoke with

Clark Clifford

most senior officials in the administration, in the Defense Department, in the Federal Bureau of Investigation (FBI), and with all the agencies of government that had dealt with the Soviet Union. The results surprised them. Elsey later remembered that "there was absolute unanimity in all of the agencies concerned as to the nature of the problems we had and the kind of response we were going to have to make." The Clifford-Elsey report put the blame squarely on Stalin for the breakdown of relations between the wartime allies. It concluded that "the Soviet Union constitutes a real menace to freedom in this world; freedom in Europe; freedom in the United States. So we must prepare for it."

On the evening that Truman read this report, he called Clifford at home and asked how many copies had been made. When Clifford said there were

George Elsey

twenty copies, the president told him to bring all of them to the Oval Office the following morning. "I don't want it to get out," Truman said. "This will blow the roof off the White House, and very likely the roof off the Kremlin." Clifford gathered all the copies and handed them over to Truman — all except one that he kept for himself. Although the president did not disagree with the Clifford-Elsey conclusion that America must be ready to act against increasing Soviet aggression, he did not think the public was ready to hear this.

The lone dissenting voice inside the administration, Secretary of Commerce Henry Wallace, had taken a more conciliatory line on the Soviet position since the end of the war. He believed that the Russians were only trying to stand up for what they had won at Yalta and Potsdam. For America to take a tough line would be to force Stalin to take a tougher line in response. His view ran counter to that of Truman, and in September the president asked for Wallace's resignation. Within the administration, agreement was now complete.

Trouble in the Eastern Mediterranean

The next flashpoint was in the eastern Mediterranean. One country that had suffered immensely, from Nazi occupation as well as from civil war, was Greece. Much of that nation's infrastructure had been destroyed. Roads, bridges, and railways had been smashed, factories had been laid waste, and the Corinth Canal had been blocked by a retreating German army. The occupation had been particularly brutal, with public executions for those accused of resisting the Nazis. By the time of the final liberation of Greece in 1944, much of that country was in the hands of resistance fighters, ELAS (the National Popular Liberation Army), and many of them were Communists. But Churchill, then still in power, was determined to restore the monarchy, along with a pro-Western government, and sent British troops to Greece.

In December 1944 civil war began between ELAS and the British puppet

This German cartoon shows the United States and the Soviet Union dividing the globe. They are smiling friendship but have their weapons at the ready. Less than two years before, they had been allies.

Cold War

government. The Greek Communists naturally looked to Stalin for support, but in his secret Moscow accord with Churchill in October that year, Stalin had already agreed that Greece was part of the Western sphere of influence. Stalin honoured this agreement because he did not choose to confront the West in Greece. The Americans wrongly believed that Stalin was behind this civil war, but in fact support for the Greek Communists came from Yugoslav leader Marshal Tito, who secretly sent supplies of arms across the Macedonian border.

The local Orthodox priest sits with pro-government forces studying a war map in Grammos, Greece, during the long and bitter civil war against the Communist left. Britain had initially supplied the anti-Communist forces, but by early 1947 could no longer afford to do so.

ELAS leaders realized too slowly that military aid from the Soviet Union would not be forthcoming. Unwisely, they boycotted a general election in 1946, further isolating themselves from the political process. The civil war was to drag on for another three years, until Tito finally gave up supplying the rebels.

Also in 1946 trouble loomed in Turkey, when Moscow demanded freedom of access for its warships through the Dardanelles into the Mediterranean. This had been discussed at Potsdam, and the Kremlin saw it as a legitimate demand, a reward for its enormous contribution to the Allied victory. Turkey had been formally neutral in the war but, sympathetic to the Germans, had closed the straits to Russian shipping. Now the United States responded to Turkey's refusal to open the straits by calling for creation of a United Nations agency to take control of the Dardanelles. An uneasy period followed, as the Soviet Union positioned twelve divisions on its border with Turkey and the United States sent warships to Istanbul. By the end of 1946 stalemate was acknowledged, which in effect meant a climbdown by the Soviet Union.

The Outcome of Winter

All these tensions were given new edge by the bitter winter that gripped the whole of Europe in 1946–1947, the worst in living memory. Everywhere, temperatures dropped to record lows. Britain's winter was especially severe, and its fragile economic recovery faltered. On 12 February 1947 a further wave of blizzards swept Britain, and the coal industry was unable to meet the extra demand for power. In the fuel crisis that followed, the government was forced to cut coal supplies to all industries by half, and electric power was limited to a few hours per day. Already impoverished by the war, and now further undermined by the energy shortage, the British economy was heading for disaster. Unemployment rose to 6 million. Hugh Dalton, chancellor of the exchequer, warned: "We are, I'm afraid, drifting in a state of semi-animation towards the rapids."

The British government decided that it could no longer cope with its responsibilities abroad, for the expense of maintaining troops throughout the world was draining resources. The British occupation of Germany alone was costing a million pounds a day. And the run on the pound, following its return to convertibility after the American loan in the summer of 1946, was draining gold reserves. Furthermore, bread rationing, which had not been necessary even in the darkest days of the war, had to be introduced because so much of the country's grain was being shipped to feed the starving Germans.

The Labour cabinet decided to speed up its plans to abandon Britain's imperial role. It announced that independence would be granted to India no later than June 1947. Earl Louis Mountbatten was appointed the last viceroy, to oversee India's transition to independence. At the United Nations, the British government unexpectedly announced that it would hand back its Mandate in Palestine. The new world body would now be left to decide how to resolve the increasingly violent conflict between Zionist Jews, to whom Britain had offered a "Jewish homeland in Palestine," and the Palestinian Arabs, who feared that their homes would be sacrificed to a Jewish state.

In late February, London also decided to end economic aid to Greece and Turkey. And in the case of Greece, where British troops were still engaged in conflict, Britain would simply withdraw. This would leave both Turkey and Greece vulnerable to falling under the sway of communism unless someone else stepped in.

OPPOSITE: *The ferocious winter of 1947 caused havoc and helped force a reduction in the UK's international role.*
ABOVE: *There had been rationing of many foods in Britain during the war, but not of bread. In 1946 bread rationing was introduced, for at the time Britain was sending much of its wheat to feed the starving Germans.*

On the afternoon of Friday, 21 February, the secretary of the British ambassador in Washington rang the State Department to ask for an urgent meeting with George C. Marshall, the new secretary of state. Marshall had already left for the weekend, but Under-secretary Dean Acheson could guess what was up. The urgent "blue paper" message from London was delivered to Acheson, and he was stunned by the announced speed of British withdrawal from the eastern Mediterranean. He later wrote of the communiqués: "They were shockers. British aid to Greece and Turkey would end in six weeks. . . . His Majesty's government devoutly hoped that we could assume the burden." Acheson began a whirlwind weekend of meetings to prepare plans for presentation to Marshall on Monday morning, as well as estimates of what costs would be involved. George McGhee, a department official, recalled this frantic weekend as "the real beginning of it all as far as the State Department was concerned." When Acheson presented the news to Marshall on that Monday morning, he told him: "We're right up against it now."

Dean Acheson

Marshall and Truman were persuaded of the need for action, but with Congress solidly Republican, Truman recognized the vital importance of first securing the support of that body. Just a week after receiving the British note, he called a meeting of congressional leaders at the White House. Truman and Marshall presented their point of view, but Acheson, sensing the moment was critical and that their case was not yet made, asked to speak. "No time was left for measured appraisal," he later recalled. Acheson explained that a Soviet takeover in the eastern Mediterranean could open three continents to Soviet penetration. "Like apples in a barrel infected by one rotten one," he told the gathering, "the corruption of Greece would infect Iran and all to the east. It would also carry infection to Africa through Asia Minor and Egypt, and to Europe through Italy and France." There was a long silence after Acheson spoke. Then Senator Vandenberg said solemnly, "Mr. President, if you will say that to the Congress . . . , I will support you, and I believe that most of its members will do the same."

Le Havre, 1949

American tractors arrive in Europe. The imaginative Marshall Plan bolstered the economies of the countries of war-ravaged Europe, but advanced the West-East division of the continent. It helped revive agriculture and manufacturing in Western Europe; it also helped US exporters.

Marshall Plan

1947–1952

Chief Justice Frederick M. Vinson (right) administers the oath of office to Secretary of State George C. Marshall as President Truman looks on. Marshall would play a crucial role in leading the West in the early Cold War.

The Truman Doctrine

On the morning of 21 January 1947, in a short ceremony at the White House, General George C. Marshall, the wartime hero and former army chief of staff, was sworn in as secretary of state. In April of the previous year James F. Byrnes had filed a letter of resignation with the president when a medical check-up revealed a heart condition. Byrnes wrote that he would leave office upon completing treaties under way with the Soviet "satellites" Romania, Bulgaria, and Hungary. When these were signed in December 1946, Truman held Byrnes to his letter; he no longer enjoyed the president's confidence.

Austere, aloof, and supremely proper, General Marshall never permitted anyone to address him by his first name. Even when the president asked to call him George, Marshall replied, "No, General Marshall will do." Through the war years he had coordinated the nation's war effort and balanced the conflicting claims of the military services fighting simultaneously in Europe and the Pacific. Churchill called him "the organizer of victory." Truman, who had worked with him throughout the war, was delighted that Marshall accepted his offer to head the State Department and would rely on him throughout his term of office.

General Marshall was not well informed on foreign affairs. He relied upon his advisers to brief him but had no love of "kicking a problem around." He approached an issue head-on and was well known for telling his staff, "Don't fight the problem, gentlemen. Solve it!" His direct, clear-cut perception of events fitted in perfectly with Truman's. When he swore the oath of allegiance on that frosty January morning, few could have imagined how momentous would be the changes he ushered in, changes that would escalate the Cold War and further divide the world into two hostile camps.

Almost immediately Marshall found himself plunged into the deep end of international controversy in the full-scale crisis over Greece and Turkey. Having gained the backing of congressional leaders, the president was determined to go on the offensive. On 12 March, before a joint session of Congress, Truman called for $400 million of funding to aid Greece and Turkey. But to get across to the Republican majority in both houses the urgency of the situation, he had to persuade the resistant isolationists that, unlike what happened after the First World War, when the United States withdrew from the

ABOVE RIGHT: *President Truman asks Congress for $400 million to aid Greece and Turkey; America would not abandon Europe and the free world.* ABOVE: *Krokodil depicts Europe crushed by the weight of US self-interest.*

international stage and turned inward, America could not this time abdicate its leadership of the free world. In addition Truman had to persuade Congress that not only was it charitable to give aid to Greece and Turkey, but fundamental American interests were directly at stake. To do this the president pitched the struggle as one between freedom and oppression, democracy and tyranny — "them" and "us." Truman declared that "the seeds of totalitarian regimes are nurtured by misery and want. They spread and grow in the evil soil of poverty and strife. They reach their full growth when the hope of a people for a better life has died. We must keep that hope alive. . . . I believe it must be the policy of the United States to support free peoples who are resisting attempted subjugation by armed minorities or by outside pressures."

This presentation of the ideological struggle in simple adversarial terms would become known as the Truman Doctrine. By focusing the defence of Western interests in Greece and Turkey on stopping the advance of communism, Truman was articulating a point of view that would dominate American thinking for a quarter of a century. No one at the time used the phrase "domino effect," but, following the logic of Dean Acheson's earlier argument to congressional leaders, it was thought that if Greece and Turkey fell to the Communists, then Western Europe, northern Africa, Iran, and the

Middle East would all be threatened. In the face of Stalin's constant probing of Western weakness, Truman wanted to draw a line and say, "No farther." The words Truman used in addressing Congress in March 1947 would echo down the decades, and the thought behind them would justify American policy at least until Vietnam.

The impact of Truman's speech was immediate. George Elsey, the Truman aide who had collaborated the previous year with Clark Clifford on surveying government attitudes towards the Soviet Union, was in the balcony and later

ABOVE: *The Marshall Plan offers a lifeline to struggling Europe, according to American cartoonist Fitzpatrick.* ABOVE RIGHT: *Refugees in a camp at Lübeck, Germany, wait hopefully for a handout of food.*

recalled how quiet Congress was when Truman spoke. "Usually there was rustling or occasional clapping, but this time the members sat in silence. There was no question in anyone's mind that this was an important historical moment." The power of Truman's rhetoric nourished the anti-Communist spirit that was just beginning to grip America. Congress voted overwhelmingly to approve aid to Greece and Turkey.

Marshall missed Truman's historic speech. He was already in Moscow for yet another foreign ministers conference, along with representatives of Britain and France. The Big Four once more tried to tackle the problem of Germany, which was left over from the disappointing Paris peace conference of a year earlier. But again ideological divisions between the Soviets and the three other countries prevented any real progress. Towards the end of nearly six weeks of meetings, Marshall asked to meet privately with Stalin, hoping to clear the bottleneck by conveying the sense of frustration America felt about the Soviet position. Marshall came out of that meeting more alarmed than before. It seemed to him that Stalin was stalling for time, waiting for the stricken European economies to collapse, knowing that communism would flourish in the fertile ground of poverty and the widespread sense of economic injustice.

On his way back from Moscow, Marshall stopped over in Germany to meet with General Lucius D. Clay, military governor of the US sector of occupied Germany. This was Marshall's direct introduction to the chaos that was post-war Europe. It alarmed him even more. Based on reports of the growing lack of food and supplies of all kinds in western Germany, he was convinced of the necessity for action.

The European Recovery Program

On his return to Washington on 28 April, Marshall felt there was no time to lose. That evening, in a radio broadcast, he reported that "the recovery of Europe has been far slower than had been expected. Disintegrating forces are becoming evident. The patient is sinking whilst the doctors deliberate." The following day, at the State Department, he put the policy-planning staff to work on coming up with ideas for an economic recovery programme. Several different strands of thinking would come together in the plan that was to bear Marshall's name. George Kennan, now director of the policy-planning staff, took the long-term view of Europe's problem as the need to contain what he identified as Soviet expansionism. He called for programmes to be organized both in Western Europe and in the United States, which when integrated would lead to European self-sufficiency in four to five years. He was hopeful that some form of union among the economies of the European states would also result from the American-led recovery.

Another crucial figure in developing the Marshall Plan was Will Clayton, under-secretary of state. Having spent much of April in Europe, and desperately worried about the appalling situation, he believed that in the face of such overwhelming economic problems, it was only a matter of weeks before Communist parties would be able to take control in France and Italy. On his flight back from Europe he sketched out some thoughts for a recovery programme. He took the position that the principal need was to save Europe from starvation and chaos rather than from the Russians.

Marshall agreed that an announcement of America's intentions could wait no longer. During the war Marshall had been invited by Harvard University to receive an honorary degree; he had made the excuse then of having no time to visit Cambridge. Now, with only a few days' notice, he told the university of his availability for the commencement ceremonies scheduled for 5 June 1947. Along with poet T. S. Eliot and physicist Robert Oppenheimer, Marshall was awarded an honorary degree, and he made a speech of about seven minutes' duration. In this short speech he presented a new initiative for economic relief to the countries of Europe, in order "to restore the confidence of the European people in the economic future of their own countries and of Europe as a whole." Marshall made it clear that he was inviting the Europeans to come forward with their own ideas and proposals. "Our policy is directed not against any country or doctrine but against hunger, poverty, desperation, and chaos. Its purpose should be the revival of a working economy in the world so as to permit the emergence of political and social conditions in which free institutions can exist." This was how the European Recovery Program, the Marshall Plan, was announced to the world.

5 June 1947. General Marshall marches in procession at Harvard University to receive an honorary degree and to deliver a short address that would make history. Among others honoured that day was J. Robert Oppenheimer, father of the atom bomb. The event received very little coverage in the press.

Rarely in history has a speech of such significance been made with so little fanfare. The presentation had been so rapidly organized that no one had thought to invite the newsreel companies. And the American press failed to accord the event front-page coverage. Many of Marshall's own State Department officials were taken by surprise, not having expected an announcement so soon. However, a few European journalists had been tipped off that something significant was going to be said. The BBC correspondent, Leonard Miall, had been alerted to attend by Dean Acheson himself and filed a report on the speech to London.

The following morning, Ernest Bevin, Britain's foreign secretary, heard Miall's report on BBC radio and was galvanized by what was said. This was what he had been praying for. Later describing the speech as "like a life-line to sinking men," he had immediately asked British Embassy officials in Washington for clarification, but they knew nothing about it. Within days, however, the embassy confirmed that Marshall was indeed inviting European nations to come forward with proposals for American aid to help their own recovery. Bevin decided there was no time to lose. He flew to Paris to meet his counterpart, Georges Bidault. They called a foreign ministers meeting in Paris for the end of the month; events would now move quickly.

At this point a new, critical issue came into play. Marshall's invitation had been framed in broad enough terms to include all the countries of Europe. This apparently left open to question whether East European nations, already under Stalin's influence, would apply for aid. And even more central, would the Soviet Union itself seek economic assistance from the United States? During the war the USSR had willingly accepted Lend-Lease aid from America. And near the end of the war, in January 1945, Moscow had formally requested a loan of $6 billion from Washington; but in the end Stalin thought better of pursuing it. The openness of Marshall's invitation now provoked further debate within the Kremlin. The Institute of World Economy, under the prominent Soviet economist Evgeny Varga, came up with a paper arguing that the Soviet economy was in real need of dollar investments. Foreign Minister Molotov appeared to be convinced, and he forwarded Varga's paper to the Politburo along with his own recommendation. Molotov believed that if the Marshall Plan was an extension of wartime Lend-Lease aid, then the Soviet Union should participate.

Stalin, however, saw the issue not only in economic but in political terms, and his suspicious nature detected an American plot. He thought that once the Americans got their fingers into the Soviet economy, they would never take them out. And going to capitalists for financial assistance was, in Stalin's view, the ultimate sign of failure for the Communist system. The socialist economies would have to find their own way forward. Nevertheless, Molotov argued in the Politburo that he should at least go to the Paris conference and assess the American offer. With some reluctance, Stalin agreed. But he made it clear that Molotov must stay in daily contact.

Molotov arrived in Paris on 26 June 1947 with a large delegation, to the great surprise of the British and French. His entourage consisted of bankers and economists as well as diplomats, all of whom were to scrutinize every

Disintegrating forces are becoming evident. The patient is sinking whilst the doctors deliberate.

— George C. Marshall,
28 April 1947

The Big Four: Ernest Bevin, British foreign secretary; George C. Marshall, US secretary of state; Vyacheslav Molotov, Soviet foreign minister; and Georges Bidault, French foreign minister, meet in Moscow to discuss the future of Germany, March 1947.

Vienna, 1947

All over Europe people struggled to find jobs and food to feed their families. The United States feared a hungry Europe would go Communist.

sentence of the American plan. Molotov would back limited American involvement in the economies of Europe with no strings attached. However, it soon became clear that the Soviet position differed from that of Britain and France, who saw Marshall's offer as a plan for aiding in the full-scale reconstruction of Europe.

New Model Spies

It was during this period that Soviet intelligence gained from penetrating the British Foreign Office in London. In the 1930s several potential spies who had come to believe that capitalism was deeply corrupt and had had its day were recruited at Cambridge University. They all believed that the Soviet Union offered a new model for society, with a fairer, more just system. This ring of spies was informally led by Harold "Kim" Philby, a remarkable figure who rose high in British intelligence but throughout his active life was a double agent, passing on information to the USSR. Outwardly a hardworking, selfless public servant, he was respected by colleagues, some of whom right up to his defection in 1963 had no idea of his double life. In the summer of 1947, although Philby was working in the British Embassy in Istanbul, others from the Cambridge spy ring in Washington and London were providing intelligence to the Soviets. As diplomatic activity increased during the meetings in Paris, British spies were passing on to their Soviet "minders" in London masses of

The Stars and Stripes logo of the European Recovery Program was stamped on every package sent abroad, so that Europeans would know where the help was coming from.

The Kremlin and the Marshall Plan: An Insider's View

In a recent interview Vladimir Yerofeyev, who served in the Soviet Foreign Ministry after the war, described the Kremlin's reaction to the Marshall Plan:

"Of course it was taken very seriously. I should say that there were conflicting feelings. On the one hand, there was a willingness to agree to discuss the question; that was Molotov's stance. He even wrote a note to the Central Committee arguing that it was necessary to start negotiations; he understood that the Soviet Union needed help. In his reply he noted that reconstruction was everyone's main aim, and the United States's offer of help should be welcomed. His reaction to the Marshall Plan was positive.

"Stalin, with his suspicious nature, didn't like it: 'This is a ploy by Truman. It is nothing like Lend-Lease — a different situation. They don't want to help us. What they want is to infiltrate European countries.'

"But Molotov insisted on his view, and Stalin said, go. So Molotov went to the Paris conference in 1946. He listened to all the proposals. He understood that it was not simple; the aid had strings attached.

"Stalin, meanwhile, received information that the Americans did not want us to take part. The Americans indicated that nobody was to be afraid to contact them. Stalin became even more suspicious and moved to stop the countries friendly to us taking part. Yugoslavia and Poland agreed. Finland too. Finland had not signed a peace treaty and didn't want to risk jeopardizing that, so it pulled back from taking part — very sharply.

"The Czechs undertook to take part in the conference, so Stalin summoned Gottwald and Masaryk, the foreign minister, to Moscow. Very severe pressure was put on them: if by 4 AM on the twelfth — the day the conference started — they had gone there, they would face the consequences.

"They understood what it meant. So at the last moment they were prevented. Nine countries refused to take part in the conference. Sixteen agreed. The Soviet Union and the socialist-oriented countries stayed away. So did Finland. . . .

"The US never really wanted the Soviet Union and its satellites to benefit from Marshall aid. They made no further effort to persuade them to take part."

Guy Burgess (TOP) and Donald Maclean (BOTTOM) were key figures in a ring of British spies recruited to world communism — which they all saw as a more just model for modern society — while at Cambridge University in the 1930s. Along with their mentor, Harold "Kim" Philby, these two occupied important positions in British intelligence and the Foreign Office and were able to pass valuable information at critical moments to their Soviet minders. From them, Molotov learned that America and Britain saw a strong Germany as the key to reviving the European economy.

detail about British and American intentions for the Marshall Plan.

Early on the morning of 30 June, Molotov received a secret cable in cipher from his deputy Andrei Vyshinsky with information obtained by Soviet intelligence. The cable dealt with meetings between US under-secretary Will Clayton and British ministers. It was clear that the Americans and the British had already agreed in advance that the Marshall Plan should not be an extension of wartime Lend-Lease or even a continuation of postwar aid through UNRRA (United Nations Relief and Rehabilitation Administration). Instead, America and Britain saw this as a new plan for the reconstruction of war-torn Europe, but with Germany the key factor in reviving the continent's economy. This was totally out of line with Soviet thinking, which was to keep Germany weak and to extract as much as possible from the German economy in reparation for wartime devastation of Russia. The Soviet Union was always anxious about what it saw as attempts to downplay its status as a victor in the war when it came to dealing with Germany, especially with regard to reparations.

Molotov cabled Stalin that all hope of effecting the Soviet restrictions on Marshall aid now seemed dead. On 3 July, Molotov, accusing the Western powers of seeking to divide Europe into two hostile camps, gathered up his papers, left the meeting, and returned that evening to Moscow. The Americans, British, and French heaved sighs of relief. With the Soviets out of the way, formal invitations were issued the following day to twenty-two countries to attend a new Paris conference, scheduled for 12 July, to frame Europe's response to the Marshall Plan.

Invitations to the new Paris conference went out to all the states of Western Europe except Spain. They went also to Romania, Bulgaria, Hungary, Albania, Finland, Yugoslavia, Poland, and Czechoslovakia. After initial hesitation, Moscow instructed its satellites to reject the invitation. On 7 July messages from Moscow informed party bosses in the East European capitals that "under the guise of drafting plans for the revival of Europe, the sponsors of the conference in fact are planning to set up a Western bloc which includes West Germany. In view of those facts . . . [we] suggest refusing to participate in the conference." Most of the Communist parties in the East European countries did just as they were told, eager to display their allegiance to Moscow. But the Polish and Czech governments found the offer of US dollars too appealing. This was exactly what their economies needed.

In Czechoslovakia about one-third of the ministers in the coalition government were Communists, reflecting the share of the vote won by the party in the 1946 election. Discussions within the government about the offer of Marshall aid produced a unanimous decision to attend the Paris conference, with even the Communist ministers voting in support. When the Soviet chargé d'affaires in Prague visited Klement Gottwald, the Czechoslovak prime minister, also a Communist, he was told that the Czech government could not now withdraw since it already had notified the British and French, and the press had been informed of the intention to attend.

Stalin was furious. He summoned Gottwald to Moscow immediately. With him on 9 July went Jan Masaryk, the foreign minister, an independent non-Communist member of the government. Stalin kept the Czech delegation waiting until the early hours of the morning and then angrily told them to cancel their decision to attend the Paris conference at once. He regarded the Czech stance as a betrayal of the Soviet Union. If an Eastern European government attended the conference, this would undermine the campaign of West European Communist parties to discredit the Marshall Plan. He told the ministers that the Paris conference was part of a Western plot to isolate the Soviet Union. He brushed aside protests and permitted no argument.

On 11 July the Czech delegation returned to Prague. A meeting of the full government was called that lasted all day. At the close of the meeting a short announcement was made. The Czechoslovak government unanimously cancelled its decision to attend the Marshall Plan conference. Jan Masaryk was distraught. He told his friends: "I went to Moscow as the foreign minister of an independent sovereign state; I returned as a Soviet slave."

Pressure on the Poles forced them into line as well, and their government announced that it too would not attend the conference. Stalin had had his way. The Eastern bloc remained united, each state taking orders from the Kremlin.

From Washington's perspective the Marshall Plan was designed to shore up the European economies, ensure the future stability of the continent by avoiding economic catastrophe, and prevent the spread of communism, which was thriving in the economic chaos of Western Europe. But from the Kremlin's perspective, the plan appeared to be an aggressive attempt to wrest from Moscow economic control of the East European nations. Stalin felt his own power threatened by the lure of the dollar.

Although Stalin saw the Marshall Plan as an attempt to divide Europe and escalate the Cold War, in Washington his opposition to the plan was seen as in itself an aggressive act. The US ambassador in Moscow described it as "nothing less than a declaration of war by the Soviet Union." Both sides were now locked in mutual suspicion and distrust. The Marshall Plan was to make the Iron Curtain a more permanent feature of postwar Europe.

The Conference on European Economic Cooperation (CEEC) opened in Paris on 12 July with sixteen European nations attending. The meetings went on through the summer, and at times it seemed to Washington that the Europeans were simply preparing shopping lists rather than acting in concert to prioritize needs for reconstruction. But perhaps that was a lot to ask from a continent that only a few years earlier had been shattered by the enmities of a terrible war. The French were still anxious about the economic revival of Germany. The British wanted to maintain the supremacy of the pound. The Italians wanted food aid as soon as possible. The Greeks sought military support to end their long civil war. And so on.

The severe winter in Europe had been followed by a summer of drought. Now the continent was suffering from harvest failures. The already bad economic situation was nearing a crisis point. George Kennan expressed the despair of many American officials at the lack of progress in Paris. Citing European national policy differences as a source of paralysis in decision making, he accused the delegates of not having the "clarity of vision" needed to frame a new "design" for Europe as a whole. In September, US officials made

Jan Masaryk

WHEN THE TIME IS RIPE—

I went to Moscow as the foreign minister of an independent sovereign state; I returned as a Soviet slave.

— Jan Masaryk,
July 1947

it clear that the CEEC risked losing the offer of Marshall Plan aid unless it addressed issues specified by Washington, including long-term cooperation and the lifting of trade barriers. This threat finally brought the Europeans to their senses.

Differences put aside, the delegations approved a programme in Paris on 22 September. This included plans to restore agricultural production to pre-war levels and to raise industrial production to levels slightly higher than prewar; to achieve financial stability; to establish an organization to promote economic cooperation; and, finally, to expand payments to overcome dollar deficits. The CEEC programme estimated that a sum of $17 billion of US aid would be necessary to achieve these goals.

The First Meeting of Cominform

The same day that West European delegates in Paris offered their programme to Washington, Communist Party leaders gathered in the village of Szkliarska Poremba in Poland. This was the first meeting of a new socialist alliance to be called the Cominform (short for Communist Information Bureau), a revival of the old Communist alliance established by Lenin, the Comintern. Cominform was a direct response by Stalin to the Marshall Plan, an attempt to consolidate his control over the Soviet satellites and to bring unanimity to Eastern bloc strategy. Andrei Zhdanov, the Soviet ideologue, was Stalin's representative at the meeting. He opened the gathering with a long speech in which he pro-claimed that there were two rival camps in the world, one dedicated to the principles of "socialism and democracy," the other dedicated to the principles of "reaction and war." Zhdanov denounced the Truman Doctrine as aggres-sive and, playing on East European fears of resurgent Nazism, accused the Marshall Plan of trying to revive German industry under the control of American financiers.

Present at this first Cominform meeting in Poland were representatives of Communist parties in France and Italy. The Soviet strategy since 1945 had been for the Communist parties in Western Europe to operate through left-wing coalitions, the Popular Front, but the Russians were now impatient with the pace of advance by various Popular Fronts. The Communist Party in France and Italy, and also the Czech Communists, were ordered to move away from these coalitions and to seize the initiative. Zhdanov insisted that no economic recovery programme could succeed if the Western Communist parties went on the offensive against it.

In Washington, Congress was beginning to consider the European response to Marshall's offer. On 8 November a commit-tee chaired by Secretary of Commerce Averell Harriman recom-mended that a large foreign aid programme was vital to US national security. Using the logic of the Truman Doctrine, Harriman's committee concluded that "if the countries of middle-western and Mediterranean Europe sink under the burden of despair and become communist, Scandinavia will fall into the same camp [as will the Middle East]. ... The transfer of Western Europe, the second greatest industrial area in the world ... would radically change the American position." If the United

Andrei Zhdanov

Conflicting cartoon images of the Marshall Plan and the Cold War. Fitzpatrick, in the St. Louis Post-Dispatch, *shows the Kremlin's noose tightening around Czechoslovakia.* Krokodil *has the Europeans on their knees before their US paymaster.*

Kingdom followed, the "shift would be cataclysmic." Truman appealed to Congress for interim aid of $600 million to "give us time to plan out our part in an economic recovery program, and it will give the peoples of Europe the strength to hold out until such a program begins."

In France the Communist Party was doing what Cominform had told it to do, working to bring the Fourth Republic to its knees. A strike at the giant Renault factory just outside Paris had led to divisions within the coalition government, and when Communist ministers supported the strike they were

expelled from government. This initiated a long period of industrial chaos. Direct agitation by the general workers union, the Communist-led Confédération Générale du Travail, compounded spontaneous outbreaks of strikes over rising prices. Through the fall of 1947 France was paralysed by industrial disputes, which forced the coal mines, the electricity industry, and the railways to shut down. In Paris the garbage collectors struck and rubbish piled up in the streets. In November a million workers went on strike, and in December this peaked at 3 million. There were dozens of political rallies, and striking workers frequently clashed violently with the police. The French Communist Party formed workers assemblies, which Washington saw as "embryonic Soviets." In Paris ministers began to express fear of the country's descending into civil war.

There were acts of sabotage in the mines and on the railways as striking workers tried to prevent management and strikebreakers from keeping things going. Then on 4 December 1947, the night express from Lille to Paris was derailed by saboteurs. Twenty people were killed. No one ever accepted responsibility, but by this point the French people had had enough. Public opinion, which had been sympathetic to the strikers, now swung against

Renault workers on strike near Paris in 1947 demonstrate for more pay, more bread, and united action on the left. The strikes gained higher wages but failed to overthrow the French government. The United States withheld Marshall aid from France until order was restored.

Krokodil shows the European leaders as puppets of the United States and contrasts their submissiveness with the activism of the peoples of Europe demonstrating in the streets for a better life and against warmongering.

Our deepest concern with European recovery is that it is essential to the maintenance of the civilization in which the American way of life is rooted.

— Harry S. Truman,
17 December 1947

them, and the momentum of the strikes was lost. Washington made it clear to the French government that there could be no prospect of Marshall aid until the Communist threat was under control. On 8 December an offer of national wage increases was made to French workers. Although it fell far below the 25 per cent increase sought by the Communist Party, most trade unions accepted it. The wave of strikes broke, and slowly French industry got back to work.

Truman Submits the Marshall Plan to Congress

On 17 December, President Truman won approval for interim aid to France, Italy, and Austria. He then submitted the full Marshall aid legislation to Congress, again presenting his case in epochal terms. Truman argued that global economic deterioration would surely result if the "vast trading system" of Europe was not revived. "The United States, in common with other nations, would suffer." He went on: "Our deepest concern with European recovery is that it is essential to the maintenance of the civilization in which the American way of life is rooted." If West Europe went Communist, "it might well compel us to modify our own economic system and to forgo, for the sake of our own security, the enjoyment of our freedoms and privileges." Truman initially asked for the entire $17 billion in aid requested by the CEEC. But because of the concerns of Arthur Vandenberg, chairman of the influential Senate Foreign Relations Committee, Marshall, in January 1948, reduced the request to $6.8 billion, to cover the first fifteen-month period.

The debate in Washington dragged on month after month. Despite the administration's claims of urgency, the Republican majority in the Congress balked at such a vast expenditure. On 17 February 1948 the request was again reduced, this time to $5.3 billion, to cover the twelve months of fiscal 1949. Marshall himself presented the case to the Foreign Relations Committee. He stressed yet again the need for action, saying that "political and economic conditions have become acute.... I urge you to help these countries to continue to eat, to work, and to survive the winter."

The situation was galvanized by news of dramatic events in Czechoslovakia. The coalition government there had operated on the principle that Czechoslovak interests were best served by looking both to the West and to the East, a notion dear to the hearts of President Beneš and Foreign Minister Masaryk. But as relations between the two power blocs worsened, the position of Czechoslovakia, straddling East and West, became ever more untenable. Masaryk, though not a Communist, felt himself increasingly cut off by the West after Prague's failure to participate in the Marshall Plan. Indeed, Washington regarded the capitulation to Stalin over the Paris conference as signifying that Czechoslovakia was now part of the Soviet bloc. Washington began to abandon Prague.

The harvest of 1947 was especially bad in Czechoslovakia, with the yield of grain just two-thirds of that expected and the potato crop only half. The need for outside aid was desperate. Masaryk appealed to Washington, but it was made clear to him that there would be no aid and no loans until Prague's political stance changed. Although Masaryk tried to convince the US government that the Soviet line had been forced on them, he failed to change the American position. Then the Soviets promised Czechoslovakia 600,000 tons of grain, which helped prevent starvation and won wide support for Stalin among the Czechs. Foreign Trade Minister Hubert Ripka said, "Those idiots in Washington have driven us straight into the Stalinist camp."

When the Soviet deputy foreign minister arrived in Prague, supposedly to oversee delivery of the promised grain, the non-Communist ministers took a gamble. On 20 February they resigned from office, hoping to force the issue and precipitate an early election. But President Beneš, who was seriously ill,

ABOVE: *Klement Gottwald, premier and leader of the Czechoslovak Communist Party, calls for a new government after the resignation of non-Communist ministers in February 1948. (President Eduard Beneš stands to his left.)* ABOVE RIGHT: *Prague Castle looms in the background as units of armed factory workers march to a mass gathering.*

wavered. Following orders from Cominform, the Communists took to the streets, organizing giant rallies, whipping up popular support. They used the police to arrest and intimidate opponents. Workers assemblies were formed at factories. Beneš feared civil war. On 25 February he allowed Gottwald, the prime minister, to form a new Communist government. In five days the Communists had taken power in Prague. Czechoslovakia would be a member of the Soviet camp for more than forty years.

Masaryk stayed on as foreign minister but was now a broken man. The son of Tomáš Masaryk, the founder of the Czechoslovak republic at the end of the First World War, he epitomized the direct line of Czech freedom. Now his attempt to bridge East and West had failed. Two weeks later, on 10 March, he mysteriously fell to his death from the window of his bedroom high in the Czech Foreign Ministry. To this day no one knows whether he jumped or was pushed. Although thousands of mourners lined the streets for his funeral, Masaryk's death marked the end of a free Czechoslovakia.

News of the Communist takeover in Prague sent shock waves through Washington, where the Marshall Plan still inched its way forward. Now the case was made: without American intervention, Europe would fall to the Communists. Had Washington not written off Czechoslovakia as an Eastern bloc state, refusing to help the non-Communists, the outcome of events might have been different. Now the administration deliberately fanned the flames of anti-communism with talk of possible immediate conflict. The secretary of the navy proposed steps "to prepare the American people for war." The Joint Chiefs of Staff drew up an emergency war plan to meet a Soviet invasion of Western Europe.

At only two days' notice, on 17 March, Truman addressed a joint session of Congress. The nation looked to him to come up with a fighting speech, and he did. "The Soviet Union and its agents have destroyed the independence and democratic character of a whole series of nations in Eastern and Central Europe," he said. "It is this ruthless course of action, and the clear design to extend it to the remaining free nations of Europe, that have brought about the critical situation in Europe today. The tragic death of the Republic of Czechoslovakia has sent a shock wave through the civilized world.... There are times in world history when it is far wiser to act than to hesitate. There is some risk involved in action — there always is. But there is far more risk in failure to act." Truman asked approval for the Marshall Plan and for the enactment of universal military training and selective service.

The American nation rallied to the president's war cry, and on 3 April Congress approved $5.3 billion in Marshall aid. Paul G. Hoffman was named head of the new Economic Cooperation Administration (ECA), the organization that would administer and distribute the aid. Two weeks later sixteen European nations signed an agreement that created the Organization for European Economic Cooperation (OEEC), the body required by America to formalize requests for aid, recommend each country's share, and help in its distribution. Within weeks the first shipments of food aid were arriving in Europe. Next came fertilizers and tractors, to help increase agricultural productivity. Then came machines for industry. At last, the tap of Marshall aid had been turned on.

The Communist Threat to Italy

Meanwhile, another drama was unfolding, this time in Italy. The Italian Communist Party had grown to nearly 2 million members, the largest outside the Soviet bloc. Its leader, Palmiro Togliatti, was a remarkable man. Although he had spent the war years in Moscow, he was no stooge of the Kremlin. He wanted Italy to develop its own form of communism, one that suited the Italian character and reflected the hostility felt by most Italians, since the fall of Mussolini, to the tyranny of a single leader. His charisma and persuasive arguments found resonance in the poverty that plagued much of Italy. In the spring of 1947, in response to pressure from Washington, the Communists had been expelled from the coalition government. Now, allied with other left-wing socialist parties, the Communists and the Popular Front were free to rally support up and down Italy. Some meetings Togliatti addressed drew crowds of over 100,000.

A general election was called for 18 April 1948. Recognizing that it would be a critical one, the government of Christian Democrat Alcide de Gasperi tried to build up support for the middle ground through the centre right. The Christian Democrats organized political rallies to rival those of the Communists, and the political temperature in Italy rose dramatically.

"Look out" says the poster. "Construction work. Things are happening with the Marshall Plan."

The US government was desperately worried about a possible Communist victory. James V. Forrestal, one of the first American cold warriors and now secretary of defence, encouraged wealthy Italian Americans to contribute funds to combat the Communists. A letter-writing campaign was organized, and in all, 10 million letters were sent to relatives in Italy, imploring them not to vote Communist. Prominent Italian Americans eagerly gathered to support the cause, including Frank Sinatra, who broadcast on the Voice of America.

But writing letters was not going to be enough. The newly created Central Intelligence Agency (CIA) viewed the situation in Italy with alarm. Admiral Roscoe Hillenkoetter, the first director, called on the agency's counsel, Lawrence Houston, to study the National Security Act, which established the CIA, to see if there was wording that might authorize foreign covert activity. Houston checked the act but could find no explicit authorization. Asked by Hillenkoetter to try to work out a way, Houston then spotted a phrase that called upon the CIA to "perform such other functions and duties related to intelligence affecting the national security as the National Security Council may from time to time direct." It was the opening the CIA was looking for. If the chairman of the National Security Council approved the action and if Congress voted funds, then the CIA could undertake covert operations abroad. The chairman of the National Security Council was the president himself, and Truman went along with it.

On 19 December 1947, at its first meeting, the National Security Council instructed the CIA to do what it could, covertly, to prevent a Communist victory in Italy. In the rapid movement of events, few at the time saw this as any sort of turning point. George Kennan cabled US embassies in Europe that "Italy is obviously key point. If Communists win election there, our whole position in Mediterranean, and possibly in Europe as well, would probably be undermined." No one challenged the need to act decisively, but the US government had now given its agents the green light to interfere in the democratic process of another sovereign state. The fear of communism had grown so intense that drastic means seemed justified to halt the further spread of Soviet influence.

The CIA immediately began its clandestine operation in Italy. Money was passed initially to the Christian Democrats and to anti-Communist trade unions, but de Gasperi urged that funds also go to other organizations opposed to the Communists, like the breakaway right-wing socialists. Among them these parties received $2 million to $3 million. The CIA's money helped fund pamphlets, posters, and election campaigning. These "black-bag" payments, as they were later called, are still the subject of controversy in Italy. De Gasperi's deputy in the Rome region, Giulio Andreotti, later one of Italy's best-known prime ministers, still denies knowledge of such payments, despite conclusive evidence that they were made, as revealed many years later in Washington.

Secretary of State Marshall certainly knew of the CIA's clandestine operation, but he kept it from the State Department's ambassador in Rome, even though the payments were going on right under his nose. The State Department made it clear that anyone openly supporting the Communists

"Vote – or he'll be your boss." Italy's Christian Democrats needed to get out the vote in April 1948. Propaganda ranged from film shows to posters. The scare tactics worked.

would be banned from ever emigrating to the United States. And Marshall declared that if the Communist alliance was elected to government, Italy would be excluded from the Marshall Plan.

Even more powerful influences now entered the election battle. On 8 February 1948 Pope Pius XII asked an old colleague, Professor Luigi Gedda, leader of an evangelical force called Catholic Action, to visit him at the Vatican. The Pope explained to the professor how important the upcoming election would be for the future of Italy. He regarded the Communists as detestable atheists and related how in the Spanish Civil War they had desecrated churches and smashed portraits of the Virgin Mary. The Pope asked Gedda to find a way to prevent a Communist victory. As he left St. Peter's, Gedda came up with the idea of creating a network of committees based on the national organization of the Catholic Church. Rapidly this network, the Comitate Civici — the Civic Committees — was put together. Committees were formed in each of the eighteen thousand parishes across the length and breadth of Italy. Above these were three hundred zonal committees, each based on a bishopric, and nineteen regional committees based upon archbishoprics. Each committee was charged with its task from the centre, from Rome; this organization proved to be the most effective political force in Italy.

Propaganda pamphlets were distributed against the Communists; people were told what demons they were. But at this time many Italians could not read, so a very effective campaign of political posters was orchestrated. Two propaganda films were made that portrayed the Communists as evil and deceitful. These were shown in village squares when there was no cinema, and they attracted great crowds. The Civic Committees never told the people whom to vote *for*, but they told everyone whom to vote *against*. And they called upon everyone to be sure they *did* vote, fearful that if Christian Democrats stayed at home the better-organized Communists might win by simply getting out the vote.

Priests and members of the religious orders were instructed to go out and preach against the sins of communism. Some priests even spoke of a "holy war," which had an immense effect on Italians, 90 per cent of whom were members of the church. The role of the clergy especially affected Italian women, who were voting for the first time in a general election. Everywhere the power of the Catholic Church was directed against the Communists; the Pope even began excommunicating members of the Communist Party.

On 18 April, the Christian Democrats won a landslide victory. For the first and only time in postwar Italian history, the Christian Democrats won an outright majority in parliament. The Communist vote was almost halved from the municipal elections of 1946. Italy had voted resoundingly to stay in the Western camp and to reject communism — for the time being at least. As the Christian Democrats congratulated themselves and the Communists wept bitter tears of defeat, the CIA reflected on the success of its campaign of covert intervention in Italian affairs. This was a lesson not lost on the future development of CIA activities elsewhere.

Since Marshall had made it clear that if the Italians voted Communist they would not receive American financial aid, they were now rewarded.

After decades of fascism, a democratic Italy went to the polls. At the general election of April 1948, the Christian Democrats, much aided by the Catholic Church, won an unprecedented overall majority. Only then did Italy begin to receive Marshall aid.

Marshall aid shipments started to flood into the country within days of the election. With congressional approval finally in place, and with the great boost of the Italian election results, the Marshall Plan now got properly under way.

The Workings of the Marshall Plan

Marshall aid was not exactly distributed to Europe like charity relief. Only 20 per cent was in the form of loans; the rest was in grants, to minimize Europe's future financial obligations. Rather than in dollars, aid was usually supplied as commodities, grain, or industrial machinery, so Washington had more control over its end use. Some of the aid came in the form of "counterpart funds," which were designed to compensate for the major dollar shortage in Europe. The currencies of most European nations at the time were not mutually convertible. A Dutch shoemaker might want to buy leather from France, but Dutch guilders were worth nothing to the French tanner; he could not change them into French francs. Any manufacturer who wanted to buy American goods could not do so without dollars, which were always scarce. So each European government set up a fund that ECA would match in dollars. An Italian company, for instance Fiat, could pay Italian lire into its government's fund for the purchase of equipment, and from counterpart funds the equivalent sum in dollars could be used to pay the producers of that machinery in the United States. This way Fiat managed to re-equip itself with the latest

Figures show funds allocated by Congress from 3 April 1948 to 30 June 1952 in millions (m) or billions (b) of US dollars. Figures have been rounded off, and scale has been compressed for amounts over $1 billion.

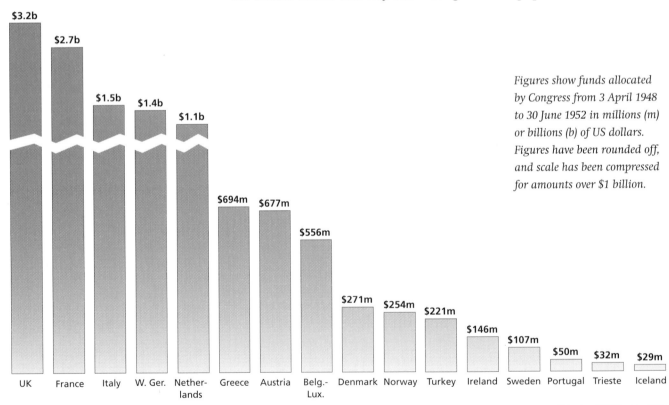

Marshall Plan Aid to Western Europe

UK $3.2b • France $2.7b • Italy $1.5b • W. Ger. $1.4b • Netherlands $1.1b • Greece $694m • Austria $677m • Belg.-Lux. $556m • Denmark $271m • Norway $254m • Turkey $221m • Ireland $146m • Sweden $107m • Portugal $50m • Trieste $32m • Iceland $29m assembly-line machinery from Detroit and Pittsburgh. The growth of Fiat in turn fuelled the overall revival of the Italian economy. For agricultural northern Greece, Marshall aid came in the form of mules. Greek farmers were given Missouri mules to work their land, though at twice the size of the Greek equivalent they at first proved hard to handle.

Economists have long debated the real value of the Marshall Plan to European economies. Some have said that the effect was only marginal. Others have argued that in certain countries, like Greece, it was decisive. Without doubt in some countries it helped economies take off into a period of growth that extended through the 1950s and 1960s. Between 1948 and 1952 a total of $13.7 billion was spent by the United States on Marshall aid (equivalent to about $130 billion in today's dollars). No one can question the generosity of the United States in allocating 1.3 per cent of its GDP to the plan, which was estimated at the time to be the equivalent of $80 for every American. However, much of this aid went straight back into the American economy. Europeans were encouraged to buy American goods with their dollars, and this is what many of them did. The grain that was shipped to feed the hungry in Europe was bought from the farmers of the American Midwest. The machines that were installed by Fiat were built in the factories of the American industrial heartland. American industry was looking for new markets to sustain the growth it had enjoyed throughout the war years, and it prospered greatly from the Marshall Plan.

The plan was political as well as economic. It grew out of the desire to prevent the spread of communism in Western Europe. No longer could European nations sit on the fence. Each country had to choose whether it belonged to the Western or to the Soviet bloc. In the immediate postwar years, the situation in Europe was still fluid, but the Marshall Plan helped accelerate the division of Europe. Forced to reject Marshall aid, Czechoslovakia became part of the Soviet sphere of influence. France and Italy were now firm members of the Western, democratic group of countries. And the Marshall Plan, by giving impetus to West European integration, was at the core of the new Europe being built.

Marshall aid for Greece included everything from goods to livestock. Missouri mules sent to help Greek farmers work their land were twice the size of the local animals, sometimes leading to awkward results.

Berlin, 1948

Berlin, where East and West confronted each other, was the epicentre of the Cold War. Two American military policemen stand guard at the Potsdamer Platz, where the Soviet, British, and US sectors of Berlin merged. In the summer of 1948, barricades went up and the division of the city became more marked.

YOU ARE LEAVING THE AMERICAN SECTO

ВЫ ВЫЕЗЖАЕТЕ И АМЕРИКАНСКОЙ ЗОН

VOUS SORTEZ DU SECTEUR AMERICA

Berlin
1948–1949

As the reichsmark, the official currency, lost value, barter and the black market took its place. Berliners traded anything for food. Cigarettes became a form of currency.

A Divided City

By the spring of 1948 the ideological division of Europe into two rival camps was almost complete, except in Germany and the two cities of Vienna and Berlin, where Britain, France, the Soviet Union, and the United States each governed a separate sector. The Potsdam Conference, which had divided Germany among the victorious Big Four into four zones of military occupation, also divided the city of Berlin. Agreements about free access to Berlin, which was deep within the Soviet occupation zone, subsequently were formalized in September 1945, when the four nations concurred on which road and rail lines would be used in supplying areas of the city occupied by the Western Allies. Then, in October, the Allies agreed to the establishment of air corridors across the Soviet zone between Berlin and the Western sectors of Germany. For three years there was free movement along the accepted routes of access to the city.

Berlin had suffered round-the-clock bombing in the war, by the US Eighth Air Force during the day and the Royal Air Force at night. The city also had suffered heavy bombardment by the Red Army during the final battle. The destruction of Germany's once great capital was almost total: whole districts had been flattened; entire apartment blocks were demolished; almost every building in the city showed signs of damage. Food was perpetually in short supply, and the official currency, the reichsmark, gradually became worthless. The black market flourished, and the cigarette became a form of currency in itself. Barter was widespread for whatever goods could be found. The citizens of Berlin had, literally, to dig in the rubble to scratch out a living.

Germany was the last unanswered question between the United States and the Soviet Union. Throughout the long negotiations of 1946 and 1947, the

Soviets had repeatedly shown anxiety over a revivified Germany. The damage caused to the USSR by the invasion and scorched-earth retreat of the Wehrmacht was so great that Russia felt justified in demanding vast reparations from Germany. Where they could, the Soviets dismantled factories they seized, almost brick by brick, machine by machine, and transported the whole lot back by train to the USSR.

The Americans and the British never put their faith in a policy of reparations. They knew what the vast and punitive reparations demanded by France after the First World War had done to keep the devastated German economy

Berlin had been bombed day and night through the latter years of the war. Berliners and refugees arriving in the city faced a constant struggle for food, warmth, and light. The US wanted to see German recovery and currency reform.

from recovering and to promote the climate in which Nazism was to flourish. Determined to prevent conditions in which extremism might grow again in Germany, the Americans in 1947 wanted to see a revived Germany at the centre of a prosperous Europe. Ernest Bevin, Britain's foreign secretary, had no love of Germany, but he gradually accepted the West's need for that country's revival as a democratic state built upon a strong industrial base, especially the iron and steel industries in the Ruhr, which lay within the British zone of occupation.

In his Stuttgart speech of 6 September 1946, James F. Byrnes, then still the US secretary of state, had called for a higher level of industrial activity within Germany, for monetary reform, and for preparations to form a German government. At the Big Four meeting in Moscow in March–April 1947, the Western powers failed to agree on any of these points with the Soviets. The USSR still demanded $10 billion in reparations and joint control of the Ruhr industrial region.

Friction newly stirred by the Marshall Plan put even greater strain on the situation in Germany. The Council of Foreign Ministers met once more in London from 25 November to 15 December 1947. Again there were major disagreements over the same issues: reparations, control over the industries of the Ruhr, and German unity. The meeting ultimately broke up in accusation and counter-accusation. Secretary of State Marshall summed up his conclusion during a broadcast to the American people: "We cannot look forward to a reunified Germany at this time. We must do our best in the area where our influence can be felt." If the Americans could not get Soviet support for their policy towards Germany, then they would go it alone in the Western zones.

In January 1948 the British cabinet discussed the situation. Bevin presented a paper that argued for slow movement towards a West German government, and for action on currency reform to undercut the rampant black market. Bevin thought of Britain as an intermediary between the French, who

were still fearful of German recovery, and the Americans, who were increasingly frustrated by what they saw as French obstructionism. For the United States, questions of national security were beginning to focus almost exclusively upon the Soviet Union. The French were haunted by an ancient rivalry with Germany and bitter memories of recent defeat and occupation.

On 23 February representatives from the UK, France, Belgium, the Netherlands, and Luxembourg, along with the United States, met in London to plan for the new West German entity, and for the participation of Germany in the Marshall Plan. News of the Communist takeover in Czechoslovakia added impetus to the urgency for creating this new state.

As before, spies within the Foreign Office in London passed reports to Soviet intelligence about secret discussions at the London conference. On 12 March, Foreign Minister Molotov was advised that the "Western powers are transforming Germany into their strongpoint" and incorporating it into a "military-political bloc" aimed at the Soviet Union. Molotov accused the Allies of violating the agreements of Potsdam, and announced that decisions made at the London conference were invalid.

The same intelligence reports were passed on to Marshal Vassily Sokolovsky, the Soviet military governor in Germany, who had been Marshal Georgi K. Zhukov's chief of staff during the march on Berlin. To the American,

French, and British military delegations who met with their Soviet counterparts as the Allied Control Council to govern Germany, Sokolovsky presented a cold, hard face. Among his aides, however, he was known for his sense of humour. Sokolovsky's opposite number on the American side was General Lucius D. Clay, the US military governor in Germany. Clay appeared to his aides to have an endless capacity for work, rarely stopping for lunch, which he considered a waste of time. He survived on coffee and cigarettes, smoking several packs a day. With boundless confidence in his own view of the situation, he had a certain impatience with his political masters. George Kennan reported that he never noticed a "yearning for guidance" on Clay's part. By the summer of 1948 Clay was convinced of the need to move ahead with a West German state, come what may. "If we mean that we are to hold Europe against communism, we must not budge," he told General Omar Bradley, the US Army chief of staff. He continued, "I believe the future of democracy requires us to stay here until forced out."

Vassily Sokolovsky

Lucius D. Clay

At a routine Allied Control Council meeting on 20 March 1948, Sokolovsky pressed Clay and his British counterpart, General Sir Brian Robertson, for information about the conference in London — already knowing, of course, exactly what had happened. When Clay stated that they were not going to discuss the London meetings, Sokolovsky demanded to know what was the point of having a Control Council. To the others' astonishment, the Soviets then got up and, in line behind Sokolovsky, walked out of the meeting, effectively ending the council.

On 12 March, prior to the Soviet walkout, Marshall had informed the British ambassador in Washington that the United States was "prepared to proceed at once in the joint discussions on the establishment of an Atlantic security system." Bevin's dream of committing America to the defence of Europe, which had first been encouraged by the offer of the Marshall Plan, was now becoming a reality, as discussions began on what would become the North Atlantic Treaty Organization. In mid-March, Britain, France, Belgium, the Netherlands, and Luxembourg signed the Brussels Defence Pact, which was the first step towards a West European union. Militarily, it bound the signatories to come to each other's defence. And they agreed to keep troops in Germany for a period of fifty years.

Petty Obstacles Grow

Meanwhile, around Berlin, Soviet authorities began applying a range of petty bureaucratic obstacles to the free movement of people and supplies in and out of the city. Restrictions were placed on traffic using the autobahn between Berlin and the British sector in the west. The bridge over the Elbe at Hohenwarte, the only other road-crossing point, was closed for "maintenance." The British offered to send engineers to build another bridge, but Sokolovsky turned down the offer. The Soviets announced that they would search military passengers and their cargo on the rail lines, and stated that no freight shipments between Berlin and the Western zones could be made without Soviet permission. On 1 April the Soviets halted two American and

If we mean that we are to hold Europe against communism, we must not budge. I believe the future of democracy requires us to stay here until forced out.

— Gen. Lucius D. Clay, summer 1948

two British trains after their commanders refused access to Soviet inspectors. All this amounted to what was later called the "mini-blockade." General Clay ordered a "baby airlift" to fly into Berlin enough supplies for forty-five days.

On 5 April a Vickers Viking of British European Airways took off from an airfield in West Germany on a scheduled flight into RAF Gatow, one of the Allied air bases in West Berlin. As it came into Berlin, in one of the agreed twenty-mile-wide air corridors, the Viking was buzzed by a Soviet Yak-3 fighter plane. It was not the first time this had happened. For a few days Soviet fighters had been carrying out mock attacks on Allied planes flying into Berlin. But this time, as the British transport plane took evasive action, it collided with the Yak fighter. Both planes crashed to the ground, killing all ten people on the BEA plane and the pilot of the Soviet fighter. The Soviets blamed the British for the collision, and the British blamed the Soviet pilot. A joint investigation of the accident broke down when the Soviets refused to allow German witnesses to testify. The British and Soviets separately concluded that the mid-air collision was an accident. But it made both sides more nervous.

With the situation in Berlin now alarmingly tense, the confrontation between Soviets and the West spilt over into Berlin's internal politics. The Berlin city council was the scene of a fierce power struggle between the East German Communists and their political foes, led by the Social Democrats. Ernst Reuter, a Social Democrat, was the leader of the anti-Communist coalition in Berlin, and a powerful orator. He and his family had been forced to flee Germany because of Hitler, but returning in 1946, he hoped to help rebuild Germany as a democratic state. His election in 1948 as mayor of Berlin (that is, of the whole city) was vetoed by the Soviets. Now Reuter feared he would have to take flight again, from another form of political dictatorship. Intimidation, blackmail, and kidnapping characterized the tactics of the Soviet-backed East German Communists, whose agents operated in both East and West Berlin. Communists and socialists came together in a new party, Socialist Unity, led by Walter Ulbricht, Stalin's man in East Germany.

Ernst Reuter

The London conference on Germany reconvened again in late April and sat through May. The British and Americans tried once more to persuade the French to agree to their plan for integrating West Germany into Western Europe, and eventually the French and the Benelux countries gave in. On 7 June 1948 the London conference issued its final recommendations. The Western powers authorized the presidents of the German Länder, the provincial assemblies, to convene a constituent assembly in the three Western zones and to draw up a constitution for a federal German state. Western military forces would remain in Germany until "the peace of Europe is secure," and prohibitions were imposed on any future German army to guarantee that Germany could never again become an aggressor. The new West German state would be economically integrated into Western Europe. Whatever the Soviet reaction, the Western nations made it clear, they intended to go ahead.

The Americans and the British, meanwhile, were secretly preparing to launch a new currency for the whole of West Germany. In the chaotic German

A Russian sentry guards the wreckage of a British civilian airliner that collided with a Soviet fighter over the outskirts of Berlin in April 1948. Debris from the plane fell 500 yards past the boundary of the Soviet sector.

economy, only the black market was thriving. Replacing the reichsmark would not only wipe out the accumulated profits of black marketeers, it would complete the integration of Germany into the West. Millions of new bank notes, the Deutschmark, were printed by the US Mint and transported in great secrecy to West Germany. Control of currency was power in Germany at this juncture, and the Western commanders decided that now was the time for the West to exert its power.

Around Berlin tensions had worsened. Soviet military authorities threatened to close down rail traffic with the West. By 15 June canal boats and freight trains were the only means left of supplying the city. In this explosive situation, the Western Allies decided to introduce their new currency, which

was announced on 18 June. West German citizens could do nothing about the devaluation of their savings and pensions, but at least the new currency brought hope of some stability against runaway inflation. Sixty old reichsmarks, which would barely buy a pack of black-market cigarettes, could be exchanged for forty new Deutschmarks. To hold down their "currency" value while the new Deutschmark established itself, the Americans wisely imported 20 million cigarettes.

The Soviet military governor, Sokolovsky, immediately issued a proclamation denouncing the new currency as "against the wishes and interests of the German people and in the interests of the American, British, and French monopolists. . . . The separate currency reform completes the splitting of Germany. It is a breach of the Potsdam decisions." He prohibited the introduction of the new currency into the Soviet zone and into Berlin.

ABOVE LEFT: *The Western Deutschmark, overprinted with the letter B for issue in Berlin by the Western powers.* ABOVE: *The Ostmark, the new currency the Soviets introduced for the Eastern zone and, they hoped, the whole of Berlin.*

The Frontiers Are Sealed

On that same day Soviet authorities sealed off frontiers with the Western zones and announced new restrictions on road, rail, and canal traffic that would come into effect at midnight. General Clay assured his staff that he was not concerned by these developments: "If they had put in a currency reform and we didn't, it would have been [our] first move."

Late on 22 June the Soviet military authorities announced that a new currency, the Ostmark, would be introduced into the Eastern zone, including all of Berlin, in two days' time. The Western military commanders then declared the Soviet order null and void for West Berlin and introduced the B-mark, a

The Berlin blockade is depicted in this American cartoon as a Soviet bear hug.

HOW TO CLOSE THE GAP?

special Deutschmark overprinted with the letter B, for the Western sectors of Berlin. Clay, who made the decision without consulting Washington, insisted it was a "technical, non-political measure." But Sokolovsky announced that the Western mark would not be permitted to circulate in Berlin, "which lies in the Soviet zone of Germany and economically forms part of the Soviet zone."

Over the next twelve hours, Berlin endured an extraordinary midsummer nightmare. On the evening of 23 June, at a meeting of the Berlin city assembly, which was located in the Soviet sector of the city, Reuter tried to persuade the assembly to approve the circulation of both the Deutschmark and the Ostmark. As thugs beat up non-Communists to intimidate them from supporting Reuter's motion, Soviet officials and Communist-controlled police stood by and watched. Nevertheless, the Berlin assembly voted to accept the Deutschmark in the Western sectors and the Ostmark in the Soviet sector.

Sokolovsky rang Molotov to ask what he should do; should he surround Berlin with tanks? Molotov told him no, this might provoke the West into doing the same, and then the only way out would be military confrontation. They decided instead to impose an immediate blockade around Berlin, and at 6:00 AM on 24 June, the barriers were lowered on all the road, rail, and canal routes linking Berlin with West Germany. That morning electricity from power stations in the Soviet sector was cut off to factories and offices in West Berlin. The official reason given was "coal shortages." So the blockade of

Berlin Occupation Zones

Germany Divided: Postwar Occupation Zones

Berlin began. The Soviets' purpose was clear. They wanted to force the Western Allies either to change their policies or get out of Berlin altogether.

In London and Washington there was firm political agreement that the Western powers would hold on to Berlin. "We are going to stay, period," said Truman. Bevin was equally determined, announcing that "the abandonment of Berlin would mean the loss of Western Europe." It was easy to make such statements, but much more difficult to decide what to do next.

West Berlin had symbolic status as an outpost of the democratic West inside the Communist East. By an agreement made at the time of Potsdam, the Soviets had excused themselves from the responsibility of supplying the British, American, and French sectors of the city. So 2.3 million Berliners, and the Allied military garrison there, were now cut off. The Western part of

The Soviets attempted a complete land blockade of Berlin. Checks were intensified at every sector crossing point; one bridge over the Elbe was declared "unsafe" by the Soviets and would remain closed until the blockade ended, 12 May 1949.

Letters stamped for posting in West Berlin were additionally marked as coming from Berlin under blockade. The bear rampant is the symbol of the city.

the city relied upon the arrival of 12,000 tons of supplies each day. At the time, there was only enough food for thirty-six days, and enough coal for forty-five. The key to keeping a Western presence in Berlin clearly lay in finding a way to supply the citizens with their basic necessities. With rail, road, and canal routes blocked, the only way to get supplies in was by air. But the American C-47 transport, the military workhorse of the day, could only deliver a payload of 3 tons. Initially the prospect for an airlift to Berlin appeared to be bleak.

On 24 June the West introduced a counter-blockade, stopping all rail traffic into East Germany from the British and US zones. Over the following months this counter-blockade would have a damaging impact on East Germany, as the drying up of coal and steel shipments seriously hindered industrial development in the Soviet zone.

On that same day General Clay rang General Curtis LeMay of the US Air Force in Wiesbaden and asked him to put on standby his fleet of C-47s and any other aircraft that could be utilized. The RAF had come forward with an optimistic plan to supply Berlin by air, but Clay was sceptical. He favoured sending a convoy of US military engineers down the autobahn to force their way through the Soviet blockade, with instructions to fire back if they were fired upon. But in Washington, Truman's advisers urged caution and restraint. The president was backed into a corner. It was an election year; the American people would never support going to war with the Soviet Union just to defend

The desperate shortage of food meant that every available square inch of ground was cultivated. This lovingly attended allotment grows vegetables as well as tobacco plants!

Berlin, 1948

Berlin, the capital of a country they had been at war with only three years earlier. But Truman had to be seen championing a firm line and not being soft on the Soviets. He made no final decision that day, but Clay was told by telephone that the president did not "want any action taken in Berlin which might lead to possible armed conflict."

During this week, by chance, General Albert Wedemeyer was visiting Europe from America. He had helped direct the airlift to China over the "hump" from India during the war. By his own calculations, he concluded that it was possible to supply all of Berlin's needs by air. Although both the

British and Americans had experience with major air supply operations, neither had ever attempted anything on this scale. Clay warned Reuter that to begin with there would be severe shortages and hardship; he did not believe initially the Allies could fly in more than 500 tons a day. Reuter assured him that the Allies could count on the West Berliners to grin and bear it. Then, without consulting Washington, Clay authorized the start of the airlift.

The Airlift Begins

On 26 June the first American transport planes flew into Berlin from air bases in West Germany. The Americans code-named the airlift Operation Vittles, and the British called it Operation Plainfare. Initially about eighty C-47s flew two daily round trips into RAF Gatow and Tempelhof, air bases in the British and American sectors of Berlin. Soon the Americans were adding fifty C-54 Skymasters, four-engined transports that each could bring in 9 tons, three times the payload of C-47s. The Allies organized willing gangs of workers to unload the aircraft and turn them around quickly. Over time these workers learned to empty each plane in just seven minutes. The citizens of Berlin were optimistic that the Allies would be able to save their city. If they had had little problem delivering bombs, they told each other, they certainly could deliver potatoes.

The Royal Air Force had nothing like enough service aircraft available for the operation, and spare planes of any type were soon pressed into the airlift.

British business executive Freddie Laker had begun to buy and sell aircraft parts after the war, and by 1948 he owned twelve converted Halifax bombers. He was asked to make them available for supplying Berlin. With little expectation that the blockade would last more than a few weeks, Laker and his team of pilots and engineers happily went to it, almost as a game to begin with. But as the months passed, the operation grew for the pilots into a crusade for freedom. They were determined to keep Berlin alive, despite the hazards of flying old, rickety aircraft, often buzzed by Soviet fighters and frequently at risk flying heavy loads in bad weather.

Lieutenant Gail S. Halvorsen rigs up candy bar and gum packets to the lines of miniature parachutes for dropping to the children of Berlin. Halvorsen was touched at the sight of children in the streets looking up to the skies for the food planes. He was nicknamed the Chocolate Bomber.

Bevin set up a crisis-management team in London to supervise this herculean effort, and early expectations were soon exceeded, as roughly 1,000 tons per day were flown into the beleaguered city. The irony was not lost on many of the veteran fliers involved; instead of destroying Berlin, they were now keeping the city alive.

In July, General Clay returned to Washington for talks with Truman. He still favoured a military convoy to break the blockade, for he believed that the Soviets would step back rather than risk confronting the West. But Truman did not want to chance it. If they chose not to let Clay's convoy through, there would be war. Instead Truman guaranteed Clay more C-54s, and they talked of doubling the airlift to 2,000 tons daily.

The American intelligence community, knowing that the Soviets still had 2.5 million men at arms, was convinced that in a conventional military confrontation the Red Army would walk right over the US forces. But they were equally confident that the Kremlin would never sanction direct military conflict with the West, which might provoke the Americans to take advantage of their atom bomb monopoly. And at this crucial time the Soviet Union was further weakened by a crisis in its own back yard. Yugoslavia split away from the Eastern camp, a defection that made the Kremlin even more nervous about its position and anxious about the support of its satellites.

During July 1948 attempts were made through diplomatic channels to bring about a settlement of the Berlin crisis. On 2 August the British,

American, and French ambassadors had a private meeting with Stalin to test his willingness to find a peaceful solution. Stalin made it clear that from the Soviet point of view the currency question was crucial, as was the London agreement to create a united West Germany. He argued that if there were two German states then Berlin was no longer the capital of Germany, and hence the Western presence in the city was no longer relevant. Stalin said the Soviet Union was not seeking conflict with the West and would lift the blockade as soon as the West withdrew the B-mark from West Berlin and agreed to four-power rule over Germany. There was in fact little the Soviets could do in the face of the West's superiority in the air and its determination to keep up the airlift. What became clear to the Western ambassadors was that the Soviet blockade of Berlin had but one principal purpose: to prevent the creation of a West German state.

Throughout the summer of 1948 the British and American governments constantly reviewed their options. Military thinking concluded that the airlift could hardly continue through the winter, that October was to be the cut-off point. The British chiefs of staff prepared a contingency plan to withdraw their troops to the Rhine in case of an emergency. In Washington the air force commanders, convinced that the airlift was doomed to fail, concluded that there was a high likelihood of war with the Soviets over Berlin.

"We Are Not Pawns"

Josip Broz Tito

The Communist Party in Yugoslavia came to power at the end of the Second World War without Soviet help, unlike what happened in the other East European states. Marshal Josip Broz Tito, the charismatic partisan leader, took power on his own initiative, and through sheer force of character held together the fragile union of the Yugoslav provinces, Montenegro, Serbia, Slovenia, Croatia, Macedonia, and then Bosnia-Herzegovina. Tito did all he could to exhibit his loyalty to the socialist cause, but there was tension in his relationship with Moscow from the start. Tito was secure at home, internationally renowned, and too independent-minded to suit Stalin.

The Kremlin dictator expected nothing less than total obedience from his satellites. But for Tito, Yugoslavia had earned the right to determine its own destiny. In foreign affairs Belgrade insisted on following its own line and did not seek advance approval from Moscow. During the Greek civil war, for instance, Tito provided military assistance to the Communist guerrillas despite Stalin's unwillingness to get involved. But on other matters, as in its rejection of the Marshall Plan, Yugoslavia was a staunch supporter of Moscow's line. Through the early months of 1948, as the split grew worse, Moscow accused Belgrade of misbehaviour and of ideological deviation from the true socialist cause. Every denial by the Yugoslavs further enraged the Kremlin. Tito refused to give way, saying in March, "We are not

pawns on a chessboard."

Then, on 28 June, only four days after launching the blockade against Berlin, Moscow expelled Yugoslavia from Cominform and called on other Communist parties to isolate Tito. An economic blockade was organized against Yugoslavia that caused great hardship, but Belgrade stood firm. Rejected by the East, Tito over the next twelve months turned slowly, and a little reluctantly, towards the West. Following a disastrous harvest in 1949, a trade agreement was signed with the United States by which Yugoslavia opened its borders. Although not technically a member of the Marshall Plan, Yugoslavia went on to receive about $150 million in aid from the United States. Throughout the Cold War, Yugoslavia would remain the only independent Communist state in Europe.

A B-29 Superfortress landing in Lincolnshire, England, in July 1948. The threat was that these aircraft carried atomic bombs. We now know that they did not.

The full machinery of Soviet propaganda turned against Tito after he broke away from Moscow and accepted US dollars in aid.

The Threat of Nuclear Retaliation

The question arose as to whether the United States would be willing to use atomic weapons in the developing crisis, for there was still no clear policy within the administration. Truman argued with his Pentagon chiefs that because they were "so terribly destructive," atomic weapons could not be treated as conventional weaponry. He urged the leaders "to understand that this isn't a military weapon. It is used to wipe out women and children and unarmed people." In September the National Security Council produced a secret report designated as NSC-30: "United States Policy on Atomic Warfare." This required the military to be "ready to utilize promptly and effectively all appropriate means available, including atomic weapons, in the interests of national security" and to "plan accordingly." However, any decision about the use of nuclear weapons would be made by the president, "when he considers such decisions to be required." Truman endorsed NSC-30. In a briefing with his chief air force commanders, he "prayed he would never have to make such a decision, but . . . if it became necessary, no one need have misgiving but he would do so."

In a dramatic gesture that summer, a fleet of sixty B-29 Superfortress bombers was flown into the United Kingdom. These were the latest American heavy bombers, designed to carry atomic weapons. The deployment of the B-29s established the US Strategic Air Command in the UK, and the arrival in Britain of "the atomic bombers" was widely publicized. The threat of nuclear retaliation was now made explicit. After a brief debate, at the height of the Berlin crisis, the British government had formally invited Washington to station the bombers in Britain. The invitation neatly fudged the issue as to who would have his finger on the nuclear trigger; the US Air Force bombers would respond to orders from the United States, but their bases would be technically under the command of the Royal Air Force. This theoretical ambivalence lasted for more than forty years. But in practice the real decision, if it ever came to that, would always be made as NSC-30 directed, by the president of the United States.

The planes in fact carried no atomic weapons, but this was a closely guarded secret. There were not enough atomic warheads in existence to equip the B-29s in Britain. Their arrival was mainly a signal to Moscow that the West meant business over Berlin, and Washington took advantage of the crisis to get congressional approval for permanent overseas military bases. The British government knew that the B-29s carried no atomic weapons, and through spies in the London Foreign Office, Moscow probably also knew the reality of the situation.

Meanwhile, the Berlin airlift was proving more successful than anyone ever expected. Tens of thousands of Berliners helped build a new airport at Tegel to reduce congestion at the other two airfields. With capacity for more flights, the Americans added another sixty C-54s to their fleet. Clay now spoke of bringing in 4,500 tons each day. On 18 September, 861 British and American flights delivered a record 7,000 tons in a single day. By this date roughly 200,000 tons of supplies had been delivered, about 60 per cent by the USAF and 40 per cent by the RAF. Coal, flour, drums of petrol, potatoes, medical

Berlin, 1948

Three hundred thousand Berliners assemble in front of the ruins of the Reichstag to hear the mayor, Ernst Reuter, call for international support for blockaded Berlin.

supplies, all were brought in by air. It began to look as if the airlift could after all supply the city on through the winter, which everyone prayed would not be severe; there were no reserves of coal.

Inside West Berlin, electricity was available only four hours a day. People got used to the limited rations and to feeling cold. The blockade in any case was not absolute. Many West Berliners registered for food rations with the Soviet authorities, and about one in ten drew food and coal from the east. There was no restriction on travel within the city. West Berliners regularly visited the

ABOVE: *A German child's drawing commemorates the airlift: "We thank the pilots for their work and effort."* RIGHT: *A new game, "Airlift."*

eastern part of the city, where there were dance halls bathed in electric light and properly heated, a magnetic attraction to the hungry citizens of the west.

West Berliners were still fearful that the West might not continue the airlift. On 6 September another meeting of the city assembly in East Berlin was broken up by Communist activists — again with violence and intimidation. The western representatives decided that the council was no longer functional, so they left and agreed to meet in the safety of West Berlin. Ernst Reuter appealed to all Berliners to help condemn the Communists, and three days later a huge gathering of 300,000 Berliners, mostly from the city's western zones, collected outside the ruins of the Reichstag. In front of the vast crowd Reuter, standing on a pile of war rubble, called on the Western governments not to abandon Berlin.

The airlift became almost a way of life. Although expensive, its cost represented only a fraction of total American aid to Europe. Despite bad weather and constant harassment by Soviet fighters, the transports continued to bring their cargoes into West Berlin. By December 1948 the goal of 4,500 tons flown in each day was reached. At Gatow and Tempelhof flights landed every 90 seconds. Enough coal was freighted in to keep West Berliners from freezing. The gamble had paid off. Production in the city picked up, and output grew rapidly. The feared economic collapse did not materialize. And the winter, fortunately, was unusually mild.

The West secured a major propaganda victory through the airlift. It was a reminder to the Soviet Union, and the whole world, of Western technological superiority, especially in the air. Conversely, the Berlin crisis showed the Soviets in a poor light; they seemed willing to threaten 2 million people with starvation.

RIAS, Radio in the American Sector, American-financed, with its mix of popular music and upbeat news, kept up Berliners' morale. Presenter and entertainer Christina Ohlsen became a celebrity.

The Soviets, operating outside the framework of American loan credits and facing the Western alliance, saw themselves to be increasingly threatened. We now know that Stalin felt less strong than was realized at the time, but in 1948 many Americans genuinely believed that Stalin sought to dominate all of Europe. The policy of containment meant confronting Communists at agreed critical points, and Berlin was one of these. As far as Western public opinion was concerned, old wartime loyalties to Russia were being replaced by fear of Soviet ambitions; a "them and us" syndrome had emerged. Marshall reported, "There has been a definite crystallization of American public and Congressional opinion over the Berlin issue. . . . The country is more unified in its determination not to weaken in the face of pressure of an illegal blockade than on any other issue we can recall in time of peace." The Berlin blockade made clear to most Americans that the new enemy was definitely the Soviet Union.

As the heavy transports continued to fly their daily missions, the constitution of the Federal Republic of Germany, popularly known as West Germany, was being drafted. Stalin's attempt to prevent the division of Germany had failed.

NATO Is Launched

In January 1949 President Truman announced his intention to provide military aid to Western Europe. Then, in April, negotiations lasting more than a year finally came to their conclusion when the North Atlantic Treaty was signed in Washington by the United States, Canada, and ten West European governments. All signatories agreed to come to the aid of each other if attacked. A common cause was formally recognized, and American leadership of the West was duly confirmed. Ernest Bevin's mission to commit the

LEFT: *On 4 April 1949 the United States, Canada, and ten Western European nations signed the North Atlantic Treaty, committing the United States to the defence of Europe. Secretary of State Dean Acheson signs as President Truman looks on.* ABOVE: *A pamphlet cover shows the NATO symbol and portrays the alliance as a shield against Soviet attack.*

United States to the defence of Western Europe by treaty obligation was accomplished. Stalin had driven the West into a formal alliance based primarily on mutual defence against Soviet aggression.

In the spring of 1949 the weather improved considerably. Food supplies in Berlin could be built up and fuel stocks maintained at a good level. The airlift increased to 8,000 tons per day. In one twenty-four-hour period, on Easter Sunday, April 1949, a record number of 1,398 flights came into Berlin, carrying a total of 13,000 tons of supplies.

As the counter-blockade of East Germany hurt more and more, the Soviets took the only course left open and tried to end the whole Berlin debacle. The Kremlin released a series of hints that it would consider ending its blockade with minimal conditions imposed. The counter-blockade would have to be lifted and the Council of Foreign Ministers be reconvened. The bellicose General Clay quietly returned to Washington and ceased to be military governor. After the tensions of the preceding year he claimed to need a break anyway. On 12 May the Soviet and Western military authorities lifted their respective blockades around Berlin. Both sides claimed a victory. Berliners were jubilant. Many thought this would be the end of the Cold War.

The sense of victory and relief felt in the West did not last long. Before summer was over an American B-29, on routine patrol at 18,000 feet over the North Pacific, picked up a radioactivity count higher than normal. Within a week more radiation was detected. Soviet scientists, led by Igor Kurchatov, had successfully tested an atom bomb. The Soviet Union had caught up. The Americans were stunned, for now there was nuclear parity between the super-powers. The balance of power would become a balance of terror.

12 May 1949. The first British truck passes the checkpoint on the British-Russian zonal border as jubilant Germans look on. The airlift has succeeded. The blockade is lifted.

Korea, 1951

The war in Korea brought tragedy to the Korean people both north and south of the 38th parallel. Civilians suffered most. This picture shows women and children taking shelter from American heavy bombing of the North.

Korea
1949–1953

General Douglas MacArthur (lower right) prepares to accept the Japanese surrender aboard the USS Missouri *in Tokyo Bay to end the Second World War. MacArthur commanded the occupation of Japan and went on to lead UN forces in the Korean War.*

End of an Empire

On 10 August 1945, the day after the atom bomb was dropped on Nagasaki, American officials worked late into the night at the State Department. With Japan on the brink of surrender, it was necessary to agree upon a future Asian policy. Poring over maps of the Japanese Empire, members of the State-War-Navy Coordinating Committee focused on occupied Korea, that remote land mass jutting out from the mainland of China. For several centuries Korea had been an independent, unified nation, but early in the twentieth century it had been overrun by an expansionist Japan. The occupation had been bitterly resented by most Koreans, who now hoped that Japan's imminent defeat would bring an end to it, leading once more to an independent Korea.

The Soviet Union, which had declared war on Japan only a day before Nagasaki was bombed, marched through Manchuria, rolling up Japanese forces still deployed there, and entered Korea. At the Potsdam Conference, the United States, then making plans to invade the Japanese mainland, had been more than happy to leave Manchuria and Korea to the Soviets. But now, with the war actually coming to a sudden end, the United States urgently reassessed its future interest in Asia and came rapidly to a decision: America must share with the USSR the occupation of Korea at the end of the war. With no appropriate natural division to the Korean peninsula, the 38th parallel, which roughly divided the country in half, was proposed to the Kremlin. The Soviet Union should occupy Korea to the north of this line, and the United States would occupy the area to the south. Dean Rusk, a member of the Coordinating Committee, pointed out to his colleagues that if the Soviets chose to ignore this proposal and continued to sweep south, they could occupy all of Korea before a single US marine was landed. However risky this policy, the Kremlin agreed to divide Korea along this artificial boundary and halted the Red Army when it was reached. In early September 1945 US soldiers landed in Korea at Inchon and set up their military occupation of the South. When the advance guard entered Seoul, the capital, the streets were filled with thousands of Koreans cheering the end of Japanese rule.

Inheriting a political vacuum that stemmed from the war's sudden end, the US occupation force, commanded by General John Hodge, was brought face to face with Korean politics when rival groups identified themselves as representing the new Korean government. Hodge ignored them all and turned instead to former Japanese officials to help him run the country. There were still more than half a million Japanese soldiers in Korea and tens of thousands of Japanese civil servants, who dutifully put themselves under Hodge's command. The Koreans were deeply offended that their new occupiers should line up with the hated Japanese.

Slowly the Japanese administrators were expelled from Korea, and the US military had to turn to a variety of collaborators in maintaining law and order. Prominent nationalists and members of the anti-Japanese resistance had formed a provisional government, but at least half of them were Communists, a powerful force in the land. However, their hectoring alienated the American generals, who now found themselves at the front line politically. They preferred a more conservative group that was made up of professionals and those educated in America or by American missionaries. This faction looked to one of Korea's most famous exiles as leader. His name was Syngman Rhee.

Rhee was born in 1875 into the Korean middle class, and studied at Harvard and Princeton, becoming the first Korean to receive a doctorate from an American university. He left Korea again in 1910, at the time of the Japanese occupation, and spent the next thirty-five years in the United States, lobbying on behalf of Korean independence. Rhee had several assets as far as the United States was concerned: he was not tainted by collaboration with the Japanese; he was strongly anti-Communist; and with his perfect English, he seemed a more comfortable figure to American soldiers and diplomats than most other Korean politicians. Rhee emerged in the winter of 1945 as the US nominee for political control over South Korea.

Although Rhee appealed to the American generals, his natural power base in Korea was small. He had to rely upon officials who, having worked with the Japanese, were discredited in the eyes of most Koreans. Ambitious for power and wealth, he became corrupt and ruthless. The United States had unwittingly transferred power to a clique with no real interest in popular democracy and to whom personal freedom meant nothing. But for the American generals Rhee offered a least-bad option.

North of the 38th parallel, under Soviet guidance and supervision, a network of People's Committees was formed. In February 1947 these committees met in Pyongyang, the northern capital, and established the People's Assembly of North Korea. Kim Il Sung, another Korean exile, was elected its chairman.

General MacArthur, seen here receiving Emperor Hirohito in the US Embassy in Tokyo, 1945, was a larger-than-life war hero. Almost as soon as the Second World War ended, the United States built up Japan.

Nearly forty years younger than Rhee, Kim had opposed the Japanese occupation during the 1930s and had gone to the Soviet Union during the war. By 1945 he was leading a Korean unit in the Red Army. When installed by the Soviets as their candidate to rule in North Korea, he advocated wholesale land reform; the great estates were broken up and most tenant farmers were given their own land. But there was no policy in North Korea of widespread collectivization of land on the Soviet model. Farming remained a small-scale activity. Kim was vicious in putting down all opposition to Communist rule, and many anti-Communists emigrated to the south.

Between 1945 and 1947, the situation in Korea polarized as the two power blocs, North and South, became more secure. Both sides constantly expressed their desire for national unity, but in practice, re-unification became a more and more remote goal. As in Europe, the difficulties of postwar reconstruction plunged much of Korea into economic chaos and hardship. With inflation, poverty, and distress came civil disturbances. A rising in Cheju Island in the South was viciously put down by soldiers of the southern government. More than a thousand died. In the North, there were public show trials of opponents of the regime.

In January 1948 the United Nations called for free elections in both North and South Korea. The Soviet Union rejected any UN involvement, and elections eventually went ahead only in the South. Amid mounting repression, and with the Communists boycotting the polls, Rhee and his right-wing supporters won a majority of seats in Korea's new constitutional assembly. In August, Rhee was inaugurated president of the new Republic of Korea. A month later the Democratic People's Republic of Korea was proclaimed in Pyongyang.

During 1949 the border between the two Korean regimes became tense as both sides made major incursions across it. Radio propaganda from the North constantly predicted imminent invasion. In the South left-wing activists by the thousands were arrested and imprisoned. Meanwhile, the Red Army withdrew from the North, leaving behind only a handful of military advisers. In June 1949 the US Army withdrew from the South. Dean Acheson, who had replaced Marshall as US secretary of state, was deeply involved with the situation in Europe and the crisis in Berlin. He had little time for Asian affairs.

Kim Il Sung, shown here relaxing with some of his officers during the Korean War, ruled North Korea for nearly fifty years.

The "Loss" of China

In the fall of 1949 the situation in Korea was transformed by events in China. From 1927 onwards the Communist forces of Mao Zedong had been engaged in a long civil war with the Kuomintang armies of Chiang Kai-shek. Since 1945 America had given $2 billion of military aid to Chiang, while Stalin had provided but grudging support to the Chinese Communists. Nevertheless, Chiang's army overextended itself in Manchuria, as it took over from Soviet troops occupying the country at war's end. Corruption and massive inflation eventually weakened the resolve of Chiang's supporters, and America began to realize that without a vast commitment it could no longer prop up Chiang's Nationalist regime. In the meantime, using captured Japanese arms, Mao's army slowly won the upper hand, and Chiang fled to Taiwan. In October

1949 Mao proclaimed the People's Republic of China: "We, the Chinese people, have now stood up."

In the United States the defeat of Chiang Kai-shek was regarded as a major disaster — the "loss" of China. In their vision of the postwar world, US policymakers had seen Chiang's China as a major player, as one of the "Big Five" members of the UN Security Council. When Mao forced Chiang to flee the mainland, it seemed to Washington that worldwide communism was given a huge boost.

The "loss" of China, coinciding with the explosion of the Soviet atom bomb, provoked a hardheaded response in Washington. At the end of January 1950, President Truman ordered the development of a hydrogen bomb. He also called for a new overview of America's foreign and defence policies, which was drafted by Paul Nitze and others at the State Department. The result was a secret National Security Council document known as NSC-68. It made alarming reading. Now that America's atomic monopoly had been broken, the paper argued, Soviet strength would have to be met by conventional power. NSC-68 concluded by calling for a massive increase of expenditure on conventional arms, from $13 billion to $50 billion. "What I read scared me so much that the next day I didn't go to the office at all. I sat at home and read this memorandum over and over, wondering what in the world to do about it," Charles Murphy, President Truman's special counsel, later said.

In December 1949 Mao went to Moscow to participate in the seventieth birthday celebrations for Stalin. Despite all the rhetoric of Communist fraternity, the first meetings of the two leaders were uncomfortable. At the end of the war, Stalin had signed a treaty of friendship with Chiang Kai-shek and had done very little to help Mao in his long campaign to win China for communism. Stalin viewed Mao, leader of the world's most populous nation, as a threat to his own worldwide leadership of communism. Mao, deeply respectful towards Stalin, deferred to him on developing communism in China. In his two months in Moscow, Mao negotiated the first Sino-Soviet Treaty of Friendship, Alliance, and Mutual Assistance, which was signed on 14 February 1950. In this momentous agreement, Stalin gave support for the re-unification of China under the Communist banner and in effect abrogated Yalta agreements to maintain the status quo in Asia. The Sino-Soviet alliance signalled the opening of a second front in the Cold War, in Asia.

Meanwhile, in Washington the Truman administration completed its review of Far Eastern strategy in NSC-48/2. This called for a hands-off policy with regard to Taiwan, and concentrated instead on essential US interests elsewhere in the Pacific, especially with regard to Japan and Southeast Asia. In January 1950, for a National Press Club briefing in Washington, Acheson outlined US interests in the Far East, and carelessly left out any mention of Korea. This sent an ambiguous signal to Pyongyang — and to Moscow.

Kim Il Sung repeatedly asked for permission from Stalin, and later from Mao, to launch an attack on South Korea to re-unite the Korean peninsula under the Red flag. But Stalin resisted this idea, doubtful of the US response. Stalin was still respecting agreements made with the United States at the end of the war, and in early 1949 he was preoccupied with the crisis in Berlin. Despite several further requests by Kim, Stalin again concluded in September

A White Book of US Imperialism stained, according to this 1949 Krokodil cartoon, with the blood of the Chinese people.

We, the Chinese people, have now stood up.

— Mao Zedong,
1 October 1949

Cold War

1949 that the risks of American intervention were too great, and he once more vetoed an invasion.

In April 1950 Kim went secretly to visit Stalin in the Kremlin. By this time, after the Communist victory in China and the Soviet development of an atom bomb, Stalin felt more confident that America would hesitate to intervene in a distant war, even if the result could be another Communist victory in Asia. Stalin felt the international situation was going his way and finally gave Kim the go-ahead. The Chinese were informed of Stalin's green light for invasion and also extended their support to North Korea. Mao assured North Korea's

ABOVE: *1 October 1949, Tiananmen Square, Beijing. Mao Zedong proclaims the People's Republic of China, uniting the country under communism after twenty years of civil war.* ABOVE RIGHT: *In December, Mao went to Moscow to celebrate Stalin's seventieth birthday. In spite of their differences, in February 1950 a Treaty of Friendship was signed between the two giants.*

ambassador that there was little to fear from the Americans, because "they would not start a third world war over such a small territory." A special protocol already had been signed between Moscow and Pyongyang, under which the Soviet Union agreed to supply military and technical assistance. By the spring of 1950 large numbers of tanks, cannons, machine guns, and planes had been delivered to North Korea. But Stalin still wanted to avoid direct military confrontation with the United States.

Kim Il Sung Moves South

Stalin gave his final go-ahead but maintained a tight rein over the North Koreans by even dictating the date of the invasion: 25 June 1950. Soviet advisers would be withdrawn from the front line a few days before, to avoid capture and disclosure of Soviet participation. Early on the morning of 25 June, on the pretext of responding to an armed incursion from the South, the North Korean People's Army attacked. Following a dawn artillery barrage, seven combat-ready divisions advanced south across the 38th parallel behind a line of giant Russian T-34 tanks. The attack achieved complete surprise.

Syngman Rhee's army was outnumbered and outmatched. Within hours his demoralized units were reeling backwards in hopeless retreat.

Sunday, 25 June, in Korea was Saturday, 24 June, in Washington, and news of the invasion reached Washington on Saturday evening. Dean Rusk, assistant secretary of state, was having dinner with Frank Pace, secretary of the army, and, still in their dinner jackets, they rushed to the State Department. There they concluded that such aggression could not go unchallenged. At the State Department's urgent request, a special session of the UN Security Council was called by Secretary-General Trygve Lie for Sunday afternoon. The

Soviet Union had walked out of the Security Council in January to protest the UN decision not to admit Communist China, and it was still boycotting the council in June. Under these extraordinary circumstances, the Security Council unanimously condemned North Korea's aggression and called for a withdrawal to the 38th parallel. Two days later, on 27 June, the UN went even further by calling on all member states to extend military aid to South Korea.

With the Soviets absent from the Security Council, the UN voted for the first time to send a military force to assist one country attacked by another. Over the next decades there would be other blatant acts of aggression, but not until the 1991 Gulf War would the UN again engage itself militarily on one side of a conflict. It was under the banner of UN legitimacy that the United States, Britain, Australia, Turkey, and the other Western allies fought the war in Korea, which Truman characterized as no more than a "police action."

To senior government officials gathered in Washington to consider the situation, the invasion fulfilled predictions of Soviet aggressiveness made in NSC-68. It was interpreted as one step in an orchestrated Soviet plot to throw the Western democracies out of Asia. To the extent that Stalin was clearly pulling Kim's strings, this judgement was justified. But it was wide of the mark to see it as part of a worldwide Communist plan. Rather, Stalin had simply taken advantage of a moment's perceived weakness in Washington to satisfy the demands of an over-ambitious ally. Without any debate in Congress,

ABOVE LEFT: *UN Security Council members discuss Korea across the empty chair of the USSR delegate at an emergency session on 25 June 1950. The council branded North Korea an aggressor and ordered both sides to cease firing. Western resistance to Communist aggression in Korea had UN backing.* ABOVE: *"Hands off Korea," says* Krokodil, *showing US soldiers there as pirates.*

whose duty it is to declare war; with hardly time to consider the implications of a conflict that could bring the United States into direct confrontation with both China and the Soviet Union, Washington set itself on a course of military involvement in Korea.

Kim and Stalin had miscalculated; they never imagined that America would choose to fight over so distant a land, nor did they foresee the speed of the West's response. For Syngman Rhee, whose corrupt regime had been on the brink of collapse, the war provided the moral legitimacy of a UN resolution, and multinational backing for his shaky government.

This South Korean poster portrays the Russian-backed Communist North as enslaving the people of Korea.

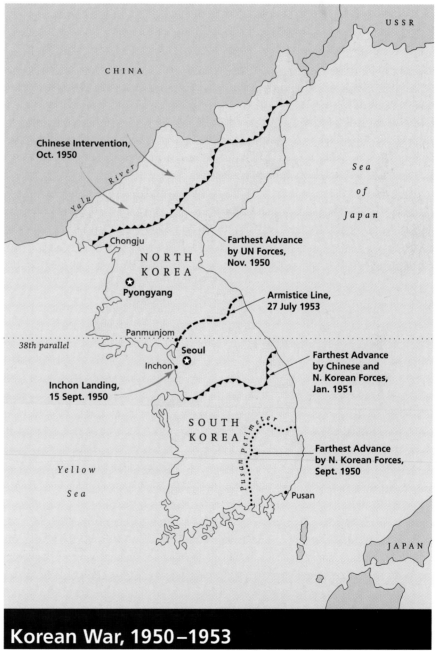

Korean War, 1950–1953

By the summer of 1950, American armed forces worldwide had been so drastically reduced that nearly every operating unit was under-equipped and under-staffed for combat. The nearest US military force to Korea was, lazily, occupying Japan, under the leadership of the legendary war hero General Douglas MacArthur. Tall and haughty, MacArthur was in many eyes the epitome of a great military commander. He had an unshakable confidence in the rightness of his own views. For some time he had argued with Washington that the real conflict with communism would be fought out in Asia and not in Europe. Now his moment had come.

MacArthur flew to Korea and met Rhee, who, preparing to evacuate Seoul, told MacArthur, "We're in a hell of a fix." It was no exaggeration. Rhee's army was as fragile as the government that led it. Without any suitable anti-tank weapons, and confronting a far better equipped North Korean army, Rhee's forces abandoned most of their equipment and fled, joining the lines of civilian refugees streaming south. On 28 June the North Korean army entered Seoul. To slow the North Korean advance, the bridges over the mighty Han River were destroyed. One of them was blown up while packed with refugees fleeing the city; more than a thousand people were killed. In a ghastly foretaste of what was to come later in the war, the Communists proceeded to round up and execute hundreds of Rhee sympathizers.

American Units Land in Korea

For soldiers stationed in Japan, the military occupation was a cushy assignment. Their relaxed training regimen failed to prepare them for what lay ahead when, with only a few hours' notice, MacArthur flew the first units into Korea as Task Force Smith. With virtually no battle plan, American soldiers were deployed east-west fifty-odd miles to the south of Seoul and told to dig in. They didn't have long to wait for action.

The first Americans in the Cold War to confront Communists directly were members of a small unit deployed in the hills near the Korean town of Osan. These soldiers, part of the Twenty-fourth Division, woke up on the morning of 5 July to the noise of a column of green T-34 tanks driving slowly through their position. With little in the way of anti-tank weapons, they could put up no resistance to the famous Russian tank that helped win the Second World War. Later in the morning came the North Korean infantry, vast numbers of them in their mustard-coloured tunics, who soon nearly surrounded the US positions. The Americans found themselves running low on ammunition and blood supplies to treat the wounded. Isolated and dazed, the GIs pulled out; in no time an organized withdrawal became a disorganized rout. Five days later, little more than half the men positioned in the hills around Osan had staggered wearily into the American lines farther south. In the first military confrontation of the Cold War, soldiers of the most powerful nation on earth had been humiliated by Soviet-equipped troops from a tiny Asian country. All the atom bombs in Washington's arsenal couldn't help the men of Task Force Smith as they reeled back in disarray. In Washington, President Truman reiterated that "aggression must be met firmly."

On 7 July the Security Council asked the United States to appoint a

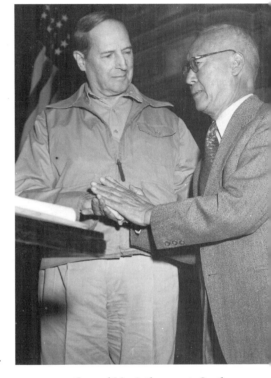

General MacArthur meets South Korean president Syngman Rhee, whose sinking regime is refloated courtesy of a UN resolution.

supreme commander of the UN force, and MacArthur was immediately installed, with his headquarters in Tokyo. Prime Minister Clement Attlee pledged to support the UN-US action with British troops, and redirected ships of the Royal Navy from Hong Kong and Singapore. In Washington, Congress gave the president powers to extend the draft and voted for an enormous increase in military expenditure. NSC-68, with its proposed fivefold increase in defence spending, was now to be implemented.

On the ground in Korea, the situation went from bad to worse. An entire US regiment, flown in from Okinawa, was ambushed and wiped out. The American units of Task Force Smith, under the command of Major General William Dean, tried desperately to hold back the North Korean advance. Deciding to make a stand at Taejon, the US forces were gradually caught up in the thousands of fleeing refugees, and the situation became chaotic. In the ensuing action General Dean himself was captured by the North Koreans, who continued to sweep southward. Their propaganda films celebrated the capture of one of the most senior US generals ever to be taken prisoner.

The only successes for the UN-US force in these early months were in the air, where US planes from carriers of the Seventh Fleet were shooting North Korea's Yak fighters out of the skies. And US air attacks throughout the South, and across the border into North Korea, harried supply lines of the People's Army. Giant B-29 bombers from island bases in the Pacific began to drop thousands of tons of high explosives on the North, driving Kim to make further requests of the Russians for military and technical assistance.

Throughout the rest of July and August 1950, Kim's forces continued to drive US and South Korean troops back into the southeastern corner of the country around the city of Pusan. There, determined to stand firm, they built a defensive line along the Naktong River in the west and eastward to the coast, near Pohang, which became known as the Pusan Perimeter. Gradually more American and allied troops were shipped in through the port at Pusan. The North Korean advance had been so rapid that the Communists, with little time to build up proper supply lines, had over-extended themselves. Although they kept up great pressure, their advance now ran out of steam.

The government of Syngman Rhee, now resettled in Pusan, called for complete mobilization of the Korean people. All males were to join the war effort. Peasant farmers were rounded up and without any training whatsoever — sometimes even without weapons — were thrown into the front lines of the Pusan Perimeter. American generals facing the prospect of defeat in Korea began to consider evacuation. Rhee made it clear there would be no Korean retreat from Pusan. His army would fight to the last man if necessary.

A Daring Landing

Even while more allied troops were assembling in Pusan, MacArthur conceived a daring plan to turn the tables on the North, with a vast amphibious invasion 150 miles behind enemy lines, along the beaches at Inchon, only 20 miles from Seoul. General Omar Bradley, chairman of the Joint Chiefs of Staff in Washington, thought the scheme was reckless and sent a team from the Pentagon to try to dissuade MacArthur. The geography was all wrong, the

Summer 1950. The first US troops in action were thrown back by the ferocious assault of the North Koreans. A wounded US soldier is carried from battle.

Inchon, 1950

Dawn, 15 September. Driven back to a shrinking perimeter around Pusan in the South, MacArthur daringly launched an amphibious invasion far behind enemy lines at Inchon, twenty miles from Seoul. After a massive bombardment, the first marines scale the seawall.

beaches too exposed, the tides too great, they argued, and there was not enough intelligence about the defences. But MacArthur's conviction never wavered. When Bradley cabled MacArthur for his withdrawal plans, should the landings fail, MacArthur cabled back that the landings would not fail.

In September a huge invasion fleet of 269 ships, the largest since D-day, gathered off the coast at Inchon. On the morning of 15 September, after a massive bombardment, US marines went ashore in vast numbers. Inchon had been flattened, the North Koreans had evacuated the city, and the landings were almost unopposed. With the beachhead secure, MacArthur went ashore, accompanied by the army of photographers and newsmen who dogged his every step. His gamble had paid off.

The military tide now turned rapidly in favour of the UN-US, and the troops marched inland from Inchon. Their first objective was the liberation of Seoul, which occurred on 25 September. Resistance was heavy, the city was devastated, and at least fifty thousand civilians were killed in the crossfire.

With Seoul threatened, the North Korean assault on Pusan crumbled. UN troops then broke out of the enclave and, within days, linked up with US units striking northward and eastward. The North Korean army was now beginning to disintegrate. Watching events from the Kremlin, Stalin was furious; he withdrew most of his military advisers and told Kim Il Sung to make plans for evacuation. To the United Nations forces it looked as though the war would soon be over.

When the UN troops reached the 38th parallel, a difficult decision presented itself. The invaders had been expelled from the territory invaded, but Rhee, burning to re-unite Korea, had no doubt that re-occupying the South was only the first step. MacArthur was fully behind him in this; he hadn't got this far just to stop where the fighting began. General Marshall, recalled to

UN soldiers, fighting building to building, liberate Seoul from the North Koreans, as they march inland from the Inchon amphibious landing.

Premature Assurances

On 15 October, President Truman summoned General MacArthur to a meeting on Wake Island in the mid-Pacific. When the president disembarked at Wake, MacArthur chose not to salute him but shook hands, a clear sign that he regarded this encounter as a meeting of equals rather than that of a field commander reporting to his commander-in-chief.

MacArthur despised the whole event and saw it, probably rightly, as an electioneering exercise by Truman, who wanted to associate himself with the fruits of victory in Korea. No real agenda had been prepared. MacArthur assured the president that all Communist resistance would cease by Thanksgiving, that the Chinese would not intervene, and that victory was imminent. The president reiterated his support for MacArthur and decorated him with another Distinguished Service Medal (MacArthur's fifth).

Irritated by being summoned to report to his political master, General MacArthur declined the president's invitation to lunch and flew back to his headquarters in Tokyo.

As he boarded his own plane, President Truman told reporters, "I've never had a more satisfactory conference since I've been president."

government service as secretary of defence, cabled MacArthur that he was to feel "unhampered" by the 38th parallel. Accordingly, on 1 October, South Korean troops crossed the line and entered North Korea. On 7 October, the UN established a Commission for the Re-unification and Re-habilitation of Korea, which added to the ambiguity of the UN's role there. On that same day, US troops crossed the 38th parallel and advanced into Communist territory. This now went well beyond "containment."

Stalin's concern about the failings of the North Korean army had grown throughout September. The Chinese also were annoyed with their North Korean allies. More than once, Mao Zedong expressed his willingness to send Chinese troops to aid their North Korean "brothers." On 1 October, Stalin, still determined to keep the Soviet Union out of the conflict, decided that China must rescue the North Korean regime. Now hesitating, China suggested that Kim Il Sung accept defeat and resort to guerrilla tactics. There was intense debate in Beijing whether China should intervene, before in mid-October Mao decided to send "volunteers" from the Chinese People's Army into Korea. It is clear that Mao thought a Chinese victory would enhance the world standing of his young Communist republic.

Meanwhile, on 19 October, Pyongyang fell to a combined force of UN and South Korean troops, the only Communist capital ever to fall to the West in the Cold War. MacArthur was jubilant. He now divided the UN forces into two different operations. The Eighth Army, under General Walton "Bulldog" Walker, would head up the west side of the Korean peninsula; the Tenth Corps, under General Edward Almond, would drive up the east. Separated by the mountains of North Korea, both units raced north towards the border with China. MacArthur was so certain of victory that spare supplies of ammunition were shipped back to Japan.

BELOW RIGHT: *On 15 October 1950 Truman summoned MacArthur to a meeting at Wake Island and pinned on him a Distinguished Service Medal, his fifth. MacArthur assured Truman that victory was near.* BELOW: Krokodil *has another view of the same ceremony.*

China Hints at Intervention

Having made the decision to enter the conflict, the Chinese now dropped various hints through the Indian ambassador in Beijing that if the UN advanced farther they would intervene. But in Washington, Dean Rusk and others in the State Department thought the Chinese were bluffing.

In mid-October the first Chinese People's Volunteers secretly crossed the Yalu River, the border between China and North Korea. Their first confrontation with UN troops came near the village of Onjong on 25 October. A battalion of the South Korean Sixth Division, encountering heavy fire, believed they

had caught up with a small North Korean force covering their retreat. That night this force counter-attacked and routed the South Koreans. Advancing south, the Chinese soon encountered units of the US Army. Some were captured. American interrogation officers were puzzled that their prisoners did not respond to questions in the Korean language. Then they understood: China had entered the war.

After several days of fighting, the Chinese forces withdrew to the hills, having given the UN troops a "bloody nose." But this warning was not heeded. In Tokyo, MacArthur refused to believe that the Chinese had entered the conflict. Still convinced that the war would be "over by Christmas," he ordered more units north, towards the Yalu River.

American soldiers enjoyed a respite on Thanksgiving Day; turkey and cranberry sauce were flown up to the front line. Three days later, on 26 November, the Chinese launched a full-scale assault. Pouring out of the mountains where they had been massing, vast numbers of Chinese soldiers engulfed the front-line UN units. Troops of the US Second Division found themselves surrounded. As they tried to move back along the roads, their retreat was blocked by knocked-out trucks and heavy equipment. Some

ABOVE: *October 1950. Unknown to the Americans, hundreds of thousands of Chinese "volunteers" crossed the Yalu River into North Korea and prepared to strike. The main Chinese offensive came shortly after Thanksgiving in a series of human-wave assaults.* ABOVE RIGHT: *This photograph was issued later and shows a re-enactment of the attack.*

American soldiers panicked, abandoning everything in their headlong rush to get away. Other units, including the Turkish, stayed put, firing into the Chinese advance until they ran out of ammunition and had to surrender. But it was all in vain. Nothing could stop the human-wave assaults of the Chinese People's Volunteers. They suffered immense casualties, but the tide of war had turned again.

Right across North Korea the UN forces were now thrown back in a rout. What the American government most wanted to avoid was taking place; the conflict was turning into a full-scale war with China. And the Chinese were

General Peng De-Huai commanded the Chinese forces in Korea. Known as a brilliant military strategist and a charismatic leader of men, Peng De-Huai was the MacArthur of the Chinese army. Mao's favourite general, he helped persuade the Chinese leadership to intervene in Korea.

hitting the UN forces with tremendous numbers, determined to throw the Americans out of Asia.

In Washington, President Truman told a press conference, "We are fighting for our national security and our survival." Pressed further by a journalist, Truman conceded that no military option would be ruled out, presumably including the use of the atom bomb. In London, Prime Minister Clement Attlee was alarmed and announced the following day that he would fly to Washington for urgent talks. He was relieved to learn from Truman that there were in fact no plans to use atomic weapons in Korea. Dean Rusk assured him the war was already larger than Washington wanted and there was no desire to enlarge it further by inviting confrontation with the Soviet Union.

Through the bitterly cold winter of 1950–1951, the Chinese forced the UN armies back. Neither side was properly equipped for such cold, and frostbite began to claim even more victims than the fighting. To the west of the mountains, the Eighth Army was falling back in shambles. To the east, the US Marines, managing a more disciplined and orderly pullback, eventually reached the relative safety of the coast. Adopting a scorched-earth policy, the Americans destroyed everything in their retreat. Having evacuated their

Korea 1950

As the war ebbed and flowed, Korean civilians were constantly on the move. These women are fleeing south with their possessions as UN forces trudge north.

marines through the port of Hungnam, US engineers then blew up the harbour as they left. Both Korean armies committed appalling atrocities, as they moved south, rounding up and massacring civilians.

On 6 December 1950 Pyongyang was recaptured by Chinese troops — at least what was left of it. Much of the city had been destroyed earlier by allied bombing, the rest was demolished by retreating UN troops. As the Communist armies continued their drive south, the UN forces faced yet another setback. Two days before Christmas, General Bulldog Walker, commander of the Eighth Army, was killed in a jeep accident.

General Matthew B. Ridgway, who had served with great distinction in the Second World War, was having after-dinner drinks with friends in

Washington when he received a call from MacArthur asking him to take immediate command of the Eighth Army. Pausing only to collect some papers from the Pentagon, Ridgway left at once and arrived in Tokyo just before midnight on Christmas Day. An inspired choice, Ridgway slowly managed to revive the morale of those under his command. Insisting on a novel strategy for defence, he ordered his troops to forsake the roads and seize the high ground, to deny the enemy that advantage. Next he introduced a new tactic to the demoralized UN army: attack.

But all this took time. Early in January 1951 the Chinese launched another offensive. On 4 January 1951 Seoul fell for the second time to the Communists. The remains of Inchon, the site of MacArthur's triumphant landing only four months earlier, were now torched by retreating soldiers. But this was the extent of this Communist advance. The momentum of the Chinese assault was running down, and they faced a newly invigorated UN army. The tide turned once more. On 10 February the Eighth Army retook Inchon, and on 14 March Seoul was recaptured. Later in March, the Eighth Army arrived again at the 38th parallel.

ABOVE LEFT: *In freezing weather conditions, US-UN forces sullenly retreat south under the Chinese onslaught. The Americans called retreating "bug-out fever."* ABOVE: *General Matthew B. Ridgway arrived to take command of the Eighth Army and dramatically improved morale. His leadership, strategy, and tactics brought results.*

MacArthur Speaks Out of Turn

Meanwhile, MacArthur had taken the position that Chinese Nationalists from Taiwan, under Chiang Kai-shek, should come to the aid of UN forces in Korea. Speaking openly of an invasion of Communist China, MacArthur advocated the bombing of Chinese cities. He called on Washington to supply him with massive reinforcements. But Washington regarded the war in Korea as a limited operation and had no wish to extend the conflict with China, or to risk direct confrontation with the Soviet Union. Increasingly, MacArthur's views were out of line with those of his political masters, and Truman decided he had to act. After a series of meetings to get support from his principal advisers and the Joint Chiefs of Staff, Truman sacked MacArthur — for "purely military considerations." General Ridgway replaced him.

In late April a new spring offensive began, as half a million Chinese and North Koreans threw themselves against the UN lines. Once more the UN forces suffered great casualties, and thousands of men were taken prisoner. In the hills around the Imjin River, British soldiers of the Gloucester Regiment, facing vastly superior Chinese numbers, displayed great heroism before being wiped out as a military force. In the west, People's Volunteers reached the suburbs of Seoul. But this time the UN line held. The Chinese were pushed back, and the war seemed to have reached a stalemate — almost exactly at the point where fighting had begun a year earlier.

In July 1951 armistice talks began at Kaesong. The US feared that the Chinese and North Koreans might use this respite as an opportunity to regroup and re-equip — which was precisely what happened. Furthermore, the North Koreans and the Chinese were determined to milk every ounce of propaganda they could from the armistice negotiations. When the UN jeeps drove up flying white flags of truce, North Korean newsreels claimed that they were signs of surrender. After six weeks of fruitless negotiations, the Communists accused the UN of violating the neutral zone and suspended the talks.

> *This was a bewildered army, not sure of itself or its leaders, not sure what they were doing there, wondering when they would hear the whistle of that homebound transport.*
>
> — Gen. Matthew B. Ridgway, December 1950

MacArthur's Dismissal

As a legendary hero of the Second World War, Douglas MacArthur enjoyed vast popular support in the United States, and Truman's exasperation with his field commander was already tempered by fear of the fallout his dismissal would provoke. After a series of secret White House meetings, the decision to remove MacArthur was made on 10 April 1951. General Bradley summed it up when he said that MacArthur was "not in sympathy with the decision to try to limit the conflict in Korea. . . . It was necessary to have a commander more responsive to control from Washington." But before MacArthur could be told of the decision, the news leaked out in the *Chicago Tribune*, forcing the White House to call a press conference at one in the morning for the announcement. MacArthur was furious at both the decision and the shabby way it had been handled. He returned to the United States to enthusiastic parades wherever he went. In his famous address to a joint session of Congress, MacArthur ironically quoted a line from an old ballad: "Old soldiers never die; they just fade away." He even considered standing as a presidential candidate in the next election, to thwart the Democrats. But most liberal opinion in the United States sided with Truman. MacArthur had got "too big for his britches."

From the fall of 1951 both sides were to confront each other from well-prepared, well-dug-in trenches. The UN forces were half a million strong, properly supplied and well armed, and their field artillery kept the Communist troops pinned down in their positions. Old soldiers observed that the fighting was now like the trench warfare of the First World War. But in the air a very advanced type of war — the first jet-versus-jet combat — was being fought, as Soviet MiG-15 fighters battled it out with American F-86 Sabers. Some of the MiGs were actually flown by Russian pilots from bases inside China. The Americans knew this but chose to make nothing of it, lest it bring the USSR fully into the war.

The US Air Force kept up a massive bombing campaign, which devastated the cities of North Korea. More than 600,000 tons of bombs fell on the North, almost as much as rained down on Germany during the whole of the Second World War. A good percentage of North Korean industry went underground, into a subterranean world of factories, shops, and hospitals. Under the slogan "The Rear Is the Front," North Korean workers were urged on to greater productivity, to be proud they could stand up to the all-powerful United States. Kim Il Sung acquired almost godlike status as he led his people in their resistance against American aggression.

Throughout 1951 Stalin was under pressure from both Mao and Kim to supply more pilots and planes to the war in Korea. Stalin flatly turned down most of these requests. But he did continue to supply considerable military hardware to the Chinese, although he insisted that the People's Republic must pay for every item in hard cash. Stalin personally supervised these negotiations, which caused great bitterness amongst Mao and the Chinese leadership. Tens of thousands of Chinese soldiers were being sacrificed for the Communist cause on the field of battle, but for every bullet supplied to their poorer Chinese comrades, the Soviets demanded payment. "What price blood?" asked Mao of the Chinese effort in Korea. This disappointment sowed the first seeds of hostility between Beijing and Moscow.

There is no substitute for victory.

— Gen. Douglas MacArthur, 20 March 1951

Armistice in Earnest

In October 1951 the armistice talks began again, this time at Panmunjom in the no-man's-land between the two armies. These talks would continue for more than eighteen months, floundering from one crisis to another. Several sessions consisted of only a few minutes of talking, then hours of silence in which each side glared at the other. One dispute focused on whether the truce lines should be along the 38th parallel, as the Communists wanted, or along the final lines of engagement, as the UN wanted. Just when some agreement was reached, a military unit would go into action, and there would be further dispute as to where the battle line then stood. Another major stumbling block was the question of prisoners. This issue delayed the cease-fire agreement even further.

In the South 132,000 Communist prisoners were kept on an island camp at Koje-Do. Here Communist activists organized training and drilling, all under the eyes of guards who found it easier to ignore what was going on than to do something about it. The UN insisted on screening all its prisoners of war (POWs), asking each if he wanted to return to the Communist mainland or to stay in the South or go to Taiwan. Inside the camps this provoked violence, as the prisoners formed into opposed political groupings. Many who said they wanted to defect were beaten or killed by hard-line Communist prisoners. There were several violent uprisings at Koje-Do. During one, the American camp commander, Brigadier General Francis T. Dodd, was captured by the prisoners. He agreed to end the screenings and was released. But then the UN authorities cracked down. Dodd was court-martialled and his agreement was overturned. UN troops entered the prison camp with tanks and flame-throwers. The Communists took full propaganda advantage, claiming that the United States was pitching armed soldiers against unarmed prisoners.

In the early days the North Koreans committed terrible atrocities against UN prisoners. Hundreds died of starvation, dysentery, or bad treatment. One in three American POWs died during the first winter of the war. In 1951, when the Chinese took control of the prison camps along the Yalu River, conditions at last improved. Although the Chinese seldom beat up their prisoners, they did try to indoctrinate them politically. All POWs were offered hours of lectures every day, to encourage them to see the virtues of Marxism-Leninism and to understand their own role in Korea as pawns of the aggressive imperialists. Men responded to this in different ways. Some went along with it for an easy ride. Others resisted any attempt at what was then called "brainwashing." A few were genuinely interested in a radical new view of the world about them.

At the Panmunjom talks, the Communists admitted to holding only three thousand US POWs, even though the UN calculated that there were another eight thousand men in captivity. When, in turn, the UN insisted that only half the Communist POWs wished "voluntary repatriation" to North Korea and to China, the Communists were outraged at this major propaganda blow. They insisted that the screening of prisoners had taken place under intimidation and violence and the results were not to be trusted.

Negotiating an end to the Korean War was held up for years by issues concerning prisoners of war. FAR LEFT: *Prisoners held in South Korea display banners and shout slogans to demonstrate their continued Communist beliefs.* ABOVE: *American POWs in Chinese hands; of GIs captured by North Koreans, one-third died in the first winter.*

The Communists accused the United States of waging germ warfare by dropping bombs on the North containing the plague bacillus and anthrax. They produced newsfilm purporting to show spider flies infected with anthrax. TOP: A shot-down American airman, First Lieutenant John Quinn, who admitted on camera, following "brainwashing," to flying missions in which he dropped germ bombs. BOTTOM: A Scientific Commission from sympathetic Communist countries examined the evidence and claimed that germ warfare had been engaged in. There is no evidence from the US side that this was ever the case.

In November 1952 Dwight D. Eisenhower was elected the new US president. Standing as a Republican, the former supreme commander of the Allied Expeditionary Force had campaigned on the slogan, "I shall go to Korea," and had briefly visited South Korea in December. Then, in March 1953, Stalin died, throwing the Kremlin into the confusion of an uncertain succession. In all the chaos following Stalin's death, the new Soviet leadership came to the conclusion, in only two weeks, that the war must be ended. By this time Mao had also decided the same thing.

In May 1953 Eisenhower, in an attempt to bully the Communists into a negotiated peace, threatened Beijing with the use of nuclear weapons. At the same time, US bombers hit a series of dams in North Korea, which led to disastrous flooding. There was bitter fighting throughout June 1953, with heavy losses on both sides. Although the United States was set on ending the war, Syngman Rhee proved recalcitrant. Trying to sabotage the armistice talks, he opened the gates of a POW camp in the South to allow Communist prisoners to defect. Eisenhower was furious, and Winston Churchill, once again Britain's prime minister, cabled the White House that Rhee should be removed from office. The armistice negotiations continued, with only the UN, China, and North Korea present. Finally, at midnight on 27 July 1953, the guns fell silent. A cease-fire came into effect.

There followed an elaborate exchange of prisoners. Twelve thousand UN POWs were released, but twenty-one Americans and one Scot chose to stay on in Communist China. Fifty thousand Communist POWs were released; approximately two-thirds of the Chinese said they wanted to go to Taiwan. Some of those who returned to the North made one final, bizarre gesture. Approaching the border, they threw off their UN-issued clothes and crossed naked, waving Communist flags they had made out of old rags, stained red with their own blood.

There was little to celebrate at the end of the Korean War. The United States had lost more than 54,000 men; a further 100,000 were wounded. The other nations of the UN force lost more than 3,000 men, with nearly 12,000 wounded. The South Korean army lost 415,000 men, and it is estimated that the North Korean army suffered nearly a million deaths. The Chinese, as the price for their relentless human-wave assaults, officially claimed to have lost 112,000 men. The figure was almost certainly double that, and possibly as many as half a million men. But the real losers in the war were the Korean people. There were terrible civilian losses from US bombing of the North, and at least 5 million refugees were homeless in the South. Seoul, Pyongyang, and most of the major cities had been flattened. The North would never fully recover under Kim Il Sung; it would remain a low-output agricultural society. The South, under Rhee, who was finally deposed in 1960, and his successors, would undergo dramatic change. A generation after the war, South Korea emerged as one of the dominant growth economies of the region.

Another major consequence of the Korean War was a huge boost to the Japanese economy. The American military spent $3.5 billion in Japan on everything from ships to trucks, from cold-weather gear to medical supplies. Japanese manufacturing output more than doubled. It was American policy to build up a strong ally in the Pacific, and Japan enjoyed a revival more dramatic than anything brought about by Marshall Plan aid in Europe. It became wholeheartedly capitalist and resolutely anti-Communist. The one positive consequence of the Korean War, ironically, was to trigger the economic growth of the whole region.

The world, during the Korean War, came near to a second Hiroshima on mainland Asia. But both sides showed restraint. Some senior American military advisers argued that the use of atomic weapons was necessary to bomb the Communists into submission. However, the United States would have been morally tarnished in using nuclear weapons to finish off a war in Asia with such confused objectives, whose only real purpose would have been to destroy communism in China. But the Eisenhower administration came out of the war convinced that it had been the US threat to use nuclear weapons against China in May 1953 that had ended the war. This had great influence on American strategic thinking. In reality, the decision to end the war had already been made in Moscow and Beijing within a fortnight of Stalin's death in March 1953. Nonetheless, the United States now saw its role in the world as defending all countries against communism, wherever they were.

ABOVE: *27 July 1953. Officers of the Canadian UN brigade receive the news that an armistice has been signed.*
LEFT: *A North Korean prisoner, stripped to his underwear, defiantly throws away his US-made POW uniform. The fighting was over; antagonism remained.*

The "Rosenberg traitors" were Julius and his wife, Ethel, convicted of passing atomic secrets to the Soviets, then an ally, during the Second World War. Both were sentenced to the electric chair. Worldwide appeals for clemency battled demonstrations for their execution. At dawn on 19 June 1953 they were "burned" at Sing Sing prison.

Reds
1948–1953

The House Un-American Activities Committee

On 3 August 1948 Whittaker Chambers, a senior editor of *Time* magazine who was a known former Communist, appeared before a meeting of the House Un-American Activities Committee (HUAC). Looking shabby and dishevelled in a wrinkled suit, he tearfully told of his own road-to-Damascus conversion and final rejection of communism. The microphone had failed, and Chambers, almost inaudible to some of the committee members, was constantly interrupted and asked to speak up. After naming six low-level government employees as members of his own Communist cell, Chambers then, to the astonishment of everyone present, named as a Communist agent Alger Hiss, a former member of Roosevelt's elite who had worked on establishing the United Nations. Several committee members regarded an accusation by such an unimpressive witness as not likely to be taken any further, but Hiss sent the committee a telegram asking to testify, under oath, in order to clear his name.

Two days later Alger Hiss presented himself before HUAC. Tall and handsome, with youthful good looks that made it hard to believe he was forty-four years old, Hiss was the epitome of the brilliant, successful East Coast lawyer. A distinguished graduate of Johns Hopkins University and Harvard Law School, Hiss had been attracted to Roosevelt's New Deal and had given up a promising private career to go into public service. At the State Department he was one of Roosevelt's closest advisers, and he had personally briefed the president before the crucial Yalta Conference on the postwar world. Following his work in setting up the United Nations, Hiss was nominated by the Soviets as someone acceptable to them as its first secretary-general. Now, before HUAC, he categorically denied all the charges made by Chambers and insisted he had never met the man. Hiss made such a contrast to Chambers that it looked as

Speaking before the House Un-American Activities Committee, Whittaker Chambers (BOTTOM), himself a former Communist, repeats his charge that Alger Hiss (TOP) was a Communist. Hiss denied the charges but was eventually convicted of perjury and jailed.

though his evidence would end the matter there and then. But after lunch the youngest member of HUAC, an ambitious first-term congressman named Richard Milhous Nixon, took over the questioning.

Nixon had been elected to the House of Representatives from California in 1946, at the age of thirty-three. He quickly realized that one way for a young Republican to gain prominence was by taunting the Democrats for under-estimating the menace of communism. The Second World War had papered over the ideological divide as America and the Soviet Union became allies in defeating Hitler. Now the old fears and suspicions were ready to be rekindled. One of Congressman Nixon's first appointments had been to the House Un-American Activities Committee, which since 1938 had been charged with pur-suing foreign subversion among federal government employees. In the fall of 1947 the committee subpoenaed a group of Hollywood writers, producers, and performers as part of an investigation into Communist infiltration of the motion picture industry. Most of those called gave evidence, but a few refused to answer questions about their political affiliations, claiming immunity under the First Amendment. This minority became known as the Hollywood Ten. They were cited for contempt of Congress and jailed for terms of four to ten months. Blacklisted by the American film industry, they could only get work by going abroad, or by using a pseudonym.

Now, on that summer day in 1948, when Nixon started to question Hiss, he saw in him all that he detested most: Ivy League privilege, East Coast estab-lishment, and calm assurance. It is not clear whether Nixon then knew that Hiss had earlier come under suspicion. In 1942 he had been interviewed by State Department security officials over claims that he was a Soviet agent but had satisfied them of his innocence. The FBI was still watching him; the attor-ney general had authorized a tap on his telephones. Nixon now seized the opportunity. That afternoon, and then in a series of further sessions, Nixon pressed Hiss hard and also extracted enough detailed evidence from Chambers to be convinced that Hiss was lying. Hiss and Chambers made claim and counter-claim in separate sessions. HUAC's chairman commented that "whichever one of you is lying is the greatest actor that America has ever pro-duced."

Hiss had powerful friends, from Dean Acheson upwards. Even President Truman, who at this time regarded most attacks on government officials as politically inspired, came out indirectly in support of Hiss by denouncing HUAC's proceedings as a "red herring." Then, on 25 August, Nixon staged a public drama starring Hiss and Chambers for the first-ever televised congres-sional hearing. In the sweltering summer heat of a packed Washington cau-cus room, made even hotter by the television arc lights, the confrontation began. As Hiss was questioned for five relentless hours, discrepancies began to emerge. Hiss now recalled that he had known Chambers as a George Crosley, a journalist to whom he had rented an apartment from 1934 to 1935. Hiss's credibility had cracked. Chambers opened his testimony by stating sim-ply, "Mr. Hiss is lying." He claimed to have introduced Hiss to his Soviet spy-master, Colonel Bykov, in 1937, and said Hiss went on to supply Bykov with a succession of State Department documents.

Hollywood goes to Washington to protest the House Un-American Activities Committee's 1947 inves-tigation of the film industry. Humphrey Bogart (centre, in bow tie) was the group's spokesman.

For Nixon, the Hiss case now became make or break. If Hiss proved to be innocent, Nixon would lose face. If Hiss was found guilty, Nixon would be a hero. When Hiss sued Chambers for libel, the case took a bizarre turn. From his pumpkin patch Chambers produced evidence he had recently retrieved from a relative who had kept it for him for ten years. It appeared to consist of copies of sixty-five pages of classified documents typed up by Hiss and his wife, and allegedly turned over to Chambers, who gave them to the Russians. Furthermore, it was proved to the court's satisfaction that these documents had been typed on the Woodstock typewriter owned by Hiss in 1938. Nixon extracted maximum publicity by being photographed with the "pumpkin papers" and by refusing to hand them over to the Justice Department, which, he said, could not be trusted to prosecute Hiss. When Truman later read this evidence, he remarked privately, "The son of a bitch. He betrayed his country." Hiss was indicted by a grand jury for perjury (the statute of limitations for espionage had expired) and bound over for trial, which ended in a hung jury. Then, in a highly publicized retrial in January 1950, Hiss was found guilty and sent to jail. When Nixon heard the verdict and sentence, he gave a whoop and danced with delight. Still protesting his innocence, Hiss served forty-four months in Lewisburg Federal Penitentiary.

The case catapulted Nixon's career, and he became a national hero. In 1950, after a bitter, mud-slinging campaign, Nixon moved up to the US Senate, now one of the Republican Party's rising stars. Two years later Eisenhower picked him as his presidential running mate, and at the age of forty Nixon became vice president. His determination in dogging Hiss had won him solid support from the right, and permanent distrust from the liberals.

J. Edgar Hoover

John Edgar Hoover was appointed director of the little-known Bureau of Investigation in 1924. This became the Federal Bureau of Investigation in 1935, and Hoover remained its guiding force. By the end of the Second World War he had made the bureau the dominant agency in the field of domestic intelligence. He developed close alliances with many conservative congressmen, who helped to sustain his personal authority and vote for the budgets needed to maintain the FBI's dominance. He also developed links with conservative reporters and newsmen. From 1946 on, Hoover ran a covert propaganda campaign against the Communist threat, leaking information to carefully selected congressmen and reporters, who would preserve the confidentiality of their source. Along with this came a major public relations campaign of radio programmes, later television dramas, and, with the support of Twentieth Century-Fox, a feature film, *The Street with No Name* (1948) — one of the few to have the agency's full participation. All this was intended to promote the work of the bureau and to build up public respect for its agents as detectives who worked miracles in the cause of justice.

Hoover himself was a conservative man of established routine, a bachelor devoted to his work at the FBI who rarely socialized or mixed with people outside the bureau. Every morning he was driven to work along the same route, often deciding to walk the last few blocks. Every evening he had a single drink on his balcony at home and then dined alone or with a friend.

In time, Hoover's reputation made it difficult for any politician to oppose him, almost immunizing him from control by those he reported to, the attorney general and the president. One of the most powerful figures in Washington, he remained head of the FBI for an extraordinary forty-eight years, until his death in 1972.

The scene in the caucus room as the House Un-American Activities Committee opens its investigation into Communist influence in the movie industry. The first witness, Jack L. Warner, a Warner Brothers executive, is the focus of attention. Seated second from right on the dais is Congressman Richard M. Nixon. "Hollywood on trial" captured public attention.

MR. PETERSON

MR. BONNER

The Hiss case served to discredit, in some quarters, the progressive social reform associated with the Roosevelt era. Many Americans began to question how it was that wartime US policy had led to the division of postwar Europe, with Communists in control of Eastern Europe. Some spoke darkly of the "treason of Yalta." In 1949 Americans had good reason to feel threatened. When the Soviets detonated their atom bomb, the United States lost its nuclear monopoly. In that same year, China was "lost" to communism under Mao Zedong. America was gripped by fear and by anti-Communist fever.

The most powerful exponent of the "Red Menace" was the director of the FBI, J. Edgar Hoover. Obsessed with hating communism and radicals, Hoover recognized an opportunity to enhance the FBI's status as the foremost national bulwark against the putative Communist conspiracy. In the hysteria he helped build up, Hoover permitted his agents the use of break-ins, wire-taps, phone intercepts, and bugging to gather evidence. Neighbours were encouraged to spy on one another. Parents were asked to inform on their children, children on their parents. Frequently, these practices created problems in bringing evidence to court, for defence lawyers could show that the prosecutions were based on inadmissible evidence. Infuriated by this impediment, Hoover launched an attack on the National Lawyers Guild as a pro-Communist organization. He relied on an extensive network of confidential informers, and in Los Angeles actor Ronald Reagan, president of the Screen Actors Guild, was one of them. Hoover secretly passed on to HUAC members evidence he knew would not stand up in court but could provide fodder for a congressional investigation. When the witch-hunt spread to Hollywood, the California office of the FBI compiled two lists for HUAC: one of Hollywood artists who were or had been members of Communist-influenced organizations, and a second list of "friendly witnesses," who would supply HUAC with further names and information.

The Passing of Atomic Secrets

The prevailing paranoia did not mean that there was nothing to be paranoid about. The Soviet Union did have active espionage agents in the United States and amply benefited from their efforts. In January 1950 the German-born British nuclear physicist Klaus Fuchs, who had worked in the US Atomic Research Laboratory at Los Alamos, New Mexico, was arrested in London. Fuchs confessed to having given atomic secrets to the Soviets and named various American accomplices; he was sentenced to fourteen years in prison. The FBI subsequently made arrests that led to a young electrical engineer, Julius Rosenberg, who was accused of furnishing atomic secrets to the Soviet Union during the war. Rosenberg was at the centre of a network of spies who felt uncomfortable that the United States was the sole owner of the key to atomic warfare, and they passed a range of industrial, military, and atomic information to the Soviets. The evidence against Rosenberg came largely from his brother-in-law, David Greenglass, who had been part of the wartime spy network. Other members, like Joel Barr and Alfred Sarant, fled to Eastern Europe at the time of Rosenberg's arrest. Even under FBI interrogation, Julius Rosenberg refused to give information, or to name any other agents. So, a

Nixon, a Republican congress-man from California, believed all along that Alger Hiss was guilty. Almost single-handedly he forced HUAC to pursue the investigation against this prominent figure. The Hiss case launched Nixon's career.

Julius and Ethel Rosenberg, photographed 19 March 1951, during their trial for espionage. Her arrest was intended to put pressure on him to name other spies, but he did not. Both were convicted and executed.

month after his arrest, his wife, Ethel, was also arrested and charged with spying, probably in the hope of breaking Julius. While Ethel must have known of her husband's activities, she most probably did not play any direct role in them. Nonetheless, Julius maintained his silence.

On evidence from Greenglass and another spy, Harry Gold, Julius and Ethel Rosenberg were both found guilty of passing atomic secrets to the Russians. Espionage in wartime was a crime punishable by death, but in this case Rosenberg had supplied information to an ally. Nevertheless, the anti-Communist mood of the day was too intense to take note of such a distinction. Judge Irving R. Kaufman spoke of the Rosenbergs' "diabolical conspiracy to destroy a God-fearing nation" and claimed that the secrets they had revealed to the Soviets gave Russia the bomb "years before our best scientists predicted." Judge Kaufman sentenced both Rosenbergs to the electric chair. A long appeal process brought requests for clemency from, among many others, Albert Einstein and Pope Pius XII. Some lawyers thought the Rosenbergs' execution was unconstitutional, but a last-minute appeal failed. At dawn on 19 June 1953 they were electrocuted in Sing Sing prison. Many Americans by now had reason to believe that their country was dangerously infiltrated by Reds.

Reds Under the Beds

Soon after Hiss had been sent to prison, at a speech in Wheeling, West Virginia, on 9 February 1950, Wisconsin senator Joseph R. McCarthy claimed that there were more than two hundred Communists inside the State Department. In response to McCarthy's accusations, the national witch-hunt took on even more virulence. Taking advantage of public frustration with Cold War reverses, and with a keen eye for publicity, McCarthy made claims of Red infiltration that included alleged conspiracies inside the Pentagon, the universities, Hollywood, Broadway, and network television. He presented long lists of "Communists" prominent in all walks of American life. He claimed that the Roosevelt and Truman administrations, soft on communism, had been guilty of twenty years of treason against the American people. McCarthy overwhelmed opponents with his hectoring, bullying style and left thousands of innocent people smeared with a stain it took a generation to wear off.

In March 1951 HUAC revived its investigation into Hollywood. The committee was seeking more and more names. Only by naming others could penitent Communists purge themselves and escape further torture by the Inquisition. The studio bosses, shaken by the earlier furore over the Hollywood Ten, pledged not to employ anyone who had ever been a Communist or had refused to declare under oath that he or she had never been a Communist. In front of newsreel cameras, many of the great names of Hollywood faced a humiliating dilemma: capitulate and become a public informer, or take the First or Fifth Amendment and be blacklisted from the industry indefinitely. Many actors, directors, and writers swallowed their pride, put aside their sense of honour, and named names.

Elia Kazan, the Academy Award—winning director who first put Marlon Brando on the screen, named eleven former Communists before the HUAC. Jerome Robbins, the successful Broadway and Hollywood choreographer,

Hollywood, responding to a national fervour, and anxious to shake off charges of un-American activities, pitched into the Cold War propaganda struggle with movies like The Iron Curtain *and* I Was a Communist for the FBI. *In these films, the good guys always won, and democracy was saved.*

agreed to co-operate with the committee. Sterling Hayden did the same. Screenwriter Martin Berkeley broke the record by naming 162 Hollywood artists as former or present-day Communists. Some 250 Hollywood personalities were blacklisted in the purge of the early 1950s. They included some of the most talented directors, writers, and performers in the industry. Some of them did not appear in a movie until well into the 1960s. Others, like Carl Foreman and Joseph Losey, went into exile in England. Some worked under pseudonyms, like Dalton Trumbo, one of the original Hollywood Ten, who, to the embarrassment of an entire industry, won an Oscar in 1956 for a screenplay written under the name Robert Rich.

Charlie Chaplin, a native of Britain, had resided in the United States for nearly thirty years but had never applied for citizenship. Throughout the war he publicly supported the Russian struggle against Hitler. In Europe for a six-month visit when the frenzy broke, he was tipped off that on his return he would face questioning of a political nature by an immigration board. He decided to stay away and did not go back to the States until 1972, and then only briefly to accept a special Academy Award.

Cinema credits throughout the 1950s would show names of some who had confessed, repented, and informed. Those who had not done so, no matter how popular, simply disappeared from the silver screen.

Elsewhere in Hollywood there was a clamour for stars, writers, and producers to proclaim their allegiance to the flag. The Screen Actors Guild, when Ronald Reagan headed it, introduced a loyalty oath and required its officers to sign affidavits that they were not Communists. After a struggle through the courts, the Screen Writers Guild eventually gave up protecting its members who had been blacklisted. It also agreed to bar Communists from membership. The Motion Picture Alliance for the Preservation of American Ideals, under the presidency of John Wayne, and whose executive committee included Gary Cooper, John Ford, and Clark Gable, published instructions for everyone in the movie business: "Don't smear the free enterprise system . . . don't glorify the collective."

As writers and intellectuals rallied to assert their American-ness, Hollywood produced a string of lightly disguised "Reds under the bed" horror movies. Fifty movies and dozens of documentaries were produced. Usually the Reds were gangsters in fast getaway cars who would brutally machine-gun anyone who stood in their way. One film, *I Was a Communist for the FBI*, won an Oscar for best documentary. With movies like *My Son John*, *I Married a Communist*, and *Evil Epidemic*, writers tried to outdo each other in their proclamation of good American values.

McCarthy also led a crusade against subversion in the universities. Again, he whipped up such hysteria that thousands lost their jobs and were unable to find new ones. Anyone failing to co-operate with a congressional inquiry was prima facie guilty. There was no formal blacklist in academia, but university departments, investigating the political background of each prospective employee, steered clear of anyone associated with political activity on the left, so as to avoid bringing down upon their heads the scrutiny of Congress. J. Edgar Hoover claimed that too many teachers were "Reducators," "tearing down respect for agencies of government, belittling tradition and moral custom and . . . creating doubts in the validity of the American way of life." Such public speech had a chilling effect.

McCarthy and his supporters also attacked the United Nations, associated by now with left-wing, liberal causes. Many of its American staff left or were purged. The UN secretary-general, the Norwegian Trygve Lie, showed no more stomach for standing up to McCarthyite smears than did his American counterparts in the movies and the universities. It was always easier to remove someone from the payroll than to fight and risk being tainted oneself.

Initially the Republican Party supported McCarthy's campaigns. But

> *Have you no sense of decency, sir? At long last, have you left no sense of decency?*
>
> — Joseph N. Welch,
> 9 June 1954

ABOVE: *Roy M. Cohn, counsel, whispers advice to Senator Joseph McCarthy as his subcommittee probes the US Army for Communist infiltration. It proved one probe too many.*
ABOVE LEFT: *McCarthy met his match in army counsel Joseph N. Welch (gesturing). Welch's courteous manner touched a sympathetic nerve in US public opinion. The McCarthy blister was lanced.*

President Eisenhower could barely conceal his dislike for the senator. As the Republican presidential candidate, Eisenhower had brought himself, just once, to shake hands with McCarthy after a half-hour meeting in McCarthy's home state of Wisconsin. Thus sidestepping a potential split in the Republican Party, he got McCarthy's endorsement for his candidacy. But McCarthy's accusations became wilder and wilder. He accused General George C. Marshall of being pro-Communist, as "part of a conspiracy so immense, an infamy so black, as to dwarf any in the history of man." To his shame, Eisenhower did nothing to defend his old wartime commander, the author of the postwar programme that was shoring up Western Europe against communism. Eisenhower even agreed to drop a paragraph defending Marshall from a campaign speech for fear of being divisive. Some supporters never forgave him.

After Eisenhower arrived at the White House, McCarthy continued to make charges, this time against members of Ike's administration. Out of control, in the climate of fear he had helped generate, McCarthy pointed the finger at whomever he wished. Eisenhower was still reluctant to act, fearful of losing the half-dozen votes in the Senate that supported McCarthy, but finally McCarthy went too far. In a series of nationally televised hearings in 1954, he made, but then failed to substantiate, claims of Red infiltration of the army. By now the senator was drinking heavily and showed signs of cracking up. The McCarthy bubble burst when army counsel Joseph N. Welch stood up to him on live television. "Senator . . . you have done enough. Have you no sense of decency, sir? At long last, have you left no sense of decency?" In December the Senate voted to condemn him, 67–22, for bringing that body into disrepute. McCarthy's career was finished.

Return of the Great Terror

The Cold War, and the reverses the nation faced, generated in the United States what has been called the Great Fear. The Soviet Union endured far worse: the Great Terror. McCarthyism, and every other American hysteria, paled in comparison to the paranoia that permeated the Soviet system and Communist East Europe in the late 1940s and early 1950s, as it had done during Stalin's reign of terror in the 1930s. Hundreds of thousands of people were sent to labour camps. Many thousands, loyal party members, were executed. In Hungary as many as one family in three had a member in jail during the Stalinist period. In the Soviet Union and Eastern Europe, conformity was everything. No dissent was allowed; independent thought was fiercely tracked down, rooted out, and repressed. What in the United States was an aberration was in the Soviet world the system itself.

In the first phase of the Soviet takeover of Eastern Europe, Communist parties, with backing from the Kremlin, had taken control of the central apparatus of each state. Sometimes there were tensions between the local Communists, who had been part of the underground struggle against the Nazis, and the Moscow Communists whom Stalin appointed over them to the party's most senior positions. Initially their energies were devoted to condemning political opponents and "class enemies." But in 1948 there began a new phase in the Sovietization of Eastern Europe; each nation was to be politically controlled by its Communist Party, and each Communist Party was to be subject to absolute control from Moscow.

The crisis that prompted this strengthening of control was the split with Tito in 1948. Tito, the wartime partisan leader of Yugoslavia, headed the only Communist country in East Europe where power was not imposed by Moscow but came from his own popularity and strength. Although Stalin's favourite for a while, Tito was soon out of favour with the Communist world leader for resisting Soviet control of both Yugoslavia's economy and its Communist Party. In June 1948 Yugoslavia was expelled from Cominform for having "placed itself outside the family of the fraternal Communist parties." Stalin even prepared plans for a military intervention, but later decided against it.

The "mutiny" in Yugoslavia now gave Stalin the opportunity he sought to reinforce his power. He could cite not just the external enemy, the imperialist powers led by the United States, but the existence of an enemy within. Titoism became the Kremlin's excuse for establishing a tighter grip on the Communist parties of Eastern Europe. Between 1948 and 1953 all the parties were forced through a crash programme of Stalinization — five-year plans, forced collectivization, the development of heavy industry, and control over the

Radio was a good way to get behind the Iron Curtain. Radio Free Europe solicited dollars to help fund its broadcasts into the Soviet-dominated countries of Eastern Europe. The broadcasts told truths but sometimes, as in Hungary in 1956, promised more than the West delivered.

army and the party bureaucracy. To maintain discipline the satellites were made to impose a vast technology of repression. A central tenet of Stalinism was that true socialism could only be constructed through intense struggle; the more enemies you revealed, the closer you were to the socialist ideal. Show trials were used to procure both public obedience and the total subservience of the local party to central control. Communist Party members who gave any hint of independence, like Tito, were now ruthlessly purged.

The most significant of the show trials was that of Foreign Minister Laszlo Rajk in Hungary. Rajk had fought in the Spanish Civil War and had spent three years in France before joining the resistance in Hungary. After the war he became the most popular member of the Communist leadership. Although he had led the Communist liquidation of the Catholic Church, he was now himself about to become a victim of Communist repression. Under the supervision of Soviet adviser General Fyodor Byelkin, confessions were concocted to do with a Western imperialist and pro-Tito plot within the Hungarian Communist Party. Rajk was put under immense pressure and tortured. He was told he must sacrifice himself for the party. János Kádár, an old party friend and godfather to Rajk's son, impressed on him that, out of loyalty, he must confess to being a Titoist spy; whatever the verdict, he and his family would be allowed to start a new life in Russia. Rajk agreed. In his public trial he admitted the pro-Tito story. But he had been betrayed by Kádár and the party. On 24 September 1949 Rajk and two other defendants were sentenced to death. A month later they were executed. The Rajk confession and trial became a model for show trials across East Europe.

Laszlo Rajk

In Czechoslovakia, where the Communist Party had seized control in February 1948, a series of trials highlighted different stages of the imposition of Communist authority. Between 1948 and 1952 death sentences were passed against 233 political prisoners — intellectuals, independent thinkers, socialists, Christians. The execution of Zavis Kalandra, an associate of the Surrealists and a Marxist who had split with the prewar Communist Party, shocked Prague. Nearly 150,000 people were made political prisoners in Czechoslovakia, 7,000 Socialist Party members among them.

The Next Phase

With real and imaginary political opponents exterminated, the next phase of Stalinization was a purge of the Communist Party itself. One out of every four Czechoslovak party members was removed. Stalin wanted to make an example of one highly placed comrade, Rudolf Slánský, the general secretary of the Czech Communist Party, who was then leading a security purge within it. Stalin personally ordered Klement Gottwald, who had replaced Eduard Beneš as president of Czechoslovakia, to arrest Slánský. When Gottwald hesitated, Stalin sent General Alexei Beschastnov and two assistants to Prague. Gottwald gave in. On 20 November 1951, Slánský was arrested. In this case there was a new ingredient in the mix: Slánský and ten of the other high-ranking Czechoslovak party members arrested at that time were Jews.

In Communist show trials the accused were forced, by torture and deprivation, to "confess" to crimes against the state. Hungarian Laszlo Rajk (second from right) was promised a new life in Russia if he admitted being a Titoist spy. In fact, when he did confess he was executed. Show trials reinforced terror; "justice" was an instrument of state tyranny.

The case against Slánský was based on Stalin's fear of an imagined Zionist, pro-Western conspiracy. Stalin appeared to believe there was a conspiracy led by American Jewish capitalists and the Israeli government to dominate the world, and to wage a new war against communism. This represented a complete turnaround by Stalin on Israel. The Soviet Union had supported the struggle of the Zionists against the Palestinian Arabs, and had supplied them, through Czechoslovakia, with essential weapons in 1947 and 1948.

Rudolf Slánský

Russia was the first nation to recognize de jure the state of Israel, within minutes of its birth in May 1948. Two years later, perhaps fearful of Israel's appeal to the hundreds of thousands of Russian Jews, and suspicious of its close ties to the United States, Stalin became convinced that Israel was in the vanguard of an international Jewish conspiracy against him.

Slánský was, in fact, a loyal Stalinist. But he was forced to confess that, because of his bourgeois and Jewish origins, he had never been a true Communist and that he was now an American spy. Slánský and his co-accused were told their sacrifice was for the party's good. Their confessions were written out in detail by Soviet advisers in Prague, and each of the accused was carefully rehearsed for his "performance" at the trial to come. They had time to learn their "confessions" by heart, for preparations took a year. In November 1952 the show trial began. One by one, Slánský and the others confessed to the most absurd charges made against them by their former friends and associates. Public prosecutor Josef Urvalek read out the indictment, condemning this gang of traitors and criminals who had infiltrated the Communist Party on behalf of an evil pro-Zionist, Western conspiracy. It was now time, he said, for the people's vengeance. The accused wondered how Urvalek could feign such conviction. The "defence" lawyers admitted that the evidence against their clients confirmed their guilt. In his last statement, Slánský said, "I deserve no other end to my criminal life but that proposed by the Public Prosecutor." Others stated, "I realize that however harsh the penalty — and whatever it is, it will be just — I will never be able to make up for the damage I have caused"; "I beg the state tribunal to appreciate and condemn my treachery with the maximum severity and firmness." Eleven were condemned to death. Three were sentenced to life imprisonment. When the sentences were announced, the court was silent. No one could be proud of what had been done. Slánský and the other ten were executed a week later.

Josef Urvalek

Stalin treated the whole of Eastern Europe as his domain, with the leaders of the Communist parties his vassals, obliged to carry out his instructions without question. Inside the Soviet Union itself, the last years of Stalin's rule saw a revival of the Great Terror that had deformed Soviet society in the 1930s. Many Russians had believed, or at least hoped, that after the war the situation would ease, that the apparatus of control from prewar years would be lifted. But Stalin was deeply suspicious of opening up the Soviet Union. At the end of the war, a general amnesty was declared for prisoners, but not for "enemies of the people." Many who had been sent to the Gulag before the war on

In the end every gangster will get his just deserts, everyone will get his well-deserved punishment. The conspiring gang standing in the dock today is a nest of rats who were caught. They are hated and despised by all honest people of our country. Citizens, you who are in the position of people's judges, in the name of our nation, against whose freedom and happiness these conspirators were subverting, in the name of peace and against the dastardly conspiracy, I demand for all accused the death sentence.

— Josef Urvalek,
November 1952

trumped-up charges now found their sentences extended by five, eight, or ten years. Of those who were released, a huge number were banished to "eternal settlement" in remote areas like Kolyma, Siberia, or Kazakhstan. Very few were allowed to return to European Russia, and even fewer to the big cities.

Stalin was obsessed by the need for total obedience to the party, which in practice meant to his will. Despite the heroic wartime suffering of the Soviet people and the immense privations still endured, Stalin called for even greater vigilance and for supreme efforts to uncover "enemies within." In 1948 he told his minister of the interior, S. N. Kruglov, to construct new camps and prisons for various deviants and dissidents. The use of torture in interrogation was increased. The "confessions" extracted only confirmed suspicions that the conspiracy to destroy the state actually existed. The evil process fed on itself.

Absolute rule demanded absolute obedience, but it helped if people loved their leader rather than feared him. In the Soviet Union the cult of Stalin was omnipresent. ABOVE: *Stalin appears as the Father of His People during the Great Patriotic War.* ABOVE RIGHT: *World Communist leaders gathered in the Bolshoi Theatre, Moscow, to celebrate Stalin's seventieth birthday on 21 December 1949.*

In 1949 Stalin intensified a purge against a group of Leningrad administrators, party officials, and artists, who he thought had dared to question the party line. After torture or the threat of torture, many of them confessed and named others. Even though many of these individuals had suffered immensely through the war and the siege of Leningrad, even though many of them were hardworking and useful party officials, that did not save them. One thousand party bosses from Leningrad were shot on charges of treason against the party. In maintaining a climate of fear and suspicion within the Soviet Union in the late 1940s, Stalin and his chief of the secret police, Lavrenti Beria, deported an estimated 6 million citizens to camps and the Gulag. Beria became one of the most feared and hated of men.

Stalin's Last Days

Stalin was suspicious of everyone around him. The Supreme Soviet no longer met, and Stalin ruled as an absolute dictator with the help of a few aides. But none of his henchmen ever felt safe. They were always under suspicion; they were not permitted to meet separately; they were not even allowed to travel to the Kremlin in the same car lest they plot together. Svetlana Alliluyeva, Stalin's daughter, described how as he got older her father "had begun to feel lonely. He was so isolated from everybody at this time, so elevated, that he seemed to be living in a vacuum. He hadn't a soul he could talk to. . . . It was the system of which he himself was the prisoner and in which he was stifling from loneliness, emptiness, and lack of human companionship."

The last months of Stalin's life were dominated by his paranoia. America's firm reaction to the invasion of South Korea and the military mobilization of NATO threw him into an alarmist, almost apocalyptic mood. The Nineteenth Party Congress, in October 1952, showed Stalinism in its final phase. Stalin did not sit with the other delegates; he sat by himself at one end of the table, alone and feared by everyone in the room. In declining health, he was absent for much of the congress. When he came in, he was greeted with a standing ovation. When he finally spoke, he was cheered as he walked to the podium. His speech was short and limited to a few clichés of Marxist-Leninist rhetoric about the world struggle for socialism. Then there was more cheering. In the meeting of the Party Plenum that followed the congress, he denounced some of his closest and most loyal supporters. He hinted that Molotov was an American agent. He revealed that he was even suspicious of Beria. In December he dismissed his loyal private secretary of many years for "passing secret documents," and had his long-term bodyguard arrested. His wife's sisters were imprisoned because "they know too much."

More than anything, Stalin feared foreign influence, what was called "cosmopolitanism." He needed a scapegoat to blame for the country's ills. Many Jews had relatives abroad, and could easily be tainted by accusations of belonging to a cosmopolitan fifth column. Several leading Jews were persecuted after the wartime Jewish Anti-Fascist Committee was dissolved in 1948. In the summer of 1952, after trials at a military court in Moscow, ten prominent Soviet Jews were found guilty of "Jewish nationalism" and shot. A hundred more were sent to labour camps. Then, in January 1953, nine Kremlin

In January 1953 Stalin had nine Kremlin doctors arrested and charged with plotting to kill Soviet leaders; most were Jews. In February when he suffered a stroke, the doctors summoned were frightened to treat him. He died on 5 March.

Beria: Stalin's Evil Genius

Lavrenti Pavlovich Beria was born in Merkhueli in the western part of Georgia on 29 March 1899. Educated in Baku, he joined the Communist Party in 1917, after deserting the Russian Army. An early revolutionary, he joined the Transcaucasian section of the Cheka, the first Soviet secret police, and rose to become its head in 1921. In the following ten years, he directed the purge of "nationalist deviationists" from the region's Communist parties and supervised the brutal collectivization of agriculture. He was made first secretary of the Georgian Communist Party in 1931.

In 1938 Stalin appointed Beria head of the Soviet People's Commissariat for Internal Affairs (NKVD), the instrument of Stalin's state terror, repression, and expansion of the Gulag prison system. We now know that Beria recommended to Stalin the 1940 execution of some twenty-five thousand Polish prisoners, including the four thousand officers whose mass grave was discovered in 1943 at Katyn Forest, near Smolensk. In 1945 Stalin put Beria in charge of the crash programme for developing a Soviet atomic bomb, and through the despotism of his absolute authority he was

able to build the bomb within four years.

By 1946 Beria had become deputy chairman of the Council of Ministers and a member of the Politburo; he began to think of himself as Stalin's successor. The other members of the Politburo had different ideas and were alarmed that he might attempt to seize power following Stalin's death. They decided to pre-empt this. Beria was arrested, tried in secret, and shot some time before December 1953, when his death was announced.

Krokodil, quick to voice the party line, however perverted, strips off the doctor's mask to reveal the murderous brute beneath; the strong arm of the state has found him out. Many Russians believed this stuff.

doctors were arrested and accused of plotting to kill Soviet leaders. Most were Jews. Stalin's anti-Semitism now became official state policy. The arrest of the Jewish doctors, called "monsters in human form, trampling the holy banner of science," unleashed a popular frenzy. In carefully prepared front-page articles, *Pravda* and *Izvestiya* erupted in hysteria about the "doctor-saboteurs — foul spies and murderers," calling them foreign agents working for America and Britain. Twenty-eight more doctors and their wives were arrested in February. In the cells of the Lubyanka prison in Moscow, under interrogation and torture, many "confessed" to heinous crimes against the state. Preparations were put in hand for a huge public show trial, the first in the Soviet Union since the Great Terror in 1938. Plans were also made to exile thousands of Soviet Jews to Siberia, and for "spontaneous" pogroms against Jews across Russia.

On the night of 28 February 1953, Stalin had his customary nocturnal meeting with members of the Politburo. Tired and irritable, he hinted at a new purge of top officials. Stalin had got into the habit of working through the night, not getting up until late in the morning. On Sunday, 1 March 1953, he did not appear at his usual time. His staff, terrified, did not know what to do, for no one was allowed to enter his rooms without his permission. Finally, at 11:00 PM, having waited all day and urged on by Stalin's housekeeper, the duty officer nervously entered the private rooms. Turning on the light in the small dining room, he was stunned to see Stalin lying on the floor wearing only an undershirt and pyjama bottoms. He had wet himself. Stalin reached out but could not speak. A stroke had paralysed his power of speech, and nothing coherent came out. The duty officer called the Ministry of State Security, for no one could call a doctor without Beria's permission. But Beria was nowhere to be found. Finally, he was tracked down, out drinking with a mistress. When Beria arrived at the dacha with Deputy Premier Georgi M. Malenkov, who would do nothing without him, Stalin was lying on a sofa and appeared to be comfortable. Beria refused to call doctors, blamed the servants for causing a panic, and left. It was not until the next morning, eighteen to twenty-four hours after the stroke occurred, that Beria returned with physicians and nurses. The doctors who had looked after Stalin for many years were now in prison. Beria warned the new physicians bustling around Stalin, "You are responsible for Comrade Stalin's health." The doctors and nurses quaked, for they could do nothing. All the senior officials of the state gathered. Beria took control and approached the patient many times, saying, "Comrade Stalin, all the members of the Politburo are here. Say something to us." At 9:50 PM on 5 March 1953, Stalin finally died. The members of the Politburo issued a bulletin announcing his death and quickly left the dacha. Had Stalin made known to someone his intentions for the succession? They sped back to Moscow in their long black limousines.

Cold War
Films

The Cold War hit the movies in 1947 when the House Un-American Activities Committee descended on Hollywood armed with the names of leading film folk suspected of being Communists or left-wing sympathizers. Their supposed treachery included such pro-Soviet movies as Warner Brothers' *Mission to Moscow* (1943) and MGM's *Song of Russia* (1944), which the White House had persuaded the studio bosses to produce as part of the war effort. HUAC's hearings resulted in ten filmmakers going to jail for contempt of Congress and hundreds of actors, writers, and directors being put on an unofficial industry blacklist. The effect on Hollywood's morale was profound and enduring.

The last moderately pro-Russian film of the 1940s, *Berlin Express* (1948), centred on a Frenchman, an Englishman, an American, and a Soviet officer uniting to protect a democratic German politician from neo-Nazi conspirators, and concluded with an edgily amicable parting beside the Brandenburg Gate. That same year the first major anti-Communist picture, *The Iron Curtain*, told in semi-documentary style the story of Igor Gouzenko, a cypher clerk at the Russian Embassy in Ottawa, who defected to the West. Over the next decade a succession of films, some bordering on hysteria, exposed Communist subversion on the domestic front: *I Married a Communist* (1950), in which Robert Ryan plays a prewar radical blackmailed into working for the Reds; Leo McCarey's *My Son John* (1952), in which a typical American couple discover their oedipal son is a party member; *Pickup on South Street* (1953), starring Richard Widmark as a patriotic New York pickpocket who stumbles across a spy ring. There were also numerous pictures about Cold War confrontations abroad,

most typically MGM's *The Red Danube* (1950), about conflicts between the occupying powers in Vienna over refugee repatriation, and *Big Jim McLain* (1952), with John Wayne playing a two-fisted HUAC investigator pursuing Communists in Hawaii. The tone of *The Red Danube* is infinitely more strident than *The Third Man* (1949), a British film with the same setting.

Meanwhile, the Cold War entered Hollywood genre movies. The western enjoyed a considerable revival as liberals used the nineteenth-century frontier for allegories on issues they could not treat elsewhere. *Broken Arrow* (1950), scripted under a pseudonym by the blacklisted Albert Maltz, used the reconciliation between Apaches and white settlers to plead for peaceful co-existence. *Storm Center* (1956), starring Bette Davis as a small-town librarian standing up for her right to stock radical texts, was the only film of the decade to speak out directly, if somewhat guardedly, against McCarthyism.

The Cold War that so preoccupied Hollywood had relatively little direct effect on the cinemas of other countries. Ingmar Bergman made *It Can't Happen Here* (1950), a crude anti-Communist allegory, and in Britain the Boulting brothers produced *High Treason* (1951), a half-baked thriller in which local Communists set out to sabotage Battersea Power Station. These, however, were exceptions, and the Eastern European cinema pretty well ignored current politics.

Then, as virulently anti-Communist pictures did poorly at the box office, Hollywood began to take a more sophisticated view of the Cold War. In the early sixties, when blacklisting came to an end, the Cold War became the subject for comedy. Billy Wilder's *One, Two, Three* (1962) starred Jimmy

Nuclear holocaust in the movies. In On the Beach, *based on Nevil Shute's novel, Gregory Peck and Ava Gardner (*TOP, *in a French poster) await the end of the human race in Australia.* BOTTOM: *Peck and Fred Astaire peek out from the safety of a submarine.*

Cagney as a wisecracking Coca-Cola Company manager in Berlin. The Cold War also provided the ironic context for espionage movies that took a jaundiced view of both sides, films such as *The Ipcress File* (1965) and *The Spy Who Came In From the Cold* (1966), made by Americans but based on British novels. The James Bond movies, unlike Ian Fleming's novels, deliberately dispensed with SMERSH, the Russian terrorist organization, and made 007's enemies apolitical megalomaniacs. The key Cold War pictures of the 1960s, and among the best of the decade, are *The Manchurian Candidate* (1962) and *Dr. Strangelove* (1963), both mordant political satires. In the former, a crypto-Communist Washington hostess plots with Russian and Chinese agents to have her husband, a right-wing Red-baiting senator, elected US president. In the latter, a deranged cold warrior in command of an American air force base unleashes a pre-emptive nuclear strike against the Soviet Union and the US president is forced to contact his Soviet opposite number on the Moscow hot line and discuss ways of averting imminent Armageddon.

Dr. Strangelove ends with a succession of nuclear explosions edited to the strains of Vera Lynn singing "We'll Meet Again." Several other films took the prospect of nuclear war and its aftermath more solemnly. In the most famous of these, *On the Beach* (1959), based on Nevil Shute's bestselling novel, the end of the world is observed from Australia, where the last remnants of mankind prepare to succumb to radiation sickness.

Hollywood, fearful of offending either hawks or doves, largely ignored the Vietnam War. Only John Wayne's *The Green Berets* (1968), a patriotic paean to the American Special Forces,

appeared while the war was on. In the late 1970s a rash of pictures — *Coming Home, The Deer Hunter, Apocalypse Now* — dwelt on the absurdity of the war and the damage it wrought on the American psyche. By then it was possible for American movies to show Russians in a favourable light, and in the sentimental *The Way We Were* (1973) the heroine, Barbra Streisand, is a 1930s Stalinist still clinging to her old convictions in the 1960s. During the 1970s and 1980s, Hollywood movies took the view that only a few renegades threatened world peace and that men of goodwill on both sides could work together. Typically, in the thriller *Telefon* (1978), a KGB officer (Charles Bronson) comes to America neither to defect nor to subvert but to defeat the diabolical plans of Communist hard-liners. The only real blast of the Cold War during the time of glasnost and perestroika was *Red Dawn* (1984), which envisaged an invasion of the United States by a combined force of Russians and Cubans. The only true resistance comes from a guerrilla force of macho teenagers, who anticipate America's backwoods militia that has emerged in the past decade.

— *Philip French*

TOP: Apocalypse Now, *1979. The Vietnam War as hell on earth, portrayed by Francis Ford Coppola, on an epic scale. Helicopters starred as the new Valkyries.*

Paranoia survives détente.
CENTRE RIGHT: *Robert De Niro stars in Michael Cimino's account of Vietnam,* The Deer Hunter, *1978. Though some thought it demeaned the Vietnam experience, it won Oscars for best picture and best director.* RIGHT: *In* Telefon, *KGB officer Charles Bronson comes to America to knock out Communist hard-liners.*

Budapest, 1956

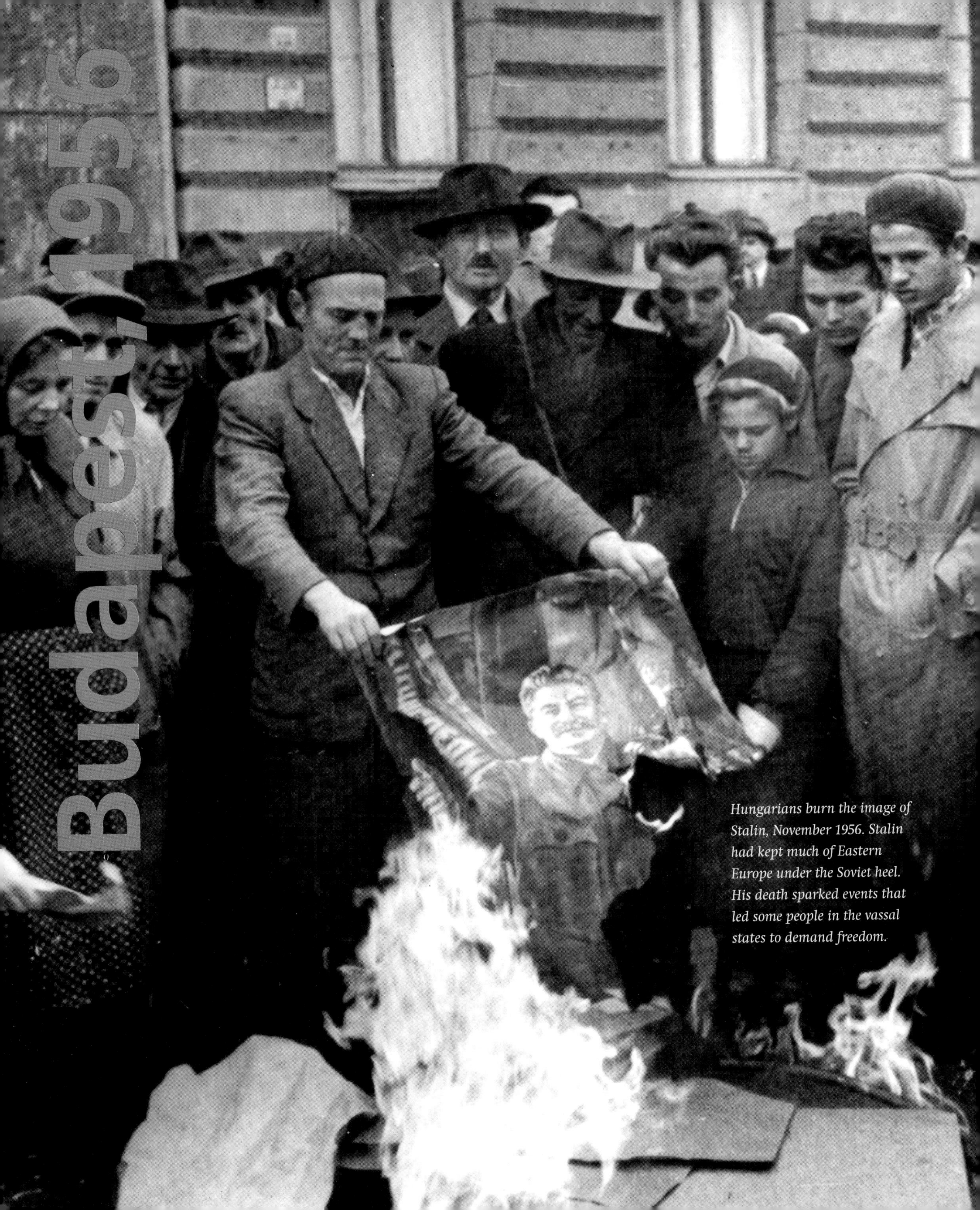

Hungarians burn the image of Stalin, November 1956. Stalin had kept much of Eastern Europe under the Soviet heel. His death sparked events that led some people in the vassal states to demand freedom.

After Stalin
1953–1956

Moscow, 9 March 1953.
Mourners weep as they watch
Stalin's funeral procession.
Many Soviet citizens genuinely
grieved at the death of the man
who had presided over their
homeland for a quarter of a
century, the man who had led
the Soviet Union to victory in
the Great Patriotic War
against the Nazis.

Uncertainty in Succession

For many millions of Soviet citizens, the death of Stalin in March 1953 was a shattering event. For decades Stalin had been the "father" of the nation, and many grieved as if they had lost a family member. Tens of thousands of ordinary Russians wept openly in spontaneous and genuine displays of public grief when crowds gathered in Moscow to pay their last respects; several mourners were killed in the crush to file past the bier. In spite of his brutal repression and his rigorous control of the economy, Stalin was still hugely popular throughout the Soviet Union. His death marked the end of an era; for most Soviet citizens it had been an era of greatness for their country.

Among the Communist leaders in Moscow, Stalin's death provoked a mixture of grief, relief, and anxiety for the future. With no clear successor evident, the Council of Ministers and the Presidium of the Supreme Soviet publicly declared a form of collective leadership. But this merely masked the beginnings of a bitter power struggle. Georgi Malenkov was appointed chairman of the Council of Ministers, in effect premier, with Lavrenti Beria as his deputy and chief of state security. Molotov returned as foreign minister and Nikolai Bulganin as minister of the armed forces. Nikita Khrushchev's role was not entirely clear initially, but his name was listed first among the five secretaries of the party secretariat. Malenkov was also appointed first secretary of the Communist Party, Stalin's old position, but nine days later he was forced to surrender this post (which in six months would fall to Khrushchev) when the new leadership decided that all the top offices should never again be held by one person. Still, to the West, it seemed that the progressive Malenkov, then just fifty-one years old, was emerging as Stalin's heir.

Dignitaries from throughout the Communist world assembled in Moscow to pay final respects to the man who had been their unchallenged leader, the generalissimo who had defeated fascism. Zhou Enlai, China's premier and foreign minister, was one of the pall bearers; the others were leading members of the Politburo. While Zhou was in Moscow, Malenkov and Molotov met with him to discuss the war in Korea, which they all wanted to end. Mao Zedong had already decided separately on this, so within a fortnight of Stalin's death, Pyongyang was ordered to resume the armistice talks in earnest.

Then, in one of his first speeches, Malenkov hinted at a new mood of coexistence with the West. "There is no disputed or unsolved question," he stated, "which could not be settled by peaceful means with any foreign country, including the United States." Less than a month after Stalin's death, the Presidium approved a general amnesty for anyone who had been sentenced to a term of less than five years' imprisonment. All those who had been arrested in Stalin's final days were released, as were tens of thousands of other political prisoners. The so-called Doctors' Plot, which had punctuated Stalin's final months, was now described as a "provocation and fake."

In the United States, Eisenhower was only weeks into his presidency when Stalin died, and he was furious to discover that there were no contingency plans for dealing with the Soviet leader's death. The new secretary of state, John Foster Dulles, stressing a "new era of liberty, not enslavement," proclaimed that "the Eisenhower era begins as the Stalin era ends. . . . For ten

Georgi Malenkov, Heir Apparent

Georgi Malenkov was the chubby figure often seen standing alongside Stalin in photographs. Born in Orenburg on the borders of Kazakhstan in 1902, he was the descendant of tsarist military officers. After the Russian Revolution, Malenkov became a political commissar on a Red Army propaganda train, and in the late 1920s he worked in the bureau of the party's central secretariat. By the late 1930s Malenkov had been promoted to the inner circle of administrators implementing the worst of Stalin's purges, the Great Terror, the elimination of dissenters or possible opponents of the regime. From 1939 to 1941 Malenkov, along with Beria, carried out the purging of newly conquered Baltic states and eastern

Poland. During the war Malenkov became one of the most important administrators in the Soviet Union, and afterwards he joined the Council of Ministers, which determined all aspects of state policy. No fiery revolutionary, he was a practical man, a manager, who presided over the core party administration at the heart of Stalin's empire. Along with Beria, Stalin assigned to Malenkov the task of building up the postwar military-industrial complex. Malenkov liked to think of himself as a technocrat, as encouraging the new science that would develop the Soviet Union's postwar greatness.

After Stalin's death Malenkov showed no desire to maintain the culture of repression and fear that were

characteristic of his master's rule. He was happy to move forward. In spite of his years of loyal service to Stalin, Malenkov was seen in the West as one of the best hopes for a new, less antagonistic leadership in the Kremlin. To his colleagues, however, he would not prove tough enough to retain the top post for long.

years the world has been dominated by the malignant power of Stalin. Now Stalin is dead. He cannot bequeath to anyone his prestige." The British prime minister, Winston Churchill, wrote to Eisenhower suggesting a meeting with Malenkov in case "both of us together or separately be called to account if no attempt were made to turn over a new leaf." But for the moment Eisenhower ruled out any direct meeting with the new Soviet leadership.

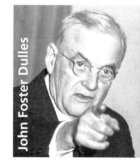

John Foster Dulles

In the meantime, Washington was sending out conflicting signals to Moscow. During the Truman administration, under the influence of George Kennan, the key word in US policy towards the Soviet Union had been "containment." Washington forged strategies to contain Soviet power — in the Middle East, in Berlin, in Europe, and in Korea. But Dulles had a new catchword: "roll-back." The United States should take the initiative in rolling back communism wherever possible. But it was never clear how this could be done without direct confrontation. On 16 April 1953, in a speech to the American Society of Newspaper Editors, Eisenhower called on the Kremlin to demonstrate that it had broken with Stalin's legacy by offering "concrete evidence" of a concern for peace. He appeared to be holding out an olive branch, hoping the Kremlin would grab it. This became known as Eisenhower's Chance for Peace speech, and it was widely reported within the Soviet Union. Only two days later, before the same group of editors, Dulles spoke in much harsher terms and declared, "We are not dancing to any Russian tune." The National Security Council backed Dulles. A secret report concluded that the Soviet interest in peace was illusory and that confrontation would be long drawn out.

In Eastern Europe the new spirit evident in the Kremlin caused concern among the various mini-Stalins who held power. In the Soviet zone of Germany, control was in the hands of Walter Ulbricht, a hard-line Stalinist of the old school who had spent most of the Nazi era in Moscow. One of Stalin's most loyal lieutenants, he had begun, in the summer of 1952, the "accelerated construction of socialism" in East Germany, aimed at building a strict command economy. A huge programme of farm collectivization was started, along with a rush towards Soviet-style industrialization, with great emphasis on heavy industry at the expense of consumer goods. Stalin intended to force the East German economy to complement that of the Soviet Union, to supply the USSR with iron and steel, of

Walter Ulbricht

which it was in desperate need. Ulbricht allowed no opposition inside East Germany. His secret police, the Stasi, were everywhere, urging friend to inform on friend, worker on worker.

Ulbricht was uneasy with changes taking place in post-Stalin Moscow. In May the collective leadership in the Kremlin summoned him to Moscow. For some time, the Kremlin had been considering a review of its German policy, supporting the idea of a re-unified but neutral Germany. The Soviets had no hope of controlling all of Germany, but a neutral Germany would at least prevent the western half, with its vast industrial base, from becoming

We are not dancing to any Russian tune.

— John Foster Dulles,
18 April 1953

Georgi Malenkov, seen here in 1956, was defeated in his power struggle with Khrushchev and put in charge of a power station in Kazakhstan.

a permanent part of the Western bloc. The Kremlin encouraged Ulbricht to follow a new course of liberalization, and to ease the pace of enforced industrialization.

Workers Demonstrate

But Ulbricht ignored the advice, and in June imposed new work quotas on industrial workers, demanding higher productivity without any increase in pay. Anger and dashed expectation combined to cause East German workers to erupt in protest. On 16 June a huge demonstration of workers in East Berlin called for a lifting of the new quotas. Like the force unleashed by opening a dam, workers' demands gushed forth. As the employer was the state, industrial protest over work norms soon became a political demand for free elections, and a call for a general strike. The American radio station in West Berlin, RIAS, publicized the demands and reported there would be major demonstrations the following day. On 17 June protests took place in East Berlin, Leipzig, Dresden, Magdeburg, and all the major towns of East Germany.

Over the next four days more than 400,000 German workers took to the streets. Ulbricht and his unpopular government were terrified by this vast display of worker power. But the demonstrations were spontaneous; they lacked any central direction or coherent organization. Lavrenti Beria called on the Soviet tank units stationed all over East Germany to confront the strikers, to prevent the Ulbricht regime from collapsing. He told the Soviet high commissioner not to "spare bullets" in suppressing the rising, and forty workers were killed, more than four hundred wounded. When thousands of strike leaders were arrested, the demonstrations ended as suddenly as they had begun. Ulbricht had learned a lesson and in time acceded to many of the workers' economic demands.

There were anti-government riots in Czechoslovakia as well, and strikes in Hungary and Romania. There was even a prisoners' strike in Siberia. The Soviets saw behind these events a well-orchestrated campaign to undermine the Soviet Union and its allies, part of Dulles's "rollback" of communism in Eastern Europe. The power struggle in the Kremlin now reached new intensity. Molotov, the old revolutionary, continued to see the Cold War as a clash between two opposing systems. He believed wholeheartedly in the Marxist-Leninist line that capitalism would ultimately destroy itself, and his diplomacy exploited what differences he could discern between the United States and its West European allies. However, for Malenkov and Beria, both of whom owed their power base entirely to Stalin, the Cold War was seen in strictly practical terms.

First of all, the Cold War was an arms race. Stalin had quickly realized how important it was to break the US atomic monopoly and in 1945 had put Beria in charge of the Soviet atom bomb project. In the summer of 1949, several years ahead of the West's predictions, the first Soviet bomb had been successfully tested. After Stalin's death Beria took more direct control of the Soviet nuclear project. Without consulting his colleagues, he ordered scientists in the closed city of Arzamas-16 to race ahead with developing a hydro-

Workers come out onto the streets in East Germany to demand better working conditions. Economic protest soon turned into political demands for sweeping reform.

gen bomb to rival America's thermonuclear weapons. If Soviet strength rested on ever more powerful nuclear weapons and he was in charge of developing them, Beria calculated, then he would control the mainsprings of Soviet power.

But this sort of arrogance was no longer acceptable inside the Kremlin. Within days of the quelling of the rising in East Germany, Khrushchev became convinced that Beria was preparing to make a grab for absolute power. Malenkov concurred, and he denounced Beria at a meeting of the Presidium. Forever tainted from heading Stalin's terror apparatus, Beria was arrested on trumped-up charges of being a Western agent. In what to many seemed a just reversal of fate, the man who had sent hundreds of thousands to their deaths was not even allowed to attend his own trial. He was found guilty and shot. Beria's removal marked a huge shift in the power balance within the Kremlin, but he was the only Soviet leader at this juncture whose fate was settled by a bullet. Times had changed.

Khrushchev Takes Charge

Beria was out of the way, but doubts about the firmness of Malenkov's leadership sent him into political decline. Khrushchev had already replaced him as first secretary of the Central Committee of the Communist Party. During the next two years Khrushchev out-manoeuvred his remaining rivals to emerge as the Kremlin's leading light. One of his first priorities was to repair Sino-Soviet relations, which, sorely tried during the Korean War, had been aggravated by mutual suspicions between Mao and Stalin. In September 1954 he visited Beijing and agreed to new trade terms that were immensely favourable to the Chinese. His new trade treaty reinforced the alliance to build socialism in Asia. In Europe, Khrushchev negotiated a farsighted agreement with Austria. Soviet troops, occupying part of the country since the end of the war, were withdrawn in return for an Austrian commitment to neutrality. In May 1955 a state treaty was signed in Vienna by the four occupying powers, and Austria remained neutral throughout the Cold War. This was a breakthrough for Khrushchev, who later said he had grown up during these negotiations, trading his "boy's pants for adult trousers." In May, Khrushchev made a dramatic visit to Yugoslavia to try to "bury the hatchet" with Tito.

Khrushchev's growing international standing was matched by popularity at home; he encouraged the development of consumer industries and called for increases to pensions and other state disbursements. Thousands more prisoners were released from labour camps. New amnesties were issued. The rigid conformity demanded of the arts was relaxed. The Kremlin was even opened to visitors, and for children's parties. All this became known as "socialism with a human face."

Seismic change also took place in the West. West Germany's chancellor, Konrad Adenauer, sought to build up his country's relationship with the NATO countries. The United States, burdened with a major military commitment in Korea, came around to supporting the idea of German rearmament, partly to lighten its load in the defence of Europe. But in Europe the notion of German rearmament was still unpopular, especially with the French, who

"Sickle"

Molotov with the sickle and Malenkov with the hammer finish off Beria, the only Soviet leader actually done away with in the jockeying for power that followed Stalin's death. (From *Herblock's Here and Now,* Simon & Schuster, 1955)

Khrushchev's dramatic visit to Tito in Yugoslavia in May 1955 represented a complete turnaround from the years that Moscow had denounced the Yugoslav leader.

United States

West Germany takes its place
again among nations. US secretary of state John Foster Dulles
directs West German chancellor
Konrad Adenauer to his
position while British foreign
secretary Sir Anthony Eden
looks on. French premier Pierre
Mendès-France is at the left.
The ministers were attending a
Four Power meeting in Paris,
October 1954.

Nikita Sergeyevich Khrushchev

Ernst Niezvestny, who created Khrushchev's memorial headstone, placed the portrait bust in a pedestal of interlocking black and white stone, symbolizing, among other things, the two sides of Khrushchev's character. At times, he was as brutal and as aggressive as Stalin, his mentor; at other times, he was a peacemaker, overawed by the destructive capacity he controlled.

Khrushchev was born in 1894, in Kalinovka, a village near the Ukrainian border, into a family of poor illiterates. The crude peasant bluntness from his hard childhood never left him. Opponents would often underestimate his cunning, seeing in him only a clowning, overweight rustic. Eccentric bluster in meetings would often obscure the shrewdness in his thought. After Stalin's death, Malenkov, Beria, and Molotov failed to perceive him as a serious rival.

Already excited by Marxism at the time of the revolution in 1917, Khrushchev served in the Red Army during the civil war as a political commissar. In 1929 he was sent by his local party to the Stalin Industrial Academy in Moscow. He studied there alongside Stalin's wife, Nadezhda Alliluyeva, through whom he got to know Stalin. At this point his career took off. During the Great Terror of the 1930s, he rose to be second in command of the Moscow party organization, and he oversaw construction of much of Moscow's underground system. In 1939 he became a full member of the Politburo. During the war against Hitler, he was a political commissar and visited the front lines several times, seeing more of the devastation of the war than most, an experience that affected him profoundly.

Although Khrushchev later censured the evils of the Stalin era, his own hands were by no means free of blood. During the late 1930s he denounced several fellow students and workers as "enemies of the people," and he willingly took part in the extermination of the Ukrainian intelligentsia. For twenty years his political vision was dominated by that of Stalin. In old age he commented, "I was infected by Stalin, but liberated myself."

Khrushchev was an instinctive, spontaneous, and often unpredictable politician, a combination that, when the stakes were high, could be immensely dangerous. But often his instinct paid off. He had no education above the elementary level of Sunday School and workers' lectures, but he had a quick mind. He was always proud of his roots in the peasant society of Russia.

Khrushchev's leadership of the Soviet Union marked a crucial transition in communism. His own political roots went back to the radical bolshevism of the revolution, and most of his career was spent under the eyes of Stalin; but as a reformer and an advocate of the "human face of socialism," he ushered in an era in which a generation would be free to reassess the entire Communist world.

TOP TO BOTTOM: *Nikita Khrushchev with Marshal Bulganin, laying a wreath to British war dead, in London, 1956; with Malenkov, gesturing with a potato during a visit to a farm; talking to workers at a tractor factory in Stalingrad.*

delayed acceptance of a new German army for several years. Eventually, Adenauer came up with guarantees that persuaded the French they could no longer block German rearmament; the manufacture of nuclear weapons would be banned in Germany. In May 1955 the Western Allies formally ended their occupation of West Germany, and the Federal Republic was admitted to NATO. The response in Moscow to this setback was to create the Warsaw Pact, a formal military alliance among the states of Eastern Europe, who agreed to come to each other's defence if any one of them was attacked. In effect the Warsaw Pact was little more than a codification of existing Soviet military control over its satellites, but now the division of Europe into two rival camps was complete.

BELOW LEFT: The Warsaw Pact is formally created at a ceremony in Prague, 14 May 1955. Vyacheslav Molotov, Soviet foreign minister, signs as East European leaders look on.

In this climate the first postwar East-West summit was held in Geneva in July 1955 — ten years after the meeting in Potsdam that marked the end of the war in Europe. Britain and France attended, along with the Soviet Union and the United States. Before leaving for the summit, Khrushchev obtained a vote of support from the Party Plenum for his innovative foreign policy. At Geneva it was clear to the West that Khrushchev was now in charge of the Soviet delegation. At last London and Washington knew with whom they should deal in Moscow. But despite a friendly atmosphere, nothing of real substance came out of Geneva. Eisenhower proposed that both sides should be free to overfly each other's territory, the policy of Open Skies. Khrushchev rejected this as "a bold espionage plot." Other proposals also got nowhere. All the same, *Pravda* was able to write about "the spirit of Geneva," implying a new thaw in superpower relations and an endorsement of Khrushchev's foreign policy.

Bulganin and Khrushchev, in India, wear turbans presented to them by the chief minister of Rajasthan. Khrushchev's visit to India in 1955 and his personal diplomacy throughout the developing world proved immensely popular.

Khrushchev was also winning friends and building support for communism in the Third World, where, in the mid-1950s, much of Southeast Asia and Africa was still dominated by the old European imperial powers. By reaching out to the newly independent states, Khrushchev made communism a beacon to those looking to liberate themselves from colonial rule. In India, Khrushchev and his close supporter Nikolai Bulganin were given a rapturous welcome during their visit in 1955. At one point the two men had to be rescued from a crowd that had grown too enthusiastic. Other visits, to Burma and Indonesia, proved equally successful. Khrushchev realized then that there were huge parts of the world, outside the zones of US-Soviet confrontation, that were eager to hear the socialist message. And the charismatic Khrushchev presented a new image — of an open, friendly, young Soviet Union — quite different from that of Stalin's day. Khrushchev himself gained prestige and self-confidence from the success of his personal diplomacy.

The process of reform, and the rejection of Stalinism, culminated at the Twentieth Congress of the Soviet Communist Party in February 1956. Delegates from throughout the Communist world, and from nations locked in "liberation" struggles with their colonial masters, were invited to Moscow for the first major Communist gathering since Stalin's death. Party congresses were always formal affairs, a forum for leaders to make set-piece statements, but in a radical public speech Khrushchev abandoned the conventional Marxist-Leninist view that war between communism and capitalism was inevitable. He claimed that because the world camp of communism had grown to be so powerful, war was no longer likely or necessary. Socialism would still be victorious, but this could come through the ballot box and would happen due to the superiority of Communist means of production.

Stalin Denounced

All this was extraordinary enough. But at midnight on the last day of the congress, Khrushchev called all the Soviet delegates together in closed session. No cameras or reporters were present. Then, for six hours, Khrushchev proceeded to denounce Stalin's reign of terror and its crimes. He revealed that the case against the so-called Trotskyite conspirators of the 1930s had been trumped up by the secret police under Stalin's orders, with the help of forced confessions made under torture. He announced that Stalin was "a flawed leader" who had acted like a pathological criminal. Such accusations, coming less than three years after Stalin's death, caused a sensation. Many old party members felt he had gone too far. Several cried, "Shame!" as he spoke. Some remembered Khrushchev's own role in the murderous repression in the Ukraine. Others heaved an immense sigh of relief that finally the clouds of fear and paranoia were to be lifted, that the truth of Stalin's horrors was coming out. Khrushchev's denunciation of Stalin marked a turning point in Soviet history. Although delivered amidst late-night theatrics, the speech was never intended to remain secret; copies were immediately made available to party officials and to foreign Communist parties. News of the speech spread by word of mouth to millions of citizens within the Soviet bloc.

The CIA obtained the speech through Mossad, Israeli intelligence. In Washington it also had huge impact, convincing the Eisenhower administration that genuine change was taking place in the Soviet Union. After being thoroughly dissected by the CIA, it was passed to the press and appeared in newspapers throughout the West in June 1956.

The shock waves of Khrushchev's speech rippled out across the entire Communist world. The Chinese Communists, who had built up their own rigidly authoritarian system under Mao Zedong, were deeply offended. Beijing began to reject Moscow's leadership of the Communist world and to

After the war . . . Stalin became even more capricious, irritable, and brutal; in particular, his suspicion grew. His persecution mania reached unbelievable dimensions. Many workers were becoming enemies before his very eyes. . . . He decided everything alone, without any consideration for anyone or anything.

— Nikita Khrushchev,
February 1956

Khrushchev addresses the Twentieth Party Congress, Moscow, February 1956. Khrushchev's historic speech denouncing the crimes of Stalin was delivered later, in a closed session after midnight. But its text was soon being quoted throughout the Soviet Union and in the West.

develop its own, independent line. In Eastern Europe many Communist party leaders, gravely upset by the impact, were concerned for the continued stability of their authoritarian regimes. But for the people of Eastern Europe, the speech was an incitement to action; at last there seemed to be an opportunity for change.

Two months after the Party Congress, the Kremlin dissolved Cominform, which Stalin had created in 1947 to impose his orthodoxy over the satellites. The hard-line conservative Molotov was dismissed as foreign minister, and later banished to Mongolia as Soviet ambassador. A loyal supporter of Stalin throughout his career, Molotov had been firmly opposed to any reconciliation with Tito of Yugoslavia, but now the door was open again. Tito visited Moscow in June for a three-week state visit, amidst much pomp. Nothing could have been more symbolic of the new attitude towards Eastern Europe. But how far would the Soviet Union go in relaxing its influence there? In both Poland and Hungary, now released from the yoke of Stalinist rule, people wanted more control over their own destinies.

On 28 June 1956, in Poznan, one of Poland's main industrial cities, workers went on strike against government-imposed wage cuts and harsh working conditions. Just as in East Germany three years earlier, strikes over specific economic grievances soon snowballed into protests against the government. On what became known as Black Thursday, the Polish government sent two divisions and three hundred tanks of the Polish army to put down the protests — bloodily. Seventy-four strikers were killed, and about three hundred wounded. For the present, order was restored.

In Moscow it was clear that the situation in Poland was unstable. Bulganin, premier since early 1955, and Marshal Zhukov, both strong Khrushchev supporters from the Central Committee, were sent to Warsaw to sort things out. There they proclaimed that the strikes had been provoked by "imperialist agitators" from the West. The Polish party reformers wanted to restore to office a popular Communist, Wladyslaw Gomulka, who had been general secretary of the party after the end of the war. At first the Soviets resisted, but slowly a compromise was reached by which Gomulka would be readmitted to power but orthodox hard-liners would be left in charge. The Soviets were torn between taking a hard line, as Stalin would have done, and allowing their satellites a degree of independence.

Gomulka, one of those East European Communists who sincerely believed in different national versions of socialism after 1945, had spoken up in favour of Tito's independent policies in 1948. When Stalin imposed his hard line on East Europe, Gomulka was expelled from the party, and in 1951, he was imprisoned. Released two months before the strikes erupted in Poznan, Gomulka was now something of a national hero. Predictably, the compromise arrangements for his return to power did not work, and discontent spread. Hopes for change had been raised, and now had to be met or directly confronted.

The Polish leaders were invited to Moscow but refused to go. Khrushchev now decided to intervene personally. Uninvited, he flew to Warsaw on 19 October. Because no warning had been given of his arrival, his aircraft was bounced by Polish fighters as it approached Warsaw. On landing, he descended from the plane, shook his fist at the hastily assembled welcome party, and spoke loudly of the "treacherous" activity of the Polish leaders. On that same day, Russian troops across Poland left their garrisons and moved in columns towards the country's main cities. In Warsaw, Soviet units took up secret positions across from the Belvedere Palace, where the Communist leaders were about to meet. These were clear threats that the Soviets were prepared for military intervention in Poland, and in the rest of Eastern Europe.

Khrushchev and the Soviet delegation met Gomulka and the other Polish leaders in a tense, tempestuous showdown. Khrushchev threatened to use force to maintain Soviet control, but Gomulka countered that the Polish army would resist and that the people would rise up against the Soviet Union.

Gomulka repeatedly stressed that Poland "will not permit its independence to be taken away." Furthermore, Gomulka made it absolutely clear that events in Poland were a direct consequence of Khrushchev's speech at the Twentieth Party Congress. During the heated exchanges, Gomulka was informed that Soviet tank and infantry units were advancing on Warsaw. He demanded that these forces be pulled back. After some hesitation, Khrushchev ordered that all troop movements be halted.

Khrushchev had miscalculated badly. Across Poland, people came out onto the streets to demonstrate against the Soviet presence. When he realized the strength of feeling in the Polish Communist Party and among the Polish people, Khrushchev, in a bad temper, conceded that Gomulka could be appointed first secretary of the party. Gomulka agreed to preserve the party organization, and promised that Poland would remain a loyal member of the Warsaw Pact. This was the main issue as far as the Soviets were concerned. Under Khrushchev the Kremlin would allow its satellites a degree of national independence, but only if the new regime was led by a trustworthy leader, loyal to Moscow. After the showdown in Warsaw, the situation calmed down. Out of the confrontation the Poles got a more popular leader who made some welcome economic concessions. And Gomulka, for fourteen years, fulfilled his promise to be a faithful ally of the Soviet Union.

Hungary Issues a Challenge

Events elsewhere, however, were moving fast. On 24 October, as Gomulka was telling a mass meeting in Warsaw that the Soviet troops were returning to barracks, students in Budapest had already begun the most serious challenge yet to Soviet rule in Eastern Europe by demonstrating in sympathy with the Poles. The Budapest students were met with bullets from the secret police. At this point several workers groups joined the students, and the giant statue of Stalin in the centre of Budapest was pulled down.

The Hungarian prime minister, Erno Gero, called on Yuri Andropov, the Soviet ambassador in Budapest, to help restore order. Andropov passed the request on to Moscow, and Khrushchev spoke with Gero by telephone. The following day, at dawn, thirty thousand Soviet troops entered Budapest and

Wladyslaw Gomulka

[Poland] will not permit its independence to be taken away.

— Wladyslaw Gomulka,
October 1956

Black Thursday, Poznan, 28 June 1956. Polish strikers carry a banner whose text reads, "We Are Hungry." Troops and tanks of the Polish army opened fire on the demonstrators; dozens were killed and hundreds wounded.

sealed off Hungary's capital city. Fierce fighting erupted. Martial law was declared, but the situation remained unstable. What was especially disturbing for governments in both Budapest and Moscow was that some of the Soviet troops fraternized with the workers. And many Hungarian army units seemed shaky in their support for the regime. As in Poland, the search was now on in Hungary for a new leader of the Communist Party, to restore confidence in the nation's leadership. The man who looked most likely to play the part of a Hungarian Gomulka was Imre Nagy, who had been prime minister until purged in 1955. Nagy was hurriedly brought back into government on the day that Russian tanks rolled into Budapest. Nagy called for an immediate end to the fighting, offering an amnesty for all participants in the uprising, and political and economic reform. On the following day, János Kádár, who had been purged from Hungary's government in the early 1950s, was also brought back and was appointed party first secretary. Nagy assured Moscow of Hungary's loyalty. But the Kremlin was split between those who wanted to accommodate the new government and those advocating a further show of strength. Khrushchev finally ordered the withdrawal of Soviet troops from Budapest on 28 October; but at the same time he deployed more divisions along the border with Hungary.

Imre Nagy

Throughout Hungary there was a mood of anger and expectation. Industrial workers seized public buildings and formed revolutionary councils. Open elections were held in villages and towns. In several government departments, new councils were formed to challenge the state. And several thousand members of the Hungarian army defected to the workers' cause, taking their weapons with them. Meanwhile Radio Free Europe, the CIA-backed station that broadcast into Eastern Europe, was dramatically talking the situation up, proclaiming the West's backing for what it called Hungary's "freedom fighters."

Carried along by the momentum of events he could barely control, Nagy announced on 30 October that he was abolishing the one-party system and would form a new coalition government. He agreed to recognize many of the revolutionary councils that had been created. Immediately, several suppressed Hungarian political parties began to reconstitute themselves, among them the Social Democrats and the National Peasant Party. On that same day the army established a revolutionary council, composed of representatives from the military and police. Its leader was also appointed to the new government.

For a while it looked as though the Soviets would give in to this massive display of people power opposing the apparatus of the state. A declaration was issued outlining the relationship between the Soviet Union and the socialist states. In it the Kremlin acknowledged that Hungarian workers were "justified" in raising issues and in pointing out the "serious mistakes" of the previous regime. The news agency TASS announced that the Soviet Union "deeply regrets" the bloodshed in Hungary, and agreed with the removal of Soviet soldiers from Hungarian soil.

At this moment, as the crisis in Hungary was still unfolding, the Israelis, in league with the British and French, launched an invasion of Egypt across the Sinai Desert. Within days British and French troops began their own well-prepared seizure of the Suez Canal, which had been nationalized by General Gamal Abdel Nasser, the Egyptian president, earlier in the year. The Suez crisis proved a disastrous venture for Britain and France, and for their prestige in the Middle East. The military intervention was universally denounced as the dying act of imperialist powers. The US government was furious; it had not been consulted on the military operation and was opposed to it. With the

British paratroopers in the Suez Canal Zone, October 1956. The Anglo-French-Israeli invasion of Suez divided the West at a critical moment of the Budapest uprising. The Soviets were happy at the distraction.

presidential elections only a week away, Washington was now presented with two international crises simultaneously.

The Suez affair distracted attention from events in Hungary as they entered their most critical phase. It split the Western camp and offered Moscow, with all eyes temporarily on Suez, a perfect cover for moving into Budapest. But at first it had the opposite effect, delaying Moscow's intervention in Hungary, for Khrushchev did not want to be compared to the "imperialist aggressors" in Egypt. After all, he had withdrawn Soviet troops in Poland when confronted by Gomulka; perhaps now he could rely on Prime Minister Nagy to bring Hungary into line.

Budapest Goes Too Far

But on 1 November, Nagy, still feeling that the initiative was with him, protested Soviet troop movements, declared Hungary's neutrality, repudiated the Warsaw Pact, and cabled Dag Hammarskjöld, the secretary-general of the United Nations, to ask that the question of Hungarian neutrality be put on the agenda of the UN General Assembly. This went much further than the Poles had dared in their revolt; it effectively faced the Kremlin with an ultimatum to get out. Deng Xiaoping was visiting Moscow at the time as an official delegate of the Chinese Communist Party. He told Khrushchev that the Hungarian rebels were not only anti-Soviet but anti-Communist, and should not be tolerated. In the face of this open revolt, the Soviet leaders decided they had to act. On 3 November fifteen Soviet army divisions, along with more than four thousand tanks, deployed within Hungary and encircled the capital. At dawn the following morning, the Russian tanks entered Budapest. The shooting began immediately.

Nagy broadcast on Radio Budapest early that morning and told the

Hungarian people: "Today at daybreak, Soviet troops attacked our capital with the obvious intent of overthrowing the lawful democratic Hungarian government." He vowed not to surrender. Two hours later Radio Budapest broadcast an SOS signal and went off the air. Many Hungarians, buoyed up by the promises of Radio Free Europe, still felt certain that the West would come to their aid. But no support was forthcoming — except that the White House issued a strong protest to the Kremlin. Eisenhower and his advisers were deeply concerned but, distracted by the Anglo-French-Israeli aggression against Egypt and the approaching climax of an election, did nothing except loudly condemn the Soviet action in the final speeches of the campaign. The *New York Times* accused the Soviet Union of "the foulest treachery and basest deceit known to man"; it claimed the invasion of Budapest was a "monstrous crime against the Hungarian people" that "can never be forgiven or forgotten."

Despite Soviet claims that the West was behind the rising, events clearly had caught the Western powers by surprise. For them the stakes at risk in intervention were too high. The National Security Council concluded that there could be no American military or political intervention in the affairs of Soviet satellites, no ventures behind the Iron Curtain. As with Poland, Eisenhower and Dulles realized they could not chance a world war over the

Today at daybreak, Soviet troops attacked our capital with the obvious intent of overthrowing the lawful democratic Hungarian government.

— Imre Nagy,
3 November 1956

Freedom fighters battled it out
with Soviet tanks for two weeks
in Budapest. This image, taken
towards the end of the battle,
shows ruined streets and the
remains of a tank, just before
the rising was finally crushed.

fate of an East European nation. The United States, in practice, could not embark on rollback. It would settle for containment. The Hungarian people were abandoned in their hour of need.

Determined this time to avoid any risk of fraternization with the rebels, the Soviets sent in tanks rather than infantry against the Hungarians. For two weeks bitter and intense street fighting scarred Budapest. The Molotov cocktail was the street fighters' only effective weapon against tanks. Nearly 700 Soviet soldiers and officers were killed and 1,500 wounded. Between 3,000 and 4,000 Hungarians were killed. The uprising was put down, and about 200,000 Hungarians fled across the borders, mostly into Austria.

The Kremlin had clearly picked the wrong man in Imre Nagy. Soviet ambassador Andropov switched his support to János Kádár as the leader who would restore authority and guarantee loyalty. On the day that Nagy went into hiding, Kádár reappeared inside Soviet-occupied territory and announced the formation of a new party, the Socialist Workers Party, and a new government. Kádár welcomed the Soviet troops; the new government could use their support in fighting the "counter-revolutionary threat." Kádár promised economic and social reforms, as well as new agreements with the other Eastern bloc nations.

The rising was crushed. But it took several months for Kádár to re-impose the hard-line centralized control the Soviets wanted. The first few arrests were made in late November. Nagy was lured out of his hiding place in the Yugoslav Embassy with a promise of safe passage. But he was betrayed, captured, and imprisoned, to be later executed. As Kádár won the upper hand, 35,000 activists were arrested, and three hundred leaders of the uprising were executed. Hungary was saved for one-party Communist rule, but the price was the spirit of the Hungarian people. For more than thirty years, Hungarians would live under a regime that had betrayed them, in a system they did not want.

From Moscow's perspective, the events of October and November 1956 had represented a major crisis; the Kremlin was seriously fearful that Poland and Hungary would both defect from the Soviet alliance. Although Khrushchev had denounced Stalin as an evil tyrant, when it came to it, he too had not hesitated to use force to ensure control of Russia's East European fiefdoms. The events of 1956 showed just how far Moscow would go in allowing liberalization. Stalin was dead, but the opportunity for national emancipation under Soviet rule was very limited. Eastern Europe was firmly back under Soviet control.

In 1957 Khrushchev consolidated his position as undisputed leader of the Soviet Union, but not before he had been nearly toppled by a palace coup in the Presidium while he was out of the country, visiting Finland. The old guard decided that the pace of reform had been too rapid, and moved to overthrow his rule. But when he returned, Khrushchev insisted that he could not be removed by the Presidium since he had been appointed by the larger Central Committee, which gave Khrushchev an overwhelming vote of support. Unlike in previous eras, those who had plotted against the leader were not rounded up and shot, nor were they sent to starve to death in a labour camp during a

Soviet soldiers object to being photographed in the streets of Budapest. The Hungarians welcomed Western photographers and journalists.

Siberian winter. Malenkov, who had led the revolt, was expelled from the party and appointed manager of an electric power plant in Kazakhstan. Lazar Kaganovich, who begged not to be dealt with as "they dealt with people under Stalin," was made director of a cement factory. There was now no opposition left to trouble Khrushchev.

There is a postscript to the process of dismantling Stalinism. At the Twenty-second Party Congress, held in Moscow in 1961, Khrushchev proposed that Stalin's body be removed from the mausoleum where it had been displayed alongside Lenin's. It was agreed that the corpse should be reinterred by the walls of the Kremlin, a far less illustrious resting place. In this final gesture, Khrushchev rid the nation of one more reminder of the tyrant who had dominated Soviet life for more than two decades.

Fleeing Hungarian refugees help one another across the "Bridge of Freedom" into Austria after the failure of the uprising. Two days earlier, a Soviet tank had fired on the bridge. Two hundred thousand Hungarians fled abroad.

Semipalatinsk, 1949

The Soviets detonate their first atom bomb. The date was 29 August 1949, astounding Western experts, who had not expected them to catch up with atomic technology for some years to come.

Sputnik and the Bomb

1949–1961

New York newspaper headlines trumpet the news following President Truman's announcement that the USSR had detonated an atom bomb.

First Lightning

On the desolate steppe of northeast Kazakhstan it was drizzling at dawn on 29 August 1949, as it had been throughout the night. At the remote laboratory settlement of Semipalatinsk-21, on the Irtysh River, a team of Soviet scientists led by Igor Kurchatov had worked through the night. Lavrenti Beria, chief of the secret police, had just joined them from Moscow. The drizzle finally stopped and, despite the overcast, the dawn light cleared visibility. Beria, Kurchatov, the other scientists, and a smattering of senior generals then assembled in the command bunker, where they were to witness the explosion of the USSR's first atom bomb. Four years earlier, the trial explosion of the US atom bomb in the New Mexico desert had been named Trinity. The Soviets code-named their trial First Lightning. Ten minutes before the countdown would reach zero, Beria, who had been put in charge of the atom bomb project in 1945, looked across at Kurchatov, the director of Soviet nuclear research, and muttered, "Nothing will come of it, Igor." But he was wrong.

At exactly 7:00 AM a white fireball engulfed the hundred-foot tower built to support the bomb. As the fireball rushed upward, turning orange then red, it sucked up debris and soil that formed an enormous mushroom cloud. In the command bunker there was elation. Beria hugged and kissed Kurchatov. "It would have been a great misfortune if it hadn't worked," he joked. Everyone knew what was meant; they might all have been shot. After a few minutes of celebration, Beria enthusiastically telephoned Moscow, even though it was two hours earlier there. He insisted on being put through to Stalin, who was still in bed. When he came on the line, Stalin asked angrily what Beria wanted. "Everything went right," said Beria. "I know already," replied Stalin, and hung up. Beria went wild. Stalin had his own source of information. Beria raged at the general in charge, screaming, "Who has told him? Even here you spy on me! I'll grind you to dust!"

Five days later a US Air Force B-29, flying a routine weather mission over the North Pacific, picked up a radioactivity count 300 per cent higher than normal. Over the next week more radiation was detected as a radioactive cloud floated east across the Pacific to the United States and Canada, then across the North Atlantic to Scotland and Norway, where it finally dissipated. At first, American scientists thought this might be evidence of a nuclear reactor explosion in the Soviet Union. But as they sifted data they found unmistakable signs of the successful detonation of a bomb with a plutonium core and a natural uranium tamper — just like the one America had dropped on Nagasaki. Initially the reaction was sceptical, for only two months earlier, in July 1949, the CIA had concluded that the "most probable date" for completion of the Soviet atom bomb would be mid-1953. President Truman remained calm when first told, and when it was certain, on 23 September, he made a public acknowledgement of the Soviet detonation. The general reaction in the United States was one of dismay and dread rather than hysteria. But everyone realized that the Soviets had caught up. How had this happened so quickly?

When the United States dropped the two atom bombs on Japan in August 1945, Stalin realized that the Soviet Union must rapidly catch up with US atomic technology. By the end of August 1945, he had created a special unit to develop the means to make an atom bomb. He put it under the control of Lavrenti Beria. In January 1946 Stalin met atomic project director Igor Kurchatov and told him he was to operate "broadly — with Russian scope." Stalin made it clear that the atom bomb project was of urgent concern and

Igor Kurchatov: Prince of Science

Igor Kurchatov was known affectionately to his colleagues as the Beard or sometimes as Prince Igor. Stalin was lucky to have in Kurchatov a scientist of immense ability who could get along with all the leading physicists working for him, and who was able to select and organize capable scientists for all stages of the momentous task of building an atom bomb. Even when demanding that they work more quickly, Kurchatov retained the loyalty of his staff. He was able also to cope with his political masters, especially Beria, who made regular menacing visits to Arzamas-16 and the other atomic research sites. But, unlike the building of a tank or an aeroplane, in atomic research there was rarely anything to see. Beria's suspicion made him fear he was being hoodwinked by Kurchatov and his team. When he wanted to see inside a nuclear reactor, he was told no, because of the risk of radiation; it was too dangerous. Beria replied, "How can we know that this isn't a deception, that it is not just your fantasy?" Kurchatov admitted that only the successful detonation of a bomb would be decisive proof.

London's Daily Express *reports on the trial of atomic scientist and spy Dr. Klaus Fuchs, March 1950. Fuchs was a German refugee who joined the US National Laboratory at Los Alamos in 1944, from where, during the war, he passed on vital information to the Soviets.*

should proceed expeditiously without regard for cost. Stalin trebled the science budget for the year and increased scientists' salaries. In the new five-year plan, the development of advanced technologies for rockets, for jet propulsion, and for the atom bomb were all given priority.

Beria organized backup for the project in his customary way. Hundreds of thousands of prisoners in the Gulag were assigned to building installations and to excavating uranium ore. At the end of 1946 the first Soviet nuclear reactor ignited a controlled chain reaction, the initial stage in the production of a bomb. In 1948 a huge secret laboratory was constructed about 250 miles east of Moscow, near Sarov, at a site later called Arzamas-16. This became the centre of Soviet atom bomb research, development, and, later, production. It grew to a vast size. As a high proportion of Soviet national product was invested in the military-industrial complex, towns like Arzamas-16, closed to the outside world, enjoyed a prosperity unique within the Soviet Union.

The cost of the bomb project mounted, and immense technical difficulties made for constant delays. Beria grew furious. But the Soviet command economy was ideally suited for a project such as this. Once its priority was established, nothing would be allowed to get in its way. So, despite chaos and devastation at the end of the war, the Soviet Union was able to develop an atom bomb in about four years, only a few months longer than it had taken the United States.

The army of scientists working under Kurchatov also benefited from intelligence acquired from the West, through Klaus Fuchs, the German-born British physicist, and, independently, an American physicist, Ted Hall. In 1944 Fuchs had joined the US atomic research programme, code-named the Manhattan Project, at Los Alamos and, along with David Greenglass, passed secrets to the Soviets through the spy Harry Gold, which helped the Soviet Union get a head start on its research and stay aware of what was going on at Los Alamos. Fuchs passed on detailed designs about the implosion process of igniting a nuclear core with high explosives, the key to making an atom bomb with plutonium. This was the bomb that had been dropped at Nagasaki, and was the type of bomb first built by Kurchatov and his team.

Klaus Fuchs

There has been intense debate as to how important the secrets captured from the West really were to building the Soviet bomb. Some experts have claimed that the Soviets would not otherwise have developed the bomb for another ten years. Fuchs himself, during interrogation following his arrest, claimed that what he passed probably speeded up the Soviet bomb "by one year at least." The latest historian of Stalin's bomb project, David Holloway, concludes that while Fuchs's detailed information was helpful, it still left an immense amount to be achieved by Soviet scientists. Most probably the timetable of the Soviet bomb had been set by the speed with which uranium was mined and further processed. Plutonium is extracted from uranium after it has been irradiated in a nuclear reactor. Here, the Soviet Union was slow, until Beria put swarms of Gulag inmates to work mining the uranium ore. Even with the secrets handed over by Fuchs, the rapid development of atomic bomb manufacture was remarkable.

Justifying the Superbomb

The catch-up by the Soviet Union led to a reassessment of defence thinking in the United States. American atomic scientists were already discussing the possibility of building a superbomb, a thermonuclear device roughly a thousand times more powerful than the atom bomb. This hydrogen, or H, bomb released tremendous amounts of nuclear energy through the fusion of hydrogen atoms, causing widespread fallout of radioactivity over a much larger area than that of an atom bomb. But the civilian scientists were split. Robert Oppenheimer, head of the Los Alamos laboratory, spoke for a group that believed it had been acceptable to develop an atom bomb during a war when

Robert Oppenheimer

it was feared (wrongly as it turned out) that the enemy was developing its own bomb, but it was immoral to develop a bomb with almost limitless destructive capacity in peacetime, when there was no identifiable need for it. To construct a superbomb would be "a danger to humanity as a whole." Oppenheimer argued that if the United States created such a bomb, the Soviet Union would be bound to copy it, which would threaten the existence of civilization, the very survival of life on earth. This body of scientists unanimously recommended to the general advisory committee of the Atomic Energy Commission that the H-bomb should not be developed; their report concluded that a superbomb was "necessarily an evil thing considered in any light."

Another group of scientists, led by Edward Teller, argued that there was a race on with a ruthless and determined enemy, and that it was the duty of the government of the day to push ahead in that race; otherwise the American people would be left vulnerable to Soviet arms superiority. Strong support for this view came from the US military. In a report that was sent directly to the president, the Joint Chiefs of Staff concluded that "the United

Edward Teller

States would be in an intolerable position if a possible enemy possessed the [super]bomb and the United States did not.... The peace of the world generally and, specifically, the security of the entire Western Hemisphere would be jeopardized."

When the issue was debated at the White House on 31 January 1950, Truman cut it short. "What the hell are we waiting for?" he asked his advisers. "Let's get on with it." For the president there was only one option. He told his press secretary that although no one wanted to use such a bomb, it was essential to have it in bargaining with the Soviets. That night Truman announced to the world that he was directing that a new "so-called hydrogen or superbomb" be developed. With this announcement, he fired the starter's pistol for the ultimate arms race. The United States committed itself to build a range of weapons that it hoped never to use.

The complete design and building of the world's first H-bomb took two years and nine months. US physicists at Los Alamos, following the concept initially worked out by Edward Teller, surmounted immense scientific difficulties to produce a bomb that was finally ready for testing on 1 November 1952, at a tiny Pacific atoll called Eniwetok in the northwest Marshall Islands, two

The top of the mushroom cloud of a US hydrogen bomb explosion in the Marshall Islands. This photograph was taken at 12,000 feet, fifty miles from the detonation site, two minutes after zero hour. Ten minutes later, the cloud stem had risen twenty-five miles into the stratosphere.

The course of the world suddenly shifted. . . . Fission bombs, destructive as they might have been, were thought of as being limited in power. Now, it seemed, we had learned how to brush even these limits aside and to build bombs whose power was boundless.

— Herbert York,
nuclear physicist

hundred miles west of Bikini Atoll. Both atolls had been designated as testing grounds for atomic weapons, and all the native inhabitants had been expatriated. By the end of October, a large US Navy task force had gathered around Eniwetok. The giant bomb, weighing 82 tons and housed in a vast refrigeration system, took six weeks to assemble. Estimates of the bomb's yield varied widely, for theoretically there was no limit to the fusion reaction of such a bomb. It was decided to evacuate all land-based scientists onto ships, to observe the explosion from at least thirty miles' distance. At H hour the bomb was detonated. The cycle of events that ignited the uranium casing worked perfectly, heating the core to a temperature hotter than the sun's centre. Within seconds it expanded to a white fireball more than three miles in diameter. The crews of the task force had been ordered to wear goggles and not to look at the explosion, but many turned to look anyway and were amazed at what they saw. The entire horizon seemed to light up. And the fireball was followed by a wall of heat, as though someone had opened a hot oven nearby. As the heat grew in intensity, observers thirty miles away began to get concerned. The wings of a B-36 flying at 40,000 feet fifteen miles from the explosion heated 93 degrees within seconds. Five minutes after H hour, the giant cloud mushrooming up from the explosion had reached the stratosphere, and it then spread out in a huge canopy that eventually was more than one hundred miles in diameter. Out of this giant canopy fell radioactive mud and, later, heavy rain. The coral atoll where the bomb exploded had disappeared entirely, vaporized by the force of the bomb, which created a giant crater more than a mile wide and two hundred feet deep. Eighty million tons of material from the atoll were sucked up by the explosion and would fall out around the world. Survey teams later picked up fish in the sea, three miles from the centre of the explosion, that had the skin burned off them. Trees fourteen miles away were scorched and wilted. The yield of the bomb was finally put at 10.4 megatons, equivalent to more than 10 million tons of TNT — one thousand times more powerful than the bomb dropped at Hiroshima. The world had now entered the thermonuclear age.

The first H-bomb, still at the experimental stage, was far too huge for even the largest bomber to carry, and the advantage Washington hoped it would bring to the United States was short lived. Nine months later, on 12 August 1953, the Soviets tested their first thermonuclear bomb at Semipalatinsk. Although this was a relatively small device, yielding some 400 kilotons, it showed that, once again, Soviet scientists had caught up. More alarming, US sampling of its radiation cloud detected elements of lithium, which probably meant that the Soviets had now taken the technological lead. In using lithium, the Soviet bomb did not require the vast refrigeration plant the American bomb needed. It would be easier to pack this bomb into a container that could be carried by a heavy bomber.

Massive Retaliation

The arms race was now speeding up. In December 1953 Eisenhower proposed in a speech at the United Nations that competition be replaced with international cooperation on atomic energy, a proposal that became known as Atoms for Peace. But this line was not pursued. Instead, John Foster Dulles proposed a hawkish new policy of "massive retaliation" against anyone who dared make a strike against the United States or its allies. While Malenkov was still pondering his response, the United States began a new series of thermonuclear tests at Bikini Atoll in the Pacific.

On 1 March 1954 the United States tested a new lithium-based H-bomb, designed to fit into the bomb bay of a B-47. Scientists at Los Alamos estimated that it would yield the equivalent of about 5 megatons of high explosives. But they had seriously miscalculated, failing to predict a secondary fusion reaction in the lithium fuel component. The fireball grew to a momentous four miles in diameter, trapping observers in their bunkers well outside the expected range of the explosion. The bomb vaporized coral from the atoll, turning it into radioactive calcium that strong winds then rained down over a large area. Eighty-two miles from the centre of the explosion, a Japanese fishing boat, the *Fukuryu Maru*, or "Lucky Dragon," was showered with this fallout. When the boat returned to Japan two weeks later, the members of its crew fell sick. All twenty-three of them had been seriously exposed to radia-

President Dwight D. Eisenhower at the United Nations, 8 December 1953, called for all countries with atomic weapons to contribute to an international atomic agency under UN sponsorship — "Atoms for Peace."

"Bombs Away, with Curtis LeMay"

Curtis LeMay, the tough, plain-talking commander of Strategic Air Command, was one of the most macho figures of the Cold War. He was rarely seen without a cigar stuck in the side of his mouth, which hid a drooping lower lip, the result of Bell's palsy he had developed while flying too high on a combat mission. In the Second World War, LeMay led an air group bombing Germany from England, and he acquired the reputation of a tough commanding officer. Transferred to the Pacific in early 1945, he reorganized the bombing of Japan, using giant B-29 superbombers — "Bombs away, with Curtis LeMay." In one night the firestorms his bombers set off destroyed much of Tokyo and killed at least 100,000 civilians, more than in any other bombing raid of the war, including Hiroshima and Nagasaki. Later, LeMay admitted that had the United States lost the war, he would probably have been tried as a war criminal. But, as that did not happen, LeMay never expressed remorse at the

civilian deaths and suffering his fire raids on sixty Japanese cities caused.

When he took charge of Strategic Air Command, he initiated a series of test bombing missions over American cities, to toughen up the flying skills of his bomber teams, and built an esprit de corps that set SAC apart.

On occasion LeMay expressed the view that he and his bomber teams should share ultimate control of the bombs with the president, in case Washington was, for some reason, paralysed or taken out in a nuclear attack. LeMay might have been tempted to push the nuclear button any number of times during the 1950s, but in the early 1960s the system was tightened up with the installation of Permissive Action Link locks. In a lecture to the National War College in April 1956, LeMay described a scenario in which SAC would go into battle tonight and "by tomorrow morning the Soviet Union would likely cease to be a major military power or even a major nation."

In his chilling vision, "Dawn might break over a nation infinitely poorer than China, less populated than the United States, and condemned to an agrarian existence perhaps for generations to come."

This line of thinking blurred the distinction between prevention and pre-emption. Official US policy was to prevent any Soviet attack through the threat of immense firepower already targeted at the heart of the Soviet Union. But in the early 1950s LeMay and others talked about pre-emptive strikes to stop the enemy from achieving any advantage in weapons over the United States. He even suggested it would be in the national interest to start the next war before the Soviet Union had fully caught up in the arms race. In discussing reconnaissance overflights of the Soviet Union, LeMay commented that if the Soviets retaliated, it would be a good way to get a third world war started. It was never clear if he was joking.

Today, shooting wars are won or lost before they start. If they are fought at all, they would be fought principally to confirm which side had won at the outset.

— Curtis LeMay,
April 1956

Pugnacious General Curtis LeMay testifies before a Senate defence appropriations sub-committee in 1962.

tion, and one of them died. There was an uproar. A Japanese newspaper claimed that "once again Japan has been poisoned by ashes of death." The United States offered to send radiation specialists to Japan but refused to give details of the fallout lest the Soviets learn that lithium was used. Lewis Strauss, head of the Atomic Energy Commission, disclaimed any responsibility, stating that "at no time was the testing out of control." He claimed, quite wrongly, that the *Fukuryu Maru* must have trespassed within the proscribed danger zone and privately suspected that the vessel was a "Soviet spy ship." In fact, "Bravo" had exploded with a yield of 15 megatons, fifteen hundred times the power of the Hiroshima bomb, and three times the power that was expected of it, the largest thermonuclear device the United States ever tested. The US H-bomb programme would now be fuelled by lithium deuteride.

In September 1954 the Soviet Union dropped a 20-kiloton bomb from an aircraft during military exercises at Trotskoye, in the southern Urals. Afterwards, Soviet troops were ordered to storm the irradiated area. The Red Army wanted to make a show of preparing for nuclear war. In the United States it was decided to manufacture small-yield tactical nuclear weapons, compact enough to fit into the nose cone of a missile. In 1955 the Soviets tested the first airborne H-bomb at Semipalatinsk, with a yield one hundred times more powerful than their first bomb. The arms race had quickened to a terrifying pace.

At the end of 1948 General Curtis LeMay had taken control of the US Strategic Air Command, and he soon built it into an elite military unit, with high morale and a strong sense of mission. LeMay turned the threatened use of offensive weapons into a strategy of defence. LeMay wanted Strategic Air Command to possess such overwhelming strength that no one would ever dare attack the United States. By determining the number of targets inside the Soviet Union, LeMay built up a case for expanding the nuclear stockpile. By 1952, he informed the president, the air force had identified "perhaps five or six thousand targets which would have to be destroyed in the event of war." These included airfields, military bases, nuclear power stations, oil fields, power plants, communication centres, and so on. In 1953 the air force was voted more than 40 per cent of all US defence funds for the year, and that level of expenditure was maintained throughout the decade. In 1950 the US military had 298 atomic bombs; by 1955 this had become 2,422 nuclear weapons; by 1962, the year of the Cuban missile crisis, the number of nuclear weapons had leapt to 27,100.

For LeMay, Strategic Air Command had to be constantly at a state of full military readiness, able to hit the Soviet Union with 750 nuclear weapons within a few hours if called upon. "Decisive victory," he claimed, would be reached in the very first stages of a nuclear war. Only a US military armed to the teeth would be a sufficient deterrent to any enemy. Strategic Air Command grew from 668 B-50 and B-29 bombers in 1951 to about 500 long-range B-52 bombers and more than 2,500 B-47 bombers capable of mid-air refuelling by 1959.

To keep up with the escalation of targeting and stockpiling of nuclear weapons, the United States needed ever more detailed information about

New York City. 1953

Two air-raid wardens survey a deserted Times Square after a civil defence exercise. Six hundred sirens wailed; two imaginary atom bombs exploded; passersby formed lines and were ushered into shelters. Most took the alert seriously.

Soviet strength, about fighter capability and bomber threat. Strategic Air Command in 1950 began its own, unauthorized reconnaissance flights over the Soviet Union in stripped-down B-29 bombers. Each of these flights was provocative and could have ignited a full-scale Soviet response. When he found out, President Truman banned them. But US reconnaissance flights began again; after July 1956 the main aircraft used for these overflights was a single-seat, high-altitude jet reconnaissance plane, the Lockheed U-2, with a range of some 2,600 miles. It carried cameras and other electronic equipment to monitor radio and radar transmissions.

Flying at a height of 75,000 feet, well out of range of Soviet fighters and anti-aircraft missiles, the U-2 spy planes looked down on the Soviet Union and photographed everything they wanted. The detail was sufficient to enable one to read a newspaper headline over the shoulder of someone on the ground. U-2 flights, organized in great secrecy, were controlled not by the US military but by the CIA. They started to crisscross the Soviet Union from US bases in Pakistan and Turkey and rapidly built up a picture of the numbers and strength of Soviet bombers and missiles. The intelligence produced by the U-2 was meat and drink to photographic interpreters in Washington. Each U-2 flight was a violation of Soviet territory and risked a violent Soviet response, but not until May 1960, just before the Paris summit, was a crisis triggered.

The first evidence brought back by U-2 spy planes made it look as though the Soviets were pulling ahead in the production of long-range bombers. The Soviet Tu-95 Bison bomber, revealed with fanfare at the Moscow Air Show in 1955, was a plane with the range to deliver a nuclear bomb all the way to the United States. A U-2 photograph of one Soviet air base showed a large number of these Bison bombers. In reality these planes constituted the entire Soviet fleet. But fears began to spread of a "bomber gap" in which the United States was being left behind by the Soviet Union.

Soviet views on the U-2.
TOP: *An unfriendly West spies on the Soviet Union.*
BOTTOM: *A picture issued at the Soviet announcement of the 1960 shoot-down and arrest of Francis Gary Powers.*

The Soviets were also seen to be striding ahead in the development of missile technology. Since 1929 Sergei Korolyov had been working on experimental rocket propulsion, and in 1933 he helped found the Research Institute for Rocketry in Moscow. In 1938 he was arrested by Stalin's secret police, charged with anti-revolutionary activities, and sentenced to ten years' hard labour in Siberia. He continued his work inside prison, as part of the war effort, and near the end of the Second World War was brought back to Moscow to head the Soviet missile programme.

In 1945 the Americans were first to reach the German rocket site at Peenemünde on the Baltic coast, from which the Nazis had launched V-1 and V-2 rockets against Britain towards the end of the war. There the Americans captured important rocket technology, and, later, Wernher von Braun, who was taken back to the United States to become the guiding light of the American missile programme. In 1946 Stalin ordered the rounding up and transporting to Moscow of sixteen thousand German rocket scientists and project engineers, who were then organized to work on the Soviet missile programme.

From the early 1950s, as nuclear weapons grew ever more powerful, the race was on to develop a vehicle that would transport a bomb to an enemy tar-

Sergei Korolyov

get in the fastest possible time. At Baikonur, in the harsh Kazakhstan desert, Soviet engineers worked on a top secret rocket project they called "the mechanism," with the intention of making a missile that would carry hydrogen bomb warheads. On 15 May 1957 they tested the world's first-ever intercontinental ballistic missile (ICBM).

Sputnik Orbits

But it was the launch of Sputnik that caught the world's imagination. Sputnik (which means "fellow traveller") was the name of a set of satellites intended to investigate outer space, and to find out if living things could survive there. At 1:28 AM local time, on 5 October 1957, the first Russian Sputnik was launched from its base at the Baikonur Cosmodrome. It was simply a test payload, an aluminium sphere about 22 inches in diameter and weighing 184 pounds, which contained a radio transmitter. Ninety minutes later Sputnik entered orbit, sending radio bleeps back to earth. The team called Khrushchev in Moscow in the middle of the night to give him the good news, but he was not at all excited. He responded, "Frankly, I never thought it would work," and went back to bed.

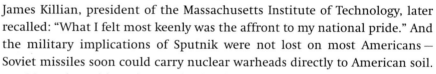

Sputnik's radio bleeps were heard round the world. In the United States the launch came as an immense shock. Although Moscow had announced its intentions, they were dismissed in the West as propaganda. Now it seemed that Soviet technology had got ahead of American, in a field that most Americans felt was their own. Edward Teller said on television that the United States had lost "a battle more important and greater than Pearl Harbor." James Killian, president of the Massachusetts Institute of Technology, later recalled: "What I felt most keenly was the affront to my national pride." And the military implications of Sputnik were not lost on most Americans — Soviet missiles soon could carry nuclear warheads directly to American soil.

More than thirty thousand scientists now worked for Korolyov in the secret Kazakhstan bases. Sputnik was ready to venture farther into the heavens. Sputnik II, launched on 3 November, the fortieth anniversary of the Bolshevik Revolution, carried a dog, Laika, the first living thing in space. Laika survived for ten days, proving that life could endure in the prolonged weightlessness of space. Americans now felt they had fallen even farther behind in the new "space race."

The Sputniks brought forth a deep sense of national humiliation within the United States. It was felt that America had gone "soft," that an obsession with material things had undermined the quality of its science, and that behind this were structural flaws in the education system. Americans turned to Eisenhower for leadership at this time of crisis. Above politics, Ike had become almost a father to the nation, winning a landslide victory for a second term in 1956. But Eisenhower was one of the few Americans not to panic in the face of Sputnik. When the news first came through, Eisenhower had left Washington for Gettysburg, Pennsylvania, where he owned a farm, and he insisted on carrying on with his golf weekend, despite the growing storm. And when he did hold a press conference nearly a week later, he failed to reassure the nation, giving what one reporter called "a fumbling apologia." Senator

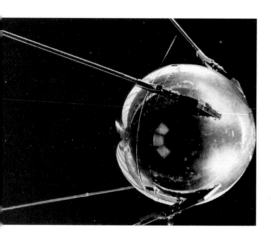

Sputnik — only 22 inches in diameter. Its launch caused Americans to fear they would lose the "space race."

Lyndon Baines Johnson, Senate majority leader, chaired a series of hearings to investigate the impact of Sputnik. One by one, top scientists and military strategists declared that the Soviet Union was ahead in science and technology, and that the United States must "wake up to the fact that we are in a tough competitive race."

The United States already had several ballistic missile programmes under way, one of which, called Vanguard, was co-ordinated by the navy. Eisenhower gave orders for this one to be speeded up. Two months after the launch of Sputnik, on 6 December, a vast crowd of dignitaries gathered at Cape Canaveral,

America's bid to launch a satellite into orbit ends in disaster as the seventy-two-foot Vanguard rocket explodes on ignition at Cape Canaveral. London's Daily Herald *jeered at the fiasco.*

in Florida, to watch the American attempt to catch up with the Russians. A mighty Vanguard rocket lifted off carrying a tiny four-pound satellite destined for orbit. In full view of the world's news cameras the rocket rose just two feet off the ground, fell back, and exploded. The national humiliation was compounded. The British press mocked, "Oh, What a Flopnik!"

Meanwhile, a panel of experts had been secretly investigating America's nuclear defences. In November the Gaither Report on Deterrence and Survival was delivered to the president. It made alarming reading, revealing what it reported as real gaps between US and Soviet science and technology. It called for increased funding for Strategic Air Command, and for a massive increase in the size of the US missile force. A month later it was leaked to the press. The *Washington Post* said that the United States was "in the gravest danger in its history," and spoke of America's becoming a "second class power," claiming that the report "finds America's long term prospect one of cataclysmic peril in the face of rocketing Soviet military might."

The Missile Gap

In the hysteria that followed, Americans saw behind the missile gap a technology gap, and behind that an education gap. A lasting legacy of the panic generated by Sputnik was the passing of the National Defense Education Act of 1958, in which at last the case for federal involvement in education was accepted by Congress. A huge programme of federal spending ushered in a vast expansion of the university system. Hundreds of millions of dollars were offered as loans to students majoring in science, engineering, and mathematics. Two billion dollars a year were spent to prevent the Russians from winning the brain race. As a consequence, through the 1960s, when the baby-boom generation reached their late teens, they advanced into higher education like a tidal wave, doubling the number of young Americans attending college during the decade.

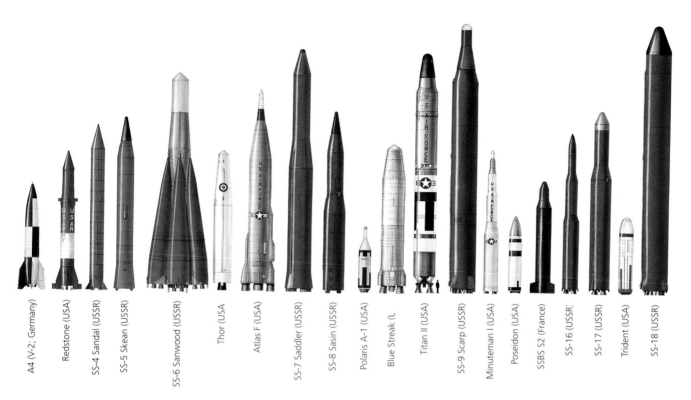

A4 (V-2; Germany) · Redstone (USA) · SS-4 Sandal (USSR) · SS-5 Skean (USSR) · SS-6 Sanwood (USSR) · Thor (USA · Atlas F (USA) · SS-7 Saddler (USSR) · SS-8 Sasin (USSR) · Polaris A-1 (USA) · Blue Streak (L · Titan II (USA) · SS-9 Scarp (USSR) · Minuteman I (USA) · Poseidon (USA) · SSBS S2 (France) · SS-16 (USSR · SS-17 (USSR) · Trident (USA) · SS-18 (USSR)

Eisenhower still refused to panic. His intelligence reports told him that the missile gap was a myth. U-2 spy-plane photographs chronicled the slow rate of Soviet missile production, and Eisenhower knew that his country had many more nuclear warheads than the Russians. He also knew that there was no bomber gap. The long-range Soviet Bison bombers captured on film were all lined up at a single air base, with the taxiways on other bases empty. But all of this was top secret, and Eisenhower did not want to reveal the extent of his intelligence about the Soviet Union, even though Dulles urged him to do so. Ike knew that massive increases in defence spending and new missile programmes were not necessary, but he chose not to reveal why. As Barry Goldwater, a conservative senator from Arizona, later put it, "Ike took the heat, grinned, and kept his mouth shut."

But the pressure on Eisenhower took its toll. He suffered a minor stroke, and for a short period was unable to talk clearly. Vice President Richard Nixon stood in for him for a few days, but Ike, determined and resilient, was soon back at his desk. Even so, to most Americans, Eisenhower appeared not to be providing the leadership the American people needed to stand up to the Soviet Union. His popularity rating dropped more than twenty points in the polls,

Preparing for the Worst

American consumers, preparing for the worst, were urged to equip themselves and their families to last out the aftermath of nuclear explosions.

RIGHT: Part of a display at New York's Grand Central Station which showed a shelter designed to accommodate a family of five or six during weeks of radioactive fallout.

ABOVE: The black-and-yellow Fallout Shelter marker made its appearance in every US city and town.
LEFT: A leading California swimming pool, patio, and barbecue dealer found business booming when he offered to build shelters for his customers. His slogan: "Due to known conditions, ACT NOW!"

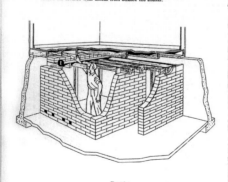

Cutaway sections of a basement shelter, from a US Office of Civil Defense booklet, The Family Fallout Shelter, published in 1959.

but his firm, guiding hand and judgement were more in line with the realities of the international arms race than anyone understood at the time.

Eisenhower knew that by 1960 the United States would have ready the new generation of Atlas and Titan ICBMs, along with new intermediate-range ballistic missiles (IRBMs) like Thor. Eisenhower turned to his European allies and successfully rebuilt the relationship with Britain and France that had been damaged by the Suez adventure in the previous year. The new British prime minister, Harold Macmillan, was an old friend of Ike's from Second World War days. At the Bermuda Conference, Britain agreed in principle to base American IRBMs in the UK, manned by British personnel, but with American control of their nuclear warheads. And in December 1957, still recovering from his stroke, Eisenhower got agreement from his European allies at a NATO conference in Paris to base IRBMs in Europe as a defence for NATO. But France's General Charles de Gaulle refused to accept that missiles on French soil could be under the control of anyone but France. De Gaulle began France's gradual withdrawal from the NATO alliance.

Slowly, during 1958, the pressure on Eisenhower forced him, against his better judgement, to increase defence spending. In a revised budget for 1959, he enlarged spending on the military to well over half the federal budget, at more than $40 billion. Much of the additional spending would go to the air force, the rest to increasing missile research and development. *Time* magazine applauded what it felt to be a long overdue response to the Sputnik crisis. And in January 1958 Wernher von Braun and his team successfully launched a modified Redstone rocket, known as Explorer, into orbit. The American nation hailed Explorer with joy and with a deep sense of relief. "That's wonderful," Eisenhower enthused when he was told the news. "I sure feel a lot better now." Two months later Vanguard finally went into orbit, along with a second Explorer rocket.

These successes raised a whole new debate within the United States about space exploration. Would it be merely an extension of mankind's natural curiosity about the stars and the universe, or would this be a race for conquest — getting somewhere before the Soviets did? One senior air force official, when asked what he expected to find on the moon, replied, "Russians." Some military men, speaking of the need to control outer space, claimed, "Whoever gains the ultimate supremacy of space, gains control — total control — over the earth." Later that year, Eisenhower set up the National Aeronautics and Space Administration (NASA), with its director reporting directly to the White House. Some Pentagon funding for missile research was diverted to NASA, and NSC-5814 gave the highest priority in the space programme to producing a spy satellite to replace the U-2. There was much talk about getting a man into space before the Russians, and of future lunar shots to probe the moon's surface. NASA would lead a programme with scientific and not military goals, although as the Cold War now reached out towards the stars it was sometimes difficult to tell the two apart.

In the West, despite evidence of the awesome destructive power of nuclear weapons, people began to believe that it still might be possible to survive a nuclear attack. In the United States a generation of schoolchildren were brought up to "duck and cover." In cartoons and musical ditties, children

"Duck and Cover." Schoolchildren in Topeka, Kansas, during a citywide civil defence drill. As sirens wailed, thirty-one thousand children left their desks and took shelter in the hallway. Incredibly, it was thought this made them safer.

were taught that during an air-raid warning, if they saw the white flash of a nuclear explosion, they should duck and cover their heads. As a strategy for surviving a nuclear explosion that could vaporize concrete-and-steel buildings, this was absurd. But many schoolchildren felt more secure in their knowledge of what to do: "duck and cover."

In the United States the leaking of the Gaither Report was followed by a crash programme for building public nuclear air-raid shelters. Soon the yellow-and-black fallout shelter symbol could be seen in every city of the land. Americans could even buy their own private family fallout shelters, which magazines advertised at $2,395 — installation extra.

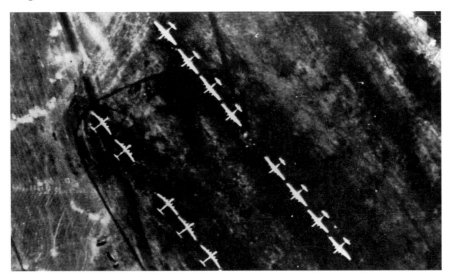

Throughout 1959 the development of the next generation of missiles, the submarine-fired Polaris, the Thor, and the Minuteman, pushed defence spending even higher. Eisenhower was furious. He spoke of the need to avoid "hysteria and demagoguery" and instead "exert some reasonable control" over defence spending. But with a presidential election coming up, the Democrats played on the supposed complacency of the Eisenhower presidency in the face of Soviet advances. Ike was still regarded as being too cautious, and *Life* magazine again wrote of a missile gap that placed the United States in a "position of great peril." Another journalist, quoting Pentagon sources, warned that military leaders were talking privately about "the future gap" between 1960 and 1963, when the Soviets would have "unchallengeable superiority in the nuclear striking power that was once our speciality." Democratic senators predicted that the Soviets would have three thousand first-strike ICBMs by 1962. It was all exaggerated, unfounded.

Secretly, U-2 flights continued to reveal the reality of the Soviet "threat." Khrushchev had decided to scrap the SS-6 missile as too large, immobile, and vulnerable to a first strike, and he gave orders to develop the more mobile SS-7 instead. U-2 photographs showed only about thirty-five ICBMs deployed in an arc along the entire trans-Siberian railway. This intelligence led Eisenhower to react wisely, as we now clearly see, to calls for a massive build-up. But his silence contributed to a public loss of confidence in the administration.

ABOVE LEFT: *A U-2 aerial photograph shows heavy bombers lined up at a Soviet air base. US intelligence believed, incorrectly, that several bases were similarly equipped, and reported a "bomber gap" that did not in fact exist.* ABOVE: *John F. Kennedy, campaigning for the presidency in 1960, made much of the "missile gap" between the United States and the USSR. He almost certainly knew from top-level briefings that there was none.*

A Summit Surprise

One of the last major events of Eisenhower's presidency was to be a four-power summit meeting in Paris in May 1960. Khrushchev regarded the regular U-2 flights over Soviet territory as symbolic of the technological inferiority of the Soviet Union. Each flight, he said to his Kremlin colleagues, "spat in the face" of the Soviet people. He instructed his air force to intercept the spy planes. But they flew too high. One air force commander said in despair that if he were only a missile, he would personally fly up and blow the damn thing to pieces. Then, on 1 May 1960, shortly before the Paris summit and the date for May Day parades in the Soviet Union, Francis Gary Powers set off from Pakistan on a

long flight across the USSR. As soon as his U-2 entered Soviet airspace it was tracked by radar. MiG fighters were launched but could not fly high enough to engage. However, over the Ural Mountains near Sverdlovsk, the U-2 came within range of the new S-75 anti-aircraft defences and was shot down. Now Khrushchev could have his say.

Before departing for Paris, Khrushchev announced that the Soviet Union had brought down a U-2 over its own territory. At first the United States denied that the plane was on a spying mission. The cover story claimed it was a high-altitude weather plane that simply got lost. Then Khrushchev produced the pilot, Gary Powers, complete with suicide needle and cameras, irrefutable evidence of his espionage mission. Realizing he was trapped, Eisenhower accepted responsibility. He admitted that the plane was operating under his broad instructions, but he would not apologize, or guarantee there would be no further spy flights. Without Eisenhower's apology, Khrushchev refused to participate in the summit, which collapsed before it had begun. US-Soviet relations, which had improved during the previous year, now slumped again. After a public and much-publicized trial in Moscow, Powers was sentenced to ten years' imprisonment. (He was exchanged for Soviet spy Rudolf Abel in 1962.)

In the new race for the White House later that year, the Democrats' can-

Francis Gary Powers

ABOVE RIGHT: *An angry Khrushchev at a May 1960 press conference. The Soviet leader demanded an apology from the United States for its U-2 spy flights, and when one was not forthcoming, refused to participate in the Paris summit.*

When Gagarin came down there was a tremendous reception in the Great New Palace in the Kremlin. There must have been about six thousand people to celebrate all this. The next day we had to drive to Leningrad, about seven hundred kilometres from Moscow, and at that time there were only two petrol stations on the whole road. They were new ones, supposed to be beautifully automated. . . . They were starting to fill my Rolls, which takes quite a lot of petrol, and the automation had gone wrong, and so they were having to do it by hand. And a jeep from a nearby farm came along and was waiting, and the two chaps were talking to each other. And one said, "Well, there you are, this is our Russia all over. Yesterday, we celebrate the first man in space; today, we can't even fill the tank of the British ambassador."

— Sir Frank Roberts,
ambassador to Moscow,
1960–1962

didate, John F. Kennedy, exploited the missile gap fears to great advantage. He campaigned hard against rival Richard Nixon and the Republican administration, playing on the frustration that had built up against Eisenhower's caution. Eisenhower was old, sometimes ill, and seemed to embody the sense of accepting second place that so many Americans resented. Kennedy was young, handsome, dynamic, and offered to make America first again. In November 1960 he narrowly defeated Nixon for the presidency.

Within weeks of taking office, the Kennedy administration found that there was indeed a missile gap — but it was in America's favour. The Soviets

were way behind in the development and deployment of their ICBM programme. After successful trials of Atlas, Thor, Minuteman, and Polaris, the United States was now far in the lead. The reverse missile gap was impassively revealed later in the year by Deputy Secretary of Defense Roswell Gilpatric, as a new crisis in Berlin was heating up. The announcement was designed to prevent Khrushchev from taking further advantage of missiles he did not possess. The missile gap slipped quietly into history.

On 12 April 1961 the Soviets celebrated the finest triumph yet for Soviet science. Yuri Gagarin became the first human being in space. His flight in the Vostok spaceship lasted one hour and forty-eight minutes, during which he made a full circle of the earth and a safe landing along the Volga River. Gagarin was given a tumultuous hero's reception as he was driven through the streets of Moscow, with Khrushchev beside him. His smile made Gagarin the most popular hero in the history of the Soviet Union. The crowds cheered as they had when celebrating their victory over Nazi Germany. True to Soviet principles, when the Nobel Prize Committee asked Khrushchev to name the scientist behind Gagarin's mission, he refused, saying it was "the Soviet people" who had launched Gagarin into space.

But President Kennedy would not accept defeat. A month later he announced his "Freedom Doctrine" and a huge programme of both military and civilian aid to the developing world. He summoned his nation to a vast global action plan to defend liberty wherever it was threatened. By now his advisers had made clear to him how illusory the Soviet scientific lead really was. America, in fact, was surpassing Russia. Kennedy pledged "before the decade is out, to land a man on the moon and return him safely to earth." The Cold War had spread into the heavens.

A Soviet poster. Man marches to the stars under the hammer and sickle.

OPPOSITE AND ABOVE:
Yuri Gagarin, the first man into space, April 1961. Gagarin's triumph made him one of the great heroes in Soviet history. His smile inspired a generation.

Berlin, 1961

Bernauer Straße

105 · 94

The Berlin Wall divided families. West Berliners, desperate to keep in touch with relatives in the East, climb high to see and be seen over the concrete barrier. The Wall came to symbolize Europe's division, at the heart of the Cold War.

The Wall
1958–1963

Walter Ulbricht, Communist leader, inspects East German police assembled in Stalinallee. Behind him, centre, is Erich Honecker, who masterminded the plan to build the Wall.

An Ultimatum

At a Moscow reception on 10 November 1958, Khrushchev launched a new round in the battle for Berlin. In a public speech he insisted that the military occupation of Berlin, which had lasted since the end of the Second World War, should now come to an end. He demanded that the Western powers join the Soviet Union in signing a peace treaty recognizing the existence of the two Germanys. Khrushchev further proposed that Berlin should become a "free city" — free, that is, from the presence of Western occupation powers. But the sting came in the tail. Two weeks later Khrushchev gave the West a six-month ultimatum. Get out of Berlin, or the Soviet Union would sign its own peace treaty with East Germany. In that case, all rights of the Western powers in Berlin and all access agreements would thenceforth be subject to negotiation with the sovereign state of the German Democratic Republic (GDR). The message was clear: agree to withdraw, or be kicked out of Berlin altogether.

Khrushchev's ultimatum landed like a bombshell in the West. A no-surrender line had been drawn at Berlin. Ten years earlier the Berlin airlift had confirmed the West's determination to hold on to this advance base more than a hundred miles inside the Iron Curtain. The view then, and still in 1958, was that to hold Europe against communism it was essential to hold Berlin and prevent a permanent division of Germany into two separate states.

Khrushchev was known to act impulsively at times, but his new threats against Berlin had been carefully calculated. He was concerned about the lack of a formal German peace settlement thirteen years after the end of the war. West Germany was then in the midst of an "economic miracle" under Chancellor Konrad Adenauer, who wanted to re-unite West and East Germany.

A unified, capitalist Germany, armed with nuclear weapons and backed by the United States, raised the spectre once again of an aggressor Germany laying waste to the Soviet Union. Memories of the horrors of the Second World War were still strong. Papers prepared for the Presidium warned the Soviet leaders of the danger of a revived Germany uniting with Poland, and the reorientation of the Polish economy westward, leaving the USSR with no buffer zone on its western border. The deployment of American intermediate-range missiles in Europe, and the buildup of nuclear weapons within NATO, further alarmed the Kremlin.

Added to this Khrushchev felt a passionate commitment to establishing a Communist state in East Germany. He was a supporter of Walter Ulbricht, the East German leader, whose hard-line Stalinist policies had nearly toppled the regime in 1953. Khrushchev believed that if the West Germans were heirs to Hitler's ambitions, then East Germany, as a Communist state in the centre of Europe, symbolically justified Soviet war sacrifices. Khrushchev's ideology told him that communism would inevitably prevail over capitalism, but he seemed blind to the obvious fact that West Germany was striding ahead economically and leaving East Germany far behind.

He was only too aware, however, that every year tens of thousands of East Germans fled to capitalist West Germany: more than 300,000 in 1953, and

Two first secretaries in harmony: Nikita Khrushchev of the Central Committee of the Soviet Communist Party and Walter Ulbricht of the Socialist Unity Party of the German Democratic Republic.

Konrad Adenauer

156,000 in 1956. A nine-hundred-mile boundary ran between the two states, and along it the East Germans had constructed a formidable frontier with watchtowers, barbed wire, minefields, and armed patrols. But Berlin, deep inside the Eastern state, offered an easy escape route. Movement around the city, in and out of the four military zones of occupation, was virtually unrestricted. Many East Berliners worked in West Berlin, and members of the same family lived in different zones. The underground train system, the U-Bahn, and the elevated trains, the S-Bahn, moved through all sectors. East Germans who wanted to emigrate, or defect to the West, slipped into East Berlin and then crossed to the Western sector. They either settled there or went to a refugee assembly point, the best known of which was Marienfelde. This vast, barracks-like reception centre processed hundreds of refugees every day, providing meals and temporary accommodation. In long lines, the refugees waited to be screened and interviewed. Many who had carefully concealed their plans for escape were astonished to find, in the next queue, neighbours or workmates who had made equally secret plans. Eventually, many were flown out to other cities in West Germany, all at the expense of the West German state, where the economic boom was generating a continuous demand for labour.

The vast majority of these refugees were young and skilled. More than half were below the age of twenty-five, and three out of four were under forty-five, the very people most needed to build the Communist state. Older people,

Two Berlins. In the West (BELOW), affluence fuelled by West Germany's booming motor car industry; in the East (BELOW LEFT), a drabber scene. Short on consumer goods, East Berliners benefited from excellent health care and free education. Very many, however, chose to leave.

Portrait of Berlin, 1960

In 1960 Berlin was a tale of two cities. In West Berlin, with a population of 2 million, the rubble of war had mostly been cleared away. Lights shone at night down the Kurfürsten Damm, which was lined with smart shops and street cafés. Kempinski's served famous ice cream sundaes. One of the first Hilton hotels in Europe dominated the skyline. Theatres, concert halls, and nightclubs were packed. Many loved the busy, throbbing, cosmopolitan air of the city; others found it hectic, frantic.

Through the Brandenburg Gate, East Berlin was another world. The vast boulevard of the Unter den Linden, still elegant, was largely deserted. The huge Soviet Embassy stood on one side. Farther along, the destruction the war had brought was still visible. Buildings stood derelict, next to empty spaces where others had been destroyed. Posters everywhere proclaimed, "Build the Socialist Fatherland." While everyone was fed and housed, the million people in East Berlin looked far from prosperous. In the drab new apartment blocks the services worked, but they were at a basic level. An East Berliner who could afford the luxury of a refrigerator would have to wait a year for one; for a washing machine, the wait was two years. Cars were not to be had on any waiting list. Consumer goods took no priority in an economy geared to earning necessary foreign currency through exports.

West Berlin had enjoyed the benefits of Western investment for fifteen years; in East Berlin, the Soviets had taken out everything they could from the economy. And it showed.

Berlin, 1950s

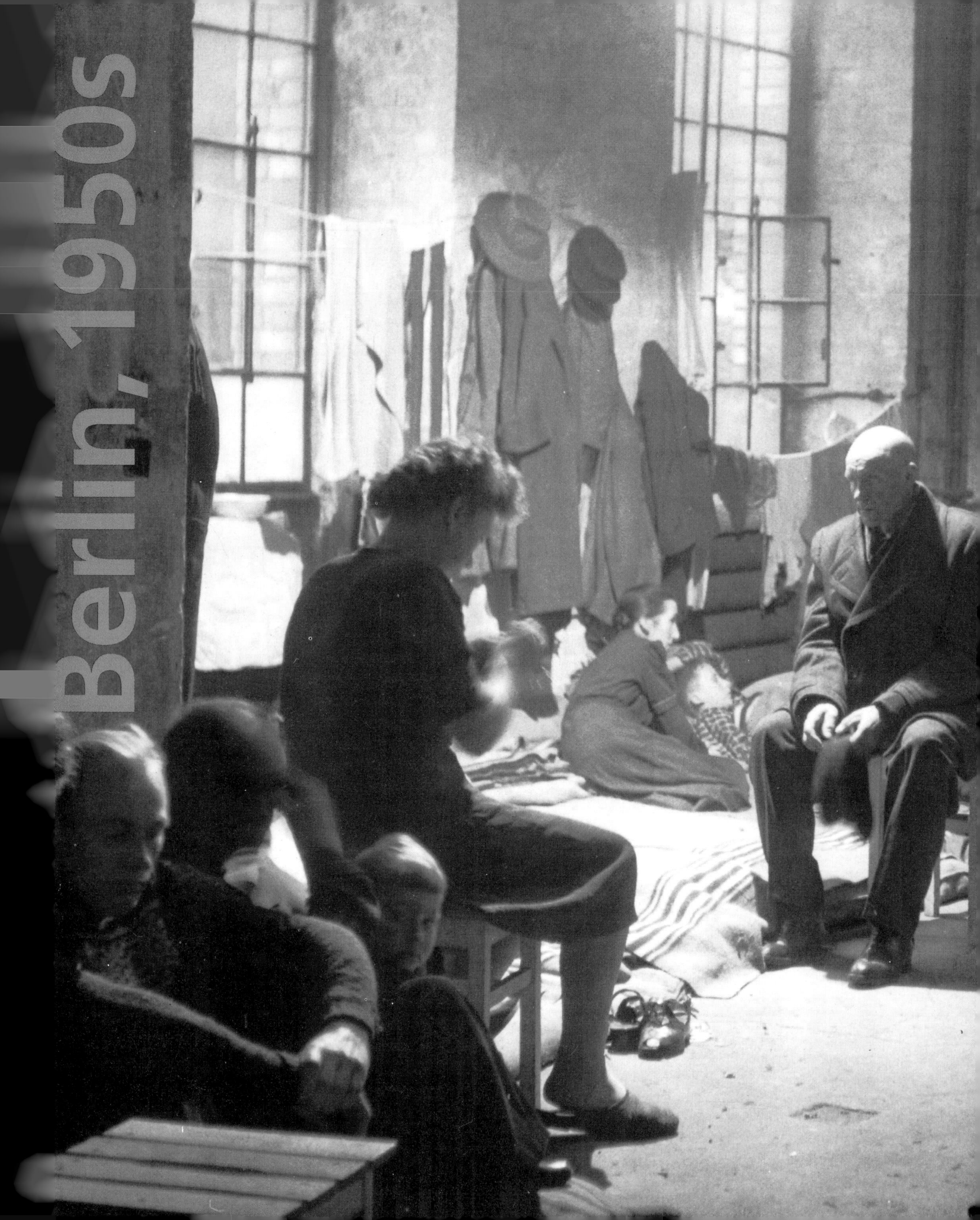

Refugees from East Germany find temporary shelter in West Berlin. Throughout the 1950s, a steady stream of Germans voted with their feet and headed to the West, in one of the largest migrations in European history.

East Germans line up to register at the Marienfelde Refugee Camp in West Berlin, 1961. Many were skilled workers. The East German government was desperate to stop this human flood.

on state pensions, were understandably less keen to start a new life in the West. The refugees numbered industrial workers, farm labourers, scientists, doctors, teachers, and other professionals. The entire law faculty of Leipzig University defected. Some came alone, some with their entire families, some even fled en masse as communities. Seventeen key engineers from one industrial plant left, taking the factory's blueprints with them. Thirty thousand students completed their studies (at state expense), received their diplomas, and then they fled. All were drawn to opportunities offered in the booming West, and the chance to escape the shortages and the restrictions of the Ulbricht regime, where every economic act was strictly controlled from the centre. Between 1949, when the GDR was created, and 1961, 2.8 million Germans crossed to the West in one of the biggest European migrations in history; one-sixth of the population abandoned the East for the good life they thought awaited them.

This exodus caused panic in the East. Not only was it a humiliating sign of the failure of the socialist utopia, but it created a serious labour shortage. Bosses, colleagues, friends were there one day and absent the next. Assembly lines were brought to a halt because a crucial worker had gone west. Skilled workers became more and more difficult to replace. Shoppers found there was no one in the store to serve them. In 1957 the GDR made *Republikflucht*, fleeing to the West, a criminal offence punishable with a prison sentence — if the escapee could be caught. The Communist-controlled press painted a lurid picture of life in the West: slave traders were capturing innocent young East Germans and selling the women into prostitution, the men into a life of drudgery. Still they went. Those who remained, under even stricter economic discipline, were called upon to make greater sacrifices. The result: another flood of workers to West Berlin.

Khrushchev Tries Personal Diplomacy

To make threats over Berlin was, for Khrushchev, to play for high stakes. And for the United States to pledge to hold on to Berlin at all costs created difficult military problems. The Joint Chiefs of Staff talked of using "whatever degree of force might be necessary" to maintain the garrison in Berlin. Dulles and Eisenhower realized, however, that any military confrontation might quickly escalate into the use of nuclear weapons. And Adenauer, who knew that Germany would be no-man's-land in any nuclear escalation between the great powers, responded by exclaiming, "For God's sake, not for Berlin." Eisenhower knew it would be difficult to ask the American people to go to war over a city that had been the capital of their hated enemy little more than a decade before. But there was a commitment, which Khrushchev recognized: "Berlin is the testicles of the West. . . . Every time I want to make the West scream, I squeeze on Berlin."

Khrushchev decided not to push his ultimatum. The West had responded to his threats with a flurry of diplomatic activity, and with speeches guaranteeing that West Berlin would not be abandoned. A four-power foreign ministers conference was called for the summer of 1959 in Geneva. By this time Khrushchev had decided to avoid confrontation, and the meetings brought no agreement. The six-month deadline passed quietly into history.

In September 1959 Khrushchev, at Eisenhower's invitation, became the first Soviet leader ever to visit the United States. He arrived in New York in the largest aircraft in the world, the Soviet Tu-114 airliner, a reminder of Soviet technological superiority. Barely three years earlier the American press had accused the Soviet leaders of committing "monstrous crimes" and "the foulest treachery" against the Hungarian people. But now Khrushchev attracted crowds wherever he went, some of them a bit frosty. In Hollywood the stars turned out to meet him. He made several television appearances. In Iowa

Khrushchev was surprised and impressed by the American standard of living when he visited the United States in 1959. ABOVE: *In Iowa, enjoying his first hot dog.* ABOVE RIGHT: *Khrushchev and his wife with Eisenhower in Washington.*

he was astonished to see the prosperity of a simple farming community. Thousands watched the Communist leader pass by in his motorcade. Khrushchev loved every minute of it.

The success of his high-profile trip made peaceful co-existence appear a real possibility. At the end of the visit, Khrushchev and Eisenhower had a few days together at Camp David, the presidential retreat in Maryland. There the leaders of the two superpowers talked frankly with each other. "There was nothing more inadvisable in this situation," said Eisenhower, "than to talk about ultimatums, since both sides knew very well what would happen if an ultimatum were to be implemented." Khrushchev responded that he did not understand how a peace treaty could be regarded by the American people as a "threat to peace." Eisenhower admitted that the situation in Berlin was "abnormal" and that "human affairs got very badly tangled at times." Khrushchev came away with the impression that a deal was possible over Berlin, and they agreed to continue the dialogue at a summit in Paris in the spring of 1960. Khrushchev felt that he got respect and recognition from Eisenhower, who made him believe he was the greatest Soviet statesman since Stalin. In Moscow propagandists applauded Khrushchev's personal diplomacy as the dynamic basis of Soviet foreign policy.

In October 1959 Khrushchev went to Beijing, to take part in the tenth-anniversary celebrations of the People's Republic of China. Mao Zedong and

Berlin is the testicles of the West. . . . Every time I want to make the West scream, I squeeze on Berlin.

— Nikita Khrushchev,
November 1958

the Chinese leadership were deeply insulted that Khrushchev came to China following a visit to the United States and not the other way around. Khrushchev, still glowing with the aura of his US tour, was beginning to believe he was infallible. However, since his denunciation of Stalin in 1956, the Chinese had grown cold to his leadership of the Communist world. As long as Stalin was alive Mao had deferred to Soviet leadership, but he had little time for Khrushchev. Mao thought his Marxism-Leninism was going soft and he was far too close to the Western imperialists. Now the Chinese leadership stormily accused Khrushchev of putting his relationship with the United States above his commitment to the Sino-Soviet alliance. After one particularly intense session of disagreement, Khrushchev shouted at foreign minister Chen Yi, "Don't give me your hand, because I won't shake it!" The minister riposted that Khrushchev's anger did not scare him. "Don't you try to spit on us," Khrushchev countered. "You haven't got enough spit." Khrushchev left Beijing furious. He had received more respect from Eisenhower, the leader of his enemies, than from his supposed comrades. But Chinese pressure on Khrushchev to display his credentials as leader of the worldwide socialist cause, and to take a hard-line stand, was an important influence on the behaviour of the Soviet premier throughout the years of crisis over Berlin.

The Paris summit that was to have resolved the Berlin question disintegrated before it began in the fallout from Gary Powers's failed U-2 spy flight. Khrushchev, ears still stinging from China's criticisms, now destroyed bridges he had built with the United States. Soviet-US relations once more took a turn for the worse.

Those most disappointed by Khrushchev's climbdown were the East Germans. Detailed preparations for a re-unification of Berlin now had to be put on hold. And the flood of citizens westward continued unabated; 144,000 in 1959, nearly 200,000 in 1960. The East German economy was being bled to death. Ulbricht again pressed Khrushchev to demand recognition for the GDR, and a peace treaty. The Soviet leader played for time; Ulbricht would set the pace in the next phase.

Kennedy Enters the Picture

Khrushchev followed the American presidential election campaign of 1960 closely. Having fallen out with Eisenhower, he backed the Democrats and was delighted when John Fitzgerald Kennedy was elected. Khrushchev seemed to believe that he would get along well with Kennedy; he dropped several hints that this presidency could usher in a new era in superpower relations. The two leaders agreed on an early summit in Vienna, only four months after Kennedy took office. A few weeks beforehand, Yuri Gagarin became the first man in space, and just days after that, the CIA-backed invasion of Cuba at the Bay of Pigs proved a fiasco, leaving Kennedy badly bruised. By this time, Khrushchev had come to think of Kennedy's youth and inexperience as serious weaknesses. He decided to take the initiative and, under pressure from Ulbricht, once more to squeeze on Berlin.

The two leaders met at the beginning of June. There was no clear agenda. On the first day they spoke about the world in general and about issues of war,

China's Mao Zedong escorts his guest, Nikita Khrushchev, to the airport at the end of a tense visit in October 1959. The Chinese resented Khrushchev's overtures to the West, and did not hesitate to tell him so.

peace, and revolution, failing to connect on almost any level. A Russian historian has written that Khrushchev had then "the complete confidence of a man riding on the crest of history." Kennedy was astonished at how strongly the Soviet leader came at him. At the end of the first day, aides of Khrushchev asked his opinion of Kennedy as a statesman. Khrushchev waved his hand dismissively, saying that Kennedy was no match for Eisenhower.

On the second day, the two men got around to the subject of Berlin. Khrushchev demanded a peace treaty and recognition for East Germany. Berlin was to become "strictly neutral"; the Western powers could have access

BELOW LEFT: *President John F. Kennedy with Khrushchev at the Vienna summit, where the Soviet leader gave him a hard time.* BELOW: *In London, on his way home, Kennedy told British prime minister Harold Macmillan that he feared losing the Cold War.*

to the city only with East German permission. Any violation of East German territory would be regarded as an act of aggression against the Soviet Union. The United States would have to withdraw by the end of the year. Kennedy was amazed. He said that the Western powers were in Berlin not on sufferance but as of right, having defeated Germany in the Second World War. He declared that the national security of the United States was directly linked to that of Berlin. Khrushchev exploded. "I want peace, but if you want war that is your problem," he shouted, banging his fist on the table. The meeting ended, ominously, with Khrushchev threatening Kennedy with the calamitous consequences of war. He announced that his decision to sign a peace treaty with East Germany in six months was irrevocable. Kennedy responded gloomily, "If that's true, it's going to be a cold winter." Neither man smiled as they shook hands for the official photographs. The two leaders never met again.

Kennedy was badly shaken by the encounter. He had been warned that Khrushchev was likely to talk tough but not that he would demand American surrender. He could scarcely believe that before even settling in at the White House he was faced with the prospect of a nuclear war. A newsman who saw him just as he left the summit said he looked "shaken and angry." Kennedy stopped in London on the way home, and Prime Minister Macmillan observed that he "seemed rather stunned — baffled would perhaps be fairer." The two men discussed the possibility of defeat in the Cold War. On his return to

Two leaders get each other's measure, according to Joseph Parish in the Chicago Tribune.

Washington, Kennedy ordered senior staff at the National Security Council, the State Department, the Pentagon, and the CIA to immerse themselves in the Berlin question and to come up with options for American policy — urgently.

As the summer wore on, the heat increased. Khrushchev announced a substantial increase in his military budget, and a resumption of nuclear testing. At a press conference in Berlin, Ulbricht talked tough, but he commented that "no one intends to build a wall." Even broaching the idea provoked a flood of more than a thousand East Germans a day to cross the border, putting further pressure on Khrushchev for a resolution.

Government opinion in the United States was divided; hard-liners argued that caving in over Berlin would be to lose the Cold War; soft-liners wanted to avoid overreacting and urged further dialogue with Moscow. As refugees still arrived in vast numbers at the West Berlin reception centres, Kennedy retired for the weekend of 22–23 July to Hyannis Port on the Massachusetts coast. There, in the family beach house, he studied all the latest position papers and reviewed the options. It was time to make his position clear, and he worked hard on a speech to be delivered on nationwide television the night of 25 July.

Kennedy reiterated that the United States was not looking for a fight and that he recognized the "Soviet Union's historical concerns about their security in central and eastern Europe." He said he was willing to renew talks. But he announced that he would ask Congress for an additional $3.25 billion for military spending, mostly on conventional weapons. He wanted six new divisions for the army and two for the marines, and he announced plans to triple the draft and to call up the reserves. Kennedy proclaimed, "We seek peace, but we shall not surrender."

The response to his speech was, in the main, positive. Army recruiting stations reported a dramatic increase in enlistments. But the president's warning that a stronger civil defence programme was needed to minimize losses in the event of nuclear attack provoked immense anxiety. Local civil defence offices were besieged with enquiries about air-raid shelters, and the sale of prefabricated home shelters boomed. Major municipalities carried out surveys of public buildings to find suitable fallout shelters. They began to test air-raid sirens regularly.

Vacationing in the Black Sea resort of Sochi, Khrushchev was furious when he heard of Kennedy's speech. He invited John Jay McCloy, Kennedy's disarmament adviser, who happened to be in the Soviet Union, to join him. He shouted at McCloy that Kennedy's military buildup was tantamount to a declaration of war against the Soviet Union. If the Americans wanted war, Khrushchev bellowed, they could have it. But if there was a nuclear war over Berlin, Kennedy would be America's last president. In Berlin, the flood of refugees became a torrent.

An Old Plan Implemented

When Khrushchev's fury abated he realized he would have to climb down once again. Intelligence reports indicated that Kennedy's threats to use his nuclear arsenal were no bluff. He had warned Kennedy, "Only a madman would start a war over Berlin," and now this applied to himself. But there was

I have heard it said that West Berlin is militarily untenable. . . . Any spot is tenable if men — brave men — will make it so. . . . We cannot and will not permit the Communists to drive us out of Berlin. . . . The endangered frontier of freedom runs through divided Berlin.

— John F. Kennedy, 25 July 1961

The City of Berlin officially certifies that Erich Honecker is a victim of fascism, not a collaborator, and clears him to be politically active in the de-Nazified city.

still the problem of East Germany's population drain. Plans to build a wall to surround West Berlin and stop the exodus had been made many years earlier. No one in the Kremlin liked the idea of fencing off West Berlin; it reflected badly on the Communist way of life. Nevertheless, Ulbricht was called to Moscow. At a secret meeting of Warsaw Pact leaders he was told to go ahead and prepare to close the border with a wall. He appointed Erich Honecker, a loyal party man, to head the team that would do it.

Meanwhile, signals were coming from Washington that the United States would not interfere with their closing borders to stem the refugee outflow, so

ABOVE: *Caught on the wrong side as barriers divide Berlin on 14 August 1961, an East German resident tries to get back home.* ABOVE RIGHT: *Workmen move in to build a more permanent wall, replacing barbed wire with concrete blocks.*

long as West Berlin was left intact. The president in his television speech had spoken only about defending *West* Berlin, not the whole city. Kennedy told his aide Walt Rostow, "I can hold the [Western] alliance together to defend West Berlin, but I cannot act to keep East Berlin open."

In the early hours of Sunday, 13 August 1961, Berliners were awakened by the clatter and clanking of military vehicles and the noise of barbed-wire coils and concrete posts being unloaded in the streets. Late-night revellers unexpectedly found the S-Bahn railway system closed, for trains were no longer crossing the border. On Bernauer Strasse, where the border between the French and Soviet sectors ran down the middle of the road, a line of army trucks gathered on the eastern side of the street, their headlights blazing, as workmen started to erect barbed-wire barricades. At Potsdamer Platz, the busiest of all the East-West crossing points, men with pneumatic drills began to pierce cobblestone streets and set in place concrete pillars.

The light of dawn revealed that East German workers, under armed guard, were slowly erecting a barbed-wire fence that zigzagged its way through the city, strictly following the borders of the American, British, and French military sectors. The fence ran down the middle of streets, it even bisected cemeteries. As the first East Berliners turned up, as usual, to go to their work in West Berlin, they were turned back. "*Die Grenze ist geschlossen,*" they were told; "The border is closed." Bewildered, they were dispersed by the police. As the morn-

Berlin, 1961

Coils of barbed wire block access to the Brandenburg Gate, August 1961. The sign, "Attention — You Are Now Leaving West Berlin," seems no longer to apply.

ing wore on, groups of West Berliners began to gather, to watch and jeer. West Berlin mayor Willy Brandt was concerned that the situation might get out of hand. The East German government also feared public protests, like those that nearly had brought down the regime in 1953. Construction of the barrier was carried out entirely by East German public works gangs, supervised by militias mobilized from all parts of the state. A few miles back, ringing the city, Soviet tanks openly took up positions — and waited. Their presence sent a message to the West not to intervene and to the East Germans not to attempt a protest. The streets of East Berlin remained eerily empty.

The moment picked to divide the city could not have been better chosen. By the time it was clear what was going on, it was still the middle of the night in Washington. As reports poured in, the three Allied military commanders in West Berlin quickly met, but they realized that nothing could be done until their political masters decided what response to make. The American commander had it drilled into him that he must take no action that might spark trouble. He and the British commander felt they ought to issue a protest to their Russian counterpart in East Berlin, but the French commander would not support even this without instructions from Paris. However, the French were in the middle of their traditional August vacation, and the foreign ministry on the Quai d'Orsay was virtually empty. It might take days to get a response.

At the State Department in Washington, officials were called out of their beds early on Sunday morning, but a decision was made not to react. The president was not even officially informed until midmorning, late afternoon Berlin time. By this point the barbed-wire fence had been largely built. Kennedy regarded the barrier as despicable, but what angered him more was

The cover of the Frankfurter Illustrierte, *23 July 1961, expresses the concern of West Germans and their chancellor as they look to West Berlin. Would it remain a free city?*

Crossing the Wall

Throughout the summer of 1961 Berlin witnessed extraordinary scenes as the Wall was completed. The dividing line ran alongside and even through several old tenement buildings, sometimes with doorways in the East and back windows looking out onto the West. As other crossing points were closed, people in despair resorted to these tenement windows as a route to escape. One fifty-nine-year-old woman threw a mattress out of her window and leapt after it. She died of her injuries. When anyone appeared ready to jump, the West Berlin fire department sent firemen with blankets to catch them. In full view of news cameras, a surreal

tug-of-war took place over one lady; the East German police tried to drag her back through the window of her border tenement, while West Berlin firemen tried to pull her safely to the street below. To cheers, she eventually reached the Western sector. Slowly, all of the tenement windows on the border were bricked up. Whole areas, up to a hundred yards behind the Wall, were levelled. A nightmarish world of searchlights, desolate watchtowers, machine-gun posts, and minefields came into being. Soon the first East German was shot dead trying to escape. There would be dozens more.

that no one had anticipated this outcome. "Why didn't we know?" he asked McGeorge Bundy, his national security adviser. Closing the borders violated four-power agreements over Berlin, but once it became clear to Washington that neither the East Germans nor the Soviets were going to move against West Berlin itself, there was a collective sigh of relief. Kennedy and his secretary of state, Dean Rusk, agreed that so long as the access routes to West Berlin were left open and the city was still free, whatever might occur in East Berlin was no cause for war. It was decided to protest "through appropriate channels" to Moscow and to do nothing more.

Fencing West Berlin's 103-mile perimeter with barbed wire took most of Sunday. During that time many East Germans decided "now or never" and made a last-minute dash to the West. Some swam across the Teltow Canal, which made up part of the border, and arrived dripping in the West with nothing but their underwear. A Volkswagen crashed through the barbed wire before it reached too high. Even a few policemen leapt to freedom as the barbed-wire barricade was being built. Dividing the city separated families in a brutal way. Some who had gone to relatives in East Berlin for the weekend now found they could not return to the West. Others could only gather along the wire barrier and wave to relatives on the opposite side.

Three days after the barbed wire went up, additional East German workers arrived and began constructing a more permanent concrete structure. Set a few yards back from the wire fence, this was the real Berlin Wall. Five to six feet high, topped with barbed wire, and eventually buttressed by gun positions and tank traps, the Berlin Wall became an obstruction almost impossible to cross. It tore the city down the middle.

BELOW LEFT AND RIGHT: *East Berliners escape to the West by climbing out windows lining the border. All of these were soon bricked up.* BELOW: *An East German policeman removes the body of Peter Fechter, shot while trying to escape across the Wall. He had lain there for hours, bleeding to death.*

The West Let Off the Hook

For a week Kennedy made no public comment. Willy Brandt was furious at the American failure to react. At a huge public rally he appealed to the West, proclaiming, "Berlin expects more than words. Berlin expects political action!" Brandt wrote directly to Kennedy, saying that the Wall "has not altered the will to resist of the population of West Berlin, but it has succeeded in casting doubt upon the capability and determination of the Three Powers to react."

Some American newspapers responded that no "mere mayor" could dictate US policy. But in any case, as it became clear that there would be no Communist threat against West Berlin itself, and no action against the access routes to the city, the Western powers felt they had been let off the hook. The leakage of the East German population had been sealed off by a crude and bizarre structure, but war had been avoided.

Kennedy sent General Lucius Clay, the bullish commander of the American sector during the 1948 airlift, and Vice President Lyndon B. Johnson to visit Berlin. They were rapturously received by the West Berliners. In front of a giant crowd outside the town hall, Johnson affirmed America's pledge "to the freedom of West Berlin and to the rights of Western access." At the same time, an American combat unit of 1,500 well-armed soldiers was sent up the East German autobahn from West Germany to reinforce the Allied garrison in West Berlin. The Soviets stopped and counted them but then let them pass. On arriving, they paraded down the main street of West Berlin, the Kurfürsten Damm, amidst cheering, weeping crowds. The unit's commander said it was the most fabulous reception he had experienced since the liberation of Paris in 1944. West Berliners now felt assured they would not be abandoned.

Berliners thought the West was slow to react to the Wall.
ABOVE: *Mayor Willy Brandt bolstered the spirits of West Berliners on 17 August 1961 and demanded action.*
OPPOSITE: *Kennedy sent his vice president, Lyndon Johnson (centre), to show solidarity with the city.*

Most of the old crossing points were closed. The East Germans allowed the use of only seven. Although West Berliners were not denied continued access to East Berlin, they needed special permits. And only one crossing point would permit other Westerners to cross into the East. This gateway would enter Cold War mythology as the place where East met West: Checkpoint Charlie, the exchange point for spies.

Rusk and Soviet foreign minister Andrei Gromyko continued to talk, into the fall, about finding a political solution to the Berlin stalemate. Khrushchev even invited Kennedy to Moscow. The president declined the invitation but agreed to set up a confidential back channel through which personal views could be exchanged. Kennedy decided to ask General Clay to return to West Berlin as his special representative, but McGeorge Bundy warned him that "Clay will be a burden to you if he takes a line more belligerent than yours." Kennedy insisted that his appointment would reassure Berliners. Clay, on the other hand, believed he was being sent to Berlin to take on the Soviets. As soon as he arrived he ordered the building of a concrete wall at a military training school, so his soldiers could practice knocking it down.

Lucius Clay

Towards the end of October a senior American diplomat and his wife were denied access to East Berlin to attend the theatre, because they refused to show the East German border guards their passports. The four-party agree-

French Sector

Tegel

Reichstag Building

Brandenburg Gate

West Berlin

British Sector

Checkpoint Charlie

Gatow

Tempelhof

East Berlin

US Sector

Schönefeld

—— Berlin Wall (28.5 miles long)
×–×–× "Country" Wall (75 miles long)

Berlin Wall

ments that governed the city guaranteed free movement of Allied and Soviet personnel without passport formalities, so Clay sent a squad of armed US soldiers to force the issue and accompany the diplomat in his car into East Berlin. Over the next few days, American jeeps started to convoy US civilians on pointless excursions into East Berlin, each jeep full of battle-ready soldiers ostentatiously flaunting rifles. Ten American M-48 tanks were pulled up near Checkpoint Charlie.

On the morning of 27 October, thirty-three Soviet tanks rolled into East Berlin and halted at the Brandenburg Gate, the first Soviet armour in the city since the uprising of 1953. Ten tanks drove on to Checkpoint Charlie and lined up facing the American armour barely a hundred yards away. For the first time in the Cold War, American and Russian tanks directly faced each other across a tense border. The American gunners loaded their cannons and awaited orders. An alarmed Kennedy spoke with Clay from the White House but assured him of his full support. As the hours passed the situation grew even more tense. The US garrison in West Berlin was on full alert, then NATO was put on alert, then Strategic Air Command. The Soviet military commander had a direct line to the Kremlin. Khrushchev told him that should the Americans use force, he must respond with force. Commanders on both sides were worried that, in all the tension, some nervous soldier would fire his weapon and trigger a shoot-out. A petty dispute over showing passports at a border crossing threatened to escalate into a global conflict.

Both sides realized that the situation had got out of hand. Through the back channel just set up, Kennedy sent a message directly to Khrushchev asking that the Russians withdraw and assuring him that the Americans would do the same.

At Checkpoint Charlie, after a sixteen-hour standoff, the first Soviet tank started up its engine and withdrew five yards. The tension was broken. A few minutes later, an American tank pulled back the same distance. One by one the tanks withdrew. There was another sigh of relief. Clay, however, was done for. General Bruce Clarke, commander of US forces in West Germany, demanded, "What in the hell did Clay think he was doing? You don't spit in the face of a bulldog." NATO's commander was furious that an unplanned dispute had threatened to engulf his forces in a conflict that could not be won. Clay remained in Berlin a few months longer and then was called home. And, without publicity, Washington ordered civilian officials not to visit East Berlin for the time being.

Both sides had decided that the dispute over Berlin was an issue of principle at the heart of their Cold War stance. This threatened the world with nuclear holocaust. Neither side had wanted the Wall, but building it was a way of avoiding direct military conflict. Kennedy said, "It's not a very nice solution, but a wall is a hell of a lot better than a war." Khrushchev too defused the situation; his threat to sign a peace treaty with East Germany was quietly forgotten. He told Ulbricht, the disappointed East German leader, "Steps which would exacerbate the situation, especially in Berlin, should be avoided." The world was left with a concrete symbol of the cruel divisions of the Cold War.

Soviet and American tanks confront each other, only gun barrels apart, at the Friedrichstrasse crossing point (Checkpoint Charlie). This was one of the tensest moments of the Cold War, but in the end both sides backed off.

> *Instructions were given to our tank commander that he was to roll up and confront the Soviet tank, which was at the identical distance across from Checkpoint Charlie. The tension escalated very rapidly for the one reason that this was Americans confronting Russians. It wasn't East Germans. There was live ammunition in both tanks of the Russians and the Americans. It was an unexpected, sudden confrontation that in my opinion was the closest that the Russians and the Allies came to going to war in the entire Cold War period.*
>
> — Col. Jim Atwood,
> US military mission, Berlin

In June 1963, at the end of a trip to West Germany, President Kennedy made a visit to West Berlin. He looked at the Wall, and over it into East Berlin, and then addressed a crowd of a quarter of a million Berliners from the balcony of the town hall, which overlooked the square that later would bear his name.

"There are many people in the world who really don't understand, or say they don't, what is the great issue between the free world and the Communist world. Let them come to Berlin. There are some who say that communism is the wave of the future. Let them come to Berlin. And there are some who say in Europe and elsewhere we can work with the Communists. Let them come to Berlin. And there are even a few who say that it is true that communism is an evil system but it permits us to make economic progress. *Lasst sie nach Berlin kommen.* Let them come to Berlin. . . . Freedom is indivisible, and when one man is enslaved, all are not free. When all are free, and we look forward to that day, when this city will be joined as one, and this country, and this great continent of Europe in a peaceful and hopeful globe, when that day finally comes, as it will, the people of West Berlin can take sober satisfaction in the fact that they were in the front lines for almost two decades. All free men, wherever they may live, are citizens of Berlin, and therefore as a free man, I take pride in the words *Ich bin ein Berliner.*" All cheered. Some smiled. *Ein Berliner* is what they called a popular local doughnut.

26 June 1963. John F. Kennedy, on a state visit, addresses hundreds of thousands of cheering West Berliners. "I am one of you," he tells them. "Ich bin ein Berliner."

Fidel Castro enters Havana
in triumph on 8 January.
The Cuban revolution, begun
with a handful of guerrillas
two years earlier, was seen by
the US government as a
threat to its security. Cuba
still stands as the only
Communist outpost in the
Americas.

Back Yard: Guatemala and Cuba

1954–1962

A Case for the Monroe Doctrine

On the evening of 16 December 1953, the newly appointed US ambassador to Guatemala sat down to dinner with President Jacobo Arbenz Guzmán. For six hours the ambassador grilled his host, questioning him about left-wing influences on his two-and-a-half-year-old government, its pro-Soviet slant, and the role of the Guatemalan Communist Party in agrarian reform. President Arbenz came up with what the ambassador regarded as lame responses. Although Arbenz was not himself a Communist, his government had been elected through the support of several left-wing parties. In a popular programme of land reform, it had nationalized 400,000 acres of uncultivated private land, much of it belonging to the largest American enterprise in Central America, the United Fruit Company, whose banana plantations were at the core of the Guatemalan economy. This unused land had been redistributed to rural peasants. After the dinner the ambassador wrote a report for Secretary of State John Foster Dulles: "If the President is not a Communist, he will do until one comes along." Arbenz had to go. The United States could not tolerate a foothold for communism in the western hemisphere.

Five months later, on 15 May 1954, a Polish ship docked in Guatemala with two thousand tons of small arms and ammunition made in Czechoslovakia. It was the first time a Latin American state had bought arms from the Eastern bloc, and the Eisenhower administration saw this transaction as the last straw. Since the days of President James Monroe, America had regarded the Caribbean as its own back yard, a source of trade and wealth, its own security zone. Of late, the Arbenz government had interfered in labour disputes between the United Fruit Company and its workers, and the company had great influence in Washington. John Foster Dulles had been a senior partner

Jacobo Arbenz, president of Guatemala, shown with his wife, confiscated land belonging to the powerful United Fruit Company and redistributed it to peasants. Months later, CIA-trained rebels invaded his country and deposed him.

in a law firm associated with the company for many years. His brother, Allen Dulles, head of the CIA, had been on its board of trustees. President Eisenhower's personal secretary was married to United Fruit Company's head of public relations. With little prodding, Eisenhower and the Dulles brothers approved a secret plan to depose Arbenz, now nicknamed Red Jacobo. But under the charter of the Organization of American States, no member could interfere in the internal politics of another. While publicly espousing this doctrine, Washington authorized the CIA to train and supply a band of Guatemalan political exiles on United Fruit property in neighbouring Honduras. The rebels were to be led by an ardent anti-Communist exile, Colonel Carlos Castillo Armas.

Carlos Castillo Armas

In June 1954 a few hundred of these rebels crossed into Guatemala. Initially they made little headway. But Arbenz had relied naively on his army's loyalty. Subjected to a campaign of radio propaganda inspired by the CIA, the officer corps defected to the rebels. Arbenz went into exile. Before long Castillo Armas led a new junta in Guatemala and was installed as president. He reversed the reforms of previous years, evicting 500,000 "squatters" from the land Arbenz's government had given them, and he executed hundreds of left-wing sympathizers, labour leaders, and co-operative farmers, unleashing an orgy of killing that would plague the small nation for decades. Castillo Armas ruled Guatemala through control of a purged army, but in 1957 he was himself murdered in a mystery that has never been solved. At the time of the Arbenz coup, the CIA was euphoric over its success. The Eisenhower administration complacently assumed that in the Caribbean and in Latin America, Pax Americana would prevail without further challenge.

Trouble Closer to Home

In 1898 the United States had been victorious in a ten-week war against Spain to liberate Cuba from Old World colonial oppression — and to protect considerable American investment there. In the following decades US businessmen bought up most of the land and industry in an independent Cuba, which, unlike Puerto Rico, could not be annexed because of an amendment attached to the declaration of war against Spain. In 1933 Fulgencio Batista y Zaldívar came to power and ruled through puppets or directly for twenty-five years. By the 1950s, however, his corrupt and dictatorial regime was losing support among many Cubans. On 26 July 1953 Fidel Castro, a young lawyer, first raised the standard of revolution against Batista, but he was arrested and imprisoned. Castro was later released and went into exile in Mexico, from where he returned to Cuba to lead a two-year guerrilla struggle. Slowly Castro and his band of rebels, which included the charismatic Argentinian Ernesto "Che" Guevara, gained popular support, as Batista's reign of terror further alienated his power base.

On 8 January 1959, a week after Batista fled the country, Castro led his armed revolutionaries into Havana, where he formed a new coalition government, which was more Cuban nationalist than revolutionary socialist. Although land reforms excited popular support, there was initially no pro-

TOP: *Ernesto "Che" Guevara, as Cuba's economic minister, delivers a speech in Uruguay in 1961. Later, the Argentina-born Che set off to stir up revolution throughout South America.* BOTTOM: *At the UN General Assembly in 1960, the old Communist Khrushchev embraces Castro, the Red hope for the future.*

gramme to nationalize American interests or take control of the all-important sugar industry. At this point Castro had not declared his allegiance to Marxism-Leninism. Consequently the Soviet Union was cautious in approaching Cuba. It was not until February 1960 that Deputy Premier Anastas Mikoyan visited Havana and signed a trade agreement. Castro then nationalized a billion dollars' worth of American investments in Cuba. Eisenhower in reprisal announced an economic blockade and stopped buying Cuban sugar, the country's principal export. However, the Soviet Union quickly agreed to buy the sugar. When the United States announced that it would not sell petroleum products to Cuba, again the Soviet Union agreed to meet the island's needs, despite the severe strain on Soviet shipping. Cuba moved closer to the socialist camp. When Nikita Khrushchev met Castro at the United Nations in September 1960, he embraced him as a fellow revolutionary.

Fulgencio Batista

To the United States a revolutionary, left-leaning government so near its coast was an unbearable affront. On 17 March 1960 Eisenhower approved another CIA programme of covert action; a Cuban paramilitary force would be trained in the jungles of Guatemala by the United States to lead a resistance movement. In December, Eisenhower also endorsed a plan for an amphibious landing by US-trained Cuban guerrillas, which, the CIA was confident, would provoke an island-wide uprising against Castro. Allen Dulles,

Americans had once flocked to Havana for a good time. The Cuban revolution and the US economic boycott ended all that.

Fidel and Che: New World Revolutionaries

FIDEL CASTRO RUZ was born in Mayarí, Cuba, in 1926. The son of middle-class parents, he was schooled by Jesuits and received a law degree from the University of Havana in 1950. In 1953 he was jailed following the failure of a coup, the July 26th uprising, against dictator Fulgencio Batista. Amnestied and then exiled, he lived in Mexico and the United States before returning in 1956 to launch a guerrilla campaign against Batista from the Sierra Maestra region of Oriente Province. In 1959 he succeeded in ousting Batista, became premier, and immediately set out to reform Cuba.

Nationalizing oil companies and sugar producers, as well as cracking down on mobsters, made him a hero in Cuba, but the seizure of American companies aroused the unremitting enmity of the United States.

Because his policies drove many middle-class Cubans into exile, the American government assumed that Castro was deeply unpopular; it encouraged and financially supported a growing band of Cuban exiles determined to overthrow him. Their attempt failed, and the disaster at the Bay of Pigs in 1961 only made Castro more powerful. He turned increasingly to the USSR for assistance and announced that Cuba was a socialist state and that he was a Marxist-Leninist. His hostility to what he saw as Yankee imperialism was implacable, and he welcomed the Soviet missiles that led to the crisis with the United States in the autumn of 1962.

ERNESTO GUEVARA DE LA SERNA, known as Che, was born near Buenos Aires in 1928. He was trained as a physician and even practised medicine briefly in Mexico City. But his first love was revolution, particularly against the United States. He was an early friend of Castro's and fought beside him in the Sierra Maestra. His nickname came from his way of addressing his buddies as "Che" — "friend" in Argentina. For a time he was president of the Cuban national bank, and his still popular portrait as a revolutionary dates from then. In 1965 he left his adopted island to begin the travels that were to take him to Bolivia, where he was killed in 1967.

the CIA director, saw a chance to repeat the kind of successful coup his agency had carried out against Arbenz.

On 19 January 1961, the day before his inauguration, the new president, John F. Kennedy, was briefed by Eisenhower on a number of topics, including the US plan to help the anti-Castro guerrillas. Kennedy was surprised by its scale but was not averse. The young president refused to let the US military intervene directly, but he continued to allow the CIA to organize Cuban exiles for an invasion. Kennedy insisted, however, that any American involvement must be concealed. In April, three days before the scheduled invasion,

RIGHT: *Before the Bay of Pigs invasion, Cuban soldiers mount anti-aircraft batteries outside Havana. Kennedy authorized the attack by Cuban exiles, but held back on promised air cover, perhaps because a CIA plan to murder Castro had failed.* BELOW: *Happy Cubans celebrate the capture of a landing craft, and victory.*

Kennedy stated at a press conference that there would not be, "under any conditions, an intervention in Cuba by United States armed forces." Privately Kennedy told his aides, "The minute I land one marine, we're in this thing up to our necks. . . . I'm not going to risk an American Hungary."

Despite the CIA's continued confidence, there were problems with the invasion plan. The morale of the Cuban exiles training in Guatemala was low; their numbers were small. And the CIA assumption that, if things did go wrong, the United States would support a failing mission by direct military involvement ran counter to Kennedy's public position. The Joint Chiefs of Staff rated the operation's chance of success as "fair" — less than fifty-fifty.

A Fiasco

From the beginning everything did go wrong. Only six American bombers, painted in Cuban colours, as if flown by rebel Cubans, took off from Nicaragua in support of the amphibious invasion, which counted on air cover for success. They damaged only three of Castro's planes on the ground. Fearful of having his role detected, Kennedy at the last minute had withdrawn US air support. Despite this, a force of about 1,500 Cuban exiles went ahead with the invasion at the Bay of Pigs. Castro sent his Soviet-made tanks against these invaders, who never won more than a beachhead half a mile wide and a quarter of a mile deep. Contrary to CIA expectations, the attack provoked no popular uprising against Castro. Kennedy called a crisis meeting and considered sending unmarked US jets to destroy the Cuban air force. The meeting broke up at 3:00 AM, after everyone recognized that the situation was hopeless. At the end of three days' fighting, the survivors surrendered. More than one hundred men were dead. Only fourteen were rescued by the US Navy.

Kennedy was distraught over the Bay of Pigs fiasco. He fully recognized that his determination to minimize political risk had fundamentally weakened prospects for a military success. And the CIA had vastly overestimated the support of the Cuban people for a military invasion to "liberate" them.

In Pravda (ABOVE)*, ravens croak for war, as Eisenhower, Nixon, and Truman urge Kennedy on against Cuba. After the invasion fiasco, Kennedy asked, "How could I have been so stupid?" But, in Miami in December 1962 (*ABOVE RIGHT*), he honoured the returned Bay of Pigs brigade.*

Kennedy took as his lesson from the Bay of Pigs that he must be considerably more critical of counsel from eager advisers. The fiasco, however, did not cause a change of mind about Cuba. He was even more determined that Castro represented a threat to the United States and must be removed.

Kennedy was now also convinced that in the battle for the hearts and minds of the developing world the Soviets were winning. When he met Khrushchev at the Vienna summit in June and admitted that the Bay of Pigs had been a mistake, the Soviet leader turned the knife in the wound by insisting that wars of national liberation would now be won by Communists, that the United States was on the wrong side of history. All this added to Kennedy's gloom; maybe the West *was* losing the Cold War.

In Cuba, the Bay of Pigs invasion helped unify the people behind the regime. Castro chose this moment to proclaim that his cause was that of socialist revolution. Communism was the only possible response to Yankee imperialism. The developing relationship with Moscow was the way forward.

Following the Vienna summit the Berlin crisis preoccupied Washington, Moscow, and their separate allies for several months. But in the United States, the open wound of Cuba did not heal. A presidential directive in November 1961 created a top secret covert-action programme against Cuba called Operation Mongoose, which had as part of its objective the overthrow of Castro. A variety of schemes were considered, including several plots to assassinate him. In March 1962 the Joint Chiefs began contingency planning for an invasion of Cuba, and for an economic blockade. Later that spring 40,000 US Marines practised an amphibious landing on another Caribbean island.

Khrushchev, paradoxically, like Kennedy, was concerned about the weakness of his own position. He worried about the humiliation for the USSR if Cuba were lost, certain that Washington would sooner or later invade again. In his memoirs Khrushchev tells how he became obsessed with the "terrible blow" that would "gravely diminish our stature throughout the world, and especially within Latin America," if Cuba fell. Khrushchev also felt the Soviet Union's military weakness. By 1962 a million US soldiers were stationed in more than two hundred foreign bases, all threatening the Soviet Union, from Greenland to Turkey, from Portugal to the Philippines. There were listening posts and USAF facilities in Iran and Pakistan, and an electronic monitoring station in Ethiopia. Three and a half million troops belonging to America's allies were garrisoned around the Soviet Union's borders. There were American nuclear warheads in Italy, the United Kingdom, and Turkey. Khrushchev felt surrounded. Despite his rhetoric about building missiles "like sausages," he knew that the missile balance was stacked against him, and that his long-range missiles were limited in their capability.

Khrushchev's Bold Idea

In May 1962 Khrushchev visited Bulgaria. Walking on the beach at Varna, the Soviet leader was acutely aware that on the opposite shore of the Black Sea, in Turkey, there were American military bases with nuclear warheads capable of wiping out Kiev, Minsk, and Moscow in a matter of minutes. It was about then that an idea formed in Khrushchev's mind of placing missiles in a base close to the United States. "Why not throw a hedgehog at Uncle Sam's pants?" Khrushchev asked.

Cuba provided the perfect site. Installing Soviet missiles in Cuba would have the double benefit of protecting the island from attack and of equalizing the balance of power in nuclear weapons. It was a bold plan. The Soviet Union had never before sited ballistic missiles outside its borders. Khrushchev talked with colleagues and then the Presidium in Moscow about implementing the idea, reasoning that it would be best to import the missiles in secret. By the time the Americans spotted them it would be too late. Even if they were able to take out some of the installations, at least a few missiles could still be fired. Washington would realize this and would not try to destroy the missiles once they were operational. Khrushchev's plan to place short- and medium-range missiles in America's back yard would, overnight, create a parity with America's long-range weapons — one of fear. The American rockets in Turkey "are aimed at us and scare us," said Khrushchev. "Our missiles will also be aimed at the United States, even if we don't have as many of them. But . . . they will be even more afraid."

Would Castro agree to the siting of Soviet missiles in Cuba? At first he was unhappy that his nation should be turned into a Soviet missile base. But, believing that the missiles would alter the worldwide strategic balance in favour of the socialist camp, Castro agreed to accept them. His brother, Raul,

> *If we and the president can agree, there will be great opportunities for cooperation in science, technology, and outer space. We will give him a choice: go to war or sign a peace treaty. It's been a long time since you could spank us like a little boy; now we can swat your ass.*
>
> — Nikita Khrushchev, to Secretary of the Interior Stewart Udall, on a visit to the Soviet Union, September 1962

BELOW LEFT: *McGeorge Bundy, US national security adviser.*
BELOW RIGHT: *Robert S. McNamara, secretary of defence, at a press conference as the missile crisis deepens. Later, he wondered privately if he'd live to see another Saturday.*

BELOW: *Photograph taken on Sunday, 14 October 1962, by a U-2 spy plane, showing a Soviet medium-range ballistic missile site under construction at San Cristóbal, Cuba.*

led a military delegation to Moscow to negotiate the terms. In July 1962 sixty-five Soviet ships sailed for Cuba, ten of them carrying military equipment. By September the installation of missile sites, from which nuclear warheads targeted on the United States could be launched, was under way. Castro wanted the missiles to be sited openly, but the Soviet obsession with secrecy prevailed. Even the Soviet ambassadors in Washington and at the UN were not told.

On the morning of Sunday, 14 October, a U-2 spy plane photographed the missile sites under construction near San Cristóbal in western Cuba. The next day the photographs were analysed, and by late evening reports hit the desk of McGeorge Bundy, the president's national security adviser. He decided to let the president get a good night's sleep before telling him the news. When Kennedy was told, he was horrified. It was, he said, "just as if we suddenly began to put a major number of [missiles] in Turkey." "Well, we *did*, Mr. President," an adviser had to remind him.

ExComm

On Tuesday, 16 October, Kennedy convened a small group of senior officials to debate the crisis. Known as ExComm, this Executive Committee of the National Security Council met almost continuously for the next two weeks. It was unanimous from the start that the missiles must be removed from Cuba. Secretary of Defense Robert McNamara calculated that they would become operational in less than two weeks, which imposed a fourteen-day maximum timetable to get the missiles out. More than just a problem with Cuba, this was a major Cold War crisis.

The first issue ExComm debated was whether to bomb the missile sites or to pursue some other option to force the Soviets to dismantle them. Could the missiles be taken out effectively by an air strike? And would the Soviets retal-

Soviet Missiles Ninety Miles Away

In early September 1962 the Soviets began to install 24 SS-4 medium-range ballistic missile launchers in Cuba, and 16 longer-range SS-5 missile launchers. All launchers would be loaded with two missiles, each with a 1-megaton nuclear warhead. With the missiles came 42 Il-28 jet bombers, 42 MiG-21 fighters, 24 advanced SAM surface-to-air missiles, coastal defences, four elite combat regiments, two tank battalions fitted out with the latest T-55 tanks, and more than 40,000 Soviet troops and personnel.

Within the 1,100-mile range of the SS-4s lay Washington, Atlanta, New Orleans, and about 40 per cent of the bases of Strategic Air Command. The intermediate-range SS-5s could travel 2,200 miles and target most American cities except Seattle. They could destroy all SAC bases. The SS-4 missiles were due to be operational by late October, and each missile possessed firepower equivalent to 1 million tons of TNT. Hiroshima had been destroyed by a blast equivalent to 13,000 tons of TNT.

The president's closest confidant was his brother Robert, the attorney general. During the crisis, Bobby Kennedy maintained a private channel of communication with the Kremlin through Soviet ambassador Anatoly Dobrynin.

iate? At first the president eagerly supported a limited air strike. As he discussed a pre-emptive air attack, his brother Robert, the attorney general, passed him a note. "I now know how Tojo felt when he was planning Pearl Harbor." On the afternoon of 16 October, the Joint Chiefs met and agreed that an air strike would have to be total to be effective, taking out not only all the missile sites but the SAM anti-aircraft missile defences and the backup facilities. ExComm met again later that afternoon but failed to agree.

Over the next few days the discussion within ExComm went back and forth as options were kicked around and analysed. The Pentagon tried to persuade Kennedy that a neat, surgical strike against the missile launchers was impractical. Air force general Curtis LeMay agreed that a major air offensive was called for, with hundreds of bombing sorties. Those opposed to this line argued that it risked American and Soviet casualties, and could jeopardize worldwide public opinion. A great deal of time was spent debating whether a surprise air attack would be a morally acceptable course of action. ExComm members fell broadly into two groups, since called hawks and doves. The hawks wanted to take Cuba and rid it of communism. Many of the military backed this line. The doves preferred to explore diplomatic options, which included approaching Castro or even Khrushchev, and wanted to avoid anything that might prompt Soviet retaliation.

On the afternoon of Thursday, 18 October, the president met with Soviet foreign minister Andrei Gromyko at the White House. Gromyko was in the United States to attend the UN General Assembly. Both men were nervous, but both tried to conceal it. Kennedy had not yet decided whether to confront

A Two-Week Meeting — On Tape!

Membership of ExComm varied throughout the crisis, but at the core were Secretary of State Dean Rusk, his deputy George Ball, assistant for Latin American Affairs Edwin Martin, and, briefly, Soviet expert Charles Bohlen; Secretary of Defense Robert McNamara, his deputy Roswell Gilpatric, and Assistant Secretary Paul Nitze; General Maxwell Taylor, chairman of the Joint Chiefs of Staff; McGeorge Bundy, national security adviser; Llewellyn Thompson, ex-ambassador to Moscow and Soviet specialist; John McCone, director of the CIA; and Attorney General Robert Kennedy, the president's younger brother and one of his key confidants.

Several other senior officials joined the deliberations from time to time, including Secretary of the Treasury Douglas Dillon; Theodore Sorensen, special counsel to the White House; Dean Acheson, former secretary of state; and Adlai Stevenson, ambassador to the United Nations.

General Taylor provided a link with the Joint Chiefs, who also met with the president throughout the crisis.

Unknown to the members of ExComm, the meetings were recorded. Tapes and transcripts of the almost hourly meetings are now available.

ExComm discussions were long, freewheeling, and unstructured, with no formality leading to decision making. Dean Acheson was appalled at the informal way in which ideas

were shared. Under President Truman personal leadership had prevailed against incessant discussion to arrive at a consensus.

Dean Rusk was suspicious that the meetings were an attempt to shift policy planning away from the State Department.

Many of the key decisions were made outside ExComm, especially by the president and his brother, who opened backdoor negotiations with Moscow through the new Soviet ambassador, Anatoly Dobrynin. Many members of ExComm were kept in ignorance of these negotiations.

> *I now know how Tojo felt when he was planning Pearl Harbor.*
>
> — Robert Kennedy,
> October 1962

ExComm, the ad hoc committee that made policy decisions during the Cuban missile crisis, operated with a loose agenda. Kennedy, with an eye to posterity, had the proceedings secretly taped. Moderate views prevailed.

Gromyko with irrefutable proof of the presence of Soviet missile sites in Cuba. But he had copies of the aerial photographs in a desk drawer ready to pull out. They discussed the possibility of another summit. Then Gromyko, in raising the issue of Cuba, charged the United States with "pestering" a small country. The president pointed out that the situation was aggravated by Soviet military aid to Cuba. Gromyko insisted that the Soviet Union's military assistance was purely defensive in nature; no offensive weapons would be introduced. Kennedy decided not to reveal US awareness of the missiles until he had his policy clearly worked out. Gromyko left the White House happy and cabled the Kremlin that "the situation is quite satisfactory. . . . There is reason to believe that the United States has no current plans for an invasion of Cuba."

That evening ExComm was told that installation of the SS-4 medium-range missiles was nearly complete and that they probably could be launched within eighteen hours. The longer-range SS-5 missile sites might not be operational until December. Talking beyond midnight, ExComm now pursued an alternative option to an air strike: a naval blockade. This would prevent the Soviets from landing any further shipments. Although stopping ships on the high seas was tantamount to an act of war, a blockade would permit better control over events and offer more options as the crisis unfolded.

For two more days the meetings continued. But with midterm congressional elections approaching, the president was needed elsewhere to campaign on behalf of the Democrats. In the meanwhile, Rusk and McNamara persuaded ExComm to come down against a military air strike, and to recommend the more cautious policy of a naval blockade of Cuba as first option.

Kennedy Backs a Blockade

On Sunday morning, 21 October, under pretext of suffering a cold, Kennedy cancelled the rest of his electioneering trip. He now decided to back the blockade. It seemed to be the step "least likely to precipitate general war while still causing the Soviets . . . to back down and abandon Castro." Acheson suggested calling this a "quarantine" around Cuba, since it sounded less aggressive. Plans were finalized at top speed, and Acheson was dispatched abroad to drum up support for America's position.

On Monday, Pierre Salinger, Kennedy's press secretary, approached the TV networks to request prime-time coverage of a speech by the president on "a matter of highest national urgency." All three networks agreed to clear their schedules. Earlier in the day the State Department officially informed America's allies of its intentions. This was the first news of the crisis in London, Paris, Bonn, Ottawa, and other capitals. Both President de Gaulle and Prime Minister Macmillan assured the United States of full support.

Meanwhile, precautionary measures were taken elsewhere. From the start Kennedy had been worried that action over Cuba would produce a reaction by the Soviets over Berlin. At noon Strategic Air Command put its B-52 nuclear bomber force on alert, ensuring that at any given time one-eighth of the force, equivalent to four squadrons, would be airborne. Each bomber was armed with four nuclear warheads. For the first time in its history, the Air Defense Command armed all its aircraft with nuclear weapons.

At 5:00 PM the president, Secretary Rusk, and Secretary McNamara met with seventeen congressional leaders from both parties to brief them on the crisis. Some expressed their support for the blockade plan. Others, including Senator J. William Fulbright, argued that the naval blockade was not enough, that an air strike or an invasion would be needed to get the missiles out of Cuba. Kennedy and McNamara assured the congressmen that they had not ruled out an invasion but would try the blockade option first. Kennedy said they would take a chance that the missiles now ready would not be fired, but he admitted that it was "one hell of a gamble."

That afternoon Soviet ambassador Dobrynin was in New York, seeing Gromyko off at the end of his American trip. A State Department official caught up with him at the airport and asked that he meet the secretary of state that evening in Washington. When Dobrynin asked that the meeting be postponed, he was told it was a matter of urgency. Accordingly at 6:00 PM Dobrynin met Dean Rusk in his office. Rusk gave the ambassador a copy of the speech that Kennedy would deliver on television that evening, along with a copy of a personal message to Khrushchev. In this letter the president told the Soviet leader that his action was a "necessary minimum" and that he hoped the Soviet government would refrain from any action that would deepen an already grave crisis. Rusk thought Dobrynin "aged ten years" before his eyes. The ambassador, who still knew nothing of the deployment of "offensive" Soviet weapons in Cuba, returned to his embassy. He sat in his office alone for fifteen minutes to calm himself before relaying Kennedy's message to a hastily assembled Presidium in Moscow, where the mood was grim. The Soviet leadership, convinced that a US invasion of Cuba would now follow, feared that the Soviet force there would be outnumbered and sent instructions to the

It shall be the policy of this nation to regard any nuclear missile launched from Cuba against any nation in the western hemisphere as an attack by the Soviet Union on the United States, requiring a full retaliatory response upon the Soviet Union. . . . I call upon Chairman Khrushchev to halt and eliminate this clandestine, reckless, and provocative threat to world peace. . . . He has an opportunity now to move the world back from the abyss of destruction.

— John F. Kennedy,
TV address,
22 October 1962

Soviet commander authorizing him to use tactical nuclear weapons in the event Americans landed. But he was told not to fire the SS-4 ballistic missiles without a direct order from Moscow. "They can attack us, and we shall respond," said Khrushchev to the Presidium. "This may end in a big war," he added.

Kennedy Addresses the Nation

An hour after Rusk met with the Soviet ambassador, President Kennedy addressed the nation live from the White House. He set out "unmistakable evidence" of the siting of Soviet missiles, and outlined the US policy of naval quarantine.

While Kennedy was speaking, the Joint Chiefs of Staff ordered all US military forces worldwide to go to DEFCON 3, a heightened state of nuclear alert. Several hundred ICBM missiles were prepared for firing, and Polaris nuclear submarines were dispatched to their pre-assigned stations at sea. In the Caribbean, the US Navy deployed 180 ships to blockade Cuba. That evening Rusk told a meeting of ambassadors in Washington, "I would not be candid and I would not be fair with you if I did not say that we are in as grave a crisis as mankind has been in."

Khrushchev's bold idea had backfired. With no contingency plan in the event the missiles were found out, all he could do now was improvise. He put Warsaw Pact armed forces on alert. On the morning of Tuesday, 23 October, TASS transmitted a statement from the Kremlin charging Kennedy with piracy, with an "unheard of violation of international law," and with measures that constituted "a serious threat to peace and to the security of nations." Moscow insisted that the weapons in Cuba were "intended solely for defensive purposes in order to secure the Republic of Cuba against the attack of an aggressor," and that the White House policy "may lead to catastrophic consequences for world peace."

That evening Robert Kennedy paid the first of several private visits to Ambassador Dobrynin. No one else was present when they met in the ambassador's living room above the Soviet Embassy. Kennedy, tense and agitated, told Dobrynin that more than anything he regretted the breakdown in the relationship between President Kennedy and Chairman Khrushchev; the president had taken grave offence at the way in which Khrushchev and Gromyko had tried to deceive him. Dobrynin, who also had not known of the missile sitings, found the talk embarrassing. As he was leaving, the president's brother asked the ambassador in a matter-of-fact way if he knew what orders had been given the Soviet ships heading for Cuba. Dobrynin told him, "Our captains have orders to continue their course to Cuba, for the actions of President Kennedy are unlawful." In fact, the Kremlin had already ordered five ships carrying missiles to return to the Soviet Union.

On Wednesday, 24 October, U Thant, secretary-general of the United Nations, under pressure from forty non-aligned states, sent identical letters to Kennedy and Khrushchev urging suspension of the blockade and the stopping of shipments to Cuba for two or three weeks. The letter pleaded with both governments to refrain from any action that would "bring with it the risk of war."

Kennedy and his colleagues, rejecting invasion or air strike, described the US action as "naval quarantine." The press called it a blockade.

22 October. The president cuts into prime-time television to tell the nation, and the world, that there are Soviet missiles in Cuba, ninety miles away, and what he intends to do about it. From here on, tensions rose.

In the Caribbean, the Soviet ship *Aleksandrovsk* arrived at the Cuban port of La Isabela. This ship was the one Soviet vessel ordered to race on to Cuba when the others were recalled. It contained twenty-four nuclear warheads, and beat the blockade by just a few hours.

Khrushchev cautioned Kennedy that should the US Navy try to stop Soviet ships at sea, his submarines would sink the American vessels. He would not be the first to fire a nuclear weapon, he said, but he warned, terrifyingly, that "if the US insists on war, we'll all meet together in hell."

ExComm went into a long, tense session. At 10:25 AM an intelligence message reported that some of the Russian ships appeared to have stopped dead in the water. Dean Rusk leaned across to McGeorge Bundy, sighed with relief, and said, "We're eyeball to eyeball, and I think the other fellow just blinked." McNamara advised Admiral George Anderson, chief of naval operations, that the blockade must carefully avoid humiliating the Russians, lest Khrushchev react in a nuclear spasm.

Later that night Kennedy received a personal message from Khrushchev, warning that the Soviet Union saw the blockade as "an act of aggression," and that "you will understand that the Soviet Union cannot fail to reject the arbitrary demands of the United States." It looked as though Moscow was, after all, going to the wire. Equally firmly, the Joint Chiefs of Staff increased the alert status of the US military to DEFCON 2, the highest alert status short of war. It was the only time in the entire Cold War that the US military would go to this level of alert.

At 7:15 AM on Thursday, 25 October, in the blue waters of the Caribbean, the first interception took place. As the Soviet tanker *Bucharest* entered the quarantine zone, it was stopped by the USS *Gearing*. Guaranteeing that it was only carrying oil, the *Bucharest* was allowed to continue to Havana. In the White House, Kennedy explained, "I don't want to push him [Khrushchev] in a corner from which he cannot escape."

To U Thant's appeal, Kennedy avoided responding directly. Khrushchev wrote that he agreed with the proposal. Meanwhile, at the UN Security Council, Adlai Stevenson confronted Soviet representative Valerian Zorin with evidence of the missile installations. At ExComm the CIA reported that the medium-range SS-4 missiles were now ready for firing.

Soon after dawn on Friday, 26 October, another ship was stopped by destroyers of the US Navy and boarded. It was the Lebanese tramp steamer *Marucla*. Intended to show US determination, this event was stage-managed for public opinion. Lebanon could barely afford to mount an international protest, and in any case, intelligence already knew that the cargo consisted of spare parts for trucks, asbestos, and other industrial goods. Three US naval officers, along with a Russian translator, boarded the *Marucla* and peered into her hold. Having assured themselves of what they already knew, they allowed the steamer to continue to Havana.

By 10:00 AM ExComm was assembled. Kennedy, under increasing political pressure to "crack down hard" on Castro before the November elections, conceded that the blockade was not going to get out missiles already in Cuba, and plans for invasion were discussed. Twenty-five thousand marines were assem-

An aerial photograph shows a Soviet ship, loaded with military deck cargo, racing for Havana, in the hopes of beating the American blockade.

Valerian Zorin, USSR delegate, listening to the UN Security Council debate on Cuba. Questioned by Adlai Stevenson (OPPOSITE), he stonewalled.

bling around the Caribbean, and 100,000 soldiers had been mobilized in Florida. Two giant aircraft carriers, *Enterprise* and *Independence*, headed for Cuba at full speed. The air force again put forward the bombing option, and presented plans for an initial strike of more than 2,000 sorties. But it was estimated that in the ten days of fighting tied to an invasion, the United States would suffer nearly 18,500 casualties. The president was aghast; to avoid catastrophe Kennedy would have to do a deal.

An Extraordinary Proposal

Later that morning ABC-TV diplomatic correspondent John Scali received a surprise phone call from Aleksandr Fomin, a press counsellor at the Soviet Embassy, suggesting they meet. Over lunch Fomin asked if the US government would accept a compromise whereby in return for a guarantee that the United States would not invade Cuba, the Soviet Union would dismantle and withdraw the missiles. Scali, amazed at the approach, immediately passed the request on to Dean Rusk, who went straight to the president with it. Scali was told to get back to Fomin and tell him that the US government saw real possibilities in the deal. Extraordinarily, it later appeared that Fomin, actually a KGB official, was acting entirely on his own initiative.

That evening the State Department received a letter from the Kremlin. In four parts, it was, in Robert Kennedy's words, "very long and emotional." It

Adlai Stevenson, US ambassador to the UN, challenges the Soviets to deny they have placed and are placing medium-range and intermediate-range missiles in Cuba.

Harsh Words

At the UN Security Council in New York, on 25 October, tensions rose. The Soviet ambassador to the UN, Valerian Zorin, challenged the US ambassador, Adlai Stevenson, to provide proof that the missiles were in Cuba. The exchange has gone down in the history books.

Stevenson: "Well, let me say something to you, Mr. Ambassador. We do have the evidence. . . it is clear and uncontrovertible. . . . Do you, Ambassador Zorin, deny that the USSR has placed and is placing missile sites in Cuba? Yes or no? [Pause] Don't wait for the translation, yes or no?"

Zorin (translated from the Russian): "I am not in an American courtroom, sir, and therefore I do not wish to answer a question that is put to me in a fashion in which a prosecutor puts questions."

Stevenson: "You are in the court-room of world opinion right now and you can answer yes or no. You have denied that they exist, and I want to know whether I have understood you correctly."

Zorin: "Continue with your statement. You will have your answer in due course."

Stevenson: "I am prepared to wait for my answer until hell freezes over. . . ."

Stevenson then turned to show close-up photographs of the missile sites on a board set up beside the council table. Zorin failed to answer and ridiculed the photographic evidence.

Stevenson: "We know the facts and so do you, sir, and we are ready to talk about them. Our job here is not to score debating points. Our job is to save the peace. And if you are ready to try, we are."

seemed to offer hope by suggesting a settlement along the lines Fomin had proposed earlier in the day; the Soviets might withdraw the missiles if the US agreed not to invade nor "support any other forces which might intend to invade Cuba." This would remove the cause for siting the missiles in the first place. The letter appeared to be directly from Khrushchev; it had his style about it: "We and you ought not to pull on the end of the rope in which we have tied the knot of war, because the more we pull the tighter the knot will be tied." At 10:00 PM, ExComm reconvened and decided to treat Khrushchev's letter as a bona fide proposal. Taken along with Fomin's approach that day, it seemed to everyone that a new Soviet position was emerging.

Later that night Castro visited the Soviet Embassy in Havana. He dictated a cable to Khrushchev predicting an imminent US invasion and assuring the Kremlin that any landings would be fiercely resisted. He suggested that the Soviets prepare a nuclear strike in retaliation. Despite protest from the Soviet ambassador, he ordered his own units to fire on any US aircraft flying over Cuba.

In the early hours of the morning, Robert Kennedy had another secret meeting with Dobrynin. The ambassador sternly pointed out that the United States had sited operational missiles in Turkey aimed at the Soviet Union. Kennedy responded that the Turkish missiles might be brought into a possible solution to the crisis and left the room briefly to make a telephone call. When he returned Kennedy told the ambassador the president was willing to "examine favorably the question of Turkey." Dobrynin passed this on to Moscow immediately.

When the sun came up in Washington that morning, Saturday, 27 October, the day was clear and bright; but it has gone down in history as Black Saturday. ExComm began a marathon session at 10:00 AM with the news that low-level reconnaissance flights indicated that six missile launchers now appeared to be operational. The next forty-eight hours would be critical. The meeting was interrupted by a report that a U-2 flight over Alaska had drifted off course into Siberian air space. The Soviet military regarded this as a "feeler" sent to test their response systems. When ExComm heard that Soviet MiGs had been launched to intercept the U-2, McNamara went white. "This means war with Russia," he yelled out. The president was calmer. "There's always some son of a bitch," he said, "who doesn't get the word."

In fact the U-2 pilot did get away safely. At this tense moment, just after 11:00 AM, reports came in of a Radio Moscow broadcast of another letter from Khrushchev. This second letter was in a much more formal tone, and it made a new proposal. For the Soviets to remove the missiles from Cuba, the United States must remove its missiles from Turkey. The hawks in ExComm were outraged. There had been nothing about Turkey in the earlier letter. Maybe Khrushchev had been overruled by hard-liners in the Kremlin, or perhaps deposed. The Kennedy brothers squirmed, for the Kremlin was only responding to the idea they had put forward the night before. The president commented, "He's got us in a pretty good spot here, because most people will regard this as not an unreasonable proposal." Bundy, Rusk, and General Taylor immediately challenged their commander-in-chief; to remove the missiles from Turkey would fragment NATO. The discussion carried on through the day, with Kennedy arguing that to start a nuclear war instead of accepting a trade over Turkey was "an insupportable position." The president was stuck. He could not move forward without risking a nuclear nightmare. He could not retreat without surrender. He had to move sideways.

Khrushchev Sees It His Way

Fears in Washington that Khrushchev had been overpowered were wide of the mark. The Soviet premier was in complete control of the Soviet leadership throughout the crisis. At the Saturday Presidium he had argued that for five days Kennedy had done nothing; by standing firm, the Kremlin had forced the White House to reconsider its invasion plans. Despite all the intelligence predictions, Khrushchev did not believe invasion would now take place. Khrushchev introduced to the Presidium the new factor, the Turkish missiles. "If we could achieve the liquidation of the bases in Turkey," Khrushchev argued, "we would win." In front of the Presidium, Khrushchev dictated the message that created the panic response in ExComm.

In Cuba, Saturday, 27 October, began badly. A powerful tropical storm lashed the island. As the Soviet technicians frantically raced to prepare their missiles, they worried that torrential rain would short-circuit their electronics. Reports that an American U-2 had been spotted over the island prompted the Soviet anti-aircraft batteries into action. Nerves were on edge. Unable to reach the Soviet commander, his deputy authorized the firing of a SAM missile. Exploding alongside the U-2 it sent the plane plunging to earth. The pilot was killed.

Cuban newspaper photograph showing wreckage of a U-2 spy plane shot down by a Cuban SAM missile battery on Saturday, 27 October 1962. US military contingency plans called for a reprisal, but the president withheld permission — a decision that may have averted nuclear war.

When this was reported in Washington, the military prepared to take reprisal against the SAM missile emplacements, as contingency plans directed. To the Pentagon's consternation, the president ordered that no action be taken. At ExComm the idea slowly emerged of ignoring Khrushchev's second letter and responding only to his first. Theodore Sorensen and Robert Kennedy prepared a reply. At just after 8:00 PM, the president signed the letter, which guaranteed an end to the blockade and no invasion of Cuba if Russia withdrew its missiles.

That Saturday evening, as he left the White House, McNamara recalled, "it was a beautiful fall evening, the height of the crisis, and I went up into the open air to look and to smell it, because I thought it was the last Saturday I would ever see." Strikingly, Martin Walker, in his book *The Cold War,* relates that on the other side of the world, at that same moment, in Moscow, Fyodor Burlatsky, a Soviet journalist with connections to the Kremlin, had similar thoughts: "That was when I went and telephoned my wife and told her to drop everything and get out of Moscow. I thought then that the American bombers were on their way." Throughout the world, as the crisis escalated, people held their breath. Parents feared for their children's future, kept them back from school, and went to bed not certain they would see another day.

A few ExComm veterans lingered at the White House, including the president, his brother, Rusk, and Sorensen. They agreed that Robert Kennedy should arrange another meeting with the Soviet ambassador and inform him directly of the president's letter. Rusk had come round to the deal over the Turkish missiles but suggested it not be made explicit since it would look like a climbdown. In case the whole business got out, Rusk telephoned an American official in the United Nations and dictated a statement that he wanted U Thant to issue the following day if so instructed by Washington. In the statement, U Thant was to call for the removal of both the US missiles in Turkey and the Soviet missiles in Cuba. If the Russians revealed the secret deal, Kennedy could pretend the suggestion had come from the UN.

Later that night Dobrynin met with Robert Kennedy at the Justice Department. Nervous and agitated, Kennedy told Dobrynin that he had not been home or seen his children for six days. He made it clear that the situation was worsening, that the military and many senior Washington officials were "spoiling for a fight." The United States would have to bomb the missile sites if the missiles were not withdrawn. However, he said, if the Soviets dismantled the missiles, the US would withdraw the blockade and would guarantee no invasion. Dobrynin asked about the missiles in Turkey. Kennedy replied that the president was willing, but the deal would have to be kept secret, since as the leading member of NATO, the United States could not appear unilaterally to withdraw them for its own purposes. However, he could guarantee that the Turkish missiles would go within "four to five months." Time was running out; there were only a few hours left. He urged that Khrushchev give a clear, substantive reply by the next day, but asked him not to mention the Turkish missile deal, which only a few people knew of.

In Moscow the Presidium had gone into session at Khrushchev's dacha, just outside the city. When Dobrynin's report of his conversation arrived, Khrushchev told his colleagues that they must take the dignified way out of the crisis. Khrushchev worried that the young president was under such intense pressure from the military to escalate that he might not be able to hold out. Fearful that air attacks on the missile sites were imminent, Khrushchev agreed to accept Kennedy's proposals.

At 9:00 AM on the following morning, Sunday, 28 October, Radio Moscow broadcast a message from Khrushchev announcing that "the Soviet government has given a new order to dismantle the arms which you describe as 'offensive' and to crate and return them to the Soviet Union." At the White House there was an immense sigh of relief. Within hours Kennedy broadcast a quick acceptance statement to Moscow over the Voice of America, and ordered that no more ships were to be boarded. In a more formal reply to Khrushchev, the president wrote of "firm undertakings on the part of both our governments which should be promptly carried out." He concluded, "I agree with you that we must devote urgent attention to the problem of disarmament. . . . Perhaps now as we step back from the danger, we can together make real progress in this vital field."

A Win-Win Outcome

In the United States the settlement was treated as a major Soviet defeat. Almost within hours everything at the White House was back to normal. President Kennedy had gone head-to-head with the Soviets, and won. Only the right-wing hawks and the military were disappointed; they had been denied a fight. Admiral Anderson, who had commanded the naval blockade, said,

Crisis over. The US press claimed victory, but Kennedy did make a deal, secretly agreeing to withdraw US missiles from Turkey. BELOW: *A Soviet ship carrying aircraft away from Cuba is inspected from the air.*

Castro and Khrushchev sign a joint Soviet-Cuban declaration in May 1963. Nevertheless, Castro was still resentful that Khrushchev had agreed to pull Soviet missiles out of Cuba without consulting him.

"We have been had." General LeMay suggested they should go ahead and bomb the Cuban missile sites anyway. The Joint Chiefs instructed the military not to relax their alert in case the Soviet line was an "insincere" ploy, designed to gain time.

In Moscow, Khrushchev too claimed a victory. "The two most powerful nations in the world had been squared off against each other, each with its finger on the button," Khrushchev later wrote. But the resolution to the crisis brought a "triumph for common sense." In portraying the settlement, the Soviets repeatedly stressed that they had achieved what had never before been possible — an agreement from the United States not to invade Cuba. Khrushchev had safeguarded the socialist revolution in Cuba for posterity. Cuba would not suffer the fate of Guatemala. Khrushchev regarded the settlement as a great victory for his diplomacy, "without a single shot having been fired."

In Havana, Fidel Castro, who had not been consulted over the missiles' withdrawal, went into a rage. He cursed Khrushchev as a "son of a bitch, bastard, asshole." He refused to see the Soviet ambassador and regarded the dismantling of the missiles as a moral defeat. In Ankara, the Turkish government, which had repeatedly made clear that it wanted US missiles sited on its territory for defensive purposes, expressed delight at the settlement and stated that it would never be party to any negotiation that involved their withdrawal. No one told the Turks that a deal already had been done.

In the legend of the Cuban missile crisis, Kennedy was the victor. Bright, young, heroic, he kept his cool and taught the Soviets a lesson. In the congressional elections ten days after the crisis, the Democrats won their biggest majority in the Senate in twenty years. In Massachusetts the president's youngest brother, Edward, was elected to that body in a landslide. Most gratifying of all to the Democrats, Richard Nixon was defeated in his bid for the governorship of California. In 1963 US missiles were quietly removed from Turkey, with cover stories that this had no connection to the Cuban crisis: the missiles were obsolete, and the president had wanted them removed long before the crisis blew up. Despite the terms of the agreement with the Soviets, Kennedy continued to discuss plans for sabotage and insurgency in Cuba. After his early humiliations over the Bay of Pigs and his uncertainty over Berlin, Kennedy had now become a statesman, a world peacemaker; his political future looked secure.

The crisis ended with a collective sigh of relief. Both Washington and Moscow had had to choose between compromise and nuclear war. Neither side chose war. Although both claimed a victory, the same important lesson was learned in the Kremlin as in the White House: never again must the superpowers risk direct nuclear confrontation.

North Vietnam, 1965

A unit of the North Vietnamese People's Army training in the North in 1965; much marching and combat lay ahead of them.

Vietnam
1954–1968

The Elephant and the Grasshopper

On 7 May 1954 French forces in the heavily fortified village of Dien Bien Phu, in northwest Vietnam near the Laos border, finally surrendered after a bitter eight-week battle with Vietnamese insurgents, the Viet Minh. The French had stationed their toughest units in the valley around the village, but the Viet Minh shelled the French troops mercilessly from the highlands overlooking the valley with artillery supplied by China. One by one the French strongholds fell. Viet Minh shelling of the airfield cut them off from reinforcements and prevented the evacuation of the wounded. After a final Vietnamese push, the French commander gave in; the red flag was hoisted over the French command post. Dien Bien Phu is one of the defining battles in history. As the Viet Minh commander, General Vo Nguyen Giap, put it, "A poor feudal nation had beaten a great colonial power. . . . It meant a lot; not just to us but to people all over the world."

The battle marked the end of an eight-year-long struggle between the French and Vietnamese nationalist forces. After the humiliation of defeat and occupation in the Second World War, the French had tried to retain their colonial empire in what they called Indochina, an area that comprised Cambodia, Laos, and Vietnam, which France had ruled since the late nineteenth century. The leader of the League for the Independence of Vietnam, the Viet Minh, was Ho Chi Minh, a wily, dedicated North Vietnamese Communist leader who had declared Vietnam's independence after the Japanese surrender at the end of the Second World War. The Soviet Union and Communist China (after 1949) supplied him with heavy weapons and ammunition, enabling Ho to transform his guerrilla bands into a powerful fighting force. Ho compared the

Dien Bien Phu, 7 May 1954. After fierce fighting and very heavy losses, French forces surrender to Vietnamese insurgents, the Viet Minh. France is ousted as a colonial power in Indochina.

struggle to that between an "elephant and a grasshopper," but the Viet Minh more than held their own in full-scale confrontations with French troops. More than ninety thousand Frenchmen were killed, wounded, or went missing in what the French public began to call *la sale guerre* — the dirty war.

In 1953, as peace talks ended the Korean War, the French considered negotiating with Ho Chi Minh. But Ho knew that his clout at the negotiating table would depend on his performance in battle. The victory he needed came at Dien Bien Phu. After the capitulation, at an international conference under way in Geneva, the French agreed to withdraw from Southeast Asia. Vietnam was divided along the 17th parallel, between the Communist North and the South; elections were to be held two years later that were intended to re-unify the country.

From Washington, President Eisenhower watched developments in Southeast Asia with foreboding. Less than a year had passed since the final negotiated truce ended the long war against communism in Korea. Eisenhower considered supporting the French at Dien Bien Phu with US planes, but, having been elected to end the war in Korea, he was reluctant to involve the United States in another conflict in Asia. Confirming his position, the Joint Chiefs of Staff concluded that "Indochina is devoid of decisive military objectives." But, the president reasoned, if Indochina were to fall, all of Southeast Asia would "go over very quickly" to the Communists, like "a row of dominoes." He added: "The possible consequences of the loss are just incalculable to the free world." Eisenhower envisaged losing Laos, Cambodia, Burma, Thailand, and possibly even India, in what would be a gigantic strengthening of the Communist power bloc.

In North Vietnam, Ho Chi Minh, as he took control, introduced land reform and education and health care to broaden popular support for the

"The Napoleon of North Vietnam," General Vo Nguyen Giap, addresses his staff. Behind him are portraits of Malenkov, Stalin's successor in the USSR; Ho Chi Minh, North Vietnamese leader; and Mao Zedong of China.

Ho Chi Minh

One of the century's most influential Communist leaders, Ho Chi Minh was born as Nguyen That Thanh in 1890 in central Vietnam, then a part of French Indochina. Ho went to school in Hue and briefly taught before working as a cook aboard a French steamship. He lived in London and Paris prior to the First World War and helped found the French Communist Party. Summoned to Moscow for training, Ho was sent to China in 1924 to work among Vietnamese exiles and was a founder of the Indochinese Communist Party (ICP). He was expelled from China for a time, but returned in 1938 as an adviser to Mao Zedong's army.

When Japan occupied Vietnam in 1941, Ho resumed contact with the ICP and was an organizer of the independence movement known as Viet Minh, which actively fought the Japanese. In 1945, following Japan's defeat, the Viet Minh established the Democratic Republic of Vietnam and named Ho Chi Minh its president. France's post-war attempt to reassert control over its colonies ended with the defeat at Dien Bien Phu in 1954, but Vietnam was left partitioned.

For the next fifteen years Ho led North Vietnam's battle for re-unification, in which the United States became totally mired. Ho died in 1969, so he did not live to witness re-unification in 1975. Saigon, the former capital of South Vietnam, was renamed Ho Chi Minh city in his honour.

struggle. In a more radical programme, the Communist regime confiscated private land and gave it to peasants. Many landlords were pilloried at public tribunals, huge numbers were forced into labour camps, and, in an excess that Ho later apologized for, thousands were executed. A million refugees fled the Communist regime for the South, in ships conveniently provided by the United States and France.

In the South, in the political vacuum left by the French departure, Ngo Dinh Diem established the Republic of Vietnam. A Vietnamese nationalist and a Catholic with strong Confucian views, Diem was an ardent anti-Communist. A very modern mandarin, he ruled through family and friends like an emperor. The United States underwrote his anti-Communist regime

A poor feudal nation had beaten a great colonial power. . . . It meant a lot; not just to us but to people all over the world.

— Gen. Vo Nguyen Giap, on the fall of Dien Bien Phu

As Ho Chi Minh's troops take over Hanoi from the departing French, 9 October 1954, school-children supplied with a Ho portrait rehearse a chorus of welcome slogans.

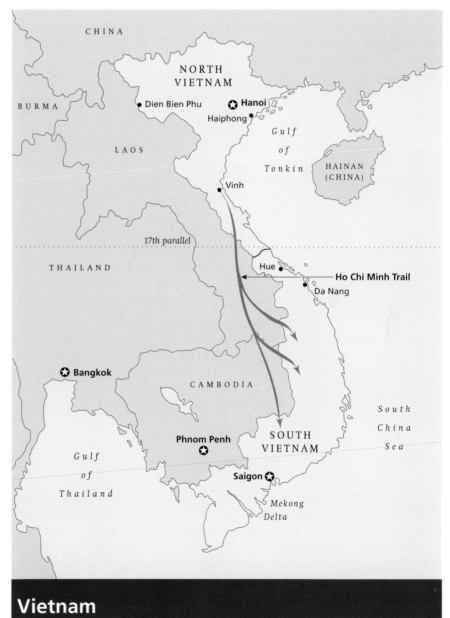

Vietnam

because, as John Foster Dulles later put it, "we knew of no one better." Diem's government took powers to arrest and detain opponents, mostly Communist sympathizers, and within a few years all the Viet Minh left in the South had been wiped out. Still fearful that the Communists would win the free elections called for by Geneva, Diem ignored the nationwide polls scheduled for 1956 and even abolished elections for municipal and village councils, announcing that in future local officials would be appointed by his supporters. The US commitment to keeping South Vietnam out of Communist clutches intensified: hundreds of millions of dollars of aid were allocated, and more American advisers were sent to Diem's government. But American sway over Diem was always incomplete; one adviser lamented, "He pays more attention to the advice of his brothers . . . than he does to me."

When Diem visited the United States in 1957, Eisenhower lauded him as the "miracle man" of Asia — praise that went right to his head. Diem presided over a narrow oligarchy; his brother Nhu, who became de facto prime minister, and his wife, Madame Nhu, were the powers in government; Diem's eldest brother, Archbishop Thuc, brought the Catholic Church behind the regime; nephews and cousins competed for lucrative American aid contracts and trade deals.

Diem's repression in the South and Ho's state terrorism in the North made the lot of the Vietnamese peasant relentlessly harsh. After eight years' struggle with France, the nation desperately needed peace and recovery. But the temporary partition that followed the Geneva Conference looked like it might become a permanent divide.

In December 1960 the National Front for the Liberation of South Vietnam was established. Usually referred to as the National Liberation Front, or the Viet Cong, this was a broad coalition of groups united in their objective to overthrow Diem's regime. It was set up as a "southern" resistance movement so as not to breach the Geneva Accords, which forbade the North from sending troops into the South. However, from the beginning, the Viet Cong was controlled by Hanoi; the Communists had long been looking at safe ways to infiltrate troops, party cadres, and supplies into the South. Gradually trails were cut through the mountains and jungles of neighbouring Laos, and along them the Communists regularly began to send supplies to insurgents in the South. They called this conduit the Ho Chi Minh Trail.

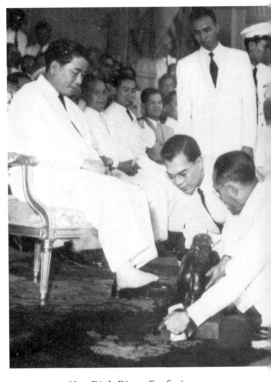

Ngo Dinh Diem, Confucian, Catholic, and anti-Communist, is installed as president of South Vietnam. Placing his bare foot on a bronze elephant will bring him strength.

A Row of Dominoes?

On the eve of his inauguration, in January 1961, John F. Kennedy and a team of senior advisers met with President Eisenhower for a briefing on the issues facing the new administration. This was the meeting at which Kennedy first learned about plans for an invasion of Cuba by a brigade of CIA-trained exiles. There are differing accounts of what advice the elder statesman passed on to the young president, but all present remember Eisenhower warning Kennedy in the strongest possible terms of the dangers of Southeast Asia's falling into Communist hands. Eisenhower does not appear to have mentioned Vietnam specifically, but he characterized Laos as "the present key" to Southeast Asia. When pressed by Kennedy for advice on how to respond to the Communist threat there, the departing president ducked the question.

Kennedy's new administration, like Eisenhower's, saw the Communist threat as monolithic, with the Soviets and Chinese cooperating in a master plan for regional domination. They saw the Communist movement in Vietnam as closely related to guerrilla insurgencies in Malaya, Indonesia, Burma, and the Philippines during the 1950s. The best and the brightest in Washington failed to recognize the nationalist component in many of these struggles. Fully cognizant of the domino theory — the belief that the fall of South Vietnam to communism would threaten the security of the United States and of the entire free world — Kennedy's circle still disagreed fundamentally on how to deal with Vietnam. Would Kennedy, to quote his inaugural address, "pay any price" or "bear any burden" to defend the South Vietnamese?

In the first months of his administration, Kennedy was preoccupied with the fiasco at the Bay of Pigs and with Berlin. Southeast Asia seemed remote. Pressed about the region's problems by a journalist, Attorney General Robert Kennedy responded impatiently, "We've got twenty Vietnams a day to handle." But as Communist infiltration of the South grew, attacks on Diem began to precipitate an air of crisis in Saigon that filtered back to the White House. The president sent Deputy National Security Adviser Walt Rostow and General Maxwell Taylor to Vietnam to assess the situation. Their report went to the core of the American dilemma: should Washington send increasing numbers of US military personnel to assist the South Vietnamese in their struggle with communism? As Defense Secretary Robert McNamara later wrote, this would "haunt us for years." The president refused to introduce US combat forces into Vietnam, but he agreed to a modest increase in the number of military advisers who were to train the South Vietnamese in counterinsurgency. As this was expressly prohibited in the Geneva Accords, it was done covertly. In November 1961 the National Security Council agreed to a stronger commitment to save South Vietnam, so long as President Diem would accept the need for reforms and broaden the base of his government. By the end of 1961 there were about three thousand US military personnel in Vietnam.

Throughout 1962 the situation in Southeast Asia worsened. Secretary McNamara was in the forefront of the debate over what to do about it. He had been the youngest-ever president of the Ford Motor Company. He was brilliant at analysing a balance sheet and wanted to set performance targets for defence policy that would measure success and failure. In July, McNamara put into place his comprehensive plan for South Vietnam. He argued that if US policy was to train the South Vietnamese to defend themselves, then this should have a time limit. If the objective was met within this time frame, the programme could be reduced; if not, an alternative policy would be needed. Corporate logic, however, did not always make sense in the jungles of Vietnam. Throughout 1962 the US military presence in Vietnam increased. Kennedy, questioned at a press conference whether any US troops were in combat in Vietnam, said no, so as not to appear in breach of the Geneva Accords. But with US pilots already flying combat missions, rumours circulated. Journalists were beginning to write about the "undeclared war." By the end of 1962 there were roughly 11,500 US military personnel in South Vietnam.

President Diem reviews an honour guard at the Pentagon with Donald Quarles, deputy secretary of defence, 9 May 1957.

During 1963 Diem's leadership of South Vietnam came under increasing American scrutiny. His religious intolerance had alienated the Buddhist population, and in a series of grotesque incidents, Buddhist monks carried out acts of self-immolation; doused with gasoline, they set themselves on fire to protest Diem's policies. While promising to be more conciliatory, Diem's brother Nhu continued to order raids on pagodas, where shrines were smashed and hundreds of Buddhist monks were arrested.

Washington was deeply divided in regard to Diem. Many senior officials still felt he was the least bad leader available in Saigon; what was lacking was sufficient pressure on him to change his ways. Others felt he must be removed; it would be impossible to win the war with Diem and his corrupt family in control of South Vietnam. But no obvious candidate to replace him had come to the fore.

"Alternative Leadership"

News of a renewed Diem crackdown on the Buddhists arrived in Washington over a late August weekend when the president and all the top members of the government were on vacation. Roger Hilsman, the smart, abrasive assistant secretary of state for Far Eastern affairs was firmly in the anti-Diem faction and chose this moment to take the initiative. He drafted a cable to the new ambassador in Saigon, Henry Cabot Lodge, Jr., saying in clipped diplomatic telegramese: "US government cannot tolerate situation in which power lies in Nhu's hands. . . . Tell appropriate [local Vietnamese] military commanders we will give them direct support. . . . Urgently examine all possible alternative leadership and make detailed plans as to how we might bring about Diem's replacement should this become necessary." The president was telephoned at his beach home at Hyannis Port, Massachusetts, and agreed to the telegram, so long as his senior advisers also approved. After a series of rapid phone-call ratifications, the cable was sent. In Saigon, Lodge, who had taken up his ambassadorship only two days earlier, interpreted it as an order from the president to organize a coup. He called on the CIA station in Saigon to go about it immediately.

The following week, in Washington, at meetings assessing the situation, tempers flared. McNamara, General Taylor, Roswell Gilpatric, and others felt they had been pushed in a new direction the United States was not prepared for. Dean Rusk, George Ball, Hilsman, and their faction argued that Diem and his family had to go. Extraordinarily, no real consideration was given to who would replace him. Kennedy was so fazed by the differences among his closest advisers that he sent an extra "eyes only" cable to his ambassador, marked "No Other Distribution Whatsoever," in which he reserved "a contingent right to change course and reverse previous instructions" up to "the very moment of the go signal" for a coup. Lodge responded: "We are launched on a course from which there is no respectable turning back." Events had developed their own momentum.

In a last attempt to assess the mood in Saigon, Kennedy sent McNamara and General Taylor on a personal mission. After a week of meetings they called on Diem himself. With a "serene self-assurance" that disconcerted

For President John F. Kennedy, Communist guerrilla activity in South Vietnam posed a threat to the free world. Covertly, he sent US military personnel to assist the South Vietnamese.

We are launched on a course from which there is no respectable turning back.

— Henry Cabot Lodge, Jr.,
August 1963

A young Buddhist monk, protesting Diem's policies, commits suicide in the streets of Saigon. Some passersby stop to watch; others simply walk by. This was the sixth act of self-immolation in four months.

After a coup against them, which Washington had encouraged, Ngo Dinh Diem and his brother Nhu were murdered. Kennedy was shaken. Three weeks later, in Dallas, he too was shot dead.

Lyndon B. Johnson, Kennedy's vice president, is sworn in as president on Air Force One before returning to Washington, 22 November 1963. LBJ is flanked by his wife, Lady Bird, and by Kennedy's widow, Jacqueline.

McNamara, Diem spoke for two and a half hours about the wisdom of his policies and the progress of the war. Diem flatly rejected any call to end his regime's repression of the people; he blamed the press for exaggerating the situation. Diem's intransigence sealed the fate of his regime. As a sign of US willingness to disengage, Washington announced it would withdraw a thousand military advisers by the end of the year.

At 1:30 PM on 1 November 1963, South Vietnamese rebel generals surrounded the presidential palace and seized key facilities in Saigon. The following day Diem agreed to stand down. Diem and his brother Nhu fled from the palace and took shelter in a church. There, an armoured personnel carrier picked them up and drove them to the rebel military headquarters. When the vehicle's doors were opened, Diem and his brother, hands tied behind their backs, had both been shot. Told of their murder, Kennedy was reportedly so shaken he had to leave his meeting. McNamara had never seen him so moved. Kennedy was profoundly troubled by the religious and moral implications of what was being done in Vietnam in his government's name.

Three weeks later President Kennedy made his fateful trip to Dallas. As he was driving through the city in a motorcade, shots rang out. The president of the United States too had been gunned down. An hour later, he was dead.

One of the most enduring questions about American policy in the 1960s is, Would Kennedy, had he lived, have escalated the war in Vietnam in the way his successor did? Kennedy had made clear to no one his long-term policy for Vietnam — he was still reacting to events. However, Robert McNamara has recently written in his memoir *In Retrospect* that he believes Kennedy would not have sent in American combat troops on a large scale. The president expressed the view that since the South Vietnamese were incapable of defending themselves, it was unwise to risk shedding American blood in support of a regime that so lacked a stable political base — even though some felt this probably would have meant the fall of Vietnam, and of all Southeast Asia, to communism.

McNamara relates how Kennedy, early in his administration, asked all his senior officials to read Barbara Tuchman's book *The Guns of August,* with its graphic portrayal of how Europe's leaders had blundered into war in 1914. "We are not going to bungle into war," Kennedy told his team. In both the Bay of Pigs incident and the Cuban missile crisis, Kennedy had demonstrated that he would stand up to belligerent advice from his closest aides. Impossible as it is to say what he would have done, McNamara believes that the longest and the most divisive war in American history might never have happened had Kennedy not been assassinated in Dallas on 22 November 1963.

"Win the War!"

Vice President Lyndon Baines Johnson succeeded Kennedy as smoothly as was possible under traumatic circumstances. Johnson inherited an unstable Vietnam that was more dangerous than at any time in the past. His advisers were deeply split over what policy to follow. Barely forty-eight hours after Kennedy's assassination, while plans for the funeral were still being made, Johnson called his most senior advisers together. The new president was con-

Secretary of State Dean Rusk, President Johnson, Secretary of Defense Robert McNamara, and General Maxwell Taylor, US ambassador to South Vietnam, in the Cabinet Room. The course they embarked on would prove neither popular nor successful.

Senator Barry Goldwater of Arizona, Republican candidate in the 1964 presidential election, charged LBJ with inaction in Vietnam. Johnson, campaigning on a peace ticket, rammed the Tonkin Gulf Resolution through Congress and won in a landslide.

vinced that behind the conflict in Vietnam lay Soviet and Chinese plans for hegemony in Asia. At this first meeting Johnson told his advisers that he had "serious misgivings" but he was "not going to lose Vietnam." He wanted to give priority to military operations over internal social reforms. "Win the war!" was his specific instruction.

Under this new president government officers spoke in increasingly bullish terms about their determination to provide "whatever help is required to win the battle." But as Communist insurgents increased their activity in the South, the situation went from bad to worse. By the end of 1963 there were twenty thousand US military personnel in Vietnam.

In the years following the coup against Diem, governments came and went in Saigon; the president is quoted as saying, "I'm getting sick and tired of this goddamned coup shit in Vietnam. It's got to stop." Policy reviews in Washington took on an even more urgent tone, and high-level delegations made a series of visits to Vietnam. Johnson told his aides he was "extremely alarmed" by the deteriorating situation. General Curtis LeMay proposed bombing bases in North Vietnam and along the Ho Chi Minh Trail. The Joint Chiefs of Staff considered using tactical nuclear weapons to hold the enemy forces at bay. Contingency plans for the bombing and blockading of the North were drawn up. In May 1964 the CIA concluded that the situation would become "untenable" by the end of the year if the tide did not turn.

In this tense context, early in August 1964, in the Gulf of Tonkin, US naval vessels came under fire from North Vietnamese patrol boats while conducting surveillance in what they regarded as international waters. Two days later, when subsequent attacks were reported, Washington reacted with outrage at what it described as unprovoked aggression. In fact, the second encounter never actually happened, but Johnson seized the moment. In the midst of a presidential election campaign, and smarting from attacks by his opponent, Barry Goldwater, and the Republican right about his inaction over Vietnam, Johnson ordered the first bombing of North Vietnamese bases as retaliation for the attacks at sea. He then went to Congress seeking a resolution that would authorize him to take "all necessary measures" to defend US or allied forces and to "prevent further aggression." In addition, the proposed resolution would enable the president to determine when "peace and security" in the area had been attained. Opinion polls showed that 85 per cent of the American public supported the administration. One senator declared, "Our national honor is at stake, and we cannot and will not shrink from defending it."

On 7 August, after only minimal debate, the Tonkin Gulf Resolution was passed in the Senate by 88–2 and in the House by 416–0. The resolution was the nearest the United States ever came to a declaration of war over Vietnam. Now the president had congressional authority to pursue the conflict as he saw fit. As Johnson later put it, the resolution was "like Grandma's nightshirt — it covered everything."

In the presidential election, Johnson won an overwhelming victory over the Republicans; he had a popular mandate for his plans to build a "great society" and to take a tougher line against communism in Southeast Asia. In the months following the election, plans were made for a dramatically increased

New York, 1963

22 November. Commuters heading home to Stamford, Connecticut, take in news of the president's sudden death. We will never know whether Kennedy, if he had lived, would have cut the United States loose from Vietnam.*

KENNEDY EXT

PRESIDENT
Shot by Ass

Highlights of Kennedy's Career

KENNEDY EXTRA
PRESIDENT DEAD
by Assassin
New York World-Telegram
ALL Sports FINAL
PRESIDENT SHOT DEAD
EXTRA
on Plane

The Tonkin Gulf Incident

During early 1964 the Soviet Union installed modern anti-aircraft missiles and radar stations across North Vietnam and at bases along the Gulf of Tonkin. The United States needed information about how this system worked for its contingency plans to bomb or blockade the North.

On the afternoon of 30 July, four South Vietnamese patrol boats left their base at Da Nang and attacked North Vietnamese radar installations along the gulf. A destroyer, the USS *Maddox*, patrolling offshore, monitored the radio and radar traffic the attacks triggered and relayed the signals back to CIA listening stations. The North Vietnamese had never established their territorial waters, so the US interpreted them as extending three miles offshore, even though China claimed twelve miles. Despite protests from North Vietnam, the *Maddox* continued its zigzagging patrol between four and eight miles offshore.

On 2 August three North Vietnamese torpedo vessels gave chase to the *Maddox*, which opened fire as it sped away. The North Vietnamese boats launched their torpedoes, all of which missed, and fired back at the *Maddox*, which now called for air support from a nearby carrier, the USS *Ticonderoga*. The skirmish lasted no more than twenty minutes and ended with one North Vietnamese torpedo boat sunk and two severely damaged. The North Vietnamese considered that they had chased away "pirates," but to the United States this was unprovoked aggression against American vessels in international waters.

Additional American fighter-bombers and another aircraft carrier were ordered into the area. The *Maddox* was joined by a second destroyer, the *Turner Joy*. On the following day, South Vietnamese boats moved once more against shore-based installations. That evening a dramatic tropical thunderstorm blew up that buffeted the *Maddox* all night and added to the tension on board. At about eight in the evening the captain of the *Maddox* intercepted messages that gave him the "impression" that Communist patrol boats were about to attack. With their equipment operating erratically in the storm, the crew of the *Maddox* believed they were under attack and had picked up sonar and radar signals of torpedoes. The captain called again for air support, but aircraft from the *Ticonderoga* could find nothing. Pilots from the *Ticonderoga* later stated that they saw no sign of a North Vietnamese naval attack.

The next day, 4 August, the president took the offensive and ordered American aircraft to bomb North Vietnamese naval bases and an oil storage depot — the first US bombing of North Vietnam. Johnson addressed the nation on television that evening and claimed, "Repeated acts of violence against the armed forces of the United States must be met not only with alert defense but with positive reply. That reply is being given as I speak to you tonight."

For many years it was believed in the United States that the Tonkin Gulf incident was an act of unprovoked Communist aggression. But even at the time, the captain of the *Maddox* admitted that none of his crew had made "actual visual sightings" of North Vietnamese vessels, and not one sailor on either the *Maddox* or the *Turner Joy* had actually heard North Vietnamese gunfire. The opening of archives in Hanoi has confirmed that there was no second attack on the US destroyers on the night of 3-4 August.

7 August 1964. President Johnson signs the Tonkin Gulf Resolution, the nearest the United States ever came to a declaration of war in Vietnam. "Like Grandma's nightshirt," LBJ said, the resolution "covered everything."

US entry into the war. By the end of 1964, there were twenty-three thousand US military personnel in Vietnam.

Meanwhile, changes were taking place in the Communist world. In October 1964 Nikita Khrushchev, who had never been forgiven for what some of his Kremlin colleagues perceived as his stand-down over Cuba, was removed from power by a palace coup. His style of idiosyncratic leadership had fallen out of favour; without fuss, he was brushed out of the way. Leonid Brezhnev and Aleksei Kosygin replaced him.

The Chinese had not readily accepted Khrushchev's leadership of the Communist world since he denounced Stalin at the 1956 Party Congress; they felt that his links with the West were diluting his commitment to Marxism-Leninism. When Khrushchev refused to share the secrets of producing an atom bomb with the Chinese, Mao Zedong took this as an insult. What had started as minor fractures in the relationship between Moscow and Beijing developed into major fissures. In 1958 Mao launched a new policy, the Great Leap Forward, by which he wanted to transform China into a wealthy world power in the shortest time possible. Land was taken over by the state; the family was to disappear; and people were organized into huge communes. Mao promised that China would catch up with Britain and ultimately with America in only a few years. The outcome was a disastrous famine in which more than 30 million Chinese starved to death.

A Chinese poster portrays the Vietnamese resisting US imperialism in South Vietnam and urges the Americans to leave. They did, eventually.

U.S. Imperialism, Get Out of South Viet Nam!
L'impérialisme américain hors du Sud-Vietnam!
¡Fuera el imperialismo norteamericano del Sur de Vietnam!

"A Bunch of Stubborn Bastards"

Tension between the Soviet Union and China led to competition between them to supply North Vietnam with aid and military assistance. The Chinese saw themselves as worldwide backers of anti-imperialism; wherever possible they championed the anti-American struggles of others. The Soviet Union, however, was pursuing a new policy of peaceful co-existence with the United States; it now wanted to be more discreet in its aid to North Vietnam. In February 1965 Kosygin visited Hanoi at the invitation of Ho Chi Minh. Kosygin was ready to give the North Vietnamese more military aid on condition that Hanoi would follow the Moscow line and not Beijing's. Kosygin then tried to persuade the North Vietnamese to consider opening negotiations with the United States, which the leadership in Hanoi bluntly rejected. The Soviet delegation's talks in Hanoi were as stormy as the American disputes with Saigon. One Soviet participant later talked of the North Vietnamese as "a bunch of stubborn bastards."

With military assistance from both Moscow and Beijing, forces of the Viet Cong were able to increase their infiltration of the South. They now had about 170,000 men and women there who could launch attacks almost at will. In November 1964 the Viet Cong attacked a US air base at Bien Hoa. In December they planted car bombs in Saigon. On 7 February 1965 they attacked the American air base at Pleiku in the Central Highlands, killing eight Americans and wounding over a hundred. This attack finally prompted the president to authorize sustained retaliation against Hanoi; in March the bombing of North Vietnam began in earnest in a campaign code-named Rolling Thunder. For eight years, heavy bombing of military positions would continue in an attempt to force the North Vietnamese to the bargaining table. It did not succeed.

High explosives, napalm, and cluster bombs rained down on North Vietnam from the bellies of giant B-52s and from ground-attack aircraft. From the early days it was clear that this was not an effective way to strike at an undeveloped nation where supplies were still transported by bicycle or on the backs of porters. However, successive American leaders believed that easing up would signal weakness. They would agree to stop only as a tactic to bring the North Vietnamese to the negotiating table. If that failed, the relentless bombing would start up again.

In addition to high explosives, the United States dropped 18 million gallons of herbicides to destroy the tropical forests that hid the Viet Cong and the rice crops on which they subsisted. The United States also used a chemical defoliant known as Agent Orange, which contained small amounts of a highly toxic dioxin. It was believed afterwards that some US soldiers who handled the chemical got cancer or skin disease. Tests subsequently revealed that the South Vietnamese had blood levels of dioxin three times that of US citizens, from Agent Orange accumulated in rivers and streams. It would take years for the poisonous chemicals to be flushed out of the fragile ecosystem.

William Westmoreland

For the first time since the Korean War, US marines go ashore in a combat zone, at Da Nang, South Vietnam.

In all, the United States dropped more tons of explosives on Vietnam than were dropped by all parties during the entire Second World War. This led to cruel absurdity: after one particularly intense raid had reduced a Vietnamese city to rubble, an American officer was quoted as saying, "We had to destroy the town in order to save it."

By the start of Rolling Thunder the United States was well down the slippery slope towards full-scale war in Vietnam. General William C. Westmoreland, the field commander in Saigon, asked for forces to protect the bases from which the air raids were carried out. General Taylor, now US ambassador in Saigon, objected, arguing that "white faced soldiers" were unsuited to "Asian forests and jungles" and would fare little better than the French. But President Johnson overruled him. On 8 March 1965 the first US ground troops, 3,500 marines in full battle kit, waded ashore at Da Nang. Their task was to defend American installations. The following month, Johnson authorized an even greater increase in US troop deployments, and agreeing with Westmoreland's view that "good offense is the best defense," he

BELOW: *Pham Van Dong, prime minister of North Vietnam, welcomes the Soviet Union's Aleksei Kosygin, February 1965.* RIGHT: *North Vietnamese anti-aircraft guns are readied; they could do little against US bombers.*

The United States dropped napalm, which burned severely. Even victims who reached a hospital rarely survived.

permitted the troops to patrol the countryside and actively seek out and kill the Viet Cong.

But Johnson decided to conceal this escalation of the war in Vietnam from the nation. He feared that a public declaration of war would undermine his domestic programme to build the Great Society. His refusal to admit to the American people what was clearly evident in every television news report from Vietnam created a credibility gap that would dog his administration.

Escalation in Vietnam did not go unchallenged in Washington. Several senior officials made spirited and emotional pleas not to increase the American stake in the war. Clark Clifford, then chairman of the Foreign Intelligence Advisory Board, worried that Vietnam would be a "quagmire" requiring "more and more ground troops without a realistic hope of ultimate victory." George Ball, at the State Department, was especially vociferous in arguing for compromise, warning that the United States would face a "protracted war" unless it could find a way to "limit its liabilities." Even the vice president, Hubert Humphrey, outlined his opposition to the war because of its impact on domestic policies. Johnson isolated Humphrey from decision making on Vietnam for the next year.

Washington, 1966

National Security Adviser Walt Rostow, Secretary of State Rusk, and President Johnson in the Oval Office, 5 May. There were now more than 200,000 US troops in Vietnam, but it was still hard to see victory — or a way out.

"We Will Stand in Vietnam"

In June the civilian government in Saigon once again disintegrated, and General Nguyen Van Thieu became head of state. Appalled, Westmoreland asked for "forty-four battalions" to fight the war on the ground, with the likelihood of his needing an extra 100,000 men in 1966. "We are in for the long pull," he told Johnson. McNamara and Rusk supported the request, and the defence secretary flew to Saigon to review Westmoreland's battle plan. Again, with cool, balance-sheet logic, McNamara gathered a multitude of statistics and predicted that Westmoreland would need all the men he had asked for, and probably a hundred thousand more. At the end of July, Johnson again went into conclave with his advisers, the "wise men." They were still deeply divided. But for Johnson the choice was clear: full-scale war or a humiliating American retreat. At a press conference on 28 July, the president announced, "I have asked the commanding general, General Westmoreland, what more he needs to meet this mounting aggression. He has told me. And we will meet his needs. . . . We will stand in Vietnam."

In November the first major confrontation took place between US and Communist forces. In the Ia Drang Valley in the Central Highlands, the two armies met head-to-head in conventional warfare. Several days of fighting left more than two thousand North Vietnamese soldiers dead. The US lost three hundred troops. Both sides saw the battle as a victory; the Americans because they had inflicted greater losses than they had suffered, the North Vietnamese because they had held their position. The Americans failed to realize that while US public opinion would not tolerate such losses for long, the Viet Cong could sustain losses for an indefinite period. The Vietnamese were willing to pay a higher price.

Over Christmas, hoping to encourage the North Vietnamese to come to the negotiating table, Johnson ordered a halt to the bombing of the North. This failed to have the desired result, and the bombing began again. By the end of 1965, there were 183,000 American troops in Vietnam.

America Transforms South Vietnam

The arrival of US forces in South Vietnam was followed by the vast panoply of a modern, high-tech army. Engineers with giant bulldozers carved roads through the jungle and built bridges across the streams of the Mekong delta. Airfields, helicopter pads, and landing strips were constructed throughout the country. Floating piers were towed across the Pacific to build new ports. Radio and communication centres went up everywhere. Oil, ammunition, and supply depots sprang up wherever American troops were stationed.

US soldiers, whether based in city office blocks or fighting in remote jungle outposts, were kept supplied with necessities from home. They got beer, cigarettes, and hot meals — including turkey and cranberry sauce on Thanksgiving. In Saigon the main US military post exchange (PX) resembled a department store; its counters were laden with sporting goods, radios, cameras, whiskey, hair sprays, shaving lotions, and condoms. Parallel to the PX, the black market flourished with goods that had gone "missing" from US supply depots. Stalls sold not only pilfered consumer goods, but rifles, ammuni-

US troops in South Vietnam were well supplied, and any surplus fuelled a thriving black market in Saigon streets. US taxpayers never intended to fund this trade.

A drug culture flourished. Heroin, grown in Laos, was easily available. GIs experimented with it, and with opium. Marijuana was widely used. Habits picked up in Vietnam were taken home.

Aftermath for B Company, 173rd Airborne Battalion, following a Vietcong attack. The wounded will be helicoptered out.

tion, flak jackets, typewriters, and office furniture. By 1967 a million tons of supplies were pouring into the country each month.

The American bombing, shelling, and defoliation drove tens of thousands of peasants from their villages into vast sprawling shantytowns that grew up along the edge of every city. Their traditional social and family structure was shattered; separated from their farms, millions of Vietnamese were condemned to a life of poverty. The young were easily tempted into a world of vice around the wealthy and luxurious American camps. An underworld appeared outside each military base offering bars, nightclubs, massage parlours, and brothels. Here, young Vietnamese women earned as much in a week as their fathers had done in a year. Many American servicemen, as well as civilians and diplomats, took Vietnamese consorts — not just from among the impoverished but sometimes from the smart sectors of Vietnamese society.

The drug trade became endemic. Heroin refined from the opium fields of Laos was sold by dealers who were often representing high-level officials in the Saigon government. In 1971 the Pentagon estimated that nearly 30 per cent of American troops in Vietnam had experimented with heroin or opium. Smoking marijuana, or dope, became commonplace. Attempts to stamp out trafficking in drugs invariably came up against resistance from Vietnamese authorities, with some officials protecting small fortunes being made from narcotics. The sale of drugs in Vietnam fed back into the United States — an even bigger potential market.

As America pushed ahead with the war, US spending in Vietnam multiplied. The gulf between the Vietnamese who prospered from this and the mil-

The Television War

Vietnam was the first television war. The American people were fed a nightly diet of news that showed scenes of carnage and destruction. During the Korean War, most of the newsreel film had been taken by official military cameramen, but in Vietnam the news film was produced by the American TV networks, allowed to move freely and operate as they wished. Using lightweight cameras, they had easy access to events, and could send their colour pictures back to the United States with great speed.

On 5 August 1965, *CBS Evening News* included a report by Morley Safer from a village called Cam Ne that showed a GI setting fire to the straw roof of a peasant's home with his Zippo cigarette lighter. The villagers meekly stood by, begging for mercy. People watching at home were shocked; must US soldiers now torch the homes of helpless peasants? What on earth was America doing in such a war? But the American public, little concerned whether Viet Cong were active in villages like Cam Ne, eventually became bored by the nightly news reviews; soon the ratings for special reports from Vietnam dropped to all-time network lows. However, for a decade, the chief source of information on the war for most Americans was the short news report served up each night with dinner in front of the television.

lions of displaced rural peasants in shantytowns became immense. Import programmes brought consumer luxuries to a privileged few. Inflation soared, further dividing the haves and the have-nots. Thieu's corrupt regime looked to the Americans to provide a lead in every aspect of policy. When Prime Minister Nguyen Cao Ky met President Johnson at a conference in Honolulu, he delivered a speech written for him by his American advisers that echoed the president's own rhetoric about the Great Society. The speech prompted Johnson to lean forward and tell the prime minister, "Boy, you speak just like an American." Ky basked in the glory. It was the ultimate compliment.

Vietnam's Buddhists opposed this Americanization. They led a series of protests in 1966, parading through the ancient capital of Hue with banners reading "Down with the CIA" and "End Foreign Domination of Our Country." This convinced Ky that Communists had infiltrated the Buddhists, and peaceful protesters were then confronted with tear gas and bayonets. Again, Buddhist monks and nuns set themselves ablaze, and horrifying images shocked the world. Eventually, in September 1967, elections for a new legislature and presidency were held. Candidates were screened to ensure that no Communists stood for election. Thieu was elected president with a low vote. Ky became vice president and chief of the military council. Now, at last, Washington could say it was fighting to defend a democratically elected government.

Search and Destroy

Westmoreland's strategy set these priorities: first, to defend US bases along the South Vietnamese coast and in Saigon; second, to launch search-and-destroy missions that would find and eliminate the Viet Cong; third, to mop up the remaining Communists to achieve final victory. As a backdrop, continued heavy bombing of North Vietnam would bludgeon the enemy into submission and sap his will to fight in the South. The Americans encouraged the Saigon government to control South Vietnam's rural population by "pacifica-

Peace Negotiations: Looking For a Starting Point

In April 1965 North Vietnamese premier Pham Van Dong outlined the Four Points that became Hanoi's basis for settlement: (1) withdrawal of the US military from South Vietnam; (2) neutrality of North and South Vietnam pending "peaceful re-unification"; (3) settlement of South Vietnam's internal affairs in accordance with the programme of the National Liberation Front (the Viet Cong); and (4) peaceful re-unification of Vietnam without "foreign interference."

The United States rejected this as a starting point for negotiations; it implied acceptance of Communist control over South Vietnam. However, it was never totally clear how willing Hanoi might be to negotiate a compromise from this position. In January 1966, Secretary of State Rusk outlined the US position in his Fourteen Points; these included welcoming unconditional discussions, considering Hanoi's Four Points, supporting free elections in the South, and allowing the

Vietnamese to determine for themselves the question of re-unification.

Later, any willingness in Hanoi to start talks was predicated upon a stop to the US bombing campaign against the North. Although Johnson halted the bombing several times, he did not hold back long if there was no immediate progress towards peace.

tion" of the countryside — an attempt to win the hearts and minds of the peasantry that increasingly became a crude bullying of village communities.

None of this worked. Search-and-destroy missions grew in intensity. Helicopter gunships roamed over the countryside firing at anything suspicious that moved. With the great difficulties they had in distinguishing between civilians and Viet Cong, it was easier for GIs to shoot first and hopefully not ask or answer too many questions later. The bombing of the North increased by more than 50 per cent during 1967. And yet report after report showed that the North Vietnamese were continually able to maintain their supply routes into the South along the Ho Chi Minh Trail and to match every increase

ABOVE: *US troops, dropped into a landing zone in the Central Highlands, hug the ground.*
ABOVE RIGHT: *At a makeshift first-aid station, wounded marines reach out to each other.*

in military effort made by the United States. Policy-makers in Washington despaired.

As the war continued to escalate, different peace initiatives were toyed with, even though the two sides seemed far apart. McNamara persuaded the president to prolong the Christmas truce on bombing North Vietnam in December 1965, and diplomatic exchanges took place for a month. Disagreement about what should be the Viet Cong's role in ending the war led the United States to resume the bombing. The North Vietnamese then closed the dialogue. Later, in 1966, the Poles began secret talks with the United States and with the North in an exercise code-named Marigold. For the first time the Soviets became involved, but again renewed bombing of Hanoi led to failure in the talks.

In February 1967 Johnson appealed directly to Ho Chi Minh. He offered to stop bombing the North if the Communists would stop infiltrating the South. Ho insisted the United States must unconditionally halt the bombing and "all other acts of war" against the North before talks could begin. Through 1967 six courses were pursued via intermediaries to establish a basis for negotiations to begin. None of them got anywhere. British prime minister Harold

Wilson approached Soviet premier Kosygin about finding ways to launch peace talks. But again this initiative foundered when the bombing of the North resumed. A major obstacle was that the United States did not always integrate its diplomatic and military actions; diplomacy frequently would be undermined by military activity at a critical moment.

When Johnson met Kosygin at Glassboro, New Jersey, in June 1967, the United States agreed to suspend the bombing as long as talks began immediately and neither side's forces made any advances. This concession from the US side was met with silence from Hanoi; despite Soviet mediation, no answer was ever received.

ABOVE: *On 31 October 1967, Nguyen Van Thieu is inaugurated as South Vietnamese head of state; behind him is Nguyen Cao Ky, vice president.*
ABOVE RIGHT: *US Ninth Division soldiers patrol what is left of a prosperous Saigon district after the Tet Offensive. Damage here was caused by US artillery and helicopter gunship fire.*

"Hey, Hey, LBJ"

Meanwhile, protest against the war at home in the United States was reaching new levels of intensity and bitterness. Many members of Congress were now suspicious of the war and its cost in lives and money. Johnson's ambitious programme of welfare reforms to build the Great Society had to be put on hold. And more and more demonstrators came out onto the streets to protest the futility of the war. In October 1967 between 50,000 and 100,000 protesters marched against it in Washington.

By the end of 1967 the US government was spending $20 billion a year on the war in Vietnam, helping to generate an annual balance of payments deficit of $7 billion. The number of US troops in Vietnam had grown to 485,000.

Despite reports of the "rapid deterioration of the strength of the Viet Cong," they regularly moved weapons and ammunition into the South, smuggling them right into the heart of towns and cities. Then, during the Tet holidays of January 1968, the Viet Cong mounted simultaneous attacks in more than one hundred cities; it was their most spectacular offensive yet. In Saigon a commando unit even penetrated the US Embassy compound; it had to be flushed out man by man. This feat, which took place in front of television cameras, stunned America and public opinion worldwide. Although the US military had intelligence that an attack was imminent, they appeared to have been caught completely by surprise. The bitterest fighting in the Tet Offensive took place in Hue, where intense house-to-house fighting and killing went on for several weeks.

The Tet Offensive was intended to inspire a popular rising across South Vietnam. It failed totally in this. Furthermore, it led to massive losses of some of the Viet Cong's best fighters. However, in propaganda terms the offensive was a magnificent victory. Before Tet, American leaders had talked of grave enemy weaknesses and of how the Viet Cong had met their masters and were

ABOVE: *Lyndon Johnson, cares showing, prepares a speech on Vietnam. Having made up his mind not to seek a second elected term as president, he announced his decision on 31 March 1968.* ABOVE RIGHT: *Hue, a normally tranquil city in central Vietnam. US marines call for assistance for those wounded in bloody fighting with Viet Cong on 1 February 1968.*

desperately hanging on. Now the Viet Cong had shown they could attack at will, and could strike even at the very nerve centre of the US presence in South Vietnam.

In Washington, President Johnson was increasingly isolated. McNamara left the Pentagon at the end of February to take a position offered some months earlier as president of the World Bank. He said he did not really know whether he had quit or been fired. The new defence secretary, Clark Clifford, opposed General Westmoreland's latest request for another 200,000 men, arguing that there soon would be further requests, "with no end in sight." He recommended pegging the level at 20,000. The president agreed. In March, Robert Kennedy announced his candidacy for the presidency and spoke out harshly against Johnson's policies. Johnson was devastated by the hostile chanting that confronted him wherever he went: "Hey, hey, LBJ; how many kids did you kill today?"

In the second half of March 1968, the "wise men" went into conclave again to review progress and consider options in Vietnam. By now the civilians of the group were openly critical of the assessments presented by the military. When told that 80,000 of the enemy had been killed and that the normal ratio of killed to wounded was 1:3, UN Ambassador Arthur Goldberg calculated that all of the enemy's manpower must be dead or injured. "Then who the hell are we fighting?" he asked. On 31 March, Johnson addressed the nation on television and announced that the United States would halt all bombing above the 20th parallel in the hope that "talks begin promptly." He went on to surprise everyone, including his own advisers, when he added: "I shall not seek, and I will not accept, the nomination of my party for another term as your president." The president had given up the fight.

A Slow Start on Talks

In May 1968 preliminary peace talks began in Paris. In the face of obdurate North Vietnamese negotiators, the talks soon ran aground. The dispute focused on whether or not the United States would halt all bombing of the North and who could sit at the negotiating table; would the National Liberation Front, the Viet Cong, sit down alongside the United States, the North, and the South? There was no agreement.

In the summer of 1968 Richard Nixon was nominated by the Republicans as their presidential candidate. Hubert Humphrey was the Democrats' choice. Nixon met with Johnson and agreed not to attack the president over Vietnam during the campaign, in return for an understanding that Johnson would not abandon Saigon. Nixon also agreed that while campaigning he would not call for a pause in the bombing. By October the Paris talks were deadlocked over representation. President Thieu, in Saigon, was deeply opposed to negotiating with North Vietnam if the Viet Cong were also present. This would imply formal recognition of his hated enemy.

With the election only days away, Johnson received FBI reports that Anna Chennault, a Nixon fund-raiser, was acting as a go-between for the Republicans with Thieu. Nixon's campaign manager had asked her to tell Thieu to

> *This confused war has played havoc with our domestic destiny. . . . The promises of the Great Society have been shot down on the battlefields of Vietnam.*
>
> — Martin Luther King, Jr.,
> 15 April 1967

Krokodil mocks Vietnam's increasing cost in American lives. The first thing Lyndon Johnson asked for each morning was the previous day's number of US casualties.

Vietnam: "What's to Be Done?"

Reporter Philip Caputo, author of the acclaimed memoir *A Rumor of War* (1977), recalled in a 1997 interview for the television series *Cold War* an incident in Vietnam, where he served in combat as a Marine Corps platoon leader in 1965–1966:

"I remember sitting at this wretched little outpost one day with a couple of my sergeants. We'd been manning this thing for three weeks and running patrols off of it. We were grungy and sore with jungle rot and everything else like that, and we'd taken about nine, ten casualties on a recent patrol. This one sergeant of mine, Prior was

his name, said, 'You know, Lieutenant, I don't see how we're ever going to win this.' And I said, 'Well, Sarge, I'm not supposed to say this to you as your officer — but I don't either!' So there was this sense, at least in my platoon and maybe in the whole company in general, that we just couldn't see what could be done to defeat these people."

oppose the cessation of bombing, and so undermine the peace talks, promising that Thieu would get a better deal under the Republicans. "That's the old Nixon," said Johnson when he heard. Thieu held out, and refused to attend talks at which the Viet Cong were present. Despite this, Johnson called a halt to the bombing on 31 October. Two days later, Radio Hanoi announced, "This is a great victory for the Vietnamese people." Still, Thieu refused to join the negotiations. Nixon talked of the "tired men" around Johnson and the need for a new team with "fresh ideas." The opinion polls showed a swing away from Humphrey, who up to this point had enjoyed a narrow lead.

On 5 November the American people came out to vote. Nixon was elected president with 43.4 per cent of the vote; Humphrey received 42.7 per cent. There would indeed be a new team at the White House. But, although the North had set out the terms on which the war would eventually end, the fighting in Vietnam would go on for another five years, and cost many thousands more lives.

May Day military parade in Moscow. The displays salute the North Vietnamese and call down destruction on the United States.

Richard Nixon, Republican candidate for president, campaigning in Savannah, Georgia. He won, narrowly, over Democrat Hubert Humphrey.

Kansas, 1963

A ten-story-tall Titan II intercontinental-range missile poised on its 150-foot-deep underground launch pad. Strategic Air Command targeted Soviet cities. The USSR responded in kind.

Looking skyward, at Vandenberg Air Force Base in California, President Kennedy, Defense Secretary McNamara, and SAC commander General Thomas Power watch an Atlas missile launch.

Mutual Assured Destruction

When Nikita Khrushchev stood up to address the delegates of the Twenty-second Communist Party Congress in Moscow on 30 October 1961, he had something special to tell them. Reminding the world of the strength of Soviet nuclear technology, Khrushchev announced that the Soviet Union had just detonated the largest bomb the world had ever seen. The explosion was equivalent to more than 50 million tons of TNT — more than all the explosives used by all participants in the Second World War. This heralded a new generation of Soviet superbombs. Khrushchev told the party members that he hoped "we are never called upon to explode these bombs over anybody's territory." He added, "This is the greatest wish of our lives." Privately, he spoke of letting the bomb "hang over the heads of the imperialists, like a sword of Damocles."

Khrushchev neatly summed up the Cold War's nuclear paradox: each side devoted huge resources to developing weapons it hoped never to use. Their strategic value lay in deterring the other side. The superpowers would refrain from attacking each other because of the certainty of mutual assured destruction, better known by its apt acronym, MAD. This theory, which underpinned the Cold War, epitomized the craziness of the nuclear balance of power: to start a war would mean almost certain self-destruction. What distinguished the Cold War from all previous conflicts was that the force now existed to destroy the entire planet and every living thing on it.

During any crisis in the nuclear diplomacy of the 1960s, the superpower leaders walked a tightrope. Although it was tempting in a confrontation to try to face down the other side, this was hugely dangerous. In the repeated crises over Berlin; during the fortnight of the Cuban missile crisis; as the conflict in Vietnam escalated; in regional conflicts that threatened to draw in the superpowers — in all these cases, pushing the enemy to the point of humiliating defeat might open up the risk of nuclear retaliation and global destruction. Kennedy for one was very aware that in nuclear gamesmanship it was necessary to give the other guy opportunity to save face in a crisis. When pressed by USAF general Curtis LeMay to bomb the Russian missile sites in Cuba, Kennedy held back, leading LeMay to believe he was a coward. What the American leaders did not then know was that, contrary to CIA estimates that no nuclear warheads had yet reached Cuba, the Soviets already had at least twenty warheads there for medium-range SS-4 missiles. The president, had he listened to his military chiefs, would very probably have instigated a nuclear exchange that could have destroyed much of North America and the Soviet Union, and caused a lethal nuclear winter to descend across Europe and most of Asia. Casualties would have been measured in hundreds of millions. As one American historian recently put it, "If John Kennedy had followed LeMay's advice, history would have forgotten the Nazis and their terrible Holocaust. Ours would have been the historic omnicide."

Meanwhile, the MAD doctrine kept both sides in a continuous state of alert. Early warning radar systems constantly scanned the skies. It was believed in the 1950s that the United States would have a warning of between two and six hours before Soviet bombers arrived. However, in the 1960s hostile missiles could reach their destinations within minutes. An entirely new warning system was needed. In 1962 the United States set up a Ballistic Missile Early Warning System (BMEWS) with three co-ordinated radar tracking stations, at Thule in Greenland, at Clear in Alaska, and at Fylingdales Moor on the east coast of England. From these, radar beams monitored all traffic from the direction of the Soviet Union, and huge multiple computer systems could process data and measure the position and velocity of any incoming missile, predicting trajectory and impact point and time. All this information could then automatically be transmitted to the North American Air Defense Command (NORAD) in Colorado Springs. From there, alerts would be passed on to Strategic Air Command (SAC) in Omaha, Nebraska.

By 1961 SAC kept at least twelve giant B-52 bombers constantly in the air, twenty-four hours a day, 365 days a year. Many of them were on twenty-four-hour patrols. They refuelled in midair, along a northern route circumnavigating the North American continent, and along a southern route crossing the Atlantic and orbiting continuously over the Mediterranean. Each B-52 was armed with three or four thermonuclear weapons, each preassigned to a target within the Communist bloc. Every bomb had a series of safety devices built into it to prevent accidental detonation. In addition to this airborne alert, code-named Chrome Dome, one-half of the entire US force of B-52 bombers was held on a constant ground-alert status; planes and crews at all times stood by, needing only a fifteen-minute scramble to be airborne.

At a host of missile silos, in remote corners of America, ICBMs were on permanent standby. During the Cuban missile crisis, 182 ICBMs were primed and ready for firing. After the first generation of Atlas missiles came a new

Curtis LeMay

"THERE'S A RUMOR GOING 'ROUND THAT WE WON..."

Restraint? Why are you so concerned with saving their lives? The whole idea is to kill the bastards. At the end of the war if there are two Americans and one Russian left alive, we win.

— Gen. Thomas Power, commander of Strategic Air Command in the 1960s generation of Titans, and by the end of 1963 the giant Titan II, weighing over 150 tons, and the even more sophisticated but smaller Minuteman missile.

From the early 1960s, too, submarines lay on the bed of every ocean, completely untraceable, waiting for the command to fire their nuclear missiles, known as submarine-launched ballistic missiles (SLBMs). At any one moment the United States could launch 144 Polaris ballistic missiles from its submarine fleet in the Atlantic, and additional salvos later from the Mediterranean and the Pacific. These deterrent weapons would, it was thought, ultimately eliminate the need for an airborne bomber assault.

A command structure was created that could operate even if a sudden first strike took out its centre. Eisenhower approved a system by which, if the conventional command and control system were destroyed, local commanders would have authority to launch nuclear weapons if, in their view, the country was under nuclear attack. In the Cuban missile crisis, accordingly, one fighter squadron of the Twenty-eighth Air Division in California, armed with nuclear weapons, flew with all safety devices removed. The division's official history noted, "Only the pilot stood between the complete weapon system and a full-scale nuclear detonation." Fortunately, the top guns desisted from starting a nuclear war.

In addition to this, the head of Strategic Air Command had specific "authority to order retaliatory attack . . . if time or circumstances would not permit a decision by the president." At the head of SAC had been the bullish Curtis LeMay. In 1957 he was replaced by the even more bullish General Thomas Power. LeMay later admitted that he was concerned about Power. "He

General Thomas Power gives evidence to a Senate committee, February 1960. Power was so tough that even Curtis LeMay, his predecessor as SAC commander, was worried by him.

The Soviet Superbomb

The explosion over Novaia Zemlya on 30 October 1961 was the single largest explosion ever detonated on the planet, equivalent to about 50 million tons of TNT. The flash was visible 600 miles away. The fireball was described as "powerful and arrogant like Jupiter"; it appeared to "suck the whole earth into it." A mushroom cloud rose forty miles into the stratosphere. The island over which the bomb was tested was levelled of snow, ice, and rocks, so that to one observer it looked like an immense skating rink.

The principal Soviet nuclear physicist behind the superbomb was Andrei Sakharov. In his memoirs, Sakharov says he was torn between the "conviction that our work was crucial in pre-serving the parity necessary for mutual deterrence" and the "bitterness, shame, and humiliation" over the biological and environmental consequences of the testing. Khrushchev, however, was determined to test the bomb as a sign to the West of Soviet power in the tense weeks that followed the building of the Berlin Wall. "We have to conduct our policies from a position of strength," he announced.

The detonation of the 50-megaton bomb was the first in a series of Soviet superbombs. Khrushchev claimed that he would detonate an even mightier, 100-megaton bomb, but in fact the bomb of 30 October 1961 would remain the largest exploded during the Cold War — or since.

Moscow, 1965

The Soviets celebrate the anniversary of the October Revolution with this display of military might.

was mean; he was cruel, unforgiving, and he didn't have the time of day to pass with anyone." LeMay used to "worry that General Power was not stable." After 1962 the system of decentralized nuclear control, with authority to attack in one man's hands, was revised. A new system of dual controls with electronic so-called permissive action link locks was introduced. Even then, SAC had the codes.

Detailed workings of the Soviet nuclear defence system still are not known, but they probably roughly mirrored the US systems. The Soviets had fewer missiles at first — in 1961 only 44 ICBMs and 155 heavy bombers against 156 American ICBMs and 1,300 bombers. The United States also had the advantage of advance bases in Europe; and two of its allies, Britain from 1952 and France from 1960, had their own nuclear weapons. After the Cuban missile crisis, Moscow decided it must try to match the US nuclear stockpile. By the mid-1960s the Soviet nuclear arsenal had risen to about 400 missiles, ranging from large SS-9 missiles, which could deliver their payload to a target 7,000 miles away, to small SS-11s, similar to Minuteman missiles. In 1968 the Soviet Union deployed its own fleet of Yankee class submarines, each one carrying 16 nuclear missiles. The Soviet Union was catching up, and would soon surpass the United States in the number of ICBMs it could deploy. By now both sides had enough nuclear weapons to destroy the world, and all life on it, several times over.

"Ban the Bomb"

People first began to question and to criticize the destructive potential of atomic and thermonuclear weapons during the 1950s. At a meeting in London at Central Hall in Westminster, on 17 February 1958, a large audience gathered to hear speeches against the manufacture and use of nuclear weapons. Speaker after speaker denounced and morally rejected the bomb; each was met with deafening applause. A new organization was established in Britain, the Campaign for Nuclear Disarmament (CND). That Easter a protest march was made to Aldermaston, Britain's principal nuclear-weapons research site. Only a few thousand took part in 1958, but the march became an annual event, a pilgrimage of protest. The Ban the Bomb protest movement spread to Holland, West Germany, and Sweden. It provided a first political experience for thousands.

One founder of CND was the philosopher and Nobel Prize winner Bertrand Russell. He saw in MAD not only the likely extinction of the human species, but a perversion of civilized morality. Russell wrote: "Nuclear warfare is an utter folly, even from the narrowest point of view of self-interest. To spread ruin, misery, and death throughout one's own country as well as that of the enemy is the act of madmen.... The question every human being must ask is 'can man survive?'"

CND called for unilateral nuclear disarmament in Britain, which had its own H-bomb, believing that if Britain gave up its bomb and evicted the United States from bases on British soil, other nations would follow suit. Many felt this did not go far enough; a more outright rejection of all nuclear weapons was needed. In late 1960 Russell split from CND and joined the militant

In February 1961, philosopher Bertrand Russell led this protest demonstration against the risks of nuclear war.

The first Aldermaston March, in 1958, from London to the Aldermaston nuclear research centre.

"Make Love Not War" circles the logo of CND, the Campaign for Nuclear Disarmament, a universal symbol of protest. A composite of the semaphore signals for the letters N and D, its central motif suggested a human being in despair.

Committee of 100, which was dedicated to inciting civil disobedience over nuclear disarmament. In September of the following year, a month after the Berlin Wall had gone up, a series of sit-down protests was planned for London and Holy Loch in Scotland, where the first US Polaris submarine had just arrived. The British police charged several of the organizers with inciting the public to civil disobedience. Many of them, including Bertrand Russell, then aged eighty-nine, were sent to prison. Russell spent a week in Brixton prison in south London (the same prison he had been sent to as a conscientious objector during the First World War). His imprisonment provoked international outrage. Sympathy helped spread the cause. A series of protests in Britain followed, including an attempt by the Oxford Committee to immobilize the military air base at Greenham Common in June 1962.

However, it was less public protest than scare inside the White House and the Kremlin — generated by the Cuban missile crisis in October 1962 — that indirectly prompted the US and Soviet leaders into action. In June 1963, during a commencement address at American University, Kennedy said that the Soviet Union as well as the United States were "both devoting massive sums of money to weapons that could be better devoted to combat ignorance, poverty, and disease." Kennedy declared that agreements to end the arms race were "in the interests of the Soviet Union as well as ours." He committed the United States there and then to a ban on atmospheric nuclear tests. Within six weeks the Nuclear Test Ban Treaty was signed in Moscow, by which the United States, Britain, and the USSR agreed to halt all but underground testing of nuclear weapons (France did not sign). No giant leap, this was more a tiny step; how-

The Aldermaston March

From 1959 the annual Ban the Bomb march started at Aldermaston; the number of protesters grew as the march, lasting the whole Easter weekend, approached the heart of London. Over the years, tens of thousands marched behind jazz bands, carrying placards and banners, singing songs, and chanting slogans. The marchers were predominantly young — about 40 per cent were estimated to be under the age of twenty-one. Every year the march ended with a rally in Trafalgar Square.

A film made of the first march captured the mood of many. One demonstrator said: "We're marching because it is all we can do to express our hostility towards a policy that is bound to lead to nuclear catastrophe and widespread devastation." A young woman declared: "I'm protesting because as a mother I don't want my children to grow up in a world whose survival is threatened by the existence of nuclear bombs."

The British establishment was profoundly shocked that thousands of ordinary citizens had taken to the streets to demonstrate. The British media were highly suspicious, treating the marchers as unwashed and irresponsible beatniks.

In many ways the Aldermaston March defined the protest movement against nuclear weapons, and it marked the beginning of a new era of protest, which would shape the 1960s.

At 1500 hours Beijing time, 16 October 1964, Communist China joined the nuclear club. The world suddenly seemed a more dangerous place.

ever, it was the beginning of a process that continued for a generation, throughout the rest of the Cold War, in which the superpowers regularly negotiated on arms limitations.

Khrushchev and Kennedy had shown restraint over Cuba; both seemed genuinely terrified by the prospect of a nuclear holocaust. The military, on both sides, appeared less terrified. American generals boasted they could bomb the Reds into the Stone Age. Of all the world leaders, Mao showed the least apparent reluctance to use nuclear weapons to destroy capitalism. When the Soviets told him of the devastation that American nuclear weapons could wreak on China, Mao responded, "We may lose more than 300 million people. So what? War is war. The years will pass and we'll get to work producing more babies than before."

For the Chinese, the stepdown over missiles in Cuba and the test ban treaty were further signs that the Soviet Union was no longer a revolutionary state in the forefront of world communism. When Khrushchev refused to supply the Chinese with the know-how to construct an atom bomb, the Chinese speeded up their own nuclear programme and exploded a first atom bomb on 16 October 1964. Less than three years later, on 17 June 1967, China exploded a 3-megaton H-bomb, making the transition from atomic to thermonuclear power faster than any other nation. There were now five countries that possessed nuclear weapons.

The Palomares Incident

One of the most dramatic nuclear accidents happened on a clear midwinter day, 17 January 1966, at 30,000 feet over Spain's Mediterranean coast. A B-52 bomber on a regular air-alert patrol from a base in North Carolina was being refuelled in midair by a KC-135 jet tanker when the two planes collided. Both blew up, igniting the 40,000 gallons of jet fuel on the air tanker. Eight of the eleven crew members of the two aircraft were killed, and four hydrogen bombs from the B-52 fell to earth around the village of Palomares. Although the safety devices prevented a thermonuclear explosion, the high explosives in two of the bombs went off; radioactive particles were scattered over several hundred acres of farmland. A third bomb landed intact near the village. The fourth landed in the sea.

There then followed what a later report called "the most expensive, intensive, harrowing, and feverish underwater search for a man-made object in world history." Thirty-three US naval vessels sealed off the area; divers and mini-subs scoured the seabed. After eighty days the missing bomb was finally found, by the midget sub *Alvin*, at a depth of 2,500 feet, about five miles offshore. It was intact and appeared not to have leaked any radiation.

At first the United States announced, "There is no danger to public health or safety as a result of this accident." However, within a few days it was realized that the two bombs that went off had leaked disturbingly high levels of plutonium radiation. About 1,750 metric tons of radioactive soil had to be removed to the United States for

burial. The main crop in the Palomares district was tomatoes, and several tons had to be buried or destroyed. After the last barrel of soil was removed, the United States left the follow-up to the Spanish authorities. Six years later an American survey revealed understaffing by the Spanish nuclear energy commission, technical deficiencies, and general lack of interest. Not until 1985 did the people of Palomares obtain access to their medical records, which were inconclusive. The US *Palomares Summary*, produced by the Defense Nuclear Agency in 1975 and eventually made public through the Freedom of Information Act, noted that a prevailing wind on the day of the accident churned up plutonium dust and that "the total extent of the spread will never be known."

Fail-Safe Devices

Each nation had its own sophisticated arrangements for the authorization and use of nuclear weapons, but no system can be completely fail-safe. The more complex the technology, the more prone it is to some form of malfunction. Although the nuclear powers claim to have had a clear safety record, the recounting of Cold War nuclear accidents and close calls is lengthy, comprising human errors, technical failures, chilling malfunctions, and appalling cover-ups. Only now, from secret military archives, is the catalogue of accidents and near misses beginning to emerge.

On 26 July 1957, while practising a touch-and-go landing at RAF Lakenheath near Cambridge, a US B-47 bomber crashed into a storage depot housing three nuclear bombs. Blazing jet fuel threatened to ignite the TNT in the trigger mechanism of the bombs, but fortunately firefighters extinguished the blaze. Had the bombs exploded, most of East Anglia would have been devastated. The event was kept secret until news of the accident leaked in the early 1990s.

On 24 January 1961 a B-52 bomber came apart in midair over North Carolina, and two 24-megaton nuclear bombs were released as the bomber fell to earth. One bomb parachuted to the ground and was recovered. The other landed in waterlogged farmland and was never found. The electrical fusing mechanism of the bombs was designed to withstand the pressure of fire or

The probability of total destruction increases with time and, in the course of the months and years throughout which we are told to expect the Cold War to continue, it becomes almost a certainty.

— Bertrand Russell,
Has Man a Future?, 1961

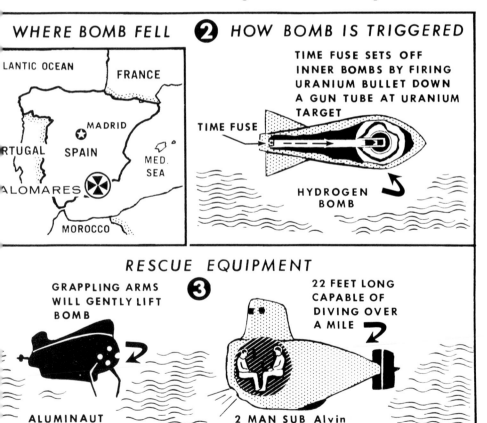

An H-bomb, complete with its white parachute, was recovered undamaged from the Mediterranean near Palomares, Spain, after the crash of a B-52 bomber in January 1966. This US Navy photograph was the first ever released of a hydrogen bomb.

explosions, and the chance of an accidental detonation was believed to be less than one in a million. However, when the recovered bomb was examined, it was found that five of its six safety devices had failed. North Carolina was saved from a nuclear explosion a thousand times more powerful than that at Hiroshima by the one remaining safety system.

On the afternoon of 21 January 1968, a fire broke out on board a B-52 as it was orbiting above the early warning radar station at Thule, Greenland. Within minutes, electrical power was lost. As dense smoke filled the plane, the captain gave orders to evacuate. Six of the seven crew members parachuted safely to the land below. The seventh was killed. The B-52, carrying four hydro-

ABOVE: *Radar towers on the US air base at Thule, Greenland. Thule was the site of a nuclear accident when a B-52 crashed making an emergency landing.*
ABOVE RIGHT: *Searchers, using dog teams on the frozen surface, found parts of one of four hydrogen bombs carried, and radioactive debris from the bomber.*

gen bombs, crashed into the ice seven miles away from the Thule base and exploded. Although the safety devices prevented a nuclear detonation, the conventional high explosives in all the bombs went off; radioactive debris was scattered over a large area. The government of Denmark, of which Greenland was a province, was outraged. Nuclear weapons were prohibited on its territory.

After the Palomares incident (see box, page 238), there was a review of the SAC airborne alert system. Defense Secretary Robert McNamara argued it was no longer necessary to keep a force of B-52 bombers constantly armed and airborne. Early warning systems had been improved by over-the-horizon radar, and the role of ICBMs had diminished the importance of the bomber fleet; the risk of accidents made the cost and the danger too high. SAC argued fiercely to defend its airborne alert status, but agreed to a compromise. Some flights were maintained, others cut back. The flights over the Thule radar base continued; SAC argued that they provided a vital fail-safe link in case communications went down, or in the event of a Soviet surprise attack on America's early warning system.

The accident at Thule provoked a crisis. There was widespread international protest against the US policy of flying bombers armed with nuclear weapons over neutral countries. There were heightened fears, too, about the environmental risks of radiation leakage. Despite reassurances from Pentagon spokesmen that "safety devices and precautions provide 'virtually 100 per cent' certainty that there will be no nuclear explosion if a plane crashes with its load of bombs," a hellish nuclear accident seemed a real possibility. Washington decided to end the airborne alert operation; henceforth SAC would rely on the early warning system to get its bombers armed and airborne.

Triggering Nuclear Retaliation

Crashes involving nuclear weapons were frightening enough. Even more terrifying were failures of the complex systems developed and designed to respond to a nuclear attack and to trigger retaliation. In Kennedy's first defence message to Congress he announced, "Our defense posture must be designed to reduce the danger of irrational or unpremeditated general war — the danger of an unnecessary escalation of a small war into a large one, or misinterpretation of an accident or enemy intention." Defence systems were designed to be infallible; civilian and military leadership were determined to minimize the effect of errors. There was never just one radar system but always two or three overlapping each other, so that if one went down the others would take over. High standards of training and a strong "culture of reliability" permeated the US military, particularly embracing nuclear systems. But ultimately all human systems are fallible. And the risks do not come higher than when error or misinterpretation of evidence can result in nuclear war.

During the Cuban missile crisis, one might have expected that with everyone at a state of heightened alert the risks of accident or close call would have lessened. The opposite was the case. With so many bombers, missile silos, submarines, and communication centres on tense, maximum standby, the potential for foul-up increased. At 4:00 AM on 26 October, at the height of the crisis, unknown to Washington an Atlas ICBM was launched from Vandenberg Air Force Base in southern California. The missile was not armed; its launch was a test that had been scheduled some time earlier and, due to bureaucratic imperative, had not been cancelled. But Vandenberg was on DEFCON 2 alert status, so the other missiles there had been fitted with nuclear warheads. Had the Soviets detected the launch of this test missile, they could easily have imagined that the firing was for real. Their response might have been to order an immediate nuclear retaliation against the United States. Again, at Malmstrom Air Force Base in Montana, the first squadron of Minuteman missiles was about to be deployed when the Cuban crisis erupted. In the haste to get them onto alert, we now know, several routine safety procedures were overlooked. Miswirings or short circuits could have led to an inadvertent missile launch. Moreover, the crews who were rushed into taking charge of their deadly payloads had not been fully trained or certified for these launchers.

In the tensest moments of the missile crisis, ground defence forces at all US air bases were vigilant against sabotage attempts by Soviet agents. On the night of 25 October, an air force sentry on patrol at a base near Duluth, Minnesota, spotted someone climbing over the perimeter fence. He fired at the intruder and sounded the alarm for sabotage. At bases throughout the region a series of synchronized alarms went off. But at Volk Field in Wisconsin, the wrong alarm was triggered. A Klaxon was sounded signalling that nuclear war had begun. Pilots ran to interceptor planes fully armed and

Control board for rocket no. 3, or how to launch a UK-based missile. The British officer would insert his key in the lock at the bottom, turn it, and push each button in turn. Only then would the American officer fit his key into the other lock, top left. If he turned it from Peace to War, the missile, and its warhead, would fly.

primed with nuclear weapons. These men, who had been told there would be no practice drills during the Cuban crisis, immediately started their engines and headed towards the runway. Fortunately, the base commander had checked with Duluth and ordered an officer to drive his car into the middle of the runway and flash his lights to abort the takeoffs.

Back at Duluth it was found that the suspect intruder was a bear.

The most chilling incident of all took place on 27 October 1962, the Black Saturday of the missile crisis, the day on which both sides felt that a nuclear confrontation looked unavoidable. Just before 9:00 AM radar operators at an advance warning station at Moorestown, New Jersey, were carrying out a regular check of their computer systems. They inserted a software test tape in which a simulated missile attack from the Caribbean activated an advanced level of alert and then aborted the system automatically, after ensuring that all responses had been correct. At the exact moment the Moorestown operators inserted their software test tape, a "friendly" space satellite crossed the horizon from the direction of Cuba. According to the command-post log, the computers and their operators "became confused" as to what was real and what was part of the test. They reacted as though under attack. Moorestown informed NORAD at Colorado Springs that a missile had just been launched from Cuba. They calculated that it was targeted on Tampa, Florida, and would detonate at 9:02 AM. The Strategic Air Command in Omaha was alerted that a nuclear attack was under way, as was the command room at the Pentagon.

What if . . . ? Stanley Kubrick's nightmare fantasy Dr. Strangelove was worryingly close to a real doomsday scenario. A US commander goes mad and orders a nuclear attack on the Soviet Union. No one can call back one of the bombers. The Soviet Union cannot not retaliate — Doomsday. George C. Scott as General Buck Turgidson, Peter Sellers as President Muffley.

Dr. Strangelove

In 1964 Columbia Pictures released Stanley Kubrick's *Dr. Strangelove, or How I Learned to Stop Worrying and Love the Bomb*. Kubrick imagined in this Cold War satirical comedy a scenario in which a US air base commander goes berserk and orders his squadron of B-52 bombers to attack the Soviet Union. Due to a series of mishaps, it proves impossible for the Pentagon to call one of the bombers back from its nightmare mission. In a hilarious sequence, the American president telephones the Soviet premier on the "hot line" to warn him. The premier informs the president that the "Doomsday machine" will now automatically launch a massive retaliation against the United States. The film ends with a macabre vision of the nuclear holocaust beginning.

Although it was denied that the series of foul-ups depicted in *Dr. Strangelove* could ever take place, the history of nuclear accidents and near misses shows how the seemingly impossible might have become the almost believable. Ideas of a Doomsday machine had actually been raised by Rand Corporation nuclear theorist Herman Kahn. He said it would be technically possible to link a giant computer to thousands of H-bombs, so that if the Soviets launched a surprise attack, the computer would go to war and fire off the bombs. Kahn thought that a Doomsday machine was an appalling notion but, theoretically, a possibility. Kahn's book *Thinking About the Unthinkable* helped inspire Stanley Kubrick to make *Dr. Strangelove*.

Looking on the bright side; missiles conquer space. Alexander Alexandrovich Dejneka called this mural design "Masters of the Universe." Technology could be used for good or ill.

President Johnson and Soviet premier Kosygin meet at Glassboro, New Jersey, in 1967. Both great powers, knowing each could destroy the other, realized they had to limit nuclear weapons. In 1969 Strategic Arms Limitation Talks began in Helsinki.

But there was no nuclear detonation in Tampa. At Moorestown they began to realize their error. Other radar tracking stations confirmed that the satellite was friendly. In the Pentagon, when assured it was a false alarm, everyone heaved a sigh of relief.

This scare sounds impossible. Who could have anticipated that during a test a satellite would come up on a radar screen at the precise moment and exact location where a missile launched from Cuba would have appeared? No fail-safe system could anticipate such a coincidence — and on the tensest day of the entire Cold War. But it happened.

Destabilizing the Balance

Apocalyptic fear of nuclear disaster gripped East Europeans and the Soviet peoples far less dramatically. All they heard was reassuring government propaganda, even if few believed it. The Cuban missile crisis scared millions in the West who followed the news of it day by day. Many key events were carried live on television. But in the Soviet Union not a hint of the crisis was revealed until it was nearly over, and then only on an inside page of *Pravda*. It was only the party elite who had any idea of what really was going on.

Aware of US superiority in missiles and bombs targeted on their homes, the Soviet leadership began to concentrate on constructing a defensive shield. In the mid-1960s Soviet scientists developed a system of anti-ballistic missiles (ABMs) ahead of their American counterparts. As the technology advanced with dramatic speed, it seemed possible to build a defence system that could intercept missiles in flight, before they reached their target. The ability to do this, however, struck at the balance at the heart of Cold War confrontation: if one side was not able to destroy the cities and missile launching sites of the other, then deterrence would not work. The superpower with the defensive shield would gain an overwhelming advantage. Mad as it sounds, successful defence was therefore a destabilizing factor.

In the United States scientists were also developing ABMs, but the costs were horrendous and the system was not thought reliable. If even a small number of missiles penetrated the shield and hit their targets, the ABM defences would prove worthless. In January 1967, fearing an impossible escalation of both offensive and defensive systems, McNamara persuaded Johnson to postpone development of the US ABM system until diplomatic initiatives had tried to limit deployment of the Soviet equivalent. Johnson agreed. He wrote to Kosygin that if the Soviets deployed their ABM system he would be under great pressure from Congress to develop a similar defensive system for the United States and to "increase greatly our capabilities to penetrate any defensive system which you might establish."

The two leaders met at Glassboro, New Jersey, following the crisis of the Six-Day War in the Middle East. Johnson raised the issue of an ABM ban. But, in a resolute voice, Kosygin protested, "Defense is moral. Aggression is immoral." How could he refuse to protect his own people from missiles attacking them? Moscow was not prepared to start ABM talks; its only real interest was in reducing the totals of offensive strategic missiles, of which the United States possessed the most.

While the debate about ABMs continued, American scientists pioneered a new system: multiple independently targetable re-entry vehicles, or MIRVs. Each missile could carry up to ten separately targeted warheads — each one capable of destroying a city. This made the problem of constructing a defensive shield infinitely more complex and immensely more expensive. The number of missiles became irrelevant; it was the number of warheads that mattered. In the very year their ABM system, called Galosh, first became operative in the Moscow region, the Soviets had to face the prospect of increasing the system tenfold. The arms race now meant that the two superpowers were spending more than $50 million per day between them on nuclear armaments. Negotiations to limit this intolerable burden became inevitable.

Worth Its SALT

On 1 July 1968 the Soviet Union, the United States, and Britain signed the Nuclear Non-Proliferation Treaty, prohibiting the transfer of nuclear technology to other countries (France and China did not sign). Alongside this, Washington and Moscow announced that "in the nearest future" they would begin "talks on arms limitations and reduction of offensive strategic nuclear weapons systems as well as systems of defense against ballistic missiles." The two nuclear giants had come to a weary conclusion: some sort of arms control was needed to prevent a cost escalation that could bankrupt them both. But despite the rhetoric, the aim of arms control would not be disarmament and a return to the unstable world before nuclear parity; it would be to ensure a stable nuclear balance between the two superpowers. Mutual deterrence would prevail.

The first arms-limitation talks were set to open in Geneva at the end of September 1968. When the Soviets invaded Czechoslovakia in August, the United States pulled out of the talks. It was not until Richard Nixon was inaugurated president in January 1969 that the stalled talks looked to be starting up again. After several months of talks about talks, both sides finally got round the table. Nixon toyed with the idea of linking the arms-limitation talks with the Middle East and Vietnam, but finally abandoned this. The need to stop the impossible spiralling of arms costs overrode all else.

On 17 November 1969 US and Soviet negotiators finally sat down together in Helsinki to begin what would be called the Strategic Arms Limitation Talks (SALT). The talking in Helsinki, and later in Vienna, dragged on for years as the negotiators tried to agree on what should be included and what excluded — and then how to verify compliance with what had been agreed. The Americans wanted to concentrate on ABM systems, choosing not to negotiate where they had superiority, as with MIRV technology. The Soviets wanted to limit strategic offensive weapons where the United States still had an advantage. The Soviet delegates were warned that the KGB was listening; anyone who offered too much or admitted more than had been agreed faced detention in the Lubyanka prison. The idea of open inspection of each other's missile sites was anathema to the military on both sides. As the negotiations inched forward, technological advances in weaponry continued, and at times even outstepped the pace of the talks.

Krokodil *is sceptical; this daisy chain kills.*

Behind the scenes, Henry Kissinger, Nixon's national security adviser, opened a back channel with Soviet ambassador Dobrynin — just as the Kennedys had done during the Cuban missile crisis. At critical points, when the talks jammed, Kissinger and Dobrynin were able to suggest ways around issues that seemed insurmountable in Helsinki and Vienna. Both delegations were kept in ignorance of these back-channel talks. Negotiators who had been patiently finding areas of agreement one by one, and then slowly building on these, felt outmanoeuvred by secret deals that broke the deadlock.

As the SALT negotiations continued at a snail's pace, the Soviet Union was narrowing the missile gap with the United States. In some cases it even surpassed the United States. This put pressure on Washington to take the talks seriously. Also, American military expenditure on Vietnam was still enormous. The United States was keen to see some breathing space in its defence spending. By 1971 Nixon and Kissinger wanted to speed up agreement, and accepted that submarine-launched missiles (SLBMs) should be included in the talks, despite US ascendancy in these.

Finally, on 26 May 1972, at a long-postponed summit in Moscow, President Nixon and Soviet leader Leonid Brezhnev signed the agreement that became known as SALT I. Both sides agreed to limit the number of ABMs; the Soviet Union was allowed to continue its buildup of ICBMs and SLBMs. But SALT was silent on the issue of MIRVs, so the Russian advantage in missile numbers was matched by the US advantage in deliverable warheads. The agreement did not cover medium-range and intermediate-range missiles, nor US bases in Europe. However, SALT I was an important first step. It would eventually usher in a new era of détente between the superpowers.

In 1972 SALT I and the ABM treaty effectively froze the military balance between the Soviet Union and the United States and codified the central philosophy of the Cold War: that each side must be able to destroy the other, but only by guaranteeing its own suicide. In its mad way, this ensured a form of nuclear stability. The Cold War had evolved through the balance of terror to a sort of balanced peace — at least between the two superpowers. But although the superpowers were learning to co-operate, the arms race was by no means at an end. It would now increasingly focus on technological virtuosity. And the nuclear arsenals continued to grow. A hundred thermonuclear warheads would have been more than enough for each side to destroy the other, and to serve as a real deterrent. By the end of the Cold War, the superpowers would have between them 40,000 thermonuclear warheads, each one at least one hundred times more powerful than the bomb dropped on Hiroshima. For forty years, total destruction of the human race, and all other life on earth, was a daily possibility.

In May 1972 President Nixon went to Moscow and, with Leonid Brezhnev, signed SALT I. There was a balance of terror, but the superpowers would stabilize it.

San Francisco, 1966

BLACK PANTHER PARTY FOR

Each Cold War power bloc contained its own counter-culture. Black Panthers, claiming the United States denied basic rights to African Americans, took up arms in big-city ghettos.

Culture Wars
1960–1968

Levittown, Long Island, from the air. The image suggests uniformity, but each family enjoys the privacy of its own home. In the Soviet Union, a family might all share one room.

The Military-Industrial Complex

The Cold War was not just a clash of military empires, but of economies, of cultures, of rival ways of life. The expenditure on armaments it entailed fuelled the American economy through the longest period of dynamic economic growth in world history, as it ushered in a new era of prosperity in the West. In 1960 defence expenditure in the United States amounted to nearly $50 billion — 52 per cent of all federal expenditure, about 10 per cent of gross domestic product. The United States had military alliances with forty-eight nations; more than 1.5 million of its servicemen were stationed around the world. The Department of Defense directly employed another 1 million civilians. Thousands of companies benefited from military contracts. Research projects were handed out to universities and research institutes by the hundred. A vast military-industrial complex developed whose interest it was to maintain or increase this level of expenditure.

Companies like General Dynamics, Lockheed, McDonnell-Douglas, or Newport News Shipping depended on defence contracts, and lobbied for continued high levels of defence spending. Many other US companies, including some of the largest, owed their high levels of production to defence work. All this public investment (much of it going to the southern and western Sunbelt states) generated profits for the shareholders. In Texas there were Bell Helicopters and the giant LTV Industries, as well as NASA in Houston. In Georgia there was Lockheed at Marietta, generating new wealth. The population of California increased sixfold; the McDonnell-Douglas and Hughes aircraft plants grew in size dramatically; nearly one-third of all defence contracts went to this single state. In the Northwest, Boeing in Seattle became one of the biggest employers. Wall Street also enjoyed the Cold War — shares in aerospace rose in value at a rate three times that of the market average.

Defence activities' spin-offs drove the civilian economy; the arms race created new metals and materials. Massive investment in radar and early warning systems helped grow the electronics and telecommunications industries. The Boeing 707, before becoming the most successful civilian airliner of all time, began life as a military refuelling tanker. American industrial technology during the 1960s produced ever more sophisticated arms, and at the same time gave consumers the items they wanted.

The military-industrial complex was all-pervasive, and all-powerful. Hardly ever did a public figure speak out against it — few congressmen dared risk the charge of shortchanging the nation's defence by objecting to military expenditure. Kennedy, campaigning against Nixon, convinced many Americans that the Eisenhower administration had allowed a missile gap to grow between the United States and USSR, thus endangering national security. Only Eisenhower himself, in his farewell address on leaving office, dared warn America against the "unwarranted influence" of the "military-industrial complex. The potential for the disastrous rise of misplaced power exists and will persist." He also warned of the "prospect of domination of the nation's scholars by federal employment, project allocations, and the power of money." It took a *retiring* president, at the end of a career that included distinguished military service, to issue this warning.

The US economy was driven also by a growing internationalism. Since the end of the Second World War, the United States looked for foreign markets to sell into. From the Marshall Plan onwards, US foreign policy encouraged free and open private-enterprise economies on the American model because this provided not only foundations for democratic societies but a marketplace for American goods. US exports quadrupled between 1950 and 1970. But US growth rates were still lower than those in Europe and Japan. Many American companies discovered they could earn more by investing their money abroad. Much of this money then remained in the economy that generated it. So the years of the Cold War saw the growth and flourishing of the multinational corporation. By 1968, 40 per cent of US investments in France, Britain, and West Germany was held by just three companies — Ford, General Motors, and Standard Oil of New Jersey. Investment decisions were made not by government officials like those who had orchestrated the Marshall Plan, but by the boards of multinational companies whose objective was profit. American multinationals extended their business throughout the capitalist world. IBM, Ford, and Exxon invested heavily in Europe, South America, and Asia. Flying the flag, every US military base became an outpost of American trade and culture. Coca-Cola and blue jeans were the symbols of modern consumerist culture worldwide, the objects that millions aspired to use and flaunt.

An American Tragedy

At home in the United States, however, prosperity was not shared evenly. Areas of deprivation remained — islands of poverty in a sea of wealth. While the Sunbelt prospered, huge numbers of jobs were lost in the old inner cities.

The American Dream, and its dark underside. For some, there's a well-stocked fridge as big as a house; in 1960s Harlem, home is a deteriorating slum that the landlord won't fix.

Robert Kennedy

At the beginning of the 1960s, more than 5 million Americans were unemployed; black unemployment was nine times the rate for whites. Across the southern states racism was still entrenched. Blacks and whites could not sit together on buses, eat in the same restaurants, drink in the same bars, or attend the same schools. Protest against this legalized apartheid built up in the 1950s; in the early 1960s it became widespread. Dr. Martin Luther King, Jr., a young black Baptist minister, was thrust into national prominence when in Montgomery, Alabama, he led the struggle against segregated seating on public buses. King preached non-violent protest and civil disobedience. Thousands of boycotts, demonstrations, sit-ins, and marches publicized the system's injustices. Well-disciplined and non-violent civil rights protesters met intense opposition from local whites and from the police. News film of policemen brutally beating peaceful demonstrators with batons, or firing water cannons at them, solicited national and international sympathy. Demands to desegregate schools and colleges led to sensational set-piece confrontations, as in Birmingham, Alabama, where Governor George C. Wallace and his racist supporters looked on and fumed as federal troops enforced black students' enrolment at the state university.

King led the massive March on Washington in August 1963, when 200,000 civil rights supporters gathered to hear him. "I have a dream," he proclaimed. "Now is the time to open the doors of opportunity to all of God's children." Folk singer Joan Baez led the chorus of "We Shall Overcome." Bob Dylan sang of the changes that were "Blowin' in the Wind." The rally called on the White House to ban racist laws and to give black Americans equal opportunities in education and jobs. After the speeches, President Kennedy invited the leaders to the White House and congratulated them. Robert Kennedy, as attorney general, urged his brother to act. The president spoke grandly: "The rights of every man are diminished when the rights of one man are threatened." But he knew he needed the southern vote, and hesitated to act decisively.

After Kennedy's assassination, Lyndon Johnson took over and brought new priorities to the White House. High on his list was the building of what he called the Great Society and an "unconditional war on poverty." In July 1964 he signed the Civil Rights Act, outlawing racial discrimination. But equality was still a long way from a reality in the South. Throughout 1964 activists were attacked, beaten up, shot at, and a few murdered in what became known as Mississippi Summer. One woman, the granddaughter of a slave, who had been so severely beaten she could no longer walk, said on television, "Is this America, the land of the free and the home of the brave . . . where our lives be threatened daily because we want to live as decent human beings?" In Alabama, King led a harrowing march from Selma to Montgomery in March 1965 to publicize the fact that only 1 per cent of eligible blacks were registered to vote in Dallas County. The marchers were attacked and beaten by angry whites until the president federalized the National Guard and instructed Governor Wallace to allow the march to proceed. "We are on the move now, an idea whose time has come," declared King.

Hollow Legs Love Foodarama Living

Raleigh, North Carolina, February 1960. White waitresses ignore two black students seated at the whites-only counter.

In the cities of the North, residential segregation concentrated deprived racial minorities into huge ghettos. In the summer of 1965 the black ghetto of Watts in Los Angeles exploded in the first of a series of inner-city race riots. Fifteen thousand troops had to be called in to restore order, and for nearly a week the ghetto burned. A thousand buildings were destroyed; 4,000 blacks were arrested; 1,000 people were injured; 34 were killed. For the next three years, northern cities experienced "long hot summers" of discontent, rioting, and outbursts of violence. These culminated in Newark, and then in Detroit

in 1967, where 43 people lost their lives and $250 million of property was destroyed. *Newsweek* headlined this "An American Tragedy." The race riots helped generate a "white backlash" against civil rights and a further division within American society. For Washington, claiming to lead the free world against the tyranny of communism, poverty, injustice, and conflict inside the United States proved embarrassing. America was at war both abroad and at home.

President Johnson's intended War on Poverty was slowing down as the real war in Vietnam ate up cash that could have gone into federal funding for anti-poverty programmes. It took as little as $50 a month to help one American out of poverty, but about $300,000 to kill one Viet Cong. King had strongly supported Johnson for his stand on civil rights; he now turned into an outspoken critic of Vietnam policy as the Great Society became a victim of military spending in Southeast Asia.

What Are We Fighting For?

The unwinnable war in Vietnam became the great polarizing issue of the era, dividing the United States more than at any time since the Civil War, a hundred years earlier. With the nightly television coverage, and as the number of casualties rose, more people questioned why America was fighting this war. The anti-war movement really got going in October 1965 with demonstrations in more than ninety cities, including Washington, where eighty thousand

ABOVE LEFT: *Martin Luther King, Jr., waves to the marchers at the Lincoln Memorial, 30 August 1963. King had a dream: that blacks would share fully in America's democracy.* ABOVE: *Lyndon Johnson shakes King's hand after signing the Civil Rights Bill into law, 2 July 1964.*

A National Guard convoy rolls into the Watts section of Los Angeles, 14 August 1965, prepared to deal with prolonged rioting. Civil rights legislation was not enough in itself to avert violent protest.

Everywhere they say "Go to California! California's the great pot o' gold at the end of the rainbow." Well, now we're here in California, and there ain't no place else to go, and the only pot I seen's the kind they peddle at Sixtieth and Avalon.

—A Watts rioter,
Los Angeles, 1965

protesters marched. The anti-war marches brought together pacifists, religious groups, and left-leaning student organizations opposed to American militarism abroad. Johnson's extension of the draft caused the protest to grow dramatically; it brought university students directly into the war, and the campuses started to erupt in a rash of draft card burnings. Over the next few years, anti-war slogans echoed around campuses and cities across the United States, and directly outside the White House and the Pentagon.

But although the number of US personnel in Vietnam increased year by year, as did the casualties, the majority of the population still supported the war effort. In September 1966 three out of four Americans supported the president's war aims. Crowds carrying banners that read "Support our men in Vietnam — Don't stab them in the back" attacked the protesters. Congressmen called on the government to clamp down on that "sleazy beatnik gang" who defaced their draft cards. A law was passed by a voice vote in the Senate ordering imprisonment for up to five years and a $10,000 fine for wilful destruction of draft cards. Ronald Reagan, then running for governor of California, gave his view of the anti-war demonstrations at Berkeley in three words: "Sex, drugs, and treason." For many in what became known as the "silent majority," it was one thing to protest over civil rights but something else to undermine the government's foreign policy during a war. When protesters started to burn the Stars and Stripes, thousands of patriotic Americans went out and bought miniature flags to display in windows and on their cars. "My Country Right or Wrong" posters began to appear throughout the nation.

The sixties generation of young Americans was the tallest, the best educated, and the most affluent in the country's history. California, where much of the aerospace industry was based, epitomized a prosperous America. It was the richest state of the union, with an economy larger than that of any foreign country except the Soviet Union, West Germany, Britain, and France. It had the highest average income in the United States and the highest provision per capita of cars, swimming pools, backyard patios, barbecues, and colour televisions. It was in California, however, that a new counter-culture first appeared, in which thousands of young people rejected the materialism and consumerism of their parents' generation.

Having grown up with the daily threat of nuclear annihilation hanging over them, young radicals wanted to turn their backs on an America they saw as racist, sexist, and imperialist. Activists started to claim that all were not equal in modern America — certainly blacks were not, nor were women. Alongside anti-Vietnam protests and peace vigils, there came a variety of sit-ins and teach-ins calling for a full-scale revolt against the American Way of Life. Some students just wanted to drop out. Others took a more ideological approach and wanted a radical overhaul of society.

Although many eloquent radicals argued forcefully for change, the movement was largely leaderless. Their organizations had names like Students for a Democratic Society, the Student Nonviolent Coordinating Committee, and, more militantly, the Black Panthers, the Yippies, and the Weathermen. Out of this counter-culture came demands for black power, and later for women's liberation. From Berkeley came the first talk of "flower power" and the call to "make love, not war." In 1966–1967, San Francisco was the hippie centre of the

Detroit 1967

In long, hot summers, US cities blazed. LBJ's War on Poverty, its resources diverted to the Vietnam War, failed to deliver to the urban poor, who bore the brunt of fighting in Vietnam anyway. One spark, or rumour of violence, could fire a city.

world. Wearing flowers in their hair and calling for free love, young people were invited to "Turn on, tune in, drop out."

"For the first time in our history," a professor wrote in the early 1960s, "a major social movement, shaking the nation to its bones, is being led by youngsters." The huge boom in the birthrate after the Second World War created in the 1960s a bulge in the national demographic: some 30 million "baby boomers." Despite immense differences among the youth-led protest movements of the 1960s, from floral peaceniks to urban guerrillas, they shared a sense of being part of the same sixties generation. In 1969 a survey revealed that 80 per cent of youth felt part of "my generation." They rejected the materialism of their parents, creating a discernible "generation gap." Hair grew longer; skirts were shorter. The birth control pill became widely available for the first time, allowing women to feel independent and enabling men to encourage girlfriends to "do it." The sexual revolution further divided the generations; parents accused the young of moral decay and degeneracy.

Music was the language of the movement. From Britain came the Liverpool sound of the Beatles, a sort of white version of black rhythm and blues. When the Beatles made their American TV debut on the *Ed Sullivan Show*, the programme got the highest rating ever in television history, and there was talk of an "invasion" of America by the Fab Four. Behind them came the Rolling Stones, the Who, and the Animals. From California came the psy-

LSD: Drug of the Sixties

The pharmacopoeia of the sixties counter-culture included marijuana, mescaline, amphetamines like "purple hearts," and a variety of "magic mushrooms"; but at its core was one unique drug: LSD — known as "acid." Lysergic acid diethylamide, LSD, was first synthesized in 1938 by a Swiss chemist, Albert Hofmann, while he was studying derivatives of alkaloids in an attempt to find a cure for migraine. LSD is a powerful hallucinogenic drug that acts on the brain to produce sensory distortions, leaving the mind free to process in its own way the evidence supplied by the eyes and ears. Frequently the drug will induce vivid visual and aural hallucinations and an entirely new experience of reality, known as a "trip." Response to the drug varies widely; it can generate apparently mystical insights at one

extreme, or intense anxiety and panic attacks at the other. The drug has been used experimentally in the study of mental illness, but its manufacture and sale are now banned in the United States, the UK, and other countries.

Dr. Timothy Leary, an instructor at Harvard University, was the first to publicize using the drug, in the early 1960s. With moves to ban its use in 1966, LSD began to acquire cult status. Beat poet Allen Ginsberg urged that every healthy American over the age of fourteen should take at least one trip in order to gain insight into "the New Wilderness of machine America." During the peak of "acid culture" in 1966–1967, many prominent figures used the drug, including John Lennon and Paul McCartney of the Beatles. Although the melody of "Lucy in the Sky with Diamonds" was thought to

have been composed under the influence of LSD, other Beatles tracks like "A Day in the Life" and "Strawberry Fields Forever" are far more redolent of acid trips. At thousands of hippie communes, university teach-ins, and innumerable love-ins and happenings, LSD tripping was commonplace. The drug does not produce physical dependence, but psychological dependency was common.

Unlike conventional drugs such as alcohol, which have the effect of numbing the senses, LSD, its proponents argued, had the effect of enhancing them, leaving the user with a heightened sense of consciousness. LSD opened up a new view of reality, transcending the material world; it provided self-oriented hallucination befitting the rejection by the counter-culture generation of older values.

Flower Power, 1968. Protesters against the Vietnam War place flowers in the rifle barrels of national guardsmen.

A "love-in" at Elysian Park, Los Angeles, 1968. The counter-culture delivered a total experience. Home was never like this.

chedelic beat of Jefferson Airplane, the Doors, the Grateful Dead, and the Mothers of Invention. During the mid-sixties almost an entire generation, in their early teens to late twenties, was affected in one way or another by the power of this music and the sense of change it sounded. Nothing expressed the optimism and the dynamism of the decade better than its music. "All you need is love," sang John Lennon and Paul McCartney; "The time is right for fighting in the street," sang Mick Jagger.

Besieged by blazing black ghettos and the ubiquitous anti-Vietnam War demonstrations, the US establishment saw the counter-culture's critique as a threat to national security. J. Edgar Hoover, the elderly, longtime director of the FBI, believed that Communists were behind the protests. The president ordered agents to infiltrate the movement and to tap the phones of its leaders. Believing that the anti-war movement had international links, the CIA was asked, illegally, to collect domestic intelligence on it. Eventually the agency reported no evidence of any international connection.

The generational conflict between parental conservatism and youthful idealism then became a head-to-head clash between seemingly repressive police forces and National Guard and anarchic youth in rebellion. The baby boom generation—who were born as the Iron Curtain descended, entered school as the first shots were fired in Korea, and were teenagers as Kennedy pledged to send a man to the moon — now reached maturity as the Vietnam War unfolded, and turned against the affluence that had helped shape their lives.

In October 1967 anti-war protesters organized a huge March on the Pentagon. A large group began a sit-down protest. For the first time since the Bonus Army riot in 1932, the federal government called in armed forces to defend the capital. Many protesters talked with the soldiers and chanted, "We'd love to turn you on"; some put flowers down the soldiers' rifle barrels. That night the troops attacked, kicking and clubbing the peace demonstrators. One eyewitness spoke of "troopers and marshals" advancing, "cracking heads, bashing skulls." This rally marked the end of the "summer of love." The curtain was up for 1968.

The protest movement, triggered often by anti–Vietnam War campaigns, was international. In Paris in May 1968, de Gaulle's Fifth Republic was nearly toppled when it came into conflict with a massed combination of workers, students, and intellectuals. In London policemen laid into anti-war demonstrators with their truncheons outside the US Embassy, in full view of television news cameras. In Germany and Japan radicals fought with the police. In Northern Ireland civil rights marches, modelled on those of the American South, sparked a new phase in the long confrontation between Irish republicanism and British rule.

The Credibility Gap

In January 1968, as President Johnson announced that the United States was winning the war in Vietnam, the Viet Cong launched the Tet Offensive within virtually every town and city in South Vietnam. The gap between what government said and what people saw on their television screens had never been greater, nor credibility lower. Support for the president's handling of the war dropped to an all-time low in the polls. Eighty per cent of Americans felt that the United States was making no progress in the war. Tet was a turning point. Senator Eugene McCarthy announced he would oppose Johnson for the Democratic Party presidential nomination. Robert Kennedy also declared he was a candidate. Then, in March, Johnson surprised everyone by saying he would not seek nor accept his party's nomination. With his crushing triumph over Goldwater only four years behind him, Johnson now recognized the deep unpopularity of his war policies.

Four days after Johnson's announcement, Martin Luther King, Jr., was assassinated on the balcony of a motel in Memphis, Tennessee. Riots swept the nation. A hundred American cities erupted; there were more than twenty thousand arrests and fifty deaths. Seventy-five thousand troops were called out to keep the peace. For many, King epitomized the dream of racial equality, but for two years his influence had been diminishing. Now leadership of the black community passed to more radical figures who wanted to go beyond passive disobedience to active resistance. The Black Panthers trained as paramilitaries in the ghetto of Oakland, California, for a civil war with racist police. Other black nationalists called openly for revolution.

Richard J. Daley

With a million college students and faculty members boycotting classes because of Vietnam, the stage was set for a showdown between McCarthy and Kennedy for the Democratic nomination. In the California primary, in June, Kennedy won by a whisker. Then, as he was leaving his hotel through a back entrance, he was shot in the head. He died the next morning. There was no rioting, just silence. The American nation was traumatized by these killings. People asked what was wrong with America. Why was the nation so violent?

Everything came to a head when the Democratic Party gathered in Chicago to choose its nominee for the presidency — now either McCarthy or Vice President Hubert Humphrey. Chicago was controlled by Mayor Richard J. Daley, a tough, old-school hard-liner who ruled the streets through a broad network of ethnic supporters. He promised, "As long as I am mayor, there will be law and order on the streets." In the riots following Martin Luther King's death he had given his police authority to "shoot to kill" arsonists. Daley was determined to keep order during the convention when rumour predicted that 100,000 activists and anti-war campaigners would assemble in Chicago. Only about one-tenth of that number arrived, but Daley had no intention of allowing any marches to go ahead. His police, some out of uniform, attacked a group of hippies and Yippies in Lincoln Park and pursued them — and anyone else who happened to be on the streets — with clubs and batons. On the night that Humphrey was to accept the nomination, the police used tear gas to break up a demonstration outside the convention hotel. More than two hundred plainclothes policemen tried to infiltrate the march. Demonstrators, newsmen, and elderly passersby were all clubbed and beaten. Tear gas got into the air vents of

Hubert Humphrey

Hope extinguished, 1968. Robert Kennedy, campaigning in California (ABOVE). He won the primary there in June, but was assassinated while leaving the scene of his victory speech (ABOVE RIGHT).

the hotel and into Humphrey's suite as he was preparing his acceptance speech. On live television, the cameras kept cutting between the convention and the extraordinary scenes outside. Humphrey left with his party's nomination but was shattered. "Chicago was a catastrophe," he said later. "My wife and I went home heartbroken, battered, and beaten."

Just a week after Soviet troops shocked the world by moving into Prague, the Chicago police, according to the *New York Times*, "brought shame to the city, embarrassment to the country." Lawyers defending those charged in the

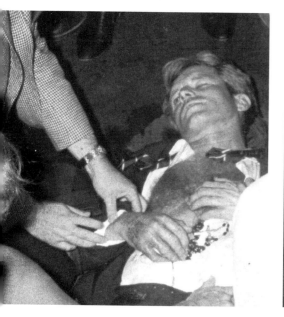

BELOW RIGHT: *Police and anti-Vietnam War protesters do battle on Michigan Avenue, Chicago, during the Democratic National Convention.*

demonstration spoke of a "police riot." Senator George McGovern denounced Daley and his "Gestapo" for creating a "blood bath." Radicals were driven even further outside the political system; they believed that the government was now totally illegitimate and led by war criminals, so that only further militancy could win the day.

"Bring Us Together" was a campaign slogan for the Nixon camp. But as the campaign heated up, there was no coming together. Governor George Wallace had declared himself an independent candidate, with Curtis LeMay as his running mate. Wallace's plan to stop the trouble on the streets appealed only to the right-wing heartlands: "We ought to turn this country over to the police for two or three years and then everything would be all right." Nixon tried to come across as the statesman and peacemaker. He spoke of a "secret plan" to end the war in Vietnam and to bring "peace with honor." With conservative Spiro T. Agnew as his running mate, Nixon tried to defuse support for Wallace. In the end, the vote was nail-bitingly close: Wallace won 13 per cent, and Nixon narrowly defeated Humphrey with just over 43 per cent. America was split into two nations.

George Wallace

The anti-war movement clearly boosted North Vietnamese morale and sustained Hanoi's will to fight on. The hostile chants had almost certainly upset Lyndon Johnson and helped persuade the president not to stand for

China and the Cultural Revolution

The Great Proletarian Cultural Revolution was officially launched by Mao Zedong in August 1966, to renew the spirit of the Chinese Revolution. Believing that the Russian Revolution had gone astray, Mao wanted to prevent the same thing from happening in China, so he unleashed a new revolution especially directed at the young. Seeing his own power slipping away, Mao wanted to purge his party colleagues and establish absolute obedience to his authority. The shock troops of the Cultural Revolution were the Red Guards, militant youth groups recruited in every town and city in China in a massive mobilization of the young. Everywhere students chanted slogans: "Chairman Mao is the red sun in our hearts!"; "We will smash whoever opposes Chairman Mao!" Wearing red armbands and waving little red books of Mao's "thoughts," they vowed to defend Chairman Mao and to fight the "Four Olds": old thought, old culture, old customs, and old habits. The Red Guards were encouraged to attack all bourgeois values and to test party officials by publicly criticizing them: "Destroy first and construction will look after itself." They started off by attacking school and college teachers. In the release of pent-up, sometimes hysterical energy, teenage Red Guards rapidly moved from verbal attacks to physical assaults: unpopular or "incorrect" teachers were tied by their ankles and flogged, or beaten to death. Often, two students would twist the arms of a victim behind his back with such force as to nearly dislocate them; this torture, known as the "jet plane," became a characteristic of Red Guard interrogations. In grotesque acts of vandalism, anything "old" — antiques, paintings, museum exhibits, books — was smashed or burned. Young Red Guards even took over traffic control; it was no longer deemed appropriate for "red" to mean "stop," or for traffic to drive on the "right." The turmoil soon turned into anarchy from one end of China to the other.

Everyone in authority came under attack — in factories, in government offices, in local Communist Party committees. Thousands committed suicide. Tens of thousands more were beaten, tortured, and murdered by Red Guards in a wave of state-supported frenzy. Every chant, every blow, every assault was carried out in the name of Mao, whose personality cult grew to religious proportions. He became known as the "Four Greats": great leader, great helmsman, great commander, and great teacher.

In February 1967 several party leaders called for a halt, but Mao escalated the purge and unleashed a new terror with more killings and atrocities. Factions of Red Guards fell out among themselves, arguing as to who represented the purest form of Mao's thought. Giant rallies were held in Tiananmen Square, at the heart of Beijing, in which a million Red Guards would gather, chanting the thoughts of Chairman Mao, waving their little red books. When Mao would wave down at them, many sobbed uncontrollably, howling out pledges of loyalty. Chaos followed in the wake of the Cultural Revolution. For many years, the education system ceased to function. Industrial output slumped. The party was decimated; officials, not wanting to take risks, became over-cautious. Many leaders were purged. Liu Shaoqi, Mao's designated successor at the time, was removed and became ill with fear and anxiety. Party general secretary Deng Xiaoping and his family were exiled to remote Jiangxi Province, where they were treated as criminals and allowed no contact with the outside world. Deng was paraded around the streets with insulting placards around his neck and was spat at and reviled. Deng's son, following efforts to make him confess the "treason" of his father, was severely beaten by a fanatical group of Red Guards. The coalition that Mao assembled to carry out the Cultural Revolution soon became immersed in a bitter power struggle over his succession. His wife, Jiang Qing, saw an opportunity to take power herself and plotted with three compatriots from Shanghai; they later became known as the Gang of Four. Zhen Boda, one of the fiercest ideological proponents of the revolution, came to the fore. As the military tightened its grip on Chinese society, Defence Minister Lin Biao emerged as Mao's successor.

In the late 1960s the Cultural Revolution began to wind down as the Red Guards were ordered into the countryside to live and work. This broke them up and restored some order to China's anarchic cities, but it transported the chaos to rural areas. Farmers who had worked their land all their lives were instructed by teenagers on how to farm in a purer ideological way. The Cultural Revolution continued to wreak its havoc on Chinese society for years, leaving scars that would take a decade and more to heal.

ABOVE: *November 1966, Beijing. A Red Guard cadre demonstrates in support of Mao's policies.*
BELOW: *This huge poster challenges China's president, Liu Shaoqi, to deliver his "self-criticism." No one escaped the Cultural Revolution's frenzied accusations.*

re-election. The anti-war movement also affected the atmosphere of decision making by which it was resolved not to broaden the conflict into a wider war in Southeast Asia. More than anything, the protests against the war in Vietnam and the reaction to them deeply divided the American people and, in the rest of the world, provoked widespread anti-American sentiment on both sides of the Cold War divide.

The United States, however, was strong enough and prosperous enough overall to hold its course in the Cold War, and to soldier on.

Keeping Abreast of the West

In East Europe and the Soviet Union, the 1960s saw some easing of governmental controls, some economic improvements. For most people, life was becoming less physically arduous. But few had money for luxuries. There was subsidized housing and food, universal free health care, free university education, and guaranteed full employment. But workers did not have the right to strike; there was virtually no freedom of speech (every typewriter privately owned had to be registered); and there were no free elections.

Full employment did not mean high productivity. Centralized state economic planning was wasteful and inefficient. Middle managers were bombarded with innumerable instructions from central committees. To one young agricultural official it was as though those at the centre were firmly convinced "that without their bureaucratic directives no grass would grow and no cow would calve." Highly qualified people did low-skilled jobs, so economic productivity was appallingly low. And there was little incentive for workers, with guaranteed jobs, to improve their productivity. Nobody worked hard. There was little to buy. The only items for sale were those the state decided to sell, at prices fixed by officials. Queues were everywhere part of Soviet life — for meat, for butter, for clothing. Every family had someone who spent much of the day queuing, so productivity declined even further.

There were constant drives for greater productivity, with new targets set by the central planning committee in Moscow and with workers exhorted to work harder and faster. The Communist Party youth organization, the Komsomol, was in the front line. Many factories had Komsomol brigades of young workers who were encouraged to compete for the honour of attaining the highest output. Across the Soviet Union, many workers shared a patriotic feeling that they were strengthening the motherland and not simply generating profits. Propaganda played on patriotism, stressing the duty of workers to strive to keep the Soviet Union abreast of the West.

Housing was still recovering from the destruction of war; everywhere there was overcrowding. Often whole families lived in a single room, sharing kitchen and toilet facilities. But people made the best of it. The future Soviet leader Mikhail Gorbachev, then in his thirties, shared a communal apartment with a welder, a retired colonel, a mechanic, and their families, along with an alcoholic bachelor and his mother and four single women. In this overcrowding, "people made friends, quarrelled, made up, celebrated anniversaries and feast days together, and played dominoes in the evenings." To reduce the housing shortage, vast pre-fabricated apartment blocks were constructed around every city. It helped the overcrowding, but only added to the drabness of most Soviet cities.

In May 1957, in a major speech, Nikita Khrushchev goaded the Soviet people to overtake the United States in per capita production of meat, milk, and butter within four years. Some of the larger collectives offered to double their output in a single year. In the Riazan district they offered to increase the production of meat fourfold. Since this was impossible to achieve, the consequences were disastrous. To meet their targets collectives bought up cattle from the peasants' smallholdings and from neighbouring villages and slaughtered them en masse. Huge numbers of cattle, oxen, sheep, and pigs were butchered; this "meat campaign" dealt a blow to the country's private agricultural sector that took decades to recover from. But targets were met and Moscow was told what it wanted to hear. Khrushchev himself handed out the Order of Lenin, and the state-controlled press called on other collectives to follow the example of these great achievements. Only later was it realized that livestock farming had been devastated by these impossible goals; the rate of Soviet meat production remained at half that of the United States well into the 1970s.

Another of Khrushchev's gigantic agricultural initiatives was the Virgin Lands campaign; at least 90 million acres of uncultivated grasslands, mostly in Kazakhstan in Central Asia, were ploughed up and planted with wheat. To farm this enormous area, nearly half a million "volunteers" were moved in from western Russia and the Ukraine and settled on huge state farms. At immense cost, the state provided credit loans and financial incentives to the new farmers. Cultivation was initially successful but, after only a few years, as the topsoil was ploughed up, the area began to turn into a dust bowl. Although new grain production kept bread prices down for a while, there were never enough fertilizers to go around, nor enough grain silos to store the wheat, nor railroad hoppers to transport it. In 1962 there was a poor harvest, and an even more disastrous one followed in 1963. People now began to curse Khrushchev, blaming him for shortages of bread. For the first time, the Soviet Union, despite myriad acres of fertile land, imported grain from the United States.

The Soviet Military-Industrial Complex

Soviet society was being dramatically transformed by two great changes. First, it was becoming less a rural peasant society and more urban. In 1939 two-thirds of the population had been rural; by the time of Stalin's death this proportion had dropped to just over half; and by the end of the 1970s it dropped to one-quarter. The other trend was more directly a consequence of the Cold War and massive continued spending on the arms race. Immense growth and prosperity were concentrated in the areas closely linked to the expanding Soviet military-industrial complex. Powerful voices inside the Soviet elite, fearful of American "militarism," continued to make insatiable demands for military investments. Advanced industries and research facilities sprang up all over the country along with dozens of "secret cities," each employing thousands of people. This military-based economy was new and much more modern, but it co-existed alongside the old agricultural and

We made sure our people were getting only what we believed they needed, and what we thought was beneficial and necessary for our state, our system, and the policy of our party, which played the leading role in our society.

—Vladimir Semichastny,
head of the KGB, 1961–1967

New apartment blocks on Lenin Prospect were welcome additions in 1968 to Moscow's housing stock. But most Muscovites still lived in cramped conditions.

Television sets arrived in Moscow's main department store, GUM, but few could afford them. Consumer frustration grew.

industrial-age Soviet Union, still recovering from the collectivizations of Stalin and the destruction of the Second World War. The Soviet Union was becoming a divided society.

Arzamas-16 was a "secret" city about 250 miles east of Moscow, specializing in nuclear weapons production. Scientists employed there on top priority work were paid well above the average. When goods were available, the citizens of the military-industrial complex had the wealth to purchase them. Billions of rubles were invested in the town. Arzamas-16 was an oasis of busy prosperity in a sea of stagnation, a widening "tale of two cities" inside the Soviet Union.

One spectacular special project was the building from 1957 of a brand-new science city alongside a lake created by a huge hydroelectric dam near Novosibirsk, the principal West Siberian industrial centre. Modelled on Western university campuses, the city was called Akademgorodok, "Academic Town." Here Soviet scientists could work on nuclear physics and pure mathematics, geology, chemistry, and hydrodynamics, cut off from daily struggles over bare necessities. Khrushchev himself oversaw the investment of 220 million rubles in the new town. Within a few years, Akademgorodok was a flourishing city of some sixty thousand inhabitants. One nuclear scientist wrote: "We felt like tsars in our enormously big (as we saw them) apartments.... While people in Novosibirsk stood for hours in line for butter, meat, and sometimes even for bread, we, the residents of Akademgorodok, were getting regular home deliveries of foodstuffs."

In this privileged, relatively open community, great scientific work was done for the first few years. However, slowly the weight of ideological and bureaucratic control pressed down on the scientists at Akademgorodok. Research institutes in the city acquired a reputation as centres of radicalism. Some scientists there even spoke out against the 1968 invasion of Czechoslovakia. Fewer young scientists were sent to join them; without renewed investment the campus declined, and scientific innovation slowly dried up. As with many other Soviet initiatives, vast financial resources had gone into something that became more a drain on resources than an engine of growth. Some Soviet citizens — dissidents, as they later came to be known — began to be critical of the way their country's economy was managed.

Khrushchev was prepared to interpret communism far less narrowly and rigidly than his predecessors. Many liberals who supported his attack on Stalinism saw this as the beginning of a new era that would offer increasing civil, political, and artistic liberty. Khrushchev's liberal period came to a climax in the middle of 1962. Many political prisoners were released, and Aleksandr Solzhenitsyn published *One Day in the Life of Ivan Denisovich*, revealing to all the horrors of life in the Gulag. Poets recited their work at events that were almost political rallies.

But for most Soviet citizens, life passed slowly, without surprises. Some young people did try to keep up with Western fashion. In the early sixties, a few young men started to narrow the legs of their state-regulated trousers, and to comb their hair back in the style of Western rock 'n' roll groups. Western visitors to Russia found there was a demand for their denim blue jeans on the black market. With new portable radios, young people began to listen to music stations broadcasting in the West — although this was strictly forbidden. In Moscow, Elvis Presley was an instant hit, and Beatlemania gripped the young. Western music represented to Soviet youth all that seemed glamorous, open, and affluent about the West. Occasionally, recordings were smuggled in. As there was no vinyl available, bootleg copies cut into plastic X-ray film were passed around, selling for one ruble — then a vast amount. All this helped generate an underground culture of the *beatniki,* especially among the children of the elite, who were more exposed to outside influences. Beatnik culture began with listening to jazz, then graduated to rock 'n' roll, then pop, percolating through Soviet society. These hints of change were never fast enough to keep up with aspirations, especially those

Yevgeny Yevtushenko

of the young. But hard-liners feared that the Communist system would be undermined by a generation pining for the trappings of consumer culture.

In late 1962 conservatives in the Communist Party persuaded Khrushchev that things were getting out of hand. The premier paid a visit to the Manezh Art Gallery and denounced non-representational avant-garde art as "anti-Soviet" and immoral. Art had to be intelligible to the people; it was supposed to inspire or encourage them, or help them to relax. If a painting communicated only to a small number of people, then it failed as art. Khrushchev followed up his attack on artists with a campaign against liberal writers. Even the popular young poet Yevgeny Yevtushenko agreed to collaborate with the authorities. In the West he was often presented as an outspoken radical, but inside the Soviet Union he kept his head down. Thousands of young people were warned to conform by Komsomol organizations or by the KGB — or risk falling afoul of the authorities.

The Thaw Generation

The young generation of Soviet poets who grew up during the 1950s, when Khrushchev unleashed his attack upon Stalin, was at the vanguard of the new liberalism in the 1960s. Huge audiences would gather to hear them recite their verse on street corners, in school and factory auditoriums, at concert halls, and at sports stadiums. Their boldness and idealism exploded across the Soviet Union, electrifying those who heard them. One hundred thousand copies were printed of first editions of works of poetry — fifty times the typical print run for a similar

book in the West. Even then, they were soon sold out and were passed from reader to reader. Yevgeny Yevtushenko, one of the best-known poets, toured extensively in the West as well, where he excited audiences with the raw energy of his verse. In the Soviet Union he was cheered at readings; ten thousand people listened adoringly as he read poems like "Babi Yar," a denunciation of Soviet anti-Semitism. Khrushchev personally authorized the publication of his poem "The Heirs of Stalin" in *Pravda* in 1962:

We removed
　　　him
　　　　　from the mausoleum.
But how do we remove Stalin
　　　　　　from Stalin's heirs?
Some of his heirs
　　　　tend roses in retirement,
but secretly consider
　　　　　their retirement temporary.
Others
　　from platforms rail against Stalin,
but,
　at night,
　　　　yearn for the old days.

Khrushchev, at a show of contemporary paintings at the Manezh exhibition hall in 1962, did not like what he saw. The thaw gave way to a renewed crackdown on liberal artists and writers.

He had a nervous breakdown; he had tears in his eyes that were dripping down his face. He couldn't quite find any comfortable place, he couldn't settle. He would go to the country, he would return. And it went on like that for a month and a half. And then he gradually calmed down.

— Sergei Khrushchev, on his father's downfall in 1964

Khrushchev Becomes a Non-Person

In October 1964 the Presidium of the Communist Party decided to oust Khrushchev from his office, partly because of his brinkmanship in the Cuban missile crisis, whose results were resented as a humiliation for the Soviet Union; partly because of the failures of his over-ambitious agricultural policies; partly because the leadership had grown impatient with his restless pace of reform. When his colleagues demanded his resignation Khrushchev was at first furious, but he was persuaded to go quietly. In return he was allowed to keep his apartment in the Lenin Hills, his dacha, and his car. *Pravda* announced that he had resigned because of "advanced age and poor health." Nikita Khrushchev effectively became a non-person, never referred to again until his death, when he was described simply as an "honorary pensioner."

In the smoothest transition since the revolution, the new leadership determined to keep a tighter grip on the reins of power. Officials toured the country and explained to party activists in closed meetings why the decision to remove Khrushchev had been taken. Leonid Brezhnev was appointed first secretary and Aleksei Kosygin chairman of the Council of Ministers. Nikolai Podgorny became president. After the hectic years of de-Stalinization and reform, they wanted to preside over an era of stability. Two years after the Kremlin coup, Yuri Andropov became head of the KGB. Brezhnev, Kosygin, Podgorny, and Andropov would rule the USSR for almost a generation.

The Soviet economy was cracking under the strains placed on it by the insatiable demands of the Cold War. The arms race helped strengthen the American economy; but it fatally weakened that of the Soviets, which suffered from chronic low productivity and an inability to meet the demand for even basic consumer goods. While the Cold War helped make America rich, it helped keep the Soviet people poor.

Prague Spring

Meanwhile, in parts of the Eastern bloc there was new thinking and concern about declining growth rates and the failure to keep up with Western levels of consumer progress. In Poland agricultural output dropped year after year; food shortages plagued the country. The economy stagnated. The regime of Wladyslaw Gomulka, so rapturously welcomed as saviour of the nation in October 1956, was growing steadily more oppressive. Intellectuals spoke out against the government, and some were imprisoned as a consequence. In March 1968 a student demonstration was brutally broken up by the police, and several days of street rioting in Warsaw followed. Gomulka had lost nearly all support in the country, but Brezhnev and the Soviet leadership stood by him. Welcomed by Poles in 1956 because he declined to submit to the Soviets, Gomulka now was able to survive in power only because the Soviets backed him. But the crises of 1968 passed in Poland; it would be two more years before food shortages and continual price increases finally brought the Gomulka regime to an end.

In Czechoslovakia there was also concern about the economy's failure to grow; in 1962–1963 national income actually fell. In 1966 the government of Antonín Novotný took the first steps towards decentralizing the economy, giving greater power to local managers and greater priority to the production of consumer goods. Profits rather than quotas were made the measure of performance, a practice dubbed "market socialism." These reforms were too slow. Against a backdrop of student revolts, Alexander Dubček was appointed party chairman in January 1968. No fiery revolutionary, he was boss of the Slovak party machine and a committed party loyalist. Dubček promised the "widest possible democratization of the entire socio-politico system," wanting to bring communism up to date. His appointment speeded change, as he widened the debate about reform to those outside the party. Censorship was eased. Amidst unprecedented debate in the press and on television, the party in April approved an Action Programme. Most newspapers published "The

ABOVE: *Alexander Dubček promised Czechoslovakia "socialism with a human face." The smiles here are genuine.*
ABOVE RIGHT: *He shakes hands with Brezhnev in Bratislava, 3 August 1968. Two weeks later, Soviet tanks crushed the Prague Spring.*

Two Thousand Words" manifesto in June, when writers and intellectuals advocated democratic reforms within a broad socialist context. Dubček's reforms became known as "socialism with a human face."

Over the months, Moscow, and other Warsaw Pact capitals, became increasingly agitated by the so-called Prague Spring. They believed that economic reform would inevitably test the party bureaucracy's ability to maintain control, and would ultimately undermine its monopoly of power. They feared that fervent debate about economic objectives would be contagious. Indeed, in Poland demonstrators did call for a "Polish Dubček." Gomulka in Poland and Walter Ulbricht in East Germany led the hard line against reforms in Czechoslovakia. Dubček continued to proclaim his commitment to the one-party system and his loyalty to the Warsaw Pact, but other Communist states grew more and more impatient.

Moscow despaired over the Prague reforms. Inside the Kremlin it was feared that Dubček's government would dismantle the internal security apparatus and evict the KGB from the country. The Soviet military was also worried about its agreements with Czechoslovakia. In the early 1960s the Soviet Union had agreed terms with its Warsaw Pact allies for stationing nuclear warheads in East Europe. Under these terms the weapons would remain

Soviet tank crews, on their way to Prague, were told they would be fighting Americans. The people of Prague let them know otherwise. But Czech hopes of change would now wait more than twenty years for fulfillment.

Prague 1968

under strict Soviet military control. The USSR had large numbers of troops stationed in Hungary, Poland, and East Germany but no permanent garrison in Czechoslovakia. When Prague went soft on communism through 1968, the Soviets delayed the deployment of nuclear warheads there, fearing they could not maintain tight control over them. This was seen in Moscow as a weak link in the Warsaw Pact defensive frontier.

In July, Brezhnev met the leaders of his East European allies in Warsaw. They shared their concerns over events in Prague. A few days later Brezhnev, Kosygin, and the senior Soviet leadership met with Dubček, and made new demands on him to re-impose censorship and tighten control over the media. An agreement at Bratislava appeared to promise a reconciliation between Prague and Moscow, but when Yugoslavia's Tito was given an enthusiastic reception in Czechoslovakia it seemed yet again that Dubček was steering the country down its own independent road. The Soviet Politburo went into a three-day session on 15 August to consider what action to take. When Brezhnev spoke to Dubček on the telephone, he shouted at him that the whole Communist system in the Eastern bloc could crumble because of what was happening in Prague.

Late in the night of 20 August 1968, Soviet paratroopers seized control of Prague airport. Over the next few hours, half a million Warsaw Pact troops crossed the borders into Czechoslovakia. In marked contrast to events in Hungary twelve years earlier, the government told the Czech and Slovak peoples to stay calm and not to resist. There were, however, still pockets of resistance, one led by the young playwright Václav Havel. But Soviet tanks moved against unarmed civilians, and again demonstrated how little prepared the USSR was to allow change, or national autonomy within the Warsaw Pact. The

Did the Czechoslovaks Invite the Russians In?

There have long been rumours that key Czechoslovak party officials invited the Soviets to invade their country to re-impose hard-line law and order. The key documents, locked in a top secret folder in the Moscow Communist Party archives, have only recently been made available. They prove that this was indeed the case. Now it is known that on 3 August the anti-reformist Slovak Communist Party chief Vasil Bilak wrote to Brezhnev a direct letter of invitation "to use all means at your disposal," including military force, to "prevent the imminent threat of counter-revolution." Bilak warned that "the very

existence of socialism in our country is in danger." Rather than risk sending the letter to Brezhnev directly, he passed it to a Soviet intermediary in a men's lavatory. When the Soviet Politburo began a three-day meeting to review options in Czechoslovakia, Bilak again dispatched a message to Brezhnev, on 17 August, not only encouraging the Soviets to act quickly and decisively, but also offering to form an alternative government that would oust Dubček and seize control in Prague when Warsaw Pact troops arrived. It is doubtful that this was a decisive factor in the Soviet decision to invade, but it must have boosted

the pro-military faction in the Kremlin, and it helped provide a pretext for the Soviets to claim that they were acting on behalf of a legitimate alternative government. In fact, the anti-reformists were entirely unable to deliver a government, and the Soviet Union ended up having to reinstate Dubček's, which survived for several months.

It takes courage to defy tanks, but to stop them anti-tank weapons are needed. The Soviets re-imposed hard-line communism on Czechoslovakia by force.

Enough Czechoslovaks spoke Russian to ask the invaders why they were there. The answer: Obeying orders.

West spoke out but did not — and, without risking nuclear confrontation, could not — intervene.

Dubček and the other leaders were arrested, taken to Moscow, and forced to accept the end of Czech moves to democracy. Over the next year hard-line Czechoslovak officials replaced their reformist predecessors at all levels. An experiment in political pluralism had come to an abrupt end. The orthodoxy of one-party rule was restored. Gustav Husák, obedient to central authority in Moscow, replaced Dubček as party secretary in April 1969. In the following year, Dubček was expelled from the party. The people of Czechoslovakia, eager for freedom, were buried alive.

Events in the mid-1960s blurred the image of the two superpowers in the Cold War. It was hard to see the United States as freedom's champion when race riots protested inequalities, and police clubbed and tear-gassed anti-war protesters outside the hotel where the Democratic leadership was gathering. On the other hand, the failure of the Communist system to feed the Soviet people without grain from the United States, and the crushing of the Prague Spring with tanks, tarnished a government that claimed to rule on the people's behalf. The Soviet invasion of Czechoslovakia ended for decades a possible third way in East Europe, and the possibility of liberal reform within the Communist bloc.

Literature

The Russian people have always been voracious readers, but during the Cold War, what they were allowed to read was strictly controlled. Classic Russian texts (except Dostoevsky, who was thought too pessimistic) and edifying socialist-realist novels like those of Maxim Gorky (*Mother*) and Mikhail Sholokhov (*And Quiet Flows the Don*) were printed in huge numbers.

When Stalin died in 1953, the floodgates seemed to open. Ilya Ehrenburg wrote *The Thaw* in 1954, and Aleksandr Solzhenitsyn published *One Day in the Life of Ivan Denisovich* in 1962, which Khrushchev personally authorized as part of his own fight against Stalin's political legacy. But there were limits to the new freedoms; Boris Pasternak could not publish his 1957 novel, *Dr. Zhivago*, in the USSR, so he allowed its unauthorized publication abroad. When he won the Nobel Prize for literature in 1958, Pasternak was told that he could go to Stockholm to collect his prize, but he would not be allowed back. He never made the trip.

More works were smuggled out of the country; those of Abraham Tertz (in real life Andrei Sinyavsky) and Nikolai Arzhak (Yuli Daniel) were among the earliest. When the two writers were put on trial in 1966 — Sinyavsky for, among other things, having written *The Trial Begins* in 1960 — and sent to labour camps, the international outcry was enormous. A few Russians too found the courage to protest (and were arrested themselves). Solzhenitsyn, who had spent eight years in labour camps after the Second World War, published *The First Circle* and *Cancer Ward* in the West in 1968 and 1969 to great acclaim. He was not sent to a labour camp this time, but in 1974, after the KGB discovered his manuscript for *The Gulag Archipelago* and he allowed its publication in the West, he was stripped of Soviet citizenship and exiled.

Writers increasingly resorted to *samizdat* ("self-publishing," as distinct from *gosizdat*, "state-publishing"). This had begun in the 1950s, when banned poetry, memoirs of Stalin's victims, and forbidden translations were first distributed as typescripts passed from hand to hand.

Not until Gorbachev came to power in 1985 were restrictions on what Russians could read gradually lifted.

The United States has never had an official censor, but this did not mean that books could not be banned during the Cold War. School boards and local libraries were keen to root out un-American beliefs and ideas, and this meant that the work of "subversive" writers like Howard Fast, Ring Lardner, Jr., Dalton Trumbo, and even Frank Baum, author of *The Wizard of Oz,* disappeared from the shelves. The United States Information Service, whose purpose was to fly freedom's flag, refused to stock Dashiell Hammett's detective stories. But repression was never co-ordinated, and even when hatred and fear of the USSR was at its most intense in the late 1940s and 1950s, books by left-wing authors could always be found somewhere. But whereas the works of Howard Fast and Dalton Trumbo were virtually unobtainable outside radical bookshops, the novels of John le Carré, Ian Fleming, and Frederick Forsyth — spy thrillers with Cold War backgrounds in which the good guys were from the West and the bad guys from the East — sold in the millions. Paranoid fantasies, like Richard Condon's *The Manchurian Candidate* of 1959, did well too.

Novels sympathetic to the Soviets were almost unheard of, but overtly anti-collectivist political works like George Orwell's brilliant satire *1984,* written in 1948, were immensely pop-

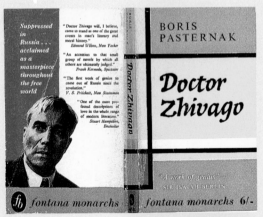

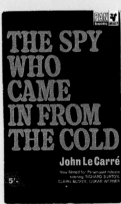

ular. Ayn Rand's *The Fountainhead,* a cult work first published in 1943, was a paean of praise to those virtues of self-reliance and rugged individualism that Americans thought they possessed in abundance and that, in their eyes, the Soviet Union was devoid of.

Novels with political events in the foreground were not very popular, apart from Orwell's dystopian visions. But American left-wing writers staged their own intramural vendettas. Who had been a Communist in the 1930s and 1940s, and why had he or she left the party? The playwright Lillian Hellman was blacklisted when she refused to co-operate with the House Un-American Activities Committee in 1952. She did so partly on the recommendation of her lover, novelist Hammett, who had been a Communist in the 1930s; his best-known works were *The Maltese Falcon* and *The Thin Man.* The lengthy quarrel that ensued involved many prominent American liberals — Mary McCarthy, Lionel Trilling, Dorothy Parker, Edmund Wilson, John Hersey — who appeared in each other's score-settling novels and articles.

By the 1960s the witch-hunt was pretty much over. Howard Fast's *Spartacus* was back on the shelves, and Hellman's plays were revived to packed houses.

In the 1980s, as Americans rearmed under the Reagan presidency, a series of best-sellers emphasized how crafty the Russian menace was. Martin Cruz Smith wrote *Gorky Park* in 1981. Frederick Forsyth's 1984 novel *The Fourth Protocol* was read not once but twice by Margaret Thatcher. Tom Clancy's *The Hunt for Red October* was also published in 1984; it sold nearly 6 million copies and was endorsed by Ronald Reagan himself.

Paradoxically, much Western Cold War literature was not even American: Fleming, Le Carré, Forsyth, and Orwell

were all British. Nevil Shute, who in 1957 wrote the first of the apocalyptic nuclear-war novels, *On the Beach,* was an Englishman who emigrated to Australia.

In the USSR's client states dissident authors — whether they were Czechs like the novelist Milan Kundera and the playwright Václav Havel, or East Germans like Christa Wolf and Stefan Heym, or Poles like Czeslaw Milosz, who won the 1980 Nobel Prize — played cat-and-mouse games with officialdom. But after Stalin's death these younger writers risked prison, house arrest, or exile rather than the Gulag if they overstepped the mark. There was one prominent exception to the pattern of state harassment: the playwright Bertolt Brecht, who went to live in East Germany after the Second World War. Brecht had an Austrian passport and the regime dared not touch him.

Blood and terror in the East, fear and loathing in the West. The Cold War was an uneasy time for writers.

— *Jerome Kuehl*

TOP: *A smile from exiled Soviet author Aleksandr Solzhenitsyn, in Paris.* BOTTOM: *Andrei Sinyavsky, bearded, and Yuli Daniel on trial for publishing anti-Soviet works in the West. Sinyavsky got seven years' imprisonment, Daniel five.*

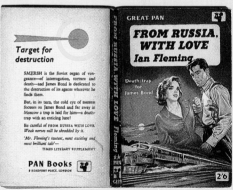

ABOVE LEFT: *Ian Fleming, author of the James Bond thrillers, meets his creation, played by Sean Connery, during filming of* From Russia with Love *in Istanbul.*

Détente is well under way as
Leonid Brezhnev and Richard
Nixon spend a June weekend at
the Soviet leader's Crimean
dacha. The superpowers were
learning to live together.

Détente
1969–1975

1966. Chinese Red Guards demonstrate against Soviet revisionism near the Soviet Embassy in Beijing. But when the chance was offered, China too made overtures to the West.

A New Number One Enemy

From Beijing, Mao Zedong and other Chinese leaders observed the Soviet military occupation of Czechoslovakia with alarm. China feared that the so-called Brezhnev Doctrine, the "right" of the Kremlin to impose its own brand of orthodoxy on another socialist state, might be attempted elsewhere — even against China itself. But China also saw this as an opportunity to alienate the Soviet Union from its satellites. Premier Zhou Enlai claimed that the "socialist camp" no longer existed, and Beijing launched a new campaign of polemics against what it described as Soviet expansionism. In the demonology of China, the Soviet leaders were now denounced as the "new tsars," replacing the Americans as Number One Enemy.

Tensions between the Soviet Union and the People's Republic of China had arisen in the Korean War, when, with no Russian ground troops at risk and with China losing nearly half a million men, the Soviets still made the Chinese pay cash for arms and armament. This grievance festered after Stalin's death. Mao Zedong never accepted Khrushchev as head of the Communist world; instead he began to see himself as leader of the international socialist revolution. To this personal rivalry was added ideological conflict. Mao felt that the Soviet Union's new policy of "mutual co-existence" with the United States, following its failure to keep missiles in Cuba, was a sign the Soviet Union was going soft. The Nuclear Test Ban Treaty was a further indication of collusion between Moscow and Washington. In addition, Beijing felt that Moscow was treating China in the same high-handed way it treated its East European puppets when it came to sharing industrial and military expertise, and this affronted proud Chinese sensibilities. The crunch came when the USSR withdrew its nuclear aid programme from China. Beijing decided to go it alone, without Soviet know-how, and despite the industrial chaos of Mao's Great Leap Forward, China still managed to test its own independent atomic bomb in October 1964, and a thermonuclear bomb less than three years later. In the immense upheaval of the Cultural Revolution, millions of Red Guards created chaos in a frenzied attempt to purify the Communist system. Moscow was terrified by what it saw. To the Soviet leaders China appeared to be wild, anarchic, unpredictable.

The long border between the Soviet Union and the People's Republic of China meanders for thousands of miles through remote Central Asia. At its

1969. Border flare-ups.
The picture, taken by a Soviet army photographer later killed here in action, is captioned, "Chinese provocateurs lie in wait for Soviet frontier guards."

easternmost point, where it divides the mountains of Russia from the plains of northeastern China, the boundary follows the graceful line of the Ussuri River. The border was a focus for Sino-Soviet disputes throughout the 1960s. In 1961 the Soviets had employed only twelve half-strength divisions to guard it. By the late 1960s this had risen to twenty-five full-strength divisions; a million Soviet troops and 1,200 warplanes were facing a million Chinese soldiers. In March 1969 the Chinese raised the level and intensity of border clashes; in one incident, at a tiny, disputed island in the middle of the Ussuri, thirty-one Russian soldiers were killed. For months clashes continued. The Soviets asked their Warsaw Pact allies for military support along the border, but the Romanians, nudged on by the Chinese, spoke out openly against Moscow and declined to offer assistance, claiming that the pact was intended only for the defence of Europe. Moscow quietly abandoned the idea.

Through the summer of 1969 the number and scale of clashes grew worse, with new flare-ups along the Kazakhstan-Xinjiang border. *Pravda* hinted that the Soviets might even consider using nuclear weapons in the dispute, and 120 brand-new SS-11 medium-range ballistic missiles were deployed along the border. Mock attacks were staged against Chinese nuclear targets. Mao Zedong fanned the flames. He ordered the accelerated building of underground tunnels and air-raid shelters with the slogan "Prepare for War — Dig

Tunnels." In Beijing, Shanghai, Tianjin, and other major cities of China, armies of volunteers, in gigantic acts of state-supported vandalism, tore down ancient city walls and historic buildings to provide stone and gravel for underground construction. The face of China's ancient cities was altered for ever.

Playing the China Card

In Washington, watching this extraordinary spat between the two Communist giants, newly elected president Richard Nixon instructed his national security adviser, Henry Kissinger, to "play the China card." Nixon and Kissinger recognized this as an opportunity to exploit the Sino-Soviet split to

BELOW: *President Nixon with National Security Adviser Henry Kissinger.* BELOW LEFT: *Nixon tells the nation he has ordered the invasion of Cambodia. The decision escalated the Vietnam War, and provoked protest.*

diminish Soviet power, and to end the hopeless war in Vietnam, from which the first US troops already had been withdrawn. Washington was convinced that China was backing North Vietnam in the war, so courting Beijing could have the effect of isolating Hanoi. Although Nixon had been one of the most ardent enemies of Chinese communism in the early 1950s, he had no trouble now changing his spots. Ideology gave way to realpolitik. Both Nixon and Kissinger were wary of the Washington bureaucracy, which they saw as monolithic and slow moving. They preferred to work in secrecy and now opened back channels of communication through Pakistan and Romania, sending the message that they wanted to establish contact with China, and end its isolation. Even senior members of Nixon's government were not privy to this major policy realignment.

At the beginning of 1970 Nixon and Kissinger began to play a double game with the Communist world. While stepping up the SALT talks with the Soviet Union, they opened secret negotiations with the Chinese in Warsaw. In Vietnam, Nixon appeared to wind down the war by handing over day-to-day combat operations to the South Vietnamese army — a process known as Vietnamization. This enabled the United States to prepare to withdraw 150,000 American ground troops. Then in May, Nixon suddenly escalated the war by invading Cambodia, which he justified with the claim that destroying the

When I was security adviser, I did not command a bureaucracy, so therefore, if the White House were to conduct any negotiation, it had to be done by a back channel. When I was secretary of state, there was in effect no back channel, because I could design the negotiation as I saw fit.

— Henry Kissinger,
US national security adviser,
1969–1975; secretary of state,
1973–1977

enemy's supply bases would speed up American withdrawal. Nixon's invasion ignited a new round of violent protests against the war. At the campus of Kent State University in Ohio, National Guard troops were called out, and they opened fire on the demonstrators, killing four students and wounding ten. At Jackson State University in Mississippi, another two students were shot dead by police. America was more divided than ever.

In protest at the American incursion into Cambodia, the Chinese cancelled the next round of secret meetings. Mao denounced the United States, calling on the "people of the world" to "unite and defeat the US aggressors and all their running dogs." But, despite this public rhetoric, Mao favoured continuing the secret talks with Washington. A power struggle took place in Beijing. Those opposed to any sort of rapprochement with the United States were led by Lin Biao, Mao's designated successor, and Zhen Boda, the ideologue of the Cultural Revolution. Zhou Enlai and Mao himself were for dialogue. At a crucial plenum of the Central Committee in August, the pro-American faction won the day. Zhou was given more freedom to manoeuvre.

In October 1970 Nixon dropped a clear hint in an interview in *Time* magazine: "If there is anything I want to do before I die, it is to go to China." The back door to talks with Beijing eased open a fraction, and this time did not swing shut even when South Vietnamese troops moved into Laos. In April 1971 the United States lifted its twenty-one-year-old trade embargo with

TOP: *US armoured personnel carriers deploy into Cambodia, in search of North Vietnamese, 2 May 1970.* BOTTOM: *Fellow students attempt to aid a Kent State victim.*

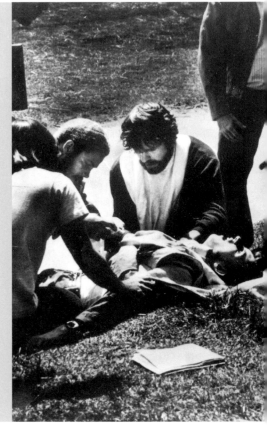

Aftermath of Kent State

In the furore following the US incursion into Cambodia, President Nixon called the anti-war demonstrators "bums," which poured fuel on the fire of protest. After the killings at Kent State and Jackson State, anger turned into fury, as teachers and administrators joined the movement against broadening the war. Five hundred campuses were closed — fifty of them for the rest of the term. The governors of four states declared their universities in a state of emergency; sixteen states called out the National Guard. But opinion polls showed that a majority of the population supported the action in Cambodia, and three out of four Americans opposed the protests against the government. Workers came out into the streets and attacked the anti-war demonstrators.

Conservatives lined up behind Nixon, while opponents called for his impeachment.

"Four Dead in Ohio," sang the rock group Crosby, Stills, and Nash in the outcry that followed the Kent State shootings. "The crisis has roots in a division of American society as deep as any since the Civil War," reported the presidential commission investigating the protests. The report went on: "A nation driven to use the weapons of war upon its youth is a nation on the edge of chaos."

Meanwhile, the president authorized wiretaps, surveillance, and "surreptitious entry," a euphemism for burglary, against the leaders of the anti-war movement. The administration had stepped onto a slippery slope that would end in Watergate.

China. In the same month an unexpected breakthrough came from the unlikely setting of a table tennis championship.

In early 1971 a US Ping-Pong team had been in Japan for the world championships, as was a Chinese team. One day an American player by mistake got on the Chinese team bus. Since talking to a foreigner was a crime, most of the Chinese players ignored the young American in their midst. However, the team captain, Zhuang Zedong, felt that this was alien to the spirit of Chinese hospi-

tality and offered the American player a gift, which broke the ice. The next day the American team captain approached Zhuang and asked if the Chinese would invite the Americans to compete in an upcoming tournament in Beijing. No American teams or official delegations had visited China for many years, but the Chinese Ping-Pong players liked the idea and passed on the request. It was soon realized that although this was sport, it was also a political issue. The request was referred to the Ministry of Foreign Affairs, but no one would take responsibility for the momentous decision. Eventually, it got to Mao himself, who did not hesitate to invite the American team to China.

In April 1971 the American table tennis players attended the tournament and were among the first Westerners to visit China in the wake of the Cultural Revolution. Against a backdrop of posters denouncing US imperialism, the young Americans received a warm welcome and played good table tennis against some of the best competitors in the world. The Chinese came up with a slogan for the tour: "Friendship First, Competition Second." They still beat the Americans easily.

The prize from Ping-Pong diplomacy presented itself in July 1971 when Henry Kissinger made a secret trip to Beijing, the first American official to visit the People's Republic of China since its founding in 1949. Kissinger was smuggled in and out from nearby Pakistan; not even Secretary of State William Rogers knew of the secret mission. Kissinger met Mao and Zhou, and was charmed by both of them. They discussed Vietnam and Taiwan, which the United States still defended and recognized as the Republic of China. In his enthusiasm to curry favour, Kissinger offered to keep Beijing informed of all Washington's dealings with Moscow — an extraordinary promise to make. In

ABOVE LEFT: *Members of the US table tennis team were among the first Westerners to go to China after the Cultural Revolution. They lost matches but won friends.*
ABOVE: *Mao Zedong — a champion at Ping-Pong diplomacy.*

China, 1972

In one of the great diplomatic surprises, Nixon and Kissinger played the China card. The first US president to go to Communist China, Nixon brought a new world power into play, and squeezed the Soviet Union.

return the Chinese invited Nixon to visit China for a summit the following year. In February 1972 the trip went ahead; Nixon went to China. Amidst great fanfare the old Red-baiter met Mao; they shook hands, toasted each other, and even looked jovial together. The key moments — Zhou Enlai proposing a toast to the American president in the Great Hall of the People in Beijing's Tiananmen Square, and a visit to the Great Wall — were all covered live on US television. The Chinese were as keen on this coverage as Nixon, who was beginning his campaign for re-election. Television coverage of world events was becoming part of the events themselves.

Nixon and Mao and Nixon and Brezhnev proved that realpolitik could bridge the ideological divide. The Soviets would have preferred Nixon to have come to them first.

The visit was more symbolic than practical; it failed to normalize full relations between the two nations, but it did mark a recognition that the two countries had common interests, and it helped lessen tensions between them over Vietnam and Taiwan. At the end of the visit, Nixon talked up the trip to historic proportions. In his toast to his Chinese hosts and the people watching back home he proclaimed, "This was the week that changed the world." The main effect, however, was to put new pressure on the Soviet Union.

Signing SALT I

For the Soviets a rapprochement between China and the United States was a terrifying prospect. They feared that an anti-Soviet coalition was being assembled, which put pressure on them to quicken agreement at the SALT talks in Helsinki and Vienna. In Washington, Soviet ambassador Dobrynin had asked earlier that Nixon go to a summit in Moscow before visiting China. But Kissinger was determined that his master visit China first. After the trip to Beijing, Kissinger made another top secret visit, this time to Moscow. Although instructed to discuss only reopening the stalled peace talks on Vietnam, he actually negotiated with Brezhnev on the final stumbling blocks over SALT. Slowly, both sides edged towards an agreement.

As Nixon basked in the success of his triangular diplomacy, Hanoi launched

To have the two Communist powers competing for good relations with us could only benefit the cause of peace.

— Henry Kissinger,
White House Years, 1979

a massive Easter offensive across Vietnam's demilitarized zone. The South Vietnamese army was overwhelmed, and even looked as if it might break up. Nixon feared that South Vietnam would be lost — and with it his presidency. His advisers argued that to escalate the war would jeopardize the upcoming summit in Moscow and the signing of the arms-limitation treaties. But Nixon decided to risk it. He knew that Moscow was arming the North Vietnamese and that these very arms were killing American soldiers. He ordered a massive escalation of the war — a new, heavy bombing campaign against Hanoi, as well as the mining of Haiphong harbour, in which many Russian supply ships were moored. His gamble paid off. In the face of appeals from North Vietnam to cancel, Brezhnev decided the summit must still go ahead. The Central Committee ratified the decision just three days before Nixon was due to arrive. In the air, en route to Moscow, Kissinger told Nixon, "This has got to be one of the major diplomatic coups of all time."

On 22 May 1972 Richard Nixon became the first serving American president to set foot inside the Kremlin. Despite the escalating war in Vietnam, the Soviets warmly welcomed the American leader. For Nixon and Kissinger, détente was a way of managing their opponent, as the USSR grew into a power that could match American military might. The Kremlin saw détente as an acknowledgement of the Soviet Union's superpower status. Nixon and Brezhnev signed the first Strategic Arms Limitation Treaty (SALT I), an event of considerable significance.

After twenty-five years of hostility, the Soviet Union and the United States had agreed to curb spiralling arms-race costs, and reduce the risks of nuclear war. Four days later Nixon and Brezhnev signed a further charter for détente: The Basic Principles of Relations between the US and the USSR. This spoke of

US Sells Grain to USSR

At the Moscow summit Nixon urged the Soviets to buy American grain, a gesture he thought would look good back home. The Soviets made no public response. However, a month after the summit a Soviet deputy minister of agriculture made an unpublicized visit to Washington and negotiated a massive purchase of 400 million bushels of wheat, worth $700 million. Along with this the USSR, on the back of the new détente agreements, negotiated $750 million worth of credit loans at the market interest rate. On the terms agreed, the price was low and, initially, the Soviets benefited from the US subsidy payments to grain dealers. The Soviets quietly purchased nearly the entire US surplus grain reserve. When this was realized there was an outcry at the scale of the sale and the favourable terms afforded the USSR. The event came to be called "the great grain robbery" and showed how shrewd the Soviets could be when operating in the capitalist marketplace. Kissinger later admitted the methods used were "those of a sharp trader skillfully using our free market system. . . . The Soviets beat us at our own game."

"peaceful co-existence" between the two superpowers, and of the need for both sides to "do their utmost to avoid military confrontations and to prevent the outbreak of nuclear war." It pledged both sides not to exploit regional tensions, nor to claim spheres of influence in different parts of the world. The Soviets attached as much importance to the Basic Principles as to SALT I, whereas to Nixon and Kissinger it was secondary; Nixon probably never even read the thousand-word text before signing it.

Both superpowers faced internal opposition to this momentous codification of arms limitation and the ringing declarations of political détente. Back in Washington, General Alexander Haig, Kissinger's military adviser, spoke of a "day of national shame." When President Nixon returned after the summit he assured Congress that the United States would continue its own defence programme to maintain its national security and to secure its vital interests. The president vowed, "No power on earth is stronger than the United States of America today. And none will be stronger than the United States of America in the future." Soviet military leaders also guaranteed that they would continue to defend the USSR and to deter attacks against it. The chief of the general staff testified to the Supreme Soviet: "The Soviet armed forces have at their disposal everything necessary reliably to defend the state interests of our motherland." But SALT I, and the long-running series of talks it sparked off, marked a historic moment. It established a working relationship between Washington and Moscow and relaxed tensions; it heralded a new era of détente. Links between the superpowers would now grow, trade would increase; the Soviet Union would be allowed credit; scholars would exchange visits, and tourists would travel, at least from West to East.

Two weeks after Nixon's triumphal return from the first summit with Brezhnev in Moscow, five men, including the security chief for Nixon's re-election committee, were arrested for breaking into Democratic Party headquarters at the Watergate apartment and office complex in Washington. This was the beginning of a drama that would come to dominate the affairs of Nixon's administration, and ultimately destroy it, overshadowing his foreign policy achievements, at least until seen in the longer perspective of history.

Finding a Way Out

The Nixon administration's primary foreign policy objective was still to find a way out of the war in Vietnam. As Kissinger put it to Dobrynin, in trying to enlist Soviet support to end the war, "A settlement in Vietnam is the key to everything." Kissinger had played the "good cop, bad cop" game in the back-channel dealings with Dobrynin: Nixon, the tough hard-liner, would escalate the war unless Kissinger was able to deliver positive results. After SALT I, Nixon and Kissinger made it clear they were keen to pull off a cease-fire before the presidential elections in November. But the United States kept up the military pressure on Hanoi, with relentless bombing of the North. More than forty thousand bombing sorties were flown over the next five months. Soviet president Nikolai Podgorny went to Hanoi to urge the North Vietnamese to settle, and Kissinger made another visit to Beijing to win China's support.

Neuilly, Paris, 6 December 1972. Henry Kissinger and chief North Vietnamese negotiator Le Duc Tho leave North Vietnamese headquarters together during long negotiations.

Now Beijing made it clear to Hanoi that the time had come to end the conflict.

Kissinger had started to hold secret meetings with representatives of North Vietnam as early as 1969, when the peace talks in Paris, which had begun in 1968, seemed hopelessly stalled. Early in 1970 he began to meet privately with Le Duc Tho, the chief North Vietnamese negotiator in Paris. In August 1972 the Politburo in Hanoi finally voted to authorize a negotiated settlement, calculating that it could obtain better terms now, before the elections, while Nixon was keen to be seen as a peacemaker. But Kissinger was

ABOVE: *Destruction in Hanoi. To get an agreement with North Vietnam, the United States used both bombing and diplomacy.* ABOVE RIGHT: *The Paris Accords were signed on 27 January 1973, and American forces left Vietnam soon after. But fighting between North and South continued.*

moving too fast. After a three-week campaign of intense negotiations, he got a secret deal with Le Duc Tho on 9 October 1972. But he had failed to consult with President Thieu in Saigon. Ten days later Thieu's government saw the deal as an impossible surrender to the North, and refused to sign. At a press conference a week later, just days before the election, Kissinger still went ahead and announced: "We believe that peace is at hand. We believe that an agreement is within sight."

Nixon was re-elected, defeating Senator George McGovern in a landslide. But a month later the talks in Paris broke down, leaving Kissinger out on a limb. Nixon responded by trying to bludgeon Hanoi into agreement and ordered a major B-52 bombing assault over Christmas. For twelve days the North came under the most sustained bombing campaign of the war. American prestige, and Kissinger's reputation, suffered immensely. But Hanoi was forced back to the negotiating table, and within a month a cease-fire agreement was formally signed. The Paris Accords brought a US troop withdrawal and the return of prisoners of war. Viet Cong troops, however, were allowed to remain in the South. Thieu's objections were ignored, but he was offered continuing US economic aid and military assistance if Hanoi resorted to military action again. Nixon spoke of "peace with honor," but the major issue of who would govern South Vietnam was left unresolved. On 29 March

1973 the last contingent of American soldiers left Vietnam.

The people of Vietnam still had two more bloody years of fighting to endure. In the South, American aid began to dry up as Nixon became embroiled in Watergate and Congress was preoccupied with other priorities. Massive inflation, heavy unemployment following the US withdrawal, and increasing corruption sapped the will of many South Vietnamese to fight on. In early 1975 the North launched another military offensive and took control of the Central Highlands. The cities of Hue and Da Nang fell. A military rout turned into political collapse, and Thieu fled. Within days the Communists finally captured Saigon. The last helicopters carrying Americans and pro-American Vietnamese took off from the rooftop of the US Embassy in Saigon on 29 April 1975. Many frantic Vietnamese were left behind.

30 April 1975. A North Vietnamese tank crashes through the gates of South Vietnam's Presidential Palace. Vietnam was re-united under Communist rule.

Ostpolitik

The late sixties and early seventies were a period of dramatic change in Europe. President Charles de Gaulle refused to permit the stationing of US nuclear weapons on French soil, loosened his ties with the West, withdrew from NATO, and looked east. This realignment can be said to have helped instigate the process of détente — which, after all, is a French word. But, though divided, Germany had been and still was at the heart of Europe. In 1966 a "Grand Coalition" of Christian Democrats and Social Democrats in West Germany began making tentative overtures to the East, moving away from the rigid position taken by Konrad Adenauer. Social Democrat Willy Brandt's accession to power in October 1969 initiated a new active policy; for the first time West Germany would recognize East Germany and the territorial changes made at the end of the Second World War. This was known as *Ostpolitik*.

Reverberations of the Vietnam War

The desperate withdrawal from Saigon, watched on television around the world, marked a sorry and humiliating end to America's longest war, whose statistics make grim reading: 2–3 million Vietnamese, Cambodians, and Laotians had been killed; 58,000 Americans were dead. Huge areas of Vietnam were devastated; jungles and farmland remained for decades poisoned by vicious chemicals. In fighting the war, the United States spent more than $150 billion.

The reunification of North and South did not bring the feared bloodbath, but the new socialist economy failed to perform; Vietnam was doomed to a poverty that it took a generation to shake off.

The South fell, but this did not immediately trigger the domino effect; only Laos and Cambodia also turned Communist. In neighbouring Cambodia the despot Pol Pot led the Khmer Rouge to power. In a three-year reign of terror the Khmer Rouge murdered or starved to death 1.5 million of Cambodia's 7.5 million people. In 1978 the Vietnamese invaded to oust Pol Pot and left an army of occupation in Cambodia — provoking the United Nations to halt most development aid to Vietnam.

The scars of the war took a long time to heal in the United States. Veterans were often shunned, rejected as reminders of a war most people agreed was a mistake. Although the United States remained undefeated on the battlefield, it had consistently underestimated its enemy's political will to fight, and overestimated the American people's willingness to support the war. After years of debate, the wounds only began to heal when, in 1982, the Vietnam Veterans Memorial was dedicated in Washington.

The first West German leader to visit East Germany, Chancellor Willy Brandt (right) is met, 19 March 1970, by GDR prime minister Willi Stoph.

In April 1975, as the last Americans evacuated Saigon, South Vietnamese refugees attempted to leave with them, hanging on to overloaded transports. Some fell to their death.

In his first speech as chancellor, Brandt accepted the existence of the East German state. He was soon the first West German leader to visit East Germany. Brandt's strategy initially was to negotiate with the Soviet Union; in August 1970 he and Kosygin signed a non-aggression pact in Moscow. In December a treaty was concluded with Poland recognizing its postwar borders on the Oder-Neisse, finally ending German claims on the lands carved from East Prussia at the end of the war. With memories of wartime atrocities still strong, Brandt made an emotional visit to the Warsaw Ghetto memorial, where he expressed contrition for Nazi crimes. At the memorial to those who died, he knelt in homage.

From the Soviet perspective these advances from their old foe were most welcome; now only the GDR's Walter Ulbricht, the last Stalinist in the East, stood in the way of further progress. Ulbricht had ordered the shooting of rioting workers in 1953, and had bullied Moscow into approving his plans for a wall through Berlin in 1961. Now, in May 1971, under pressure from Moscow, he finally resigned. He was replaced by Erich Honecker, the loyal party man who planned the operation that built the Berlin Wall; he was more willing to accommodate Soviet wishes. The breakthrough came in December 1972, when the two German states finally signed a treaty of mutual recognition. The reality of the postwar settlement was now at last formally accepted by the key players. Simultaneously, agreement in Berlin removed the city from the focus of Cold War quarrels. The Soviets guaranteed civilian access to West Berlin from West Germany, and recognized the continuing role of the three Allied powers in the Western part of the city. The Western powers accepted that East Berlin was now an integral part of East Germany, which they formally recognized. The new mood of détente penetrated even into the heart of NATO, where there was talk of mutual force reductions and the "twin pillars" of defence and détente. All this coming together transformed the politics of Europe, and provided the backdrop against which Nixon's visits to China and the Soviet Union took place.

In the 1970s, "convergence" became a buzzword of the Eastern bloc countries. In the hope of kick-starting their stagnant economies, they imported Western technology. This created a legacy of debt that would later come home to roost. Détente continued to roll. At the end of 1972 negotiations began to extend the SALT agreements. In June 1973 Brezhnev visited the United States for the first time, for a second summit. A series of bilateral trade agreements came from this, along with a high-flown agreement, The Prevention of Nuclear War, by which both superpowers pledged to do all they could to prevent the outbreak of nuclear war between them. The Soviets again put great emphasis on this document as a landmark agreement at the core of the Cold War conflict; the Americans regarded it as little more than hot air. The *Philadelphia Inquirer* called it "Ballyhoo." Kissinger later doubted "whether the result was worth the effort."

At the summit Brezhnev warned Nixon that America's strong pro-Israeli stance in the Middle East was making it difficult for the Soviets to hold back their Arab allies. Another war there was a possibility. Four months later Egypt and Syria attacked Israel. The October War brought a major crisis to US-Soviet

Warsaw, 1970

On 7 December, West German chancellor Willy Brandt visits the Warsaw Ghetto Memorial. Expressing contrition for Nazi crimes, he kneels in homage.

Flying high. Henry Kissinger was awarded a Nobel Peace Prize in 1973 for his work in negotiating the cease-fire with North Vietnam.

Bowing out. On 8 August 1974 Richard M. Nixon, brought low by the lies of Watergate, tells the American people he is resigning the presidency. Soviet leaders could not believe that the most powerful man in the world could be forced out of office for so little.

relations, and nearly succeeded in derailing détente. The superpowers co-operated in trying to bring about a cease-fire, while both rushed to reinforce their own allies in the region. When the cease-fire was breached, a major flare-up between Washington and Moscow even threatened the possibility of nuclear confrontation. The cease-fire finally took hold, and the crisis blew over. For the next year Kissinger, the frequent flyer, shuttled between the capitals of the Middle East. He obtained minor Israeli concessions, but did not address the key issue of Palestinian nationalism and the Palestinian people's need for a homeland. The conflict came no nearer to resolution. However, it was clear that now the key player in the Middle East was the United States, not the Soviet Union.

The October War was followed by a cutback in oil production by OPEC (Organization of Petroleum Exporting Countries), and a massive hike in oil prices. The ensuing energy crisis threw Western economies into chaos. In the United States motorists were enraged by having to wait in line for gasoline, the commodity that had always been cheap and freely available, and which had helped fuel the American dream. In Britain, where the crisis was followed by a miners' strike, the government introduced a three-day work week to cut down on the use of energy. The Western world suddenly came to realize how reliant it had become upon one single source of energy — of which a vast proportion came from Third World countries, and from beneath the deserts of the Arab Middle East.

In 1973 Congress had begun to consider granting the Soviet Union most favoured nation trade status. This provoked a curious coalition against the process of détente. At one extreme, liberals tried to tie most favoured nation status to the emigration of Soviet Jews, which was still severely restricted. At the other end of the spectrum, right-wing hawks, already opposed to reconciliation with Moscow, also argued against it. Their treatment of the USSR's Jewish population became a thorn in the side of the Soviet leaders. Dissident Soviet Jews, *refuseniks,* demonstrated in Moscow streets for the right to leave the Soviet Union. Elsewhere, Jewish groups drew attention to the refuseniks' plight at every Soviet appearance, political or cultural, in the West.

Watergate Plays Out

Throughout Richard Nixon's last year in office, the Watergate drama, and the attempt to cover up, absorbed virtually all of the president's attention. Détente made little headway; the whole process became tainted as the growing Watergate scandal imploded on its author. Senator Henry Jackson, a potential candidate for the presidency, stepped up his campaign against further measures of détente, including SALT. Jackson opposed improved trade relations with the USSR unless Moscow would relax its line over the emigration of Soviet Jews and the treatment of political dissidents. Détente became bound up with domestic American politics.

On 8 August 1974 Nixon finally resigned and left the White House. Soviet leaders, as Anatoly Dobrynin later commented, looked on in amazement as the most powerful man in the Western world, who had led the rapprochement with the Soviet Union, was hounded out of office for what they characterized

Leaving the White House for the final time, Richard Nixon and his wife, Pat, say farewell to Nixon's successor, Gerald Ford, and his wife, Betty.

as "stealing some silly documents." Soviet history knew no parallel, said Dobrynin. Some people inside the Kremlin even suspected that the whole Watergate issue had been staged by those opposed to détente. Gerald R. Ford — appointed vice president in 1973 after Spiro T. Agnew resigned in the wake of a scandal of his own — now replaced Nixon, and tried to pick up the pieces of the détente policy. One of his first acts was to call Kissinger, now secretary of state, and say, "Henry, I need you. The country needs you. I want you to stay. I'll do everything I can to work with you." To this Kissinger dutifully responded, "Sir, it is my job to get along with you, and not yours to get along with me."

Ford strongly affirmed his faith in détente in a summit with Brezhnev in November. The two leaders met, at short notice, at a military base outside Vladivostok, after Ford had paid a visit to Japan and Korea. A framework for a new arms-limitation agreement was quickly worked out; it would attempt to balance out aggregate numbers of missiles and MIRVs, and ultimately curb both nuclear arsenals. The fact that both leaders agreed to equal levels of warheads was a major breakthrough — to which the military in both countries objected. Ford was "euphoric" about the agreement, and hoped that, after a few remaining problems had been ironed out, a new SALT treaty could be signed in a matter of months. Unfortunately, the military problems proved more complex than the two leaders had optimistically imagined. Negotiations over details of definition and verification dragged on, as before, for month after gruelling month.

Despite delays in the second round of SALT negotiations, by 1975 the Kremlin was in a confident mood. The Soviet leaders believed, hopelessly over-optimistically, that their economic progress was pushing the Soviet Union ahead of the West. SALT I had relieved the worst strains of the arms race. The links with Europe were bearing fruit in new trading relations. In the spring final victory for the Communist-led nationalist movement in Vietnam showed up American weakness. And a new American president had agreed on the principles for another round of arms-limitation treaties.

The only US president who had not been elected to either the presidency or the vice presidency, Gerald Ford would pursue continuity in US foreign policy.

Détente's High Point

The process of détente culminated in the Final Act of the Conference on Security and Cooperation in Europe, signed in Helsinki in the summer of 1975. Representatives from thirty-three European countries, along with the United States and Canada, gathered to settle the postwar European borders, thus recognizing the division of Europe between East and West. The German policy of Ostpolitik now reached fruition. The final accord, drafted after more than two years of discussion, consisted of three main sections, or "baskets." The first dealt with security in Europe, and confirmed existing borders; it dealt with territorial integrity, co-operation between states, and the need for the peaceful settlement of disputes. The second basket, in the full spirit of détente, encouraged trade and cultural links and scientific and industrial co-operation between states. The third basket dealt with humanitarian issues; it guaranteed the free movement of peoples, and the free circulation of ideas and information.

Kremlin leaders were delighted with the first and second baskets, which

In Helsinki, August 1975, Leonid Brezhnev signs the agreement on Security and Cooperation in Europe. President Ford signed also.

In the new situation, the leaders of the bourgeois world have also come to realize that the Cold War has outlived itself and that there is need for a new, sensible, and realistic policy. Our calls for peaceful co-existence have begun to evoke serious responses in many capitalist countries.

— Leonid Brezhnev,
May 1975

recognized the political status quo in Eastern Europe, confirmed what the Soviet people had shed so much blood for during the Second World War, and largely assuaged their long-standing fears of the threat from a resurgent Germany. However, they were horrified at the third basket, human rights, which they regarded as unnecessary and interfering. During a fierce debate in the Politburo, many members had argued against signing. However, Brezhnev and Gromyko persuaded the rest that because the Soviet Union would get so much real benefit out of the Final Act, and because it had pursued the objectives of the conference for so long, they must sign up — and then overlook the clauses they objected to. As Brezhnev stated on human rights, "We are masters in our own house, and we shall decide what we implement and what we ignore."

Many Americans, fearing the implications of recognizing the political status quo in Eastern Europe, had also opposed elements of the agreement. Senator Jackson, now declared as a Democratic presidential candidate for 1976, opposed it. Ronald Reagan, soon to declare as a Republican candidate, said, "All Americans should be against it." But Washington, like Moscow, balanced out the pros and cons and concluded that overall it was advantageous to sign. In Europe, a generally positive feeling towards the agreement saw it as bringing together the processes of European détente with a broader East-West reconciliation.

On 1 August 1975, the leaders gathered in Helsinki to sign the Final Act. Brezhnev had overcome the doubts of his colleagues. It would be his finest hour. President Ford flew from Washington to sign in person for the United States. As if to symbolize this new spirit of goodwill, the American Apollo and Soviet Soyuz spacecraft docked together in outer space, 140 miles above the earth. For two days the astronauts of rival systems carried out joint experiments while orbiting the earth. Détente had replaced decades of confrontation.

In space, US-Soviet co-operation flourished as Apollo and Soyuz spacecraft docked.

Angola 1975

West and East took sides in the Angolan civil war. Jonas Savimbi (right), head of the CIA-supported UNITA, prepares to question a captured Cuban soldier, one of many fighting for the Marxist MPLA.

Surrogates

1967–1978

Egypt's Gamal Abdel Nasser inspired the Arabs. Crowds hailed him throughout the Arab world — as here in Damascus, capital of Syria.

An Unsettling Presence

On 14 May 1964 a high-level international delegation assembled in the roasting heat of Upper Egypt to launch the final stage in completing the Aswan High Dam power plant, which when fully operational would generate electric power to fuel a new programme of industrialization and development in Egypt. General Gamal Abdel Nasser, the president of Egypt, was there, accompanied by Soviet premier Nikita Khrushchev, for it was Soviet money that was largely financing the dam and Soviet engineers who were building it. Nasser and Khrushchev together triggered an explosion that closed the old river channel and diverted the Nile's waters through the power plant's giant turbines. Eventually the turbines would generate enormous amounts of electricity, as the Aswan Dam continued to back up the mighty waters of the Nile into a vast lake three hundred miles long.

Far distant from more obvious points of confrontation and tension, the building of the Aswan High Dam was still one of the key events of the Cold War. Initially, it was the United States, along with the World Bank, that had offered the loans that would finance this enormous project destined to transform the Egyptian economy. But in 1956 the United States became unhappy with Nasser's radical politics and withdrew its offer of economic aid. To Washington's amazement Nasser shrugged this off and turned to the Soviets for financial and technical assistance. For the first time, a Third World leader played the United States off against the Soviet Union. It would not be the last time, for as the old European colonial empires broke up, dozens of new states appeared across the globe, looking for allies and aid.

Nasser was the hero of Arab nationalism, the leader who stood up to superpower bullying and still got what he wanted. Throughout the region

Nasser's image roused popular support for Arab freedom and independence. But the Arab nations themselves were divided by bitter antagonisms. They had never been able to unify politically in the way the rhetoric of their leaders suggested. Nasser kept his country aloof from the regional alliances of the Baghdad Pact between Iraq, Iran, Turkey, and Pakistan, partly because of Egypt's traditional rivalry with Iraq. In Lebanon in 1958, a civil war between the pro-Western government and Arab nationalists had to be resolved by the landing of American marines in Beirut. Although Egypt and Syria came together in a mutual defence pact (the short-lived United Arab Republic), the

The Six-Day War, 1967; Israel wins a crushing victory over the Arabs. Israeli troops, BELOW, celebrate the capture of East Jerusalem from the Jordanians and, BELOW LEFT, ride through the wreckage of an Egyptian convoy in the Sinai.

Syrians were deeply suspicious of the Egyptians, as they had been throughout history, and were also often at loggerheads with their neighbours the Jordanians. Added to these tensions was the unsettling presence of the State of Israel, created in 1948 when the British withdrew from the area they controlled as Palestine. For the Jews, the creation of a safe haven after the appalling tragedy of the Holocaust was a vital necessity. To the Arabs, who had played no part in Hitler's extermination of the Jews, the creation of an alien state in the midst of what they saw as Arab land was a hurt that must be remedied. Along with this came a burning sense of the injustice done to Palestinian refugees, who were forced to leave their homes in the war that followed Israel's creation.

Overlying all these tensions was the superpower rivalry of the Cold War. Following the Suez debacle in 1956, which sealed the demise of Britain's influence in the region, Washington and Moscow jockeyed for influence and power in the political vacuum of the Middle East. The Soviets felt that the course of history was flowing their way; under Khrushchev they offered help to emerging nations all around the world, seeing them as allies for the socialist cause in their struggle against the West. Assistance with building the Aswan High Dam fell neatly within this objective; the mighty concrete structure became a symbol of Soviet support for developing nations. The Americans wanted to limit Soviet expansion in the Middle East, contain Arab radicalism, and buttress friendly pro-Western regimes. And the United States had a growing commitment to Israel, which as the years passed came into conflict with its other interests in the region. Some policy-makers in Washington saw Israel as a natural ally, and as a bulwark against Soviet penetration of the Middle East. Others believed that support for Israel would drive its Arab enemies into the arms of the Soviet Union and promote more radical, militant Islamic attitudes that might destabilize the entire region.

The defining moment came with the Six-Day War of June 1967, which firmly established Israel as the principal military power in the Middle East. Reacting to the fanatical rhetoric of Nasser, who repeatedly threatened to throw the Israelis into the sea, and a series of menacing Arab moves, the Israeli army attacked the Arabs on three fronts. In the first few hours of combat, the Israeli air force destroyed the Egyptian air force while it was still on the ground. With total control of the air, Israeli forces won a series of spectacular military victories in only days of lightning war, capturing the Sinai

Our soldiers [understood] that only their personal stand against the greatest dangers would achieve victory for their country and for their families, and that if victory was not theirs the alternative was annihilation.

— Gen. Yitzhak Rabin, Israeli commander-in-chief, June 1967

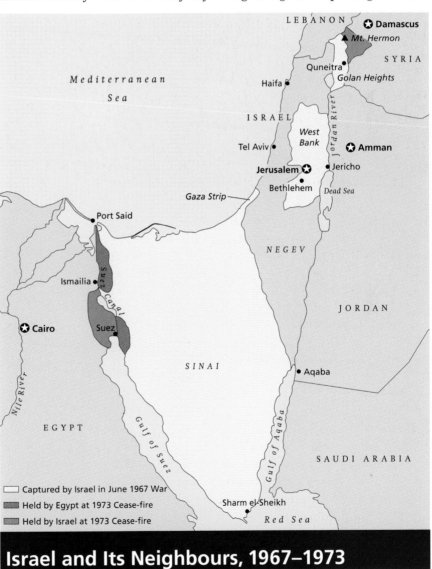

Israel and Its Neighbours, 1967–1973

□ Captured by Israel in June 1967 War
▨ Held by Egypt at 1973 Cease-fire
▨ Held by Israel at 1973 Cease-fire

Aswan, 1964

from Egypt, the West Bank from Jordan, and the Golan Heights from Syria. Divided Jerusalem was re-unified under Israeli control. After six days of fighting, the UN got all sides to agree to a cease-fire. David had become the military Goliath of the Middle East. Israel was now the ruler of more than a million stateless Palestinians, who passed on an intense hatred of the Zionist state from one generation to the next.

A Special Relationship

A consequence of Israel's victory in the Six-Day War was that the "Israel first" proponents gained a dominant hold over American foreign policy. The special relationship between Israel and America rested on a foundation of common values; many Americans admired Israel's pioneering spirit and supported its democratic ways in a region often hostile to democracy. The powerful domestic Jewish lobby in Washington, organized through the American Israel Public Affairs Committee (AIPAC), ensured that a strategic alliance developed between the United States and Israel. Under Richard Nixon and Henry Kissinger, Washington offered Israel diplomatic support, economic assistance, and an ever-growing supply of armaments.

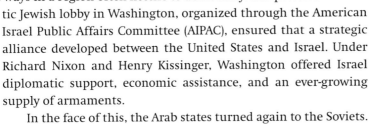

Anwar al-Sadat

In the face of this, the Arab states turned again to the Soviets. Syria and Egypt requested further military supplies from the Soviet Union. Having left the Baghdad Pact (now called the Central Treaty Organization), Iraq went on to sign a treaty of friendship and co-operation with the Soviets. New revolutionary regimes came to power in Sudan and Libya, both of which looked to Moscow. The Russian fleet entered the eastern Mediterranean in an attempt to counter the sway of the US Sixth Fleet. Some nations tried hard to remain neutral, but the Middle East became an armed camp that was divided between pro-Soviet and pro-US clients.

When Nixon and Leonid Brezhnev signed the Basic Principles of Relations at their summit in Moscow in May 1972, they agreed not to take advantage of each other in the Third World. This annoyed Anwar al-Sadat, who had succeeded to the leadership of Egypt after Nasser's death. Sadat came to believe he could no longer rely on Soviet help to win back the territory lost to Israel in 1967. When Moscow refused to provide Egypt with advanced military technology, Sadat expelled fifteen thousand Soviet military advisers from his country, along with the Soviet reconnaissance aircraft based there. At the same time he made secret approaches to the United States, playing the superpowers off against each other. After a brief hiatus, he continued to receive arms from Moscow, even while pursuing secret talks with Washington. In April 1973 Sadat met Syrian leader Hafez al-Assad. They decided the only way to win back the land they had lost to Israel was to prepare their own war plans. Brezhnev continued advising the Egyptians against war; however, at their 1973 summit, he warned Nixon and Kissinger of the danger that war might break out.

On 6 October 1973, which was Yom Kippur, the Jewish Day of Atonement, Egypt and Syria launched a combined attack against Israel, achieving almost

Egypt and Syria came close to winning the 1973 October War. ABOVE: *Israeli artillery, recovering from a surprise attack, hits back at Syria.* OPPOSITE: *A wounded Israeli tank commander is given first aid.*

total surprise. The United States and the USSR supported opposing sides, so the war threatened to undo the process of détente that was well under way between Moscow and Washington. Egyptian tanks and armour rolled back the Israeli advances of the Six-Day War. But after initial Arab successes, the Israelis slowly began to win the upper hand. Both superpowers called for cease-fires when it appeared that the tide of battle favoured their own side. In the war's second week — "the week of the airlift" — the superpowers openly resupplied their allies with arms. On 16 October, Kosygin flew to Cairo to persuade Sadat of the need for a cease-fire, and as the war turned against the Arabs, Sadat finally agreed. Brezhnev then invited Kissinger, who had recently been sworn in as US secretary of state, to Moscow for urgent talks, which began on 20 October. On the following day Kissinger and Brezhnev agreed to terms for a cease-fire, and Kissinger flew to Israel to persuade America's ally to accept the agreement. With Israeli forces poised to destroy the Egyptian Third Army in the Sinai, Prime Minister Golda Meir only reluctantly agreed to halt the fighting. It is clear now that Kissinger was vague about when the cease-fire should take effect. On 22 October the UN Security Council adopted a resolution, jointly sponsored by the United States and the USSR, calling on all sides to accept the cease-fire. By this point Kissinger was directing US policy almost single-handedly, for Nixon was preoccupied with the Watergate scandal and Gerald Ford had just been appointed to the vice presidency after Spiro Agnew's resignation.

Within hours of the cease-fire's taking effect, it collapsed. Claiming provocation, the Israelis mounted a major offensive against the Egyptian Third Army, which was now cut off on the east bank of the Suez Canal. Fearing their client would be wiped out on the battlefield, the Soviets protested frantically, and called on Washington to impose the cease-fire on the Israelis. Another UN resolution called for a second cease-fire; this too was ignored as the Israelis advanced into the city of Suez. The Soviets warned the Israelis of the "gravest consequences" if they did not halt their advance. Sadat called upon both America and Russia to send in forces to implement the cease-fire. Kissinger feared the Israelis' actions risked humiliating the Soviet Union in front of the Arab world; he was desperate to spare Brezhnev the loss of face that might make him "look like an idiot."

The Risk of Unilateral Action

Kissinger's policy in the Middle East had been to talk with Arab states as well as Israel, and to marginalize the Soviet Union in the region. He wanted the United States to emerge as the central player in the peace process. Now, by making the Arabs stare defeat in the face, Israel had backed the Soviets into a corner. On the evening of 24 October, Brezhnev called upon the United States to assist the Soviets in sending troops to impose the UN cease-fire. Kissinger made it clear, he later wrote, that "we had not worked for years to reduce the Soviet military presence in Egypt only to cooperate in reintroducing it as the result of a UN resolution." In his letter Brezhnev hinted that if the United States did not agree to act jointly, the Soviets would consider acting unilaterally. This Washington would never tolerate. Kissinger did not inform Nixon of

The October War

The October War in the Middle East in 1973 has been variously called the Yom Kippur War, as it began on the Jewish Day of Atonement; the Ramadan War, after the Islamic festival with which it coincided; or the Fourth Arab-Israeli War.

The first assaults on 6 October were made against Israeli positions that were understrength because many soldiers had been allowed home to celebrate the religious holiday with their families. The Arab armies achieved almost total surprise. In the north, in the first hours of the attack, following heavy bombardment, Syrian commandos stormed the radar-surveillance fortress on the top of Mount Hermon. Eight hundred Syrian tanks, including a few of the latest Soviet T-62s, backed by three infantry divisions, then poured through gaps in the defences into the Israeli-occupied Golan Heights.

In the south, 600,000 men in the Egyptian armed forces, backed by 2,000 tanks, 160 SAM missile batteries, and 2,300 artillery pieces, launched a furious attack across the Suez Canal, throwing themselves against the supposedly impenetrable Bar-Lev Israeli defence line. Within twenty-four hours, five Egyptian infantry and armoured divisions had overrun Israeli defences and begun to press forward into occupied Sinai. Elated with their initial success, the Egyptian chief of staff declared, "The war has retrieved Arab honour."

The Israelis on leave quickly returned to their units, reserves were mobilized, and the whole nation was put on a war footing. Blood donors were lined up; volunteers came forward to do the jobs vacated by reservists; Jews from around the world arrived to volunteer. Realizing that Israel was fighting for survival, the government issued anguished pleas to the United States for military assistance.

After three bitter days of fighting, the Israeli general staff made a critical decision to move most of the reserves from the Sinai to the Golan Heights, where a furious rearguard action was being fought by Israel's Seventh Armoured Brigade. The fighting was intense, but the line held. "You have saved the people of Israel," radioed the commander to his men. In the south, as more Israeli forces hurriedly crossed the Sinai to rebuild their defences, the line stabilized. The Egyptians began to dig in.

On 9 October the Soviets began to airlift supplies to their allies, flying in an average of thirty huge Antonov-12 aircraft each day to Damascus and to Cairo, with thousands of weapons and tons of ammunition. Two days later, Nixon and Kissinger decided they must respond by supplying Israel with sufficient arms to turn the tide of war, rebuff the Soviets, and provide Washington with the diplomatic leverage to shape the postwar negotiations. Nixon ordered the Pentagon to organize an emergency airlift. The next morning Phantom jets were dispatched to Israel. Giant C-130 and C-5 cargo planes started round the clock to fly in tanks, helicopters, electronic jamming equipment, and vast supplies of shells and bombs.

As the military balance swung in Israel's favour, a huge offensive was launched against Syria. For several days there was fierce fighting. Then the Israelis broke through and advanced to within twenty-two miles of the suburbs of Damascus. The Soviets threatened to intervene directly with airborne divisions if Israel menaced the Syrian capital, which now was within range of its guns. The Israeli army halted and consolidated.

Meanwhile, in the south, at a furious tank battle on 14 October, the biggest since the Second World War, the Israelis defeated a huge Egyptian armoured assault in the Sinai and inflicted heavy losses. After this defeat Kosygin flew to Cairo to urge Sadat to agree to a cease-fire. As they were talking, the Israelis began to cross the Suez Canal near Ismailia and establish a bridgehead on the western side, separating the Egyptian Third Army in the south from the rest of the Egyptian forces. Intense diplomatic activity led to a cease-fire agreement sponsored by Washington and Moscow in an emergency session of the UN Security Council on 22 October. The cease-fire prevented the Israelis from inflicting the worst defeat on Egypt in all the wars between them. On the following day the cease-fire was broken; Israel continued its advance southward, cutting off the twenty thousand men of the Egyptian Third Army. With Moscow threatening to act unilaterally to preserve the cease-fire and save the Egyptian army from defeat, Kissinger responded by calling a global nuclear alert. The October War threatened to explode again, possibly bringing the superpowers into direct, even nuclear, conflict. But this time the cease-fire held.

Israeli troops, under fire, cross into Egypt to clinch victory.

Frequent flyer Henry Kissinger shuttled between the cities of Cairo, Tel Aviv, and Moscow to secure a cease-fire. He is seen here with Golda Meir, Israeli premier, and Egypt's president, Anwar al-Sadat.

the Brezhnev letter, for that same day the House Judiciary Committee announced that it would go forward with an impeachment investigation. Nixon had been drinking heavily, Kissinger wrote, and was "too distraught to participate in the preliminary discussion." That night, in the president's absence, Kissinger convened a meeting (there is some dispute as to whether it was of the National Security Council or the Washington Special Action Group); it was decided to issue a DEFCON 3 military alert — the first since the Cuban missile crisis. Strategic Air Command was mobilized for action, as were US field commands in Europe and around the world. The Eighty-second Airborne Division was placed on standby at Fort Bragg, North Carolina; two more aircraft carriers were ordered to join the *Independence* in the eastern Mediterranean. A note was dispatched to Brezhnev spelling out that the United States could "in no event accept unilateral action" by the USSR.

The signal for a US worldwide nuclear alert was given in such a way as to make clear to Moscow that Washington was serious. We now know that Brezhnev never properly considered taking unilateral action; this veiled threat had only been added to his letter as an afterthought. The Kremlin did not respond to the US alert in any confrontational way and tried to defuse the tension. Two days later the Americans lifted the alert. But the crisis still took a few days to wind down before the United States compelled Israel to accept the cease-fire and allow the Egyptian Third Army, surrounded in the Sinai, to be supplied with food and water. Sadat, in turn, agreed to accept a UN multinational force to monitor the cease-fire, instead of a joint US-Soviet force.

Kissinger had won a great diplomatic victory; America had achieved leverage over the Arabs through preventing a decisive Israeli victory. But America had also pledged its support to Israel through its arms airlift when the battle was going badly and by the offer of a $2.2 billion arms package. Both sides now looked to Washington to resolve their differences through negotiation. Kissinger spent months shuttling between the cities of the Middle East, negotiating disengagement agreements and establishing UN buffer zones between the warring parties in the Sinai and on the Golan Heights. The Soviet Union was effectively exiled from a position of influence in the region.

A brief, highly dramatic flare-up had threatened to engulf the superpowers in a direct conflict, but it had blown over in a couple of days. The United States was winning the Cold War in the Middle East. And, for the moment, the process of détente survived.

Threats on the Doorstep

The United States considered Latin America and the Caribbean as its own back yard; any insecurity on its doorstep posed a threat. From the advent of the Cold War, "insecurity" meant a Communist government or a left-wing government infiltrated by Communists, which ultimately would look to the Soviet Union for aid and assistance, and which could offer a base for military subversion throughout the region. So for Washington the CIA-led plan to remove President Arbenz in Guatemala in 1954 had been a resounding success — even though it left that country divided and faction-ridden for decades. Castro's revolution in Cuba had caused considerably more anxiety in the White House, and the Bay of Pigs fiasco did nothing to blunt Washington's determination to oust the revolutionary dictator. Operation Mongoose, whose objective was to remove Castro, was never cancelled, despite the agreement with the Soviet Union not to invade Cuba that resolved the missile crisis in 1962. Cuba continued to export its own brand of revolution throughout Latin America and to Africa.

A coup in the impoverished Caribbean state of the Dominican Republic in 1965 was thought to have been inspired by Havana. President Johnson, not

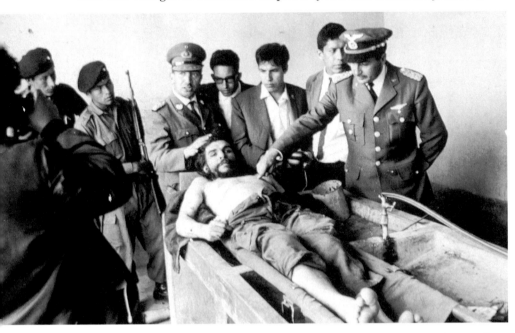

wanting to risk another Cuba, ordered twenty-three thousand American marines to invade the Dominican Republic. It was subsequently learned that there had been no Cuban involvement, so the United States was left to withdraw from what National Security Adviser McGeorge Bundy described as an "interrupted civil war." Elsewhere, the Cuban threat was more real. In 1965 Che Guevara, one of the heroes of the Cuban revolution, left for Bolivia to try to stir up a commotion he hoped would inspire the whole South American continent to rise against American imperialism. But the rising failed to materialize. Two years later, leading only a small force of men, ill and exhausted, Guevara was tracked down in a mountain hideout and surrounded by a troop of government soldiers. In the shootout, Guevara was wounded and surrendered. On direct orders of the Bolivian president, Guevara was executed without trial. His hands were cut off and sent away for positive identification via fingerprints. His battered and beaten body was photographed and dragged off for burial; the image of his face in death went round the world.

Cuba was only a small island, but the prospect of a major South American nation like Chile joining the Communist camp was bound to provoke a strong reaction from Washington. The United States had extensive interests in Chile's copper and silver mines, and the conglomerate ITT controlled much of the telecommunications system. Chile had one of the longest traditions of

ABOVE LEFT: *Che Guevara's body, shown to the press after his capture and execution in Bolivia in 1967. Che failed to stir up the revolutions he had planned in South America, but his image came to symbolize revolution worldwide.*

Socialist Salvador Allende was elected president of Chile in September 1970, much to the chagrin of the CIA. He had wide support among the poor (BELOW RIGHT), but provoked protest from the middle class (BELOW).

democracy in South America, but when it looked likely that socialist Salvador Allende Gossens would win a victory through the ballot box for a left-wing coalition of Communists and socialists, Washington decided it had to act. Kennedy approved a secret fund to be used to influence the outcome of the 1964 Chilean election, which Johnson later supplemented. The Christian Democrats won the election. At the time, the CIA operation to defeat Allende was classed as "very successful," although how much difference it made is unclear. The justification for the use of secret American funds to influence

other people's elections was simple: the Soviets also spent money to support others' political parties and trade unions, and as long as this went on, the United States should do the same. The CIA had been doing this since the Italian elections of 1948.

CIA director Richard Helms proposed another covert operation in Chile in 1969, a year prior to the next election, in which Allende would stand again. But Kissinger, preoccupied with events elsewhere, was not interested. In September 1970 Allende came out on top at the polls, but lacked the necessary majority for election. Nixon was "beside himself" and blamed the State Department and the CIA. Having chided the Democrats for years over their policy on Cuba, he now faced the prospect of Chile's going Communist during his presidency. Nixon insisted, Kissinger later recalled, on "doing something, *anything,* that would reverse the previous neglect." Under Chile's constitution, there was a fifty-day runoff before Chile's congress would finally select the president from the two leading vote-getters, Allende and the conservative Jorge Alessandri. So there was time to act. On 15 September, Nixon summoned Helms and Kissinger to the Oval Office. The CIA director's notes of the meeting include phrases barked at him by Nixon: "One in 10 chance perhaps, but save Chile!"; "not concerned risks

Richard Helms

involved"; "no involvement of Embassy"; "full-time job — best men we have"; "make the economy scream." Kissinger now believed that in Allende they were facing another Castro. A plan was quickly drummed up for a twin-track approach: track 1 was a programme of CIA covert operations to persuade the Chilean congress not to vote Allende into office; track 2 was a top secret plan to incite and prepare a military coup. CIA agents with forged foreign passports made their way into Santiago to establish contact with right-wing military officers. This attempt, way beyond the bribing of politicians, was known only to a tiny group of senior officials; it was kept secret from the Departments of State and Defense, the embassy in Santiago, and even from the Washington committee that supervised sensitive, covert operations — the 40 Committee.

Means to an End

On track 1, the CIA enlisted tame journalists to put out stories against Allende in the Chilean and the international press. A hostile cover story in *Time* appears to have been influenced by CIA briefings. Booklets were printed, posters distributed, and walls painted with slogans. ITT offered to fund Allende's opponents. CIA operatives even approached the retiring president, Eduardo Frei. Although under the constitution Frei could not stand again, they tried to persuade him to seize power. Failing to convince him, they had to regard Frei as a "lost cause" in the campaign to stop Allende.

That left track 2: fomenting a military coup. Even the CIA agent in charge wondered, "Should the CIA . . . encourage a military coup in one of the few countries in Latin America with a solid, functioning democratic tradition?" The commander in chief of Chile's army, General René Schneider, was a straight military man, a constitutionalist who had no interest in involving the army in politics. The CIA looked for other coup-minded officers and found a dissident retired general, Roberto Viaux, with whom they developed plans to kidnap General Schneider. One CIA official, who contacted Viaux and his co-conspirators, travelled with $50,000 bundles of currency stashed in his riding boots. However, Viaux was not thought to be reliable, and at the last minute Washington decided to cancel the coup attempt. But by this time Viaux had decided to go on ahead with or without American support. After two botched attempts, on 22 October, two days before the congressional decision, Viaux tried again to abduct his commander in chief. Three cars drew up outside General Schneider's house at dawn, as he was leaving for work, and opened fire. Schneider drew his own pistol in self-defence but was mortally wounded. Viaux was arrested and the coup backfired totally, as Christian Democrats switched their votes to support Allende. Despite Washington's attempts against him, Salvador Allende became the first democratically elected Marxist president in the western hemisphere, or anywhere in the world.

Allende's government redistributed 7 million hectares of land to about forty thousand families organized in farm co-operatives. The banks were nationalized, along with the copper industry. In retaliation for these blows at American interests, Washington, over the next few years, did all it could to destabilize Allende's government. Kissinger personally took charge of the

We are the victims of a new form of imperialism, one that is more subtle, more cunning and, for that reason, more terrifyingly effective. . . . External pressure has tried to cut us off from the world, to strangle our economy. . . . We find ourselves facing forces operating in the twilight, without a flag, with powerful weapons.

— Salvador Allende, addressing the United Nations, 4 December 1972

September 1973. Chile's presidential palace, La Moneda (BOTTOM), burns after being bombed in the military putsch that toppled Allende. Allende was killed. Many Chileans were rounded up and taken to the Santiago football stadium (TOP). Thousands "disappeared."

campaign across several government departments. Millions of dollars were allocated by the 40 Committee for opposition to Allende, and ITT offered a million dollars to undermine the government. Bank loans were cancelled. The World Bank had earlier lent Chile more than $234 million, but under Allende not a single loan was approved. American aid dried up. Allende turned to the Soviet Union, which provided some industrial assistance but failed to come up with the credit the nation needed. Fidel Castro visited Allende in late 1971, intending to stay ten days, but spent three weeks in Chile, urging the government to move further to the left. Allende refused; as leader of a democratically elected government, he wanted to pursue his own path to socialism.

Slowly, however, the strains on Chile's economy began to tell. Without credit loans, industry slumped and farming stagnated. Inflation began to get out of control. The rich withdrew their money from the banks. There were not enough jobs, and before long people began to go hungry. In 1972 the CIA encouraged a truck drivers' strike that brought the country to a standstill. The following year physicians and teachers went on strike. There were riots and disorder. Rebels seized control of downtown Santiago, and the streets became battlefields. People began to say that communism was not working in Chile.

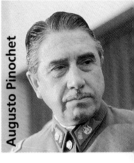

Augusto Pinochet

In August 1973 General Augusto Pinochet Ugarte took control of the army and plotted against Allende. On the evening of 10 September, Pinochet called his senior commanders into his office and made them swear an oath of secrecy on his ceremonial sword. The following day, they executed a well-prepared military takeover. In the fighting inside the presidential palace, Allende was killed; it was reported that he committed suicide, but those closest to him believe he was murdered. Allende's widow, Hortensia, fled the country; the rest of his cabinet was arrested.

The military had taken power and put an end to Chile's record of nearly fifty years of democracy; the roundups began. Thousands of Allende's sympathizers were arrested and taken to the national football stadium. There they were tortured, or put up against a wall and shot. Many people simply disappeared; their families never found out what happened to them. The killings went on for years as the military junta worked to eradicate the "cancer of Marxism." The Organization of American States reported "grievous violations of human rights" in Chile. But the killings did not stop. There are estimates that as many as 800,000 people were arrested. Expropriated land, control over banks, and nationalized factories were all returned to private owners. The United States had achieved its objective in Chile. But when President Ford was forced to admit the use of covert operations to stir up trouble for Allende, there was outrage at the tactics employed. In 1975, as part of an investigation of CIA involvement in assassination plots abroad, a Senate committee slowly pieced together the story of conspiracies, bribes, and violence. The US government, whose identity and Cold War posture were bound up with the pursuit of freedom, admitted to undermining the democratically elected government of a foreign state, out of fear that that state would become a base for Communist subversion in its own back yard.

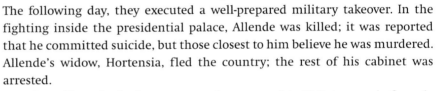

Winds of Change

Another major theatre of the Cold War, where the superpowers opposed each other through their proxies, was Africa. "Winds of change" had been blowing through the continent since the 1950s, as the old European colonial powers that had ruled over most of Africa since the late nineteenth century were replaced by newly independent states. More than thirty African countries declared their independence during the fifties and sixties; some made the transition peacefully, others only after years of struggle. Various conflicts divided the continent. In the south, the white, racist, apartheid regime in South Africa, isolated by the rest of the world, was engaged in a struggle with the outlawed African National Congress (ANC), which looked to neighbouring African states for support.

The last European power to sustain its rule in Africa was Portugal, whose right-wing dictatorship maintained military control of its possessions. In April 1974 a coup in Lisbon ousted the dictatorship, brought a return to democracy, and launched the first steps towards independence for Portugal's colonies. The new regime announced its intention to grant independence for Angola, in southwest Africa, where three groups were feuding over power. The Popular Movement for the Liberation of Angola (MPLA), headed by Agostinho Neto, was committed to the creation of a Marxist state. The Front for the National Liberation of Angola (FNLA) was headed by Holden Roberto, a committed anti-Communist who had long been receiving small-scale support from the CIA, usually through neighbouring Zaire. The National Union for the Total Independence of Angola (UNITA), headed by Jonas Savimbi, had broken off from the FNLA and developed its own power base in the south of Angola. Each group had a tribal connection from which it derived part of its

The most frequently used Cold War weapon around the world, the Soviet-designed AK-47.

The AK-47 Kalashnikov Automatic Rifle

The AK-47 automatic rifle was produced in greater numbers than any other weapon in history. The Soviet army first commissioned it as an assault rifle after the Second World War, when there was still a need to concentrate a vast amount of conventional firepower on the battlefield. The advantage of the AK-47 is that it is accurate with a heavy rate of fire and also easy to use and maintain. Issued in the 1950s to the armies of the Warsaw Pact, the AK-47 became by the sixties and seventies the principal weapon used by Soviet-backed guerrilla forces throughout the world; light-weight and reliable, it can be used by troops with relatively little training. From Angola to Lebanon, from Nicaragua to Mozambique, the AK-47 was the ubiquitous symbol of the freedom fighter. And in the Soviet Union, a whole generation of school-children were brought up able to assemble this rifle in twenty seconds — the time limit required for passing the basic civil defence exam.

The rifle is often called by the name of its designer, Mikhail Kalashnikov, a Soviet weapons engineer, who never received a ruble for the sale of the weapon in the hundreds of thousands worldwide.

The AK-47 fires a 7.62mm cartridge. When operated fully automatic, it fires at a rate of 90 rounds per minute and is accurate to about 300 metres. The rifle has been used in at least thirty-five armies and has been manu-factured in at least four countries outside the Soviet Union. Millions were produced during the Cold War.

Angola, October 1975. Marxist-oriented government troops of the MPLA, in their camp near the northern front. Helped by Cuba, the MPLA held on to power.

support, as well as an ideological commitment that attracted external allies. The bitter civil war, and the struggle for freedom in Angola, became bound up with the superpower rivalry of the Cold War.

After a tense few months following the Portuguese coup, the Organization of African Unity — an organization of independent African states — negotiated a partial agreement, confirmed in the Alvor Accord of January 1975. The three feuding parties agreed to collaborate in holding elections and in aiding the transition to independence, set for November. But outside interests soon affected the situation. Like the CIA, the Chinese had given the FNLA

We were young and the children of a revolution. We dreamed of revolution. We wanted to be part of it, to feel that we were fighting for it.

— Cuban guerrilla,
fighting in Africa, 1970s

limited support through neighbouring Zaire. The Soviets provided small arms to the MPLA. One week after the Alvor Accord, the US secret intelligence and covert operations committee, the 40 Committee, met and decided to provide the FNLA with $300,000. Encouraged by US support, the FNLA, despite the agreement reached at Alvor to collaborate peacefully, made a bid for power. A motorized column of FNLA troops left Zaire and attacked MPLA forces, killing fifty to sixty activists at a training camp. US backing for its client threw a match into dry timber, and it encouraged the Soviets to increase their modest support for their client. More Russian arms were sent to the MPLA.

In the mid-1960s Fidel Castro had made a tour through Africa and offered Cuban backing for several nationalist revolutionary movements on the continent. From that point, the Cubans had backed the MPLA. Hundreds of Cuban guerrillas secretly fought in Africa and acted as military instructors — more than had fought in Latin America during the same period. In 1975 the MPLA revived its association with Cuba and requested further military aid. After some delays a high-level Cuban military delegation visited Angola in August as the fighting grew more intense. The Cubans decided substantially to increase their military support for the MPLA; three shiploads sent to Angola consisted of twelve thousand Czech rifles, food and clothing, and about five hundred military instructors.

Meanwhile, the CIA decided to bring UNITA, under Savimbi's charismatic leadership, into the American sphere alongside the FNLA. In July, Secretary of State Kissinger persuaded the 40 Committee to increase the level of US backing. President Ford agreed to send $25 million in supplies to Angola along with $16 million in arms by the end of August. Weapons were flown to Zaire and from there distributed to both the FNLA and UNITA. President Mobutu Sese Seko of Zaire also sent paracommando battalions to support his brother-in-law, Roberto, who controlled the FNLA. Now, reinforced and in good spirit, the FNLA marched south towards the capital, Luanda.

Bloodletting Reaches New Pitch

Then, during the summer of 1975, South Africa entered Angola's civil war, concerned that a left-wing government would make the country a base for ANC attacks against the apartheid state. Initially, South Africa supplied arms and advice to UNITA, whose power base was in the south of Angola. For Washington, which had just witnessed the final fall of Vietnam to the Communists, direct intervention by American troops was ruled out. Instead the United States turned secretly to South Africa. In October, prodded by Washington, Pretoria decided to dispatch several thousand South African regular troops, backed by a band of European mercenaries, into Angola. Denying that they were directly involved in the conflict, the South Africans moved north towards Luanda. They advanced rapidly, covering some fifty miles a day. Soon they were within one hundred miles of the capital. Bloodletting in Angola reached a new pitch as the countdown to independence on 11 November approached. The stakes got higher, for neither superpower could easily stand by and watch its players in the battle being defeated.

With their opponents closing in, the MPLA appealed again to the Cubans, who sent elite troops to prevent a rout of the revolutionary forces in Angola. These Cuban troops, flown straight from the Caribbean into battle, put up determined resistance and halted the South African advance. To support the Cubans, Moscow started to send tanks, missiles, and other arms. Within months some seven thousand Cuban troops had arrived in Angola, and more were still on their way. In a valley in the Angolan bush southeast of Luanda,

LEFT: *Holden Roberto, FNLA leader (in white shirt), rides a Mercedes convertible into Huambo, surrounded by white mercenary and Angolan troops.* BELOW: *The British-Cypriot mercenary known as Colonel Callan was later captured by the MPLA and executed for atrocities.*

at a place called Ebo, on 23 November, the South Africans confronted a well-armed Cuban brigade. The Cubans won a resounding victory. The South Africans, who suffered heavy losses, abandoned vehicles and weapons as they left the scene. The Cubans held their ground despite heavy counter-attacks along the front over the next two weeks. These battles proved a turning point.

In Washington the administration had exhausted its CIA funds and had to turn to Congress to request additional aid for its allies in Angola. When the request leaked out, there was widespread opposition. Both the Senate and the House voted against allocating more resources to the lost cause of Angola, in which even Kissinger had to admit the United States had no national interest. Ford and Kissinger regarded the disastrous congressional votes as tying their hands and allowing the Cuban-backed Marxists to go on to victory. Sporadic outbursts of fighting in the bush would prolong the civil war for many years; thousands more would be killed, maimed, and wounded. But within three months, the overall outcome was clear, and the fighting between the proxies came to an end; South Africa and Cuba soon withdrew their forces.

The MPLA declared an independent People's Republic of Angola in Luanda. The Soviet Union and several African nations, outraged by South Africa's direct intervention against the MPLA, recognized this government. The FNLA-UNITA faction declared its own government, but won little support from other African nations. In February 1976 the Organization of African Unity chose to recognize the People's Republic, and later that year the Soviet Union signed a twenty-year treaty of friendship. The United States still

Kid soldiers, but the guns are real. Recruited by the FNLA.

Dogs of War

Mercenaries had been employed in the civil wars of Africa since the fighting in 1960 that followed independence in the Congo. French, British, and other European mercenaries fought there and in Biafra, Angola, and the Seychelles. Some of them became legends, like "Mad Mike" Hoare and Rolf Steiner. The world's press regarded them as "the last soldiers of fortune"; African leaders called them "human vermin" and "gangsters in the service of Western imperialist capitalism." These soldiers, who fought for the highest bidders, often proved to be the cruellest fighters in what were already bloody and bitter civil wars. Some of them claimed they fought a crusade against communism; others were there because they loved the

thrill of combat; others simply because they could find no other jobs.

The most famous of the mercenaries who fought in Angola was a Cypriot, Costas Georgiou, who had served in one of the toughest units of the British army, the First Parachute Regiment, until being dishonourably discharged for raiding a post office in Northern Ireland. Known as "Colonel Callan," Georgiou was recruited by the FNLA as part of a gang of British and American mercenaries hired with money supplied by the CIA. Georgiou personally executed suspect spies and deserters, terrifying the men he commanded, who themselves freely used violence and torture against both soldiers and civilians. Some colleagues claim Georgiou was a psychopath, oth-

ers that he was a brave leader of men. He became famous for leading frontal assaults against superior forces, relying on speed and surprise. In one suicidal assault against a far larger Cuban brigade, he was wounded and later captured. To publicize the mercenaries' crimes, ten Britons and three Americans were put on trial by the MPLA in Luanda. They were accused of being "paid assassins" and "dogs of war." "Callan" and three others were executed. The trial and the brutality it revealed attracted international press attention and prompted widespread revulsion against the mercenaries and those who traded in them. When Georgiou's body was flown back to Britain, handlers at Heathrow Airport refused to unload it.

opposed the Marxist government, and vetoed its application for membership in the United Nations.

Although Kissinger liked to call Cuban troops the "mercenaries" of the Soviet Union, it is now clear that Cuba acted out of its own revolutionary zeal and not, in the initial stages at least, as the Soviet Union's client. Fidel Castro was his own man, whose ambition to spread communism around the world played a crucial role in extending the Cold War into Africa from the mid-1960s onwards. Often, the passions unleashed by ideology coincided with the energies harnessed for nationalist struggles. Some nationalist parties perceived themselves not as pawns or as hapless victims of the superpowers but as major players; they saw the Cold War as an opportunity to advance their own cause.

The United States, as Kissinger admitted, "lost" the battle for Angola and failed to prevent the advance of communism in this part of the Third World. Expressing his frustration in a major speech in March 1976, the American secretary of state said détente could not "survive any more Angolas." Although he denied encouraging the South African military incursion into Angola, it is now clear that the approach to Pretoria came from the highest level in Washington.

Although Kissinger's standing had never been higher — he had shared a Nobel Peace Prize with Le Duc Tho in 1973 for his work in negotiating the cease-fire in Vietnam — revelations of undercover operations in Latin America and Africa led many people to question the means used to obtain Washington's ends. Many Americans felt that, in addition to a more honest and open administration in the wake of Watergate, a new, cleaner, more principled foreign policy was also needed. Democratic presidential candidate Jimmy Carter talked about "human rights" as a cardinal goal in foreign policy. Carter vowed to reverse eight years of Republican rule and at the end of 1976 was elected president.

The Sands of the Ogaden

The first flare-up for the new Carter administration came in the Horn of Africa, when Ethiopia, once a Western outpost, fell under the Marxist government of Colonel Mengistu Haile Mariam. The Ethiopian revolution opened up new opportunities for the Soviet Union in East Africa. As Ethiopia sided increasingly with Moscow, its traditional enemy Somalia, which had signed a treaty of friendship and co-operation with the Soviet Union, now changed sides and looked for an alliance with Washington. Soviet diplomats tried hard to keep Somalia within the socialist camp, but Somalian leader Mohammed Siad Barre had territorial ambitions for the Ogaden region of eastern Ethiopia. In July 1977 Barre launched an attack on the Ogaden, and within three months he had captured much of this sandy, arid region. Mengistu appealed to the Soviet Union for help.

Addis Ababa, Ethiopia, 13 September 1978. Fidel Castro is dictator Mengistu Haile Mariam's guest of honour on the fourth anniversary of the socialist revolution. They are seated in armchairs that once belonged to Emperor Haile Selassie.

Moscow and its allies, notably Castro in Havana, decided they could not stand by and watch this strategically important country be defeated by a country that now appeared to be an ally of the West. Between November 1977 and February 1978, Soviet planes and ships transported some fifteen thousand Cuban troops and masses of Soviet arms to Ethiopia, and the Somalis were thrown out of the Ogaden. Washington now charged Moscow with using Cuba as a proxy to expand its power in Africa. National Security Adviser Zbigniew Brzezinski maintained that the crisis in the Horn of Africa, coming on the heels of the Soviet-Cuban intervention in Angola, showed a new assertiveness in the Kremlin.

These accusations came just as the Carter administration was beginning to improve relations with Brezhnev, especially in the SALT II negotiations. Carter was keen on a summit with Brezhnev, but the Kremlin made it clear that a meeting would have to include signing the new arms-limitation treaty, which had been under negotiation for more than five years. The crisis in Africa threatened to unhinge this progress. It began to tilt the balance of influence in the White House away from Secretary of State Cyrus R. Vance, who favoured reconciliation with the Soviets, toward Brzezinski, who wanted to link advances in the SALT talks to Soviet conduct in the Third World. Amidst charge and countercharge, relations between Moscow and Washington rapidly deteriorated in the first half of 1978. Incidents in areas where neither the Soviet Union nor the United States had any direct interest had been fanned into major Cold War disputes that threatened progress towards global arms reduction and world peace. As the Cold War spread around the globe, the remains of détente, it was said, lay "buried in the sands of the Ogaden."

ABOVE: *14 September 1979. Aleksei Kosygin, Soviet premier, was in Addis Ababa to watch this parade honouring heroes of Marxism-Leninism.* RIGHT: *Cuban tanks faced invading Somalis in the Ogaden region of Ethiopia. Fifteen thousand Cubans went to fight for Marxist Ethiopia in a war for land.*

Moscow, 1979

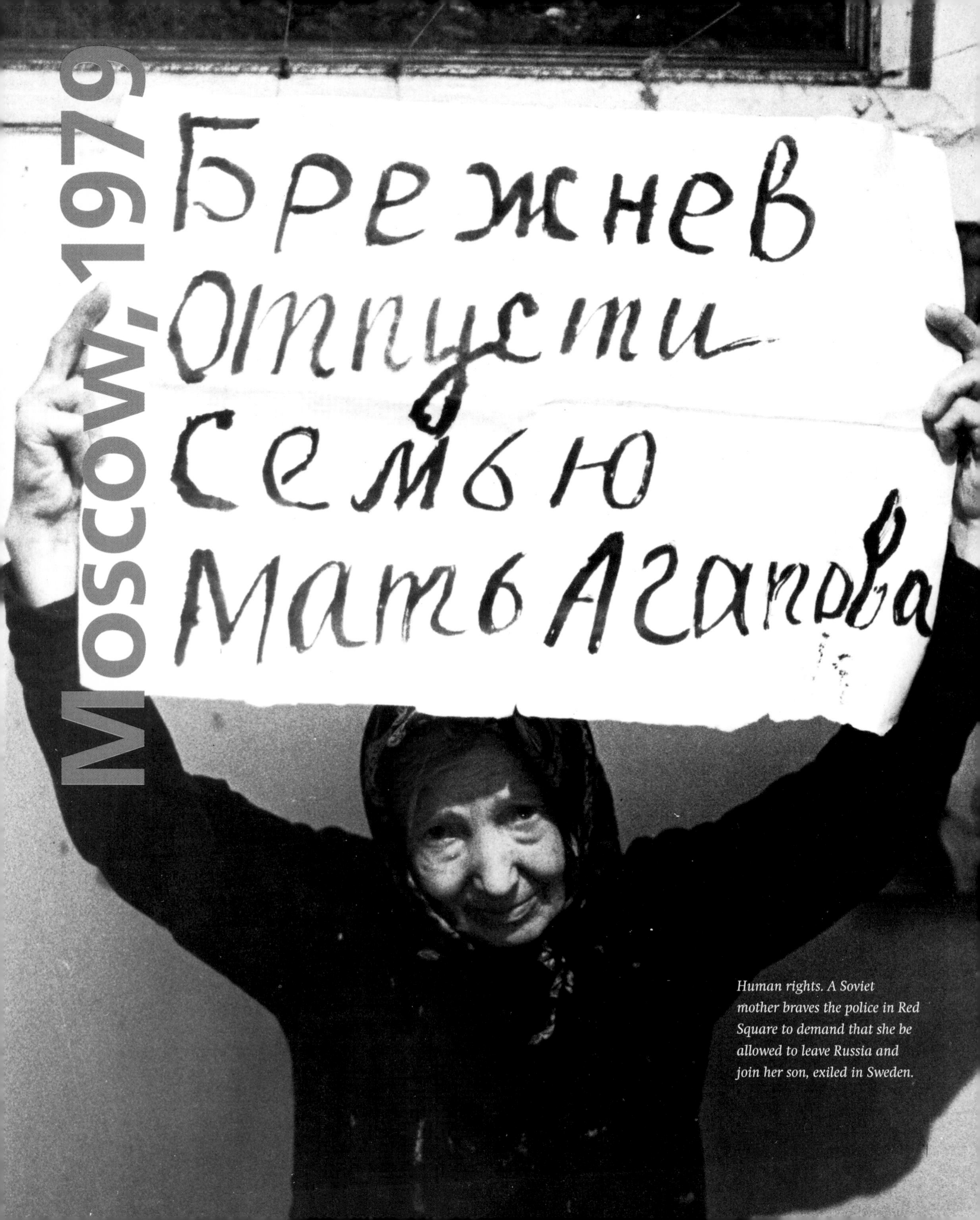
Брежнев
Отпусти
Семью
Мать Агапова

Human rights. A Soviet mother braves the police in Red Square to demand that she be allowed to leave Russia and join her son, exiled in Sweden.

Freeze
1977–1981

The new team. President Jimmy Carter flanked by Secretary of State Cyrus Vance (left) and National Security Adviser Zbigniew Brzezinski. Vance and Brzezinski would often disagree.

Détente Goes on Hold

It was bitterly cold on 20 January 1977 when Jimmy Carter walked down Pennsylvania Avenue to the White House following his inauguration as thirty-ninth president of the United States — a harbinger of the chill that would affect US-Soviet relations over the next few years. Carter was an outsider to Washington, his political career having been confined to his home state of Georgia, where he'd been a state senator and then governor, on his second attempt. In the wake of Watergate he campaigned for bringing a new honesty to political life. He talked morality and spoke of promoting human rights around the world. His administration would mark not only a change of party, but, with regard to the Cold War, a clear transition from the era of Nixon and Ford — and Kissinger.

Détente effectively had been stalled since the spring of 1976. Public opinion in the United States was turning against a policy that seemed to contrast American weakness with Soviet strength. For the duration of the presidential election campaign, Kissinger and Ford had given up trying to advance the SALT II negotiations in Geneva. Ford even stopped using the word détente in public. From Moscow, the Soviet leaders watched with some concern as Carter formed the first Democratic administration since détente. In the Kremlin, Democratic administrations were more to be feared than Republican: Nixon and Ford had, at times, been conciliatory; Truman and Kennedy had led major confrontations with the Soviet Union.

Two days before Carter's inauguration Brezhnev welcomed the new president with a speech promising that the Soviet Union would "never set out on a path of aggression; never shall we raise a sword against another nation."

Andrei Sakharov and his wife, Yelena Bonner, banished from Moscow, are photographed in his apartment in Gorky, 250 miles away. Sakharov and Bonner were fearless in their criticisms of the Soviet regime.

And at his inauguration Carter spoke grandly about his "ultimate goal, the elimination of all nuclear weapons from earth." But the political innocence that had made Carter so appealing as a presidential candidate proved a hindrance in the White House. With almost no experience in international affairs, Carter, who saw détente as a mix of competition and co-operation, would pursue policies that zigzagged between the recommendations of his major advisers. When Secretary of State Cyrus Vance favoured reconciliation, the president was pulled towards the Soviet Union; when National Security Adviser Zbigniew Brzezinski argued for a tougher line, the president was persuaded into a more hostile attitude. Within days of his inauguration Carter sent a warm letter to Brezhnev proclaiming that his goal was "to improve relations with the Soviet Union on the basis of reciprocity, mutual respect and benefit." But a few days later he sent a letter of support to Soviet dissident Andrei Sakharov, provoking Brezhnev to respond with a hard-line rejection of "interference in our internal affairs."

Disarmament and arms control were a high priority for the new administration, and it was soon agreed to propose to Moscow radical cuts in arms levels, reductions that went far beyond those negotiated between Ford and Brezhnev at Vladivostok in November 1974. When Secretary Vance took the proposal to Moscow it was flatly turned down. This hastily calculated initiative gave the Soviets reason to feel that the new Carter administration was not entirely serious in its relationship with Moscow. The rejection itself boosted the position of Brzezinski, a firm believer in the overarching "geopolitical struggle" between the United States and the Soviet Union.

> *I know from my experience collecting signatures for Charter 77 how anguished people were until they decided to sign. When they finally signed it, they found themselves in a state of euphoria. It was a community of free people in the middle of an unfree society, and they had a feeling of harmony with themselves.*
>
> — Václav Havel, signatory of Charter 77, later president of the Czech Republic

Charter 77

The third basket of the Helsinki Accords, on human rights, proved to be a time bomb in relations between the socialist bloc and the West. On 7 January 1977 a group of 242 dissident Czechoslovak intellectuals and former government officials issued a charter demanding that the Helsinki Accords and the UN Declaration on Human Rights be put into practice in Czechoslovakia. Charter 77 was smuggled to the West, where it was given widespread publicity. The authorities came down hard on the signatories, and many of them were imprisoned. One, the playwright Václav Havel, was put under house arrest.

After the defeats inflicted by Communists in Vietnam, Angola, and Ethiopia, the West found in human rights a battleground on which it could score moral points. As brave campaigners demanded that their governments implement the declarations they had affirmed at Helsinki, they faced tough reactions by the Communist regimes that further aggravated Western demands for better practice. The issue generated the atmosphere of hostility against the Soviet Union that later enabled Ronald Reagan to describe it as the "evil empire."

Human Rights on the Agenda

The so-called third basket of the Helsinki Accords, signed in 1975, had put the issue of human rights on the political agenda, but Kissinger had not made much of this. Under Carter the White House sent messages of encouragement to individual dissidents who challenged the Soviet Union and Eastern European governments on their civil rights abuses. The Department of State announced its support for Charter 77, a dissident human rights document put together in Czechoslovakia. Encouraged by Carter, groups of courageous and determined campaigners set up Helsinki Watch committees to monitor abuses and to raise awareness. Carter hoped that his approach would help unify left and right behind his government. In fact it failed to do so.

Inside the Soviet Union, the knee-jerk reaction of the authorities to Helsinki Watch was a strict clampdown. Dissident Anatoly Sharansky was accused of being an agent of the CIA. Many others were arrested on charges of passing state secrets to foreigners and imprisoned or exiled. Several were sentenced to labour camps and long periods of hard physical labour. Some activists were labelled as insane and sent to mental hospitals, where they could be drugged and tranquillized. This was tame by comparison to practices of the Stalin era, when criticism would have been met with a bullet through the back of the head, but news of these abuses leaked into the West and generated real outrage. Although the dissidents did not see themselves as a political party, the authorities feared that their specific criticisms would spread to a broader critique of the socialist system and the government.

One clause of the Helsinki third basket guaranteed people's right to move

Prison was not the only way of punishing and locking up dissidents. Soviet state mental hospitals (BELOW) and labour camps (BELOW RIGHT) were used to confine political prisoners also.

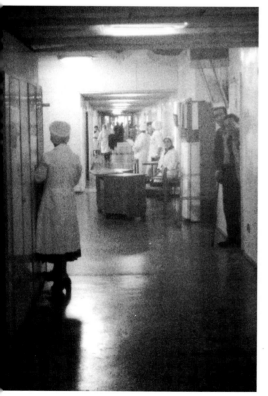

MOSCOW, 1973

A plainclothes policeman
(light coat) rips a sign held by
a Soviet Jew demonstrating
outside the Ministry of Internal
Affairs for the right to leave
Russia and for an exit visa to
Israel. On the left, wearing
a hat, is another plainclothes
policeman, who later tried to
seize the photographer's film.

freely. Soviet Jews who campaigned for their right to emigrate to Israel or the United States became a distinct group among the dissidents, known as refuseniks. Their devoted bands of supporters in Jewish communities of the West seized every opportunity to publicize their plight and to attack the policies of the Soviet Union. Under pressure from the West, the numbers of Soviet Jews permitted to emigrate rose, from a low point of fourteen thousand in 1975, the year of the Helsinki signing, to fifty-one thousand in 1979 (although the number then plummeted in the aftermath of the Soviet invasion of Afghanistan).

Despite all the signs of increasing Soviet irritation, Carter seemed genuinely to believe that because human rights was an ethical issue, constant denunciations of abuses would not affect Washington's relations with Moscow. Ambassador Dobrynin protested to the president in person that this was an interference in Moscow's internal affairs. But Brzezinski recognized the political advantage to be had from the human rights issue, for it put pressure on the Soviet Union and rallied opposition to Moscow.

A New Threat for NATO

In 1977 the Soviets began to install new solid-fuel SS-20 missiles in Eastern Europe. These were replacements for the ageing liquid-fuel SS-4 and SS-5 missiles that had been in place for twenty years. The intermediate-range SS-20s represented a new generation of Soviet missile technology; they were more accurate and reliable than previous missiles and were capable of carrying three MIRV warheads each. They could be moved around on giant transporters to avoid detection. Moreover, they were permitted under the terms of the SALT negotiations, which did not prohibit the modernization of existing missile systems. To the Soviets the new SS-20s were merely replacing obsolete systems with more effective and reliable missiles.

To the West, however, the SS-20s marked a fresh threat. The United States found it hard to understand why the Soviets wanted to install a new intermediate-range missile system when intercontinental missiles that could be fired from land or beneath the sea had become the principal nuclear weapons of the day. However, for NATO and Western Europe, the SS-20 represented something much more alarming. Here it appeared that, while pursuing détente with the United States, the Soviet Union was developing the means to wage a limited nuclear war in Europe, the ability to take out airfields, bases, and cities in a pre-emptive first strike. If Europe alone were hit by nuclear missiles, would the United States intervene and risk the possible destruction of its own cities? By limiting its targets to Western Europe, Moscow could decouple the security of Europe from that of the United States. To NATO it seemed that a response was required to bolster deterrence and to reassure Europe of America's strategic backing.

Soviet SS-20 missiles on their launchers, ready to fire.

The ongoing SALT talks were intended to bring about nuclear parity between the United States and the USSR, but Chancellor Helmut Schmidt of West Germany believed this would leave Western Europe not only vulnerable to Soviet superiority in conventional weapons but to the SS-20 missiles as well. He wanted the United States to include the SS-20s within the SALT talks, and felt particularly let down when the Americans failed to do so. With little confidence in Jimmy Carter as leader of the Western world, he implied that the White House could not be trusted with the defence of Europe, concluding that "strategic arms limitations confined to the United States and the Soviet Union will inevitably impair the security of the West European members of the Alliance."

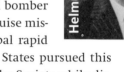

While still calling for greater arms reductions, Carter simultaneously advocated a new arms buildup for the Western alliance. NATO was encouraged to expand its conventional forces, and member states agreed to increase their defence expenditures by 3 per cent per annum. In June 1977 Carter cancelled the B-1 bomber but then gave the go-ahead for the development of the cruise missile. The following month he approved plans for a global rapid deployment force. For two and a half years, the United States pursued this twin-track approach, negotiating arms reductions with the Soviets while discussing the deployment of new missile systems with its European allies.

A series of international incidents managed to set the superpowers against each other. Washington talked of admitting the Soviet Union back into the Middle East peace process. However, cutting right across this, in November 1977 Anwar al-Sadat of Egypt decided to visit Israel in person and, by this dramatic gesture, to recognize Israel and make peace with an old enemy. The Soviets suspected that the United States was behind this move. Several months later Sadat and Menachem Begin, the Israeli prime minister, signed the Camp David Accords, mediated directly by Carter. Again Moscow was marginalized. Meanwhile, in the Horn of Africa, Cuban troops and Soviet supplies assisted Ethiopia in its struggle with Somalia; this Kremlin involvement in the Third World annoyed Washington. The spirit of détente ebbed away.

Siting New US Missiles

Throughout 1978 the governments of Western Europe debated the installation in Europe of the new generation of American missiles: Pershing II ballistic missiles and intermediate-range, ground-launched cruise missiles. At a summit meeting in Guadeloupe in January 1979, Chancellor Schmidt and British prime minister James Callaghan both agreed to accept the siting of these missiles in their countries. The United States lobbied hard in Europe, and eventually Italy and, after some persuasion, the Netherlands and Belgium also agreed to take the new weapons. Because of their first-strike capability, the missiles were seen by some to be especially aggressive, as yet another dangerous proliferation of arms to which the Soviets would almost certainly respond. The total number of new US missiles in Europe would amount to fewer than 600, a number thought to be small enough not to be provocative but large enough not to appear weak. West Germany would get 108 Pershing IIs, replacing on a one-to-one basis the 108 Pershing IAs that preceded them — as permitted by SALT I. Of the 464 cruise missiles to be sited in Europe, 160 would go to Britain, 96 to West Germany, 112 to Italy, and 48 each to the Netherlands and Belgium.

The proposed deployment of these new missiles prompted mass demon-

Triple handshake. To the world's applause, Carter brokers the Camp David agreements with Anwar al-Sadat of Egypt and Menachem Begin of Israel.

strations across Western Europe. The most vocal of the peace movements was in Germany, where hundreds of thousands took to the streets in protest. In England, outside Greenham Common air base, west of London, a women's peace camp was set up to protest against the cruise missile deployment. Throughout the next decade the women maintained a continuous vigil for peace. The Labour Party in Britain and the Social Democrats in West Germany were deeply divided on the issue.

In Moscow the siting of the missiles was regarded as an escalation of the arms race, and an attempt by the United States and NATO to tip the balance

BELOW LEFT: *Tomahawk, the General Dynamics cruise missile, is launched at a US test site. Stationed in Europe, cruise missiles drew protest.* BELOW: *Demonstrators concerned about US missile deployment in Europe take to the streets.*

of nuclear weapons against the Soviet Union. The Soviets feared that the Pershing could be used as a first-strike weapon to hit strategic targets deep within the USSR. They did not accept that the deployment of these missiles was a response to the installation of their own SS-20s, which the Kremlin continued to insist represented merely a modernizing of existing weapons.

In the spring and summer of 1978 relations between the United States and the Soviet Union worsened further when the Soviet authorities cracked down on dissidents with a string of punishments by the courts. Yuri Orlov, one of the organizers of the Helsinki Watch committee in Moscow, was sentenced to seven years' imprisonment. Sharansky was convicted of treason and anti-Soviet activities and sentenced to thirteen years' hard labour. Outside the court, to publicize the case to the Western media, was Andrei Sakharov, the distinguished nuclear scientist. Anatoly Filatov was sentenced to death for espionage. Washington responded with expressions of shock. Several high-level delegations cancelled visits to the Soviet Union. The sale of a large computer system for use in the upcoming Moscow Olympics was annulled, and licences were withdrawn for the export of equipment for oil and gas exploration. The Sharansky case, particularly, hit a nerve in the United States; protests were organized, inflaming anti-Soviet feeling throughout America. The case against Filatov never became a similar cause célèbre — he had in fact been working for the CIA.

If we really want to place curbs on the Russian bear, the only realistic thing is for us to unite.

— Deng Xiaoping,
to Jimmy Carter,
January 1979

Another China Card

At this moment Washington decided, once again, to play the China card. Although relations between the two countries had been reopened by Nixon's spectacular visit in 1972, they had developed only sluggishly since then. Following the death of Zhou Enlai in 1976, China had been thrown into turmoil as the Gang of Four, radical figures of the Cultural Revolution led by Mao's wife, Jiang Qing, forced out moderates, including Deng Xiaoping, and temporarily assumed power. After Mao's death in the same year, the Gang of Four were purged and later put on trial. In July 1977 Deng Xiaoping was rehabilitated and appointed deputy chairman of the party and vice premier. Deng had been exiled and publicly tormented at the height of the Cultural Revolution; his return to power now marked a major shift in China towards a policy of economic reform and modernization. Deng saw links with the United States as a vital means of acquiring technical aid and helping the economy to modernize.

Carter sent Brzezinski to China in May 1978 with secret instructions to begin a new phase in American-Chinese relations. The visit was a great success. Brzezinski discussed a variety of issues with the Chinese, including US views on the SALT talks and China's attitudes towards the Soviet Union. Brzezinski saw improved relations with China as scoring a major strategic advantage over the Soviet Union, and as a means of punishing Moscow for its perceived aggression in Africa and elsewhere. At the same time, the Chinese had fallen out with the Russians, particularly over their policy of support for Vietnam. Deng needed a breakthrough with the West to justify his programme of reform. The time was right on both sides to do a deal. In response to a Chinese stand-down over US support for Taiwan, Carter announced that relations between the two countries would be normalized from 1 January 1979. The Soviets were disturbed by the realignment and, as in 1972, felt isolated by Sino-American reconciliation.

The decision to normalize relations with China marked a victory for Brzezinski in the internal White House debate over foreign policy. At the end of January, Deng made a state visit to the United States. He was frank, telling Carter, "If we really want to place curbs on the Russian bear, the only realistic thing is for us to unite." Carter, delighted with the visit, wrote, "To me, everything went right, and the Chinese leader seemed equally pleased."

Two weeks after Deng's visit, China invaded Vietnam, in response to Vietnam's invasion of Cambodia. Deng had made both public and private threats while in the States to "teach a lesson" to the Soviet-allied Vietnamese, expressions that were not rebuffed by his American hosts. Clearly Deng was now playing his own "American card," by relying upon tacit US backing to prevent Soviet intervention on behalf of Vietnam. While announcing, "We will not get involved in conflict between Asian Communist nations," Carter did not appear to realize how much he had been compromised by the Chinese; he had been given advance notice of their intention and done nothing to prevent the action.

The Soviets were critical of the American position. Gromyko warned Washington that the "Chinese leaders are striving with particular eagerness

China's leader, Deng Xiaoping, leading a new overture to the United States, wears a cowboy hat during his visit, January 1979.

to set the Soviet Union and the United States at loggerheads." But Brezhnev, now ageing visibly, made no reference to the United States in his comments on Vietnam, and instead reported that the SALT talks were nearing completion. He looked forward to a summit with President Carter "in the not distant future."

The Arc of Crisis

The focus of international events now shifted to what Brzezinski described as the "arc of crisis." America's closest ally in the Persian Gulf region was Mohammed Reza Pahlavi, shah of Iran. For twenty-five years the shah pursued an ambitious policy of modernization of Iran, including rapid industrialization and the emancipation of women. American and British oil companies negotiated profitable concessions to exploit the vast reserves, and oil revenues earned by Iran helped fuel the process of change. Some spectacular engineering and construction projects were undertaken with Western help, but the benefits of economic growth were restricted to a tiny elite within Iranian society. Opposition to the shah's policy began to centre on the *ulama*, the Islamic clergy, who were hostile to any process of westernization that overrode traditional Islamic values.

In the late 1970s the shah became increasingly tyrannical in exercising power, relying upon the army and the CIA-trained secret police. Despite this, Carter kept up his support and called Iran "an island of stability." When resistance erupted it was Islamic clerics who led the opposition. They called for a wholesale rejection of Western values. In massive street rioting dozens were killed, and in November 1978 the shah declared martial law. Schools and universities were closed. Newspapers ceased publishing. In the capital, Tehran, public meetings of more than three people were proscribed. As strikes paralysed the oil industry, demonstrations against the regime continued to grow. In December more than a million marched through the streets of Tehran, demanding the removal of the shah and the return from exile of fundamentalist religious leader Ayatollah Ruhollah Khomeini.

In January 1979 the shah was forced to abdicate and flee. Shortly afterwards Ayatollah Khomeini returned to Tehran to a tumultuous reception. He denounced the United States as the "Great Satan," and within weeks an Islamic republic was declared. Hundreds of the shah's supporters were arrested and executed. The process of westernization was rapidly reversed. The Sharia (the sacred law of Islam) was instituted, women were forced to wear the veil, and revolutionary committees patrolled the streets enforcing strict Islamic codes of behaviour and dress. In a new constitution, supreme authority was vested in a religious guide, a position Khomeini was appointed to for life.

The Iranian revolution unsettled the whole region. The United States had lost a crucial ally. The Soviet Union looked with alarm at excesses of Islamic fundamentalism on its southern border. Iraq, Iran's neighbour, feared the germ of religious fervour would spread to its own territory. In June OPEC, the oil export cartel, reacting to the chaos in Iran, raised the base price of petroleum by 24 per cent, plunging the Western world into another fuel crisis. Motorists formed long lines outside petrol stations; once again the Western

TOP: *Demonstrators against the shah burn rubbish in the streets and attack the US embassy.* BOTTOM: *Ayatollah Khomeini greets his followers at his home in Tehran. They reach out to touch him.*

A massive demonstration against the shah by Iranian women. Wearing traditional Islamic dress, the chador, women of Tehran make their voices heard.

economies went into recession. The giant "gas guzzlers" produced in Detroit and Cleveland, so much a part of the American way of life, became dinosaurs of the road. The crisis had real effects on the US economy. By 1980 inflation in the United States was running at 17 per cent, and the Federal Reserve Bank rate climbed to 20 per cent. The price of gold nearly doubled.

The Vienna Summit

In the early months of 1979, the Carter administration decided that the SALT talks must now come to a conclusion. Brzezinski announced that SALT II was "essential" and would be a "historic achievement." In the light of the Sino-US realignment, Moscow too was keen to sign a SALT treaty. The long-awaited summit would go ahead in Vienna.

The first and only meeting between Carter and Brezhnev took place at the Vienna summit, 15–17 June 1979, but the sole item of real business achieved was the signing of the SALT II treaty. Brezhnev was not at all well. When the Soviet leader described the importance of arms limitation he declared, "God will not forgive us if we fail." This remark from the leader of atheistic world communism not only stunned Carter but clearly shocked Gromyko, who was by Brezhnev's side. Carter had hoped to discuss a broad range of issues, but the Soviet leader was not up to it. The president had wanted to take a strong line against the use of Cuban troops in Africa, which he saw as proxies for the Soviets, and other destabilizing actions in the Third World. But Brezhnev responded by reaffirming Soviet support for national liberation struggles; they were part of an unstoppable process of history, he said. The two leaders discussed briefly the terms within which SALT III talks would commence;

My initial reaction was to do something. [But] none of us would want to do anything that would worsen the danger in which our fellow citizens have been placed.

— Jimmy Carter,
following seizure of
US hostages in Tehran,
November 1979

SALT II

The SALT II treaty signed in Vienna in June 1979 basically codified the agreements reached at Vladivostok between Ford and Brezhnev in 1974. Both sides accepted an upper limit to their nuclear arsenals of 2,400 missiles, to be reduced to 2,250 by 1981. Both sides accepted a ceiling of 1,200 ICBMs and SLBMs. MIRVs were drawn into the agreement, with a maximum number of ten warheads allowed per missile, and existing missiles were restricted to the number of warheads they already carried. Heavy bombers were to count against the total number of launchers when they carried cruise missiles with a range of more than 600 kilometres.

Each side agreed not to impede the other from verifying tests and deployment.

The SALT II talks had dragged on for seven years, since the signing of the first arms-limitation agreement, but there had been long periods when one side or the other stalled the talks. The final signing of the SALT II treaty came too late to reverse the breakdown of détente, and the US Senate never completed the process of ratifying the treaty. After the Soviet invasion of Afghanistan in December 1979, Carter gave up hope for SALT II and announced major increases in defence spending.

Tehran, 4 November 1979. Militant students armed with sticks take hostage the entire US Embassy staff. Blindfolded and humiliated, the Americans were marched off to a detention that lasted fourteen months.

Carter and Brezhnev at a ceremony to sign SALT II in Vienna, 18 June 1979. The body language makes clear that nothing else was achieved here; Brezhnev was too ill.

Carter proposed an annual reduction of nuclear arsenals by 5 per cent per year on the SALT II levels. At a private meeting Carter raised the issue of human rights practices but got nowhere. Much attention was focussed upon whether the elderly Brezhnev would kiss Carter in the Russian fashion at the signing ceremony. He did, and Carter got stick for it when he returned home. The summit, which had been a success in a limited way, came far too late to be more than a blip on the downward path of détente. Interestingly, the final communiqué made no reference to "the principle of peaceful co-existence" that had been extolled at previous summits between Brezhnev and Nixon and Ford.

Carter returned to Washington flushed with what he regarded as a solid foreign policy achievement, but was condemned by the right and by those who regarded SALT as an "appeasement" of the Soviet Union. Ronald Reagan, the emerging voice of the Republican right, accused Carter of going soft on the Soviets. The treaty had to be ratified by the Senate, and immediately changes were called for, some of them designed to be "killer amendments." After several months of deliberation, the hawkish Senate Armed Services Committee recommended against ratification, stating that without "major changes" SALT II was "not in the national security interests." Meanwhile, wanting to be seen as tough, Carter gave the go-ahead for the new-generation MX missile system. In December he called for an increase in defence spending of 5 per cent per annum, which would take defence expenditure to $165 billion in 1981 and up to $265 billion by 1985. At the same time NATO agreed to the siting of Pershing and cruise missiles in Europe. All of this convinced the Soviets that SALT II was lost and that Carter had abandoned détente.

The Iranian Hostages

While SALT II foundered in the US Senate, the Iranian crisis returned to centre stage when, on 4 November 1979, the US Embassy in Tehran was taken over by militant Iranian students on instructions from the religious leaders. Sixty-six Americans, including diplomats and their guards, were taken hostage, and the Ayatollah Khomeini demanded that the United States agree to extradite the former shah, who was undergoing medical treatment in New York.

The US government responded to the crisis by suspending Iranian oil imports, freezing official Iranian assets in the United States, and, eventually, warning Iran of military action if the hostages were not released. The ayatollah refused to budge, and countered with the threat that some of the embassy personnel would be tried for espionage. Fourteen hostages, either female or black, had been released within a few days, but the regime held on to the remaining fifty-two. The failure of Washington to succeed in coercing their release highlighted for many frustrated Americans the impotence of Carter's administration. The humiliation was further compounded in April 1980, when a rescue mission went horribly wrong in the Iranian desert. A helicopter and a refuelling aircraft collided at a staging area; eight servicemen were killed and the operation was aborted. Americans learned of the failed rescue attempt from their president, who, as commander in chief, accepted ultimate responsibility for it. Carter's credibility as a superpower leader crashed. The hostages would spend a total of fourteen months in captivity, before being released on the day of Reagan's inauguration as president in January 1981.

As this crisis unfolded and SALT II collapsed, the Kremlin was stumbling towards the fateful decision to intervene militarily in Afghanistan. Many Western commentators would see this as the first step in a co-ordinated master plan by Moscow towards its presumed real target: the oil fields of the Persian Gulf and domination of the entire region. This response failed to take into account the tangled and faction-ridden history of Afghanistan, which the Soviet leaders had long grappled with, and the deep divisions within the Kremlin over the wisdom of intervening.

Mujahedeen, soldiers of God. Muslim rebels against the pro-Soviet Afghanistan government show off their weapons in a mountain stronghold they control.

Afghanistan Becomes a Battleground

In the "great game" of the nineteenth century between the superpowers of the day, the Russian tsars had tried to annex northern Afghanistan, while the British Raj had conquered parts of southern and eastern Afghanistan to defend the northwest frontier of India. Afghanistan had inherited links with both Russia and the West, but they were coloured by a fierce nationalism and a suspicion of outside intervention. After the king Zahir Shah was overthrown by his cousin Mohammed Daoud Khan in 1973, Afghanistan became a battleground in Cold War politics. When the United States and Iran tried to bring Afghanistan into the Western sphere of influence with offers of aid for economic development, Daoud's government turned against the Soviet presence, dismissing several advisers and banning the Communist Party. In Moscow in April 1977, Brezhnev met the Afghan leader and objected to the presence of American interests in Afghanistan. Daoud walked out of the meeting. It was the final break with Moscow.

A year later, in April 1978, Daoud was deposed and murdered in a coup led by Soviet-trained Afghan officers — a coup that went ahead without direct Soviet participation. Nur Mohammed Taraki was appointed president of the new, pro-Soviet regime. The Afghan leaders, displaying a mix of nationalism and revolutionary Marxism, were divided into factions based on tribe and party that now feuded for power. The left-wing government initiated reforms of land ownership and encouraged women to join literacy classes alongside men. The reforms soon provoked a reaction from Islamic clerics, the mullahs, who regarded the new government as ungodly. After the Iranian revolution Ayatollah Khomeini gave support to the Islamic fundamentalist rebels — known as Mujahedeen, or soldiers of God — who were fighting the new "godless" regime. In an armed uprising at the Afghan city of Herat, the Mujahedeen killed hundreds of Afghans, along with many Soviet advisers and their families. Their bodies were paraded through the streets.

In March 1979 the Afghan leader Taraki issued an urgent appeal to the Kremlin: "The situation is bad and getting worse. We need practical help in both men and weapons." The Politburo met for three days in emergency session. The Soviet leaders were fearful that a revival of Islamic fundamentalism on their borders would destabilize the Muslim population of the Soviet Union's southern republics. KGB director Yuri Andropov declared, "We cannot

Mohammed Daoud Khan

afford to lose Afghanistan under any circumstances." However, most Politburo members came out against direct military intervention. Gromyko said, "The Afghan army is unreliable, and our army would become an aggressor. With whom will it fight? With the Afghan peoples! Our army would have to shoot them!" Kosygin added, "The negative factors would be enormous. Most countries would immediately go against us." From the minutes of the meeting it is clear that these arguments held sway. There was a real fear in the Politburo that Soviet military intervention would achieve nothing. As Gromyko summed up: "It would place us in a very difficult position in the international arena. We would ruin everything we have constructed with such great difficulty, détente above all."

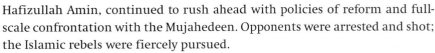

The decision was made not to intervene directly. Kosygin told Taraki that Moscow would help with advisers and military matériel, but that "it would be a fatal mistake to commit ground troops." However, three Soviet divisions were gathered near the border, just in case, and the Soviets did send to Kabul some helicopter gunships and seven hundred paratroopers disguised as aircraft technicians. Meanwhile, the strongman of the new regime, Hafizullah Amin, continued to rush ahead with policies of reform and full-scale confrontation with the Mujahedeen. Opponents were arrested and shot; the Islamic rebels were fiercely pursued.

In Washington the Communist coup in Afghanistan widened the divide between Brzezinski and Vance. Brzezinski argued that the United States must support the fundamentalist rebels; Vance believed that nothing must be done to drive the Kabul regime into "a closer embrace with the Soviet Union." The new US ambassador, Adolph Dubs (later kidnapped and killed), met Amin and found him "a tough cookie who thinks of himself as a 'nationalist Communist.'" For the moment Washington kept out of direct involvement, but the CIA encouraged the Pakistani leader, Mohammed Zia ul-Haq, to supply and help train the Islamic rebels — despite the fact that Carter had earlier broken off trade links with Zia's military regime for its record on human rights, for tolerating drug trafficking, and for trying to develop its own nuclear bomb.

Increasingly desperate appeals to Moscow from Afghanistan for military assistance continued throughout 1979. The evidence now coming out of the Soviet archives shows how resistant the Kremlin was to these Afghan appeals for help. The Russian armed forces themselves objected to any form of military intervention, arguing that a war would be unwinnable — "Russia's Vietnam."

In September, Taraki visited Moscow and met with Brezhnev. They decided to slow the pace of reform and to remove Amin. However, when the Afghan president returned to Kabul the secret plans leaked out and, in another bloody coup, Taraki himself was overthrown by Amin, imprisoned, and suffocated with a pillow by three of Amin's agents. Brezhnev was "rudely shocked" by the murder of the man who had not long before been his guest.

In Kabul, Amin now seemed to want to realign his government with the West. He gave interviews to American journalists. The KGB in Kabul reported

A Muslim fighter of Paklia Province cleans his weapon to fire at the Soviets. Ironically, it is the ubiquitous Soviet-manufactured automatic rifle, the Kalashnikov AK-47.

him more hostile to Moscow and said the CIA was becoming active in the country. Washington was in fact still opposed to Amin, but at the Kremlin the Soviet leaders feared that Amin would "do a Sadat" — make a sudden break with the Soviet Union and go over to the West. The Kremlin was alarmed by the militant Islamic regimes of Southwest Asia and feared that Amin would make an alliance with Pakistan and then with China, Pakistan's principal Communist ally. Added to this was the growing sense that détente was breaking down, that a new arms race with the West was about to begin. Politically, at least, Moscow now had little to lose.

ABOVE LEFT: *Mujahedeen on the move in the hills.* ABOVE: *Soviet armoured forces deploying in Kabul, December 1979. The heavy vehicles, confined to the roads in mountainous country, were easy targets for the Mujahedeen guerrillas.*

A Decision to Invade

The Politburo met in the evening of 12 December 1979, the very day that NATO announced it would introduce cruise and Pershing missiles into Western Europe. In this atmosphere of heightened Cold War tension, the Politburo finally settled Moscow's line on Afghanistan. Brezhnev's health was failing; he was drunk and, we now know, unable to lead the meeting effectively. He tottered in on Gromyko's arm, kissed everyone, and took his seat. After a few minutes of hearing denunciations of Amin, he banged his fist on the table, shouted, "Dirty man," and left the room. Kosygin, who opposed intervention, was absent. Andropov, at the eleventh hour, was won over. Brezhnev's chief ideologue, Mikhail Suslov, in favour, argued that the collapse of the Afghan revolution would imperil Communist regimes everywhere. Eventually the Politburo made the historic decision to use Soviet troops to overthrow Amin and establish a more broadly based pro-Soviet regime. The general staff still advised against military action, but was not listened to.

Ten days later elite KGB anti-terrorist troops flew into Kabul, and on 25 December hundreds of Soviet tanks and tens of thousands of motorized infantry began to cross the border into Afghanistan, the first time during the Cold War that Soviet troops would violate a neutral border. It was decided to invade over the Christmas period when the West's guard would be down and the Red Army would have a few days' grace to do its work. Within forty-eight hours Soviet commandos occupied the Afghan radio and television station, and on the evening of 27 December they stormed the royal palace on the edge of the city. There they killed Amin and his son. Moscow now installed a new leader, Babrak Karmal, whom they regarded as more manageable. The Western belief that the Soviet invasion was part of an orchestrated plan to dominate the region as far as the Persian Gulf was wide of the mark. The decision to intervene was the act of a divided and leaderless clique that was already beginning to lose its grip on power.

ABOVE RIGHT: *Zbigniew Brzezinski, US national security adviser, with Pakistan's minister of defence, General Fazul Haq, on the Afghan frontier. Brzezinski offered $400 million in aid. Pakistan asked for, and got, much more.*

But in Washington an administration previously challenged for policy weakness responded with outrage. On 28 December, Carter sent Brezhnev a message on the hot line stating that the Soviet invasion was a "clear threat" to peace and "could mark a fundamental and long-lasting turning point in our relations." Carter denounced the invasion and called for trade sanctions against the Soviet Union. Grain sales were suspended. Inside the White House, Brzezinski and Vance were once more in dispute over how to respond. The national security adviser wanted to make the Soviet Union "bleed" over its military incursion; Vance preferred to link withdrawal to a broader policy of "mutual restraint" over both Iran and Pakistan. Carter, torn, eventually came down on the side of Brzezinski.

In his State of the Union address on 23 January 1980, Carter called the Soviet invasion "the most serious threat to peace since the Second World War" and then warned that "an attempt by an outside force to gain control of the Persian Gulf region will be regarded as an assault on the vital interests of the United States, and such an assault will be repelled by any means necessary, including military force." Carter let it be known to the Soviets that this would not exclude nuclear force.

The United States dramatically increased arms shipments to Pakistan. Brzezinski went there on a high-profile visit and appeared at the Khyber Pass on the Afghan border, where he posed for television cameras ominously waving a Chinese submachine gun. After some bargaining, President Zia agreed that Pakistan would act as the conduit for secret weapons supplies to the Afghans, who were fiercely resisting the Soviet occupation. Brzezinski also offered economic aid to help prop up Zia's regime, which earlier in his administration Carter had denounced. The CIA began to supply the Afghan rebels with weapons bought on the open market with funds from the United States and the Saudis, America's closest allies in the region.

The administration now dropped its support of the SALT II treaty and initiated a rapid increase in arms spending. It was resolved to maintain a permanent naval presence in the Indian Ocean. US military chiefs, looking at the problems of responding to events in Southwest Asia, had asked, "How the hell are you going to get there?" The strength of the Rapid Deployment Force was increased until, a decade later, it absorbed some $45 billion of defence expenditure each year.

The Kremlin's response to all this sabre rattling was to dig in deeper. Brezhnev denounced Carter's "lies" about Afghanistan and insisted that Soviet troops had entered Afghanistan at the request of the Kabul government, and that there was no intention of withdrawing them. But as the resis-

The Moscow Olympics

During the 1960s and 1970s, the Eastern bloc came to see international sport as an opportunity for the socialist world to prove its superiority over the capitalist system by winning more medals. Athletes became pawns in the superpower rivalry. The International Olympic Committee awarded the Summer Games of 1980 to Moscow, the first time the Olympics would be held in the socialist bloc. The Soviets were determined to make them the best ever. A huge new facility was built, the Lenin Stadium. The cost of staging the Games was absorbed within the military budget.

Following the invasion of Afghanistan, President Carter issued an ultimatum: the Soviets must withdraw or the United States would boycott the Moscow Games. When this policy came under criticism, Carter called on the IOC to reallocate the Games to another city, something never done before. In any case there were only six months left before the Games were due to open. Carter could not legally impose a US boycott, so he threatened the US Olympic Committee; under pressure it capitulated. Athletes felt aggrieved; "These are *our* Games," declared hurdler Edwin Moses. Following the lead of the United States, several other countries, including Canada, West Germany, China, Japan, and Kenya, did not send teams to Moscow. But most did. Britain's prime minister, Margaret Thatcher, supported the call for a boycott, but the British Olympic Association showed its independence from government and defiantly sent a team.

The Olympics went ahead without the Americans and the others and were a limited success. The Soviets and East Europeans won a huge tally of medals. Two British middle-distance runners, Sebastian Coe and Steve Ovett, each won a gold medal.

Soviet television coverage of the Games never admitted to Russian viewers the real reason for the boycott. Rumours were spread that CIA spies would mingle with the crowd and offer poisoned chewing gum. Fearing that Soviet youth would be contaminated by mixing with Westerners, the Kremlin sent most Moscow schoolchildren out of the city while the Games were on.

Four years later the Soviet leadership got back at the United States; they announced a last-minute tit-for-tat boycott of the Los Angeles Summer Games. Again the Olympics went ahead, this time without thousands of athletes from the Soviet Union, East Germany, and the socialist bloc. Although sport claims to be beyond politics, the Cold War left deep scars on the Olympic Games.

ABOVE: *Pope John Paul II, near Krakow in Poland. His visit to his homeland evoked a huge wave of national sentiment.* BELOW: *Misha the Bear, mascot of the Moscow Olympics, sheds a tear at the closing ceremony.*

tance grew more bitter, Moscow had to send in more and more troops. By the end of 1980 there were about 125,000 Red Army soldiers in Afghanistan. Although their commanders initially wanted to leave the fighting to the Afghan army, Soviet soldiers soon got sucked into combat. They initially adopted vast "sweep offensives," tactics devised to defeat NATO forces in Europe and the Chinese army in Manchuria. These parade ground manoeuvres proved futile against guerrilla fighters operating in mountainous countryside. Mechanized forces moving by road made easy targets for guerrillas and for mines. Motorized convoys were attacked, and the Soviet soldiers massacred. The casualties rose. Just as in Vietnam, once troops had been deployed it would prove difficult to find a way to get them out.

To Washington's irritation, America's allies did not see the need to abandon détente because of events in Kabul. Helmut Schmidt went ahead with a visit to Moscow despite Carter's attempt to prevent it. Margaret Thatcher, Britain's prime minister since May 1979, pledged support for Carter but nothing more. And through the spring and summer of 1980, France, West Germany, Italy, and Japan all embarked on bilateral trade talks with Moscow. As US trade with the Soviet Union dropped from $4.5 billion to $2 billion per year, other Western nations stepped in; huge trade deals cancelled with American companies were picked up by European firms. That summer the Olympic Games were due to be held in Moscow, an event for which the Kremlin had great ambitions. Carter called for a boycott, and when that proved unpopular he asked for the Games to be restaged elsewhere or cancelled. This request was mocked by the International Olympic Committee. The games went on despite the American-led boycott, and a majority of nations competed. Washington, it seemed, was powerless either to reverse the Soviet aggression or to force its allies into line.

Solidarity at the Lenin Shipyards

The end of détente had a particular impact on Poland, which had become dependent on the West for trade and technology. Shortages of food and consumer goods intensified. But when Cardinal Karol Wojtyla became Pope John Paul II, the Polish people felt a surge of pride. The return to his homeland by the first-ever Polish-born Pope in June 1979 was inspirational; half a million people in Victory Square, Warsaw, heard him proclaim, "The exclusion of Christ from the history of man is an act against man." He concluded his sermon: "Let your Spirit descend, and renew the face of this land. Amen." As many as one in four of the entire population saw the Pope during his nine-day visit. John Paul II did not attack the government directly, but by invoking the spirit of an ancient Christian nation, the Pope helped to reawaken the Polish people. He gave them a new self-confidence.

In July 1980 the Polish government announced increases in meat prices by as much as 100 per cent. Strikes and factory stoppages spread across the country in protest. On 14 August a strike broke out in the Lenin Shipyards in Gdansk. More than seventeen thousand workers put down their tools and walked out. Strikes spread to Szczecin and other Baltic towns, and within a week 250 factories were out. Although the government agreed to the Gdansk

August 1980. A strike at the Lenin Shipyards in Gdansk, Poland, brings Lech Walesa, leader of Solidarity, into the spotlight. Here, carried on his comrades' shoulders, he returns their enthusiasm.

workers' demands, the strikers there now recognized the importance of unity and formed Solidarnosc, or Solidarity. It began as an Inter-Factory Strike Committee with a broad coalition of interests, calling for the legalization of strikes and the opening up of Catholic Church worship. Gradually, political demands, such as the abolition of censorship, were added to economic demands like higher pay. The highly articulate and keenly astute strike leader of the Lenin Shipyards was Lech Walesa, an unemployed electrician. He became head of the Solidarity trade union and spokesman for the Polish working people. It was clear that a major confrontation with the

I said to the gentleman who came to arrest me, "This is the moment of your defeat. These are the last nails in the coffin of communism."

— Lech Walesa,
leader of Solidarity

Polish state was imminent; the concessions won by the strikers were a beginning and not an end.

Washington followed developments closely; in a campaign speech on Labor Day, Carter expressed US sympathy for the Polish workers in their struggle, declaring that "the working men and women of Poland have set an example for all those who cherish freedom and human dignity." Solidarity was given massive coverage in the Western media; the US provided covert support. Washington warned its allies that the Soviets might intervene in Poland, but decided to do nothing more that might provoke Moscow.

In the Kremlin, Solidarity was perceived as potentially the biggest threat to the Communist system in Eastern Europe since the Prague Spring. Economic protests were developing into a programme for sweeping political change. Joint East German and Soviet troop manoeuvres took place along the Polish border and, in a clear warning to the Poles, were given great publicity on television. Support for Solidarity within Poland soared. As the crisis worsened, detailed plans were made for Warsaw Pact military intervention; if the plans were implemented, eighteen divisions would take part: fifteen Soviet, two Czech, and one East German. On 2 December, CIA director Stansfield Turner sent an urgent note to President Carter stating, "I believe the Soviets are readying their forces for military intervention in Poland."

But Moscow, deeply involved in Afghanistan and worried about its relations with the West, decided against using troops. The immediate crisis passed.

ABOVE LEFT: Poland avoided Soviet military intervention by appointing hard-line minister of defence General Wojciech Jaruzelski (second from right) as premier. ABOVE: Students confront riot police, Warsaw, 1 December 1981. Jaruzelski cracked down hard on strikers and demonstrators and later that month imposed martial law.

Over the following year, Solidarity membership grew to 10 million; it became much more than a trade union, rather a national platform for opposition to the Communist regime. However, to Moscow's relief, General Wojciech Jaruzelski, the defence minister, who promised to take a hard line, was appointed prime minister and first secretary of the Polish Communist Party. The economy declined; factories stopped work because of a lack of spare parts, the currency lost value; everywhere people queued for food. Another wave of strikes swept the country. When Solidarity demanded a popular vote on the future of the Communist Party and relations with the Soviet Union, Jaruzelski, under pressure from the Soviets, knew he had to act.

On 13 December 1981 Jaruzelski announced that the country was in a "state of war" and proclaimed martial law. A twenty-one-man Army Council of National Salvation was established to run the country. The press was closed down and the right to free association proscribed; strict curfews were imposed, and key economic enterprises were taken over by the military. All links with the outside world were cut, and the domestic telephone system was closed down. Solidarity was banned. Lech Walesa and all its leaders, along with thousands of activists, were arrested. Tanks and armoured vehicles poured out onto the streets. Solidarity was taken by surprise and leaderless; there was no general uprising. There were a few isolated battles between strikers and the internal police force, who used tanks and tear gas, and several workers were killed. By the end of December the last of the strikers in the Silesian coal mines had returned to work. Jaruzelski, acting decisively, had avoided direct Russian intervention. But with ten thousand activists imprisoned or interned, he could not bring about the national salvation he sought. It was impossible to build a new power base. Martial law continued for two years, and economic conditions grew even worse. Opposition went underground and rallied around the Catholic Church. The Communist state survived in Poland for a few years longer.

In the United States, as the 1980s began, the sense of weakness had been all-pervasive. The hostages were still being held in Iran; the hike in OPEC oil prices had brought fuel shortages; interest rates were high; Afghanistan had been invaded. Carter's opponent in the 1980 presidential campaign, Ronald Reagan, claimed that "America has lost faith in itself. . . . We have to recapture our dreams, our pride in ourselves and our country."

On 23 March 1983, President Ronald Reagan, addressing the nation from the White House, calls for a major shift in defence strategy: a space-age shield to intercept missiles and replace the deterrent of instant retaliation. The Strategic Defense Initiative, SDI, was immediately christened Star Wars.

Reagan
1981–1984

Reagan takes charge. The new cabinet poses for its official portrait in the Oval Office. Vice President George Bush gets to sit on the table with the president.

A New Role for Reagan

When President Ronald Wilson Reagan and his team took up office in January 1981, they were brimming over with confidence and optimism. Reagan had campaigned on a pledge that he would reinvigorate America with new strength and the will to lead the free world in its struggle against communism. A modestly successful Hollywood actor and a leading figure in the Screen Actors Guild, Reagan had been the governor of California. He was inaugurated president within a few days of his seventieth birthday — the oldest US president ever. Never wanting to be tied down with detail, he required that papers prepared for him be double-spaced and no more than a page and a half long. For Reagan the presidency was intuitive and inspirational, a "role" he would play. He would offer a broad strategy; it was for others to follow through on policy details and implementation.

Reagan was further to the right than many Americans on both domestic and foreign policy issues, but he was a genial, gutsy communicator, with a way of phrasing ideas that made them appealing. Prosperity would come from "getting the government off our backs." At his first press conference he announced that "détente is a one-way street the Soviet Union has used to pursue its own aims." Since dealing with accusations of Communist infiltration of Hollywood in the late 1940s, he had been a fervent and outspoken anti-Communist. Now he attacked the morality of the Soviets; they believed they could do anything to "further their cause, meaning they have the right to commit any crime, to lie, to cheat in order to attain that [end]." Reagan's world was like an old Hollywood movie; he saw things in simple terms of right and wrong, with the Communists as the bad guys and the West leading a "crusade for freedom" that would dump the whole Communist system on the "ash heap of history." Two years into his presidency he described the Soviet leaders as "the focus of evil in the modern world" and their domain as "an evil empire." Jimmy Carter, his predecessor, had begun the process of rejecting détente and increasing defence spending. Reagan wholeheartedly embraced this way forward in foreign policy.

Many of Reagan's ideas came from a right-wing think tank, the Committee on the Present Danger, which was strongly anti-Communist, opposed to the SALT II agreement, and in favour of increased military expenditure. Fifty members of the committee took senior positions in the new administration. This nucleus within government believed that negotiating with the Soviets was a sign of weakness; what was needed was a determination to contain Soviet expansion by building up American economic and military strength.

Immediately Reagan began a new phase of rearmament, on a colossal scale. Within two weeks of taking office, he increased the defence budget by $32.6 billion. The new secretary of defence, Caspar Weinberger, announced that his mission was "to rearm America." Defence spending increased by nearly 50 per cent during the first Reagan term, rising to 7 per cent of gross domestic product. The Pentagon got almost everything it wanted, including the B-1 bomber, which Carter had scrapped, an enlarged navy, and reinforcements of conventional weaponry. New defence guidance directives called, alarmingly, for preparations to wage a nuclear war "over a protracted period." They advocated "nuclear decapitation" of the Soviet political and military leadership in the event of war and stressed that the United States must "prevail" in any nuclear conflict. They also identified the need for using "special forces" in covert counter-insurgency operations. All these hawkish plans were funded by immense budget deficits and by cutting back on domestic welfare programmes. Through the decade the national debt would soar from $1 trillion to $4 trillion.

Reagan reasoned that the United States could afford the cost of a new escalation in the arms race but the Soviet Union could not. A few months before his election he had told the *Washington Post:* "Right now we are hearing of strikes and labor disputes because people aren't getting enough to eat. They've diverted so much to military spending that they can't provide for consumer needs." He was convinced that the way to defeat the Soviets was to outspend and outperform them. He concluded: "So far as an arms race is concerned, there's one going on right now, but there's only one side racing."

In Reagan's view the Soviet Union was the source of "all the unrest that is going on" in the world; national liberation struggles were nothing less than instruments for Soviet expansion. Both Reagan and his first secretary of state, Alexander Haig, believed that the Soviets were behind most acts of international terrorism. So local problems anywhere became issues that threatened the stability of the entire free world and needed an appropriate response. Haig claimed that Moscow had a "hit list" for the "takeover of Central America," with El Salvador and Nicaragua at the top.

America's nuclear deterrent. FB-111 swing-wing fighter-bombers line the tarmac.

So far as an arms race is concerned, there's one going on right now, but there's only one side racing.

— Ronald Reagan, 18 June 1980

"Our Son of a Bitch"

The Somoza family had ruled Nicaragua, the largest nation in Central America, since the 1930s. By exploiting the country mercilessly, they accumulated a vast fortune, becoming the richest family in the whole area. For several decades the Somozas were known as staunch allies of the United States, even though American leaders were aware that they were despotic and greedy. As Franklin Roosevelt is supposed to have said of the founder of the dynasty, "I know he's a son of a bitch but he's our son of a bitch." With US military backing, the Somozas overpowered all opposition and ruled through a tough national guard. During the Cold War, American strategic interest in Nicaragua was to maintain stability; so when hostility to dictator Anastasio Somoza Debayle grew in the mid-1970s, President Ford doubled military aid to him. But Somoza's record of human rights violations was abysmal, and President Carter, trying to distance his administration from this repressive regime, reduced American aid to Nicaragua.

General Anastasio Somoza, with his wife and son, greets American visitors. The family dynasty he established in 1937 ruled Nicaragua for four decades.

During 1977 opponents of Somoza came together in a broad alliance, of which the Sandinistas, who began as Cuban-supported guerrillas, represented the rural poor. The more moderate opposition, from the business classes, was led by Pedro Joaquin Chamorro. On 10 January 1978 Chamorro was assassinated — a spark that set Nicaragua on fire. There followed weeks of rioting and calls for a general strike. The opposition to Somoza now comprised businessmen, journalists, students, and intellectuals as well as poor peasants. They all hoped Washington would put pressure on Somoza to compromise. Carter had said he would not intervene in Latin America, but as the disturbances worsened, he decided to try to prop up the moderates to avoid power going to the radicals, the Sandinistas. It was too little too late. Nicaragua was polarizing rapidly; the fighting soon escalated into civil war. In mid-1979, the Sandinistas finally took control of the capital, Managua. A bloody civil war had cost nearly fifty thousand lives. The dictator Somoza, America's long-time ally, fled the country and was later murdered in Paraguay.

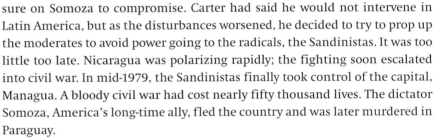

Daniel Ortega

Sandinista guerrillas stand over the body of a Somoza national guardsman killed in hard fighting in the south of Nicaragua in 1979.

Modelling itself on the Cuban revolution, the new left-wing government led by Daniel Ortega Saavedra began a policy of land reform and the nationalization of key industries, as well as a literacy campaign to raise educational standards. Thousands of Cubans arrived to assist in the revolution — doctors, teachers, agricultural experts, and military advisers. But the old business classes soon fell out with the Sandinistas, and in 1981 another civil war began when the paramilitary *contrarevolucionarios* (known as the Contras) launched brutal attacks from neighbouring Honduras. The Contras looked for outside support and naturally turned to Reagan's White House.

In November 1981 the National Security Council authorized substantial funds to assist the Contras. The CIA began arming and training a force that grew from a few hundred in 1981 to about fifteen thousand by the mid-eighties. The stated objective for the NSC in becoming involved in Nicaragua was, in the short run, to "eliminate Cuban/Soviet influence in the region," and, in the longer term, to "build politically stable governments able to with-

The Israeli Invasion of Lebanon

In 1975 the fragile balance of cultural and religious diversity in Lebanon fractured into civil war between Christian and Muslim forces. The civil war was aggravated by a large Palestinian refugee population, forced out of Israel, whose government-in-exile, the Palestine Liberation Organization (PLO), operated almost as a state within a state. The Palestinians controlled southern Lebanon and used their bases there to launch rocket attacks into northern Israel, to which the Israelis usually responded with heavy counter-attacks. A United Nations peacekeeping force was sent to southern Lebanon to try to keep the two combatants apart, since the Reagan administration was reluctant to become involved in the Israeli-Palestinian conflict.

In June 1982, on the pretext of retaliating for a terrorist attack in London, the Israelis launched a full-scale invasion of Lebanon. With overwhelming firepower, the Israelis stormed the PLO guerrilla bases in southern Lebanon and within days sped past UN peacekeepers, who could do nothing more than note registration numbers of the invaders' tanks.

In the early days of the invasion, the Israelis, using US weaponry, came into conflict with the Soviet-armed Syrian air force in a classic Cold War "proxy" confrontation. Using US missile technology to fight Soviet air technology, the Israelis shot the Syrians out of the sky. Within hours hundreds of Soviet advisers had arrived in Damascus to assess whether the defeat was due to the superiority of American weaponry or the failure of Syrians to use Soviet technology effectively. Moscow rapidly rearmed the Syrians but at the same time warned the United States on the hot line against direct intervention.

American exasperation with Israel grew as its commanders occupied West Beirut and, after a month of stalemate, stood by while Christian militiamen massacred hundreds of Palestinian civilians at the Sabra and Chatila refugee camps, supposedly under Israeli control. This prompted a flurry of diplomatic activity. Both Israel and the PLO agreed to withdraw from Beirut. US marines, along with French, Italian, and British troops, were sent to West Beirut to keep the peace.

The Soviets believed the United States wanted to turn Lebanon into a protectorate, but this was never Washington's intention. Sucked into the Lebanese civil war to prop up a pro-Western leader, Amin Gemayel, the Americans became unpopular with all sides. In October 1983 an Islamic terrorist drove a truck packed with explosives into an American military barracks and detonated his cargo, killing 241 marines. As a consequence, within four months, the Reagan administration had withdrawn American troops from Lebanon.

Israeli armoured vehicles invade Lebanon, June 1982. UN observers can only watch them go by.

Burial of Palestinian victims of a massacre in Sabra refugee camp, Beirut, Lebanon.

stand such influences." The US Navy patrolled Nicaragua's coast. US aircraft flew reconnaissance missions over the country, and American troops staged manoeuvres in Honduras, just to the north. The campaign against the revolutionary government in Nicaragua became a rallying cry for Reagan, who saw the Sandinistas as the Soviet Union's advance guard in the western hemisphere.

In El Salvador a guerrilla war had been waged by leftist fighters against a right-wing military regime for many years. The guerrillas were supported by Cuba with small arms supplied through Nicaragua. Reagan increased aid to El Salvador's military junta from $36 million in 1981 to $197 million in 1984. The junta viciously pursued the opposition, sending "death squads" through the countryside looking for peasants who had given support to the guerrillas. Tens of thousands of people were killed or simply went missing: the "disappeared." Almost one in five of the population fled abroad for refuge. The conflict ended in stalemate, with neither side able to defeat the other. But Washington preferred the right-wing military junta to a left-wing revolutionary government, and to this extent was satisfied that El Salvador remained free from communism.

El Salvador. Rightist government forces exhibit bodies of dead revolutionaries.

"Freedom Fighters"

In Afghanistan the Reagan administration inherited a programme of covert assistance for the Mujahedeen, which it substantially increased by supplying arms to the rebels fighting the Red Army there. Most arms were channelled through the Afghan refugee camps in Pakistan, where the rebels recruited their fighters. The Pakistanis hoped to encourage the creation of a fundamentalist Islamic state in Afghanistan. Before long Reagan and his people were describing the Mujahedeen, the Islamic "soldiers of God," as "freedom fighters" in the US struggle with the forces of evil, and Pakistan as a "front line" state in the war. President Carter's national security adviser, Brzezinski, had offered Pakistan $400 million of US aid, which President Zia rejected as "peanuts." He wanted tanks and high performance aircraft like the F-16 that he could use against Pakistan's traditional enemy, India. Realizing that at the Reagan White House he was pushing on an open door, Zia talked up his demands for aid. He eventually agreed to a five-year $1.5 billion military aid package from the United States that included forty F-16 jets, along with $1.7 billion of economic aid. In return the United States got permission to replace the radar listening posts it had lost in Iran with new monitoring stations in northern Pakistan, near the Soviet border. However, despite the CIA, the Pakistanis controlled the distribution of weapons to the Mujahedeen. Three out of four rifles went only to a small group of resistance leaders, adding to divisions within the heavily factionalized Mujahedeen.

In addition the new CIA director, William Casey, also wanted the Saudis to increase the sums they were contributing to the Mujahedeen war chest. King Fahd of Saudi Arabia would not be drawn further until Washington offered to sell him five airborne warning and control system aircraft (AWACS), in a deal worth $8.5 billion. The sale was delayed by Congress, under pressure from the Zionist lobby, but it went through eventually, when the Saudis

San Salvador 1984

DESAPARE-
CIDO

Tonio
bina
el 7-6-1982

MARIO REYNALDO
RAY GOMES

WALdo
ELVIDIO
Yonzalez. 22 años
saparecidos 7 agosto 1981

tan Nuestros Hijos?

Before the March general election in El Salvador. A hundred women demonstrate in front of the cathedral with pictures of their missing menfolk, the disappeared. They would never see them again.

agreed to support large-scale covert anti-Communist operations in Afghanistan and Nicaragua.

The fighting in Afghanistan grew more intense through 1981 and 1982. After heavy casualties in the early phase of the war, the Red Army moved away from massive armoured sweeps to smaller-scale land operations backed with air support. Soviet planes would bomb a village or a valley thought to be infiltrated by rebels, and Soviet commandos would come in by helicopter to block Mujahedeen escape routes. There were some large set-piece battles, but the results were inconclusive; and once the Soviets had withdrawn, the Mujahedeen would gradually return. The Soviets continued to sustain high losses; by the end of 1982 nearly five thousand Russian soldiers and airmen had died in Afghanistan.

Soviet leader Yuri Andropov said he was prepared to offer a timetable for withdrawal, if the United States and Pakistan agreed to stop supplying the Mujahedeen with arms and if a regime broadly along the lines of the existing one in Kabul remained in place. Peace efforts began under UN envoy Javier Pérez de Cuéllar (who shortly became UN secretary-general). Afghanistan and Pakistan were brought into the mediation process through "proximity talks"; the different sides did not meet face to face but through a UN intermediary. These talks began in Geneva in June 1982. From the archives in Moscow, we now know that the Soviets were trying to disengage honourably, leaving behind a friendly regime in Kabul. However, the talks were premature. Pakistan did not want peace; like the United States it preferred to see the Soviets tied down in Afghanistan. The United States never had any real expectation that Moscow would withdraw. It concentrated instead on supplying arms to the Mujahedeen and in letting the Soviet Union "bleed." Talks dragged on for year after year, but got nowhere.

A New Generation of Leaders

In the early 1980s, as conflicts continued, Cold War fears intensified. In Europe the peace movement, galvanized by opposition to cruise and Pershing missiles, mobilized ever larger numbers; across the continent 300,000 protesters marched during one weekend. But peace movement motives varied enormously, ranging from radical feminism at Greenham Common in England to Green Party politics in Germany. In Britain many people opposed the deployment of cruise missiles while still welcoming the NATO nuclear umbrella. In Germany some protested against the existence of nuclear weapons, others the use of nuclear energy for power. Statements from Moscow of Soviet support played into the hands of critics of the peace movement; they claimed that the KGB was behind every demonstration for peace.

Despite this groundswell of popular hostility to Cold War ramifications, a new generation of leaders in Europe brought increased vigour to the Atlantic alliance. In Margaret Thatcher, already British prime minister for a year and a half when the new administration took over in Washington, Reagan found a soulmate. Dubbed the Iron Lady by the Russians, Thatcher was resolute in her determination to deregulate government and allow the benefits of capitalism to flourish. Although the UK was now committed to

Kunar, Afghanistan. Mujahedeen clamber over a Soviet helicopter they have shot down.

BELOW: *A young Soviet soldier, captured by the Mujahedeen, shows his identity cards.*
BELOW RIGHT: *The women of Greenham Common, England, tied together, block the gates of the US air base in an Easter 1983 protest against nuclear weapons.*

Europe, Thatcher was also a strong believer, she said, in Britain's "enduring alliance" with the United States. Reagan and Thatcher saw eye to eye on many key issues. In François Mitterrand, France elected a president who wanted to return his country's nuclear capability to the Atlantic fold; discussions about bringing French troops back under NATO military control began. In West Germany, Helmut Kohl, who became chancellor in 1982, feared the Soviet threat and had a mandate to proceed with the deployment of cruise and Pershing missiles.

In the Soviet Union the early 1980s marked a period of stagnation. Leonid Brezhnev, in his mid-seventies, had been too ill even to lead the ageing band

President Ronald Reagan and British prime minister Margaret Thatcher. The Iron Lady stands by her man.

of Kremlin bosses effectively. Soviet policy became almost entirely reactive and devoid of initiative. At the Twenty-sixth Party Congress in February 1981, a month after Reagan took office, Brezhnev announced that the USSR wanted "normal relations with the United States" and said, "We are ready for dialogue." But as relations worsened over the next year, Politburo members claimed the buildup of arms by NATO was "exceeding all reasonable limits" and was "intensifying the danger of war." But it was beyond Moscow's ability to reverse this. It had no alternative policy but to reiterate a belief in détente and strategic arms control. These, as far as Washington was concerned, were now dead and buried. Reagan was accusing Moscow of lying, cheating, and using any means to achieve the objective of "world revolution"; the Kremlin merely noted that the new team in Washington lacked "political tact and courtesy." Moscow was not looking for any further commitments. Afghanistan was proving a major drain, and economic aid for Cuba and Vietnam was costing the USSR dearly. The Soviet economy was now falling seriously behind the West. It could not keep up with the demands of new technologies, and it was incapable of supplying the consumer needs of its people, outside of the tiny *nomenklatura*, the bureaucratic elite.

Brezhnev's death in November 1982 ended the era of his eighteen-year rule. The succession passed smoothly to Yuri Andropov, formerly head of the

KGB and Moscow's man in Budapest in 1956. Everyone expected a hard-line approach, but instead Andropov's first months brought a peace offensive. He talked of the 1970s, the decade "characterized by détente," not as a "chance episode in the difficult history of mankind," but as the key to the future. Andropov called for arms reductions, offered to cut back SS-20s in Europe, and proposed a new East-West summit. He went on to suggest nuclear-free zones in parts of Europe and the Mediterranean and a ban on arms sales to the developing world. At a Warsaw Pact meeting in January 1983, Andropov proposed a non-aggression undertaking in which NATO and the Warsaw Pact would agree not to use force against each other, or against members of their own bloc. His adviser Georgi Arbatov described this as "a crucial breakthrough . . . a break with the Hungarian syndrome that had so plagued him. Of course, it was also a break with the 'Brezhnev Doctrine.'"

A New Initiative: Star Wars

In Washington, Reagan was of no mind to compromise. Within days of Andropov's offering his olive branch, Reagan made his famous speech calling the Soviet leaders "the focus of evil in the modern world." Two weeks later, on 23 March 1983, in a speech calling for support of the defence budget, Reagan rejected the whole concept of mutual deterrence that had prevented nuclear war for more than three decades. Instead he argued for the Strategic Defense Initiative (SDI), an ambitious project to construct an anti-missile system in space, a programme instantly dubbed "Star Wars." Without any analysis of the technological problems or the costs involved, Reagan put forward a vision of a defensive shield that would intercept and destroy any incoming hostile projectiles through laser beams in space. Such a defensive shield, had it ever become a practical prospect, would have been as unsettling to the nuclear balance as anti-ballistic missiles were in the 1960s and early 1970s. If successful as designed, SDI could have nullified the Soviet nuclear threat. But had it gone ahead, most likely the Soviets would simply have increased the number of their ICBMs, with the idea that if enough were launched some of them would certainly get through. However, in Reagan's crusade against the forces of darkness, Star Wars was a powerful new weapon in the rhetorical arsenal.

Andropov responded to the Strategic Defense Initiative with a clear message of defiance. He claimed: "All attempts at achieving military superiority over the USSR are futile. The Soviet Union will never let that happen. It will never be caught defenceless by any threat, let there be no mistake about this in Washington. It is time they stopped devising one option after another in the search for the best ways of unleashing nuclear war in the hope of winning it. Engaging in this is not just irresponsible. It is insane." Andropov repeatedly described Washington's rhetoric against the Communist world as "flippant" and "irresponsible" and blamed the United States for failing to commit to the new Strategic Arms Reduction Talks (START), a follow-up to SALT, and to the Intermediate-Range Nuclear Forces (INF) talks.

America's European allies were also alarmed. A protective shield over America would leave Europe as the principal vulnerable target. Even Reagan's

"I'm willing to discuss the arms race whenever those Russian devils are!"

A cartoon targets the Reagan of 1984. By 1986 they were talking plenty.

All attempts at achieving military superiority over the USSR are futile. The Soviet Union will never let that happen.

—Yuri Andropov,
27 March 1983

Red Square, 15 November.
An era ends. Politburo members
carry Leonid Brezhnev's coffin;
his successor, Yuri Andropov,
is on the right. Andropov began
a process of change but was
dead himself within two years.

Moscow 1982

staunchest supporter, Margaret Thatcher, was troubled by SDI and tried to persuade Reagan to modify the plan to include the NATO allies. When Thatcher visited the White House to discuss SDI, Reagan spoke later of the "handbagging" he received.

"A Forward Strategy for Freedom"

Reagan's aggressive pronouncements against communism became known as the Reagan Doctrine. In 1983, in a speech to the Heritage Foundation, he once again described "the struggle now going on in the world" as "essentially the struggle between freedom and totalitarianism, between what is right and what is wrong." He went on to say, "We must go on the offensive with a forward strategy for freedom." The United States, he argued, must support forces fighting for freedom everywhere, "in all continents." Reagan even spoke of supporting "the forces of freedom in Communist totalitarian states," implying that the United States would actively encourage insurgents in Eastern Europe or even inside the Soviet Union itself. Reagan provided substantial covert support for Solidarity in Poland, in alliance with the Catholic Church. But apart from this, Washington did no more than alarm Moscow by these threats. US policy, however, did include an increased level of covert support for "freedom fighters" in Afghanistan and Nicaragua, and later, to a more limited degree, in Angola, Ethiopia, Mozambique, and Cambodia. The whole aim was an attempt to roll back communism — not just to contain the Soviet Union but to try for outright victory in the Cold War.

Any conflict, anywhere in the world, was liable to be overlaid with this

Reagan, flanked by Vice President George Bush and Defense Secretary Caspar Weinberger, makes his case for the Strategic Defense Initiative with a joke.

Star Wars

Ronald Reagan, in spite of his macho posture, was actually terrified by the prospect of a nuclear war that could be triggered in only minutes and seconds of response time. He had nightmares about mutual assured destruction and the possible need one day to press the nuclear button. But his Strategic Defense Initiative both destabilized the balance that had endured for thirty-five years and threatened an anxious Soviet Union.

The so-called Star Wars programme was intended to exploit the huge gap that already existed between American and Russian technology. An electronic shield would be constructed across the United States, and laser beams in space would intercept hostile missiles. Reagan's vision had a parallel in a popular 1977 space fantasy movie in which the force for Good pits deadly rays against an Evil Empire; its vocabulary was entirely apt for use by Reagan against the Communist bloc.

But such a system flouted the basic terms of the Anti-Ballistic Missile Treaty of 1972, which had stabilized the nuclear balance by ensuring that both sides would guarantee their own destruction if either launched a nuclear attack on the other. If Star Wars worked, the thinking went, the United States might be more likely to launch a first nuclear strike, knowing it would be inviolable to retaliation. Reagan got around that threat by offering to share the technology with the Soviets.

Soviet scientists believed that if only they built enough missiles no defensive system could stop them all. They imagined that by spinning the missiles on launch they could deflect the laser beams. And, with all the talk in Washington of the Soviet Union as the "evil empire," they were suspicious of Reagan's intentions ever to share the technology with them. It all seemed a trick intended to dupe them. Star Wars, it appeared, would make a new arms race inevitable — this time in space.

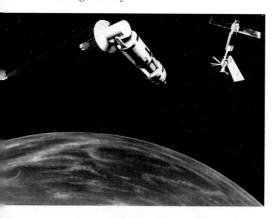

"May the force be with you." Models of laser technology to come. Reagan prophesies it will change history.

simplistic vision of an ideological crusade against communism. This created strange bedfellows for the United States. The Contras in Nicaragua were trained by, among others, a terrorist bomber, Luis Posada Carriles. Carriles had blown up a Venezuelan airliner in 1976, with heavy loss of life, and was never turned over to the Venezuelan authorities; instead he went on the US payroll. Yet Reagan described the Contras as "the moral equal of our Founding Fathers." In Cambodia the United States, lining up with the non-Communist forces, found itself allied with the genocidal Khmer Rouge. Right-wing military juntas, despite their despicable treatment of opponents, received US support. President Zia of Pakistan made it clear that, even with US aid, he still wanted to develop his own nuclear weapons. Before the Falklands War between Britain and Argentina in 1982, the United States supported the Argentine generals, with their cruel record on human rights, because of their anti-Communist stance, as well as the support they gave the Contras. In El Salvador, Guatemala, and Honduras, covert US aid helped arm the death squads that terrorized the countryside. America's share in the international arms trade increased during the Reagan years. All this came as a consequence of Reagan's "noble cause" of fighting communism.

The extent to which the administration was prepared to go in advancing this cause was seen in Nicaragua, where congressional support for backing the Contras waxed and waned. In 1984, after a CIA-sponsored programme to mine the Nicaraguan ports damaged ships of neutral and friendly countries, Congress cut off funds for covert support of the Contras. Private sources in the United States provided some financial help, but not enough. So the White House eventually channelled to the Contras revenues from the illicit sale of arms to Iran. When the Iran-Contra scandal was revealed in November 1986, it made the only serious dent in the popularity of the Reagan administration in its final years.

A rare example of direct US military intervention came in October 1983, when the United States invaded the tiny Caribbean island of Grenada after that country's prime minister was murdered in a military coup. Reagan feared the island would become a Communist base in the region and, on the pretext of rescuing American medical students there, acted decisively. A 7,000-strong US invasion force overcame the 600-man Grenadan army in a matter of hours. The evidence for Cuban-Soviet infiltration of Grenada was minimal; there were about forty-three Cuban military advisers on the island. The airport runway being built by a British company was for tourism, not for long-range Soviet supply aircraft as Washington claimed. The invasion was welcomed by some on the island, but widely criticized internationally; condemned in the Security Council, the United States had to deflect censure with a rare use of its veto. And since Grenada was a Commonwealth country, the invasion prompted a rebuke of Reagan from Margaret Thatcher. But at home in the United States the invasion was popular. Most Americans accepted the president's line: Grenada was "a Soviet-Cuban colony, being readied as a major military bastion to export terror and undermine democracy. We got there just in time."

We now know that the Soviets were so alarmed at this time that they put the KGB onto a special alert. Andrei Gromyko, Soviet foreign minister, warned: "The world situation is now slipping towards a very dangerous precipice. Problem number one for the world is to avoid nuclear war." Moscow began to believe that a US attack upon its allies, perhaps Cuba, or even against itself, was a possibility. KGB officers were instructed to observe closely whatever was going on in the West; any unusual activity — the movement of money, the setting up of blood banks, the sudden return of servicemen to active duty — was to be reported to Moscow. This intelligence operation lasted for some years; it reflected the Kremlin's growing paranoia.

KAL 007. ABOVE: *The captain of the doomed Korean airliner (front row, centre) and the president of the airline (right).* ABOVE RIGHT: *A victim's family, holding her picture, grieves at an altar at Seoul Airport.*

An Airliner Well Off Course

In late August 1983 came the most traumatic event of this period to affect US-Soviet relations: the shooting down of a Korean Air Lines jumbo jet, flight 007 from New York via Anchorage to Seoul, with 269 persons on board. When it was shot down by a Russian Su-15 fighter, the Korean airliner had strayed 365 miles off course and was inside Soviet airspace, well into a security zone of particular sensitivity. At the time of the incident another aircraft was also in the area, a US surveillance plane packed with electronic listening and monitoring devices. It has never been established whether the tragedy was connected to some American-sponsored intelligence mission that went terribly wrong, or whether it was just the incompetence of Soviet defence system personnel in firing on a civilian plane gone astray.

The response in Washington, however, to the loss of innocent life was instant outrage. Secretary of State George Shultz said he could see "no explanation whatever for shooting down an unarmed commercial airliner, no matter whether it's in your airspace or not." Reagan expressed "revulsion at this horrifying act of violence." He called it a "terrorist act," "a crime against humanity," and "an act of barbarism." At the United Nations the US representative described the shooting down of the civilian airliner as "wanton, calculated, deliberate murder." These furious condemnations were met with silence and evasions. For six days, as a full investigation was carried out, Moscow even refused to admit that the aircraft had been shot down. It now seems that although the Soviet military wanted to admit its error, the Kremlin refused to do so to avoid losing face. But the delays and denials made the Soviets look guilty to the rest of the world.

In Washington tapes were produced of the conversation between the Soviet pilot and his ground control station. The pilot, ordered to carry out the attack, fired his missiles and reported back to base: "The target is destroyed." However, we now know that the tape extracts produced by US intelligence

Military buildup in the Pacific. ABOVE: *Backbone of the US Seventh Fleet in the South China Sea.* ABOVE RIGHT: *The Soviet navy's new Typhoon-class submarine.*

were edited very selectively. The rest of the tape reveals that the Soviet fighter pilot followed all the international protocols for warning a civilian airliner that it was off course. Having gone through all these manoeuvres, the Soviet pilot, as a final warning, then fired tracers across the bow of the airliner. When, astonishingly, this still failed to get a response, Soviet military ground control concluded that the Korean jumbo jet must be a US military reconnaissance plane on a spying mission and ordered the shoot-down. However, this part of the tape was not revealed by Washington. Moscow was so slow to get its story together that it never managed to reverse the successful US propaganda campaign.

Following the KAL 007 incident, Washington banned all Aeroflot flights into the United States — even preventing Foreign Minister Gromyko from landing in New York to attend the UN General Assembly. Both sides believed the worst about the other, and US-Soviet relations reached a new low. Andropov, unwell and confined to a kidney-dialysis machine at a clinic outside Moscow, saw all his hopes for peaceful co-existence shattered. Four weeks after the Korean airliner shoot-down, he finally decided to go on the attack and accused US policy of taking a "militarist course that represents a serious threat to peace." Sticking to the position that flight 007 had been used by the United States for a deliberate surveillance provocation to test Soviet

The Shoot-down of KAL 007

Mysteries still surround the shooting down of Korean Air Lines flight 007 during the night of 31 August 1983. KAL 007 was on a regular flight from New York to Seoul. It stopped to refuel at Anchorage where, unusually, it took on more fuel than it needed before continuing its journey. From there, Captain Chun Byung-in, a veteran of the Korean War and one of the airline's most experienced pilots, flew the aircraft on a route that from the start began to drift off course, as if the highly sophisticated Inertial Navigation System was either switched off or had been wrongly programmed. Before long KAL 007 was hundreds of miles from its intended flight path. However, when Captain Chun reported his position to several ground control relay stations, he did so as if he were in fact flying along his designated route. For several navigation computers not to have caught this error adds up to an extraordinary malfunction in itself. The odds that all the different radar navigation systems could separately have failed to spot KAL 007's incorrect route have been calculated by one writer as "literally billions of trillions to one against."

While these double-check systems were, apparently, failing, KAL 007 was straying, perhaps deliberately, into some of the most dangerous skies in the world. At this tense moment in the Cold War, the Soviet Pacific Fleet had grown into the largest of the USSR's four fleets; it included several 25,000-ton Typhoon-class submarines, each of which carried eighty nuclear warheads, along with the newest Delta submarines. There were 2,400 Soviet combat aircraft in the region, and nearly half a million men, mostly along the Chinese border. Against this, the US Seventh Fleet patrolled the western Pacific with four giant aircraft carriers. It was backed by air and naval bases along the Aleutians, in Japan, in South Korea, and on several Pacific islands. From these flew the latest F-16 fighter-bombers, unmatched in the Soviet air force. Large-scale naval exercises had been held in the region earlier in 1983. Admiral Robert Long, commander-in-chief of the US Pacific forces, was convinced that the Pacific was where "a confrontation with the Soviet Union is most likely to take place."

Both sides employed a variety of surveillance platforms to observe the other: ground listening stations, reconnaissance ships and planes, and spy satellites. The United States had an overwhelming technological superiority in its electronic monitoring equipment. Occasionally it would mount surveillance missions in which an intruder aircraft flew into Soviet airspace while an RC-135 aircraft, packed with tons of listening equipment, recorded data about how the Soviet command structure responded, and how its radar and electronic facilities operated. The purpose was to find out if there were any gaps in the Soviet defensive system. The Soviets had protested about one of these intrusions only a few months before. On the night of 31 August, over the Kamchatka Peninsula, KAL flight 007 appears to have passed near such a US RC-135 surveillance aircraft, there to monitor tests of a new Soviet PL-5 missile due to be fired that very night. Perhaps the Soviet radar controllers got the two aircraft muddled and, as the civilian airliner crossed Soviet airspace again, over Sakhalin Island, scrambled their defences.

But there are still unanswered questions about what happened. Was the flight off course due to some extraordinary coincidence of navigational accidents? Had the Soviets jammed its navigation system for some reason? Was Captain Chun deliberately trying to take a short cut to reduce fuel costs? If so, why was he not extra vigilant as he knowingly crossed Soviet airspace? Why, above all else, did KAL flight 007 not respond to international warning signals from the Soviet fighter, the waggling of wings and then the firing of tracers across its bow? The Soviet pilot has said that he had identified the plane as a Boeing-747 civilian jet, so why, then, was the order given to shoot it down?

The Soviets alleged that KAL 007 was on a spy mission to provoke the Soviet defences in a way that could then be observed by US electronic surveillance systems. This has never been proved. Nine years after the incident, a Russian investigation concluded that the shoot-down was a genuine accident by panicky and incompetent Soviet Air Defence Command operators.

In any case, at a particularly tense moment in the Cold War, the tragic loss of KAL flight 007 made each side even more suspicious of the other. Reagan exploited the anti-Soviet sentiment generated in the United States to win support for his increased military spending.

Russian Su-15 fighter like the one that shot down KAL 007.

responses, he apologized for the loss of life but accused Washington of "extreme adventurism" in this "criminal act." The Soviet press denounced America heavily. Ordinary Russians began to fear the worst. One local party chief, in a remote agricultural region, was approached after a meeting by several women in tears, asking if war with America was now inevitable, and if their sons would have to die.

Relations Blow Hot and Cold

A few weeks later, as the United States deployed Pershing and cruise missiles in Western Europe, the Soviets walked out of the stalled INF talks and the START talks in Geneva. They had threatened to do so before. Now they felt it was the only option left open to them. They hoped to shock Western opinion

ABOVE LEFT: *NATO exercises in November 1983 convinced the Kremlin that an attack by the West was imminent.* ABOVE: *US-USSR talks in Geneva on missiles in Europe are suspended on 23 November. No date was set for a resumption.*

into forcing a change in US policy. The plan backfired badly. Washington seized the opportunity to blame Moscow for breaking off arms-limitation talks that had been going on for fourteen years.

The situation had got so bad late in 1983 that a large-scale NATO exercise in Western Europe led the Kremlin to believe that an American first-strike offensive was imminent. Both the killing of US marines in Beirut and the invasion of Grenada in late October had prompted US military alerts that had been closely monitored in Moscow. Then, in early November, came a ten-day NATO exercise code-named Operation Able Archer 83 that was designed to practise high-level command co-ordination during a nuclear attack. As the NATO forces went through the various stages of alert from conventional to nuclear, Moscow became more and more nervous. Soviet defence thinkers had often imagined that a real attack, when it came, might be launched during what purported to be military exercises. Again, the KGB was put on special alert. At air bases in East Germany interceptor aircraft were placed on standby. This panic in Moscow was the Kremlin's blackest time since the Cuban missile crisis. Many in the Soviet leadership were genuinely afraid of the US Pershings, which, newly deployed in Europe, could reach the Kremlin in only a few minutes.

The deputy KGB chief in London, Oleg Gordievsky, was a double agent who also worked for British intelligence. When Gordievsky passed on news of the KGB alert and the fact that the Kremlin seriously feared an American first-strike offensive, initially no one believed him. However, the information was passed from London to Washington. When the new national security adviser, Robert McFarlane, told Reagan, the news had a strong impact on the president. Reagan was puzzled, but also seriously disturbed, to learn that the Kremlin could really believe that he would launch an offensive assault against the Soviet Union. He felt a real need for a face-to-face meeting with the Soviet leaders. This feeling influenced his thinking over the months ahead.

In early 1984 the White House decided to take a more conciliatory tone.

The Hall of Columns, 11 February 1984, Moscow. Dignitaries of the Soviet Communist Party pay their last respects to Yuri Andropov. Another ill old man, Konstantin Chernenko, replaced him.

In a major policy speech to kick off his campaign for re-election, Reagan announced that he was ready to "meet the Soviets halfway." He still spoke about building "credible deterrence" but also of the need to "avoid war and reduce the level of arms." He even talked of engaging in "constructive co-operation" and in a new "dialogue" with the Soviets. A few days later, Secretary Shultz met Gromyko in Stockholm. Instead of the usual recriminations, they enjoyed five hours of reportedly "serious" discussions together. And in Washington, the backdoor negotiating channel with veteran Soviet ambassador Anatoly Dobrynin was opened up again.

Throughout 1984 Reagan and Shultz blew hot and cold towards Moscow. Reagan, convinced that America had grown strong again, felt secure enough to begin talking with the Soviets. On the other hand, in his election campaign he kept up some of the old anti-Soviet rhetoric. The Kremlin was still cautious about the new line coming out of Washington and was not sure what to make of it. In May the Soviets called a boycott of the Los Angeles Olympic Games, citing fear for their teams' safety. Groups from the American right wing had formed a Ban the Soviets coalition that threatened acts of violence against Russian athletes; they also announced their intention to induce defections with the use of "safe houses," supposedly all prepared and waiting. The Soviets imagined that their boycott would make Reagan less popular in America. However, the president opened an Olympic Games in which the

United States indulged in an orgy of national pride and flag-waving. Without the stiff competition from the Eastern bloc, the United States won more gold medals than in any previous Games. Later in the year Moscow suggested it would consider restarting arms-limitation negotiations. The Kremlin wanted to prevent the militarization of outer space and called for a ban on "space weapons." Washington, still committed to the Star Wars initiative, SDI, agreed to a meeting in Vienna. And Reagan met Gromyko after he had addressed the United Nations. This, the first encounter between Reagan and any senior Soviet official, was treated in the United States like a mini-summit. A slight thaw began to affect the frosty relations between Moscow and Washington.

On 9 February 1984 Andropov died; he was replaced as general secretary by Konstantin Chernenko, another elderly Soviet leader who had been close to Brezhnev. Chernenko's appointment disguised changes that were gathering pace inside the Soviet Union. In his short rule Andropov had started the process of reform, initiating a campaign against corruption in the bureaucracy and trying to find ways to improve the dreadful inefficiency of Soviet industry. This included an attempt to reduce the chronic alcoholism that afflicted the country like a plague. He tried to decentralize economic decision making and to delegate planning decisions to local managers. Andropov also promoted a younger generation of party reformers, including Mikhail Gorbachev and Eduard Shevardnadze. They wanted to pull the Soviet Union out of its stagnant mire. Through Chernenko, the old guard would cling to power for a little longer. But Chernenko was old and frail. In the wings, the new generation gathered.

In London, Margaret Thatcher's advisers looked at these new, younger members of the Soviet Politburo. They wondered with whom they would be dealing next and issued a series of invitations to visit Britain. By chance, the first to accept was Mikhail Gorbachev, who at the end of the year visited Thatcher in London. He came with his wife, Raisa, itself remarkable, as Soviet leaders rarely travelled with their wives. By comparison to the old men who had led the Soviet Union for twenty years, the Gorbachevs were young, lively, and glamorous. The visit was a great success. After Thatcher and Gorbachev met, the British prime minister was asked by reporters what she thought of her guest. "I'm cautiously optimistic," she replied. "I like Mr. Gorbachev. We can do business together." Mrs. Thatcher's verdict ushered in the final stage of the Cold War.

I like Mr. Gorbachev. We can do business together.

— Margaret Thatcher, December 1984

Looking ahead, Margaret Thatcher invited Mikhail Gorbachev to London. He brought his wife, Raisa, and a new style in Soviet leadership.

Cold War Spies

Slipping in and out of the shadows, busy with cypher and with micro-dot, stealing and concealing, betraying and being betrayed, intelligence agents of the great power blocs risked their lives to obtain and pass on information. Spies came to personify the very image of the Cold War. But how much did they influence its course?

Early Cold War spies — Kim Philby, Guy Burgess, and Donald Maclean in British intelligence and the Foreign Office — acted from political conviction. They believed what they were doing was right. Late in the Cold War, Aldrich Ames, the KGB's mole in the CIA, acted only for money. In between, both agencies expanded vastly; the CIA and KGB came to employ thousands. All the while, rival technologies of signals interception, known as Sigint, and of satellite photography — mechanical, impersonal, increasingly efficient — threatened to render the human spy redundant.

Spies operating before the Cold War began gave the Soviet Union an early advantage. Klaus Fuchs and Ted Hall were scientists employed at Los Alamos on the project to make the atomic bomb. They passed to their Soviet controllers detailed drawings of the implosion method of exploding the bomb. Partly as a result, the Soviet atomic bomb was ready in 1949, two years earlier than expected.

Burgess and Maclean delivered a flow of information on Western policy to Moscow in the 1940s, including the West's intentions on the Marshall Plan. Maclean and Philby had high clearances in British intelligence. Philby revealed details of Western Sigint to his KGB controllers and betrayed agents infiltrating the Balkans, who were apprehended and shot. The effect of this spectacular treachery, the knowledge that the KGB had an officer in the heart of

Western intelligence, was debilitating and dismaying. Americans would not trust British intelligence for twenty years. Burgess and Maclean defected to Russia in 1951; Philby, under suspicion for another decade, finally defected in 1963.

Agents on both sides told their employers what they wanted to hear. Consistent US over-estimates of Soviet missile strength fuelled the high defence expenditures and spiralling programmes of the 1950s and 1960s. But the CIA failed to predict North Korea's attack on South Korea in June 1950, or China's entry into the Korean War in November of that year. The CIA had the information needed, but did not want to believe it. The USSR, it reasoned, was known not to want to get involved. China was a client of the USSR; therefore China would not involve itself either. And the CIA's aerial intelligence could not then reach farther than an enemy's border. The CIA's Korean debacle led to the setting up of the National Security Agency (NSA), soon to be equipped with the biggest bank of computers in the world.

In Berlin, the front line of the Cold War, the CIA in 1954 dug a long tunnel under the Soviet sector, to tap telephone cables. The KGB let it go on for eleven months — its spy George Blake had warned them of the tunnel's existence.

Mossad, Israeli intelligence, obtained a copy of Khrushchev's Twentieth Party Congress speech of 1956, denouncing Stalin's crimes, and passed it to the CIA, which broadcast it behind the Iron Curtain. This helped provoke risings in Poland and Hungary later in 1956 and general turmoil elsewhere in the Communist camp.

As Khrushchev threatened and blustered, Oleg Penkovsky, an active agent, briefed the West repeatedly on

TOP: *Rudolf Abel, Soviet master spy operating in New York, was arrested in the United States in 1957, and exchanged for U-2 pilot Francis Gary Powers five years later.* BOTTOM: *Oleg Penkovsky after capture in 1962. Penkovsky's work helped brief the West during the Cuban missile crisis. He was shot in May 1963.*

the true state of Soviet military pre-paredness. Eisenhower and Kennedy had the benefit of his advice and knew that Khrushchev was bluffing. Penkovsky was accidentally spotted by the KGB after meeting a British contact in Moscow and was executed by a bullet in the head.

Oleg Gordievsky, of the London branch of the KGB, gave valuable service to the West for years, till he defected in 1985. He reported the Soviet Union's genuine fears of Western aggressive intentions in 1983.

Eisenhower was the first US president to understand how productive aerial intelligence and satellite photography could be. In 1962 U-2 overflights revealed to Kennedy that there were Soviet missile installations in Cuba. This came as a shock to administration officials; no one had warned them Khrushchev would put them there. Nor did any US agent, in Moscow or Havana, reveal another crucial fact: the Cuban army was equipped with tactical nuclear weapons. Had the United States invaded, as some urged, the use of these weapons would have come as a total surprise, and might well have triggered all-out nuclear war.

The United States had aerial photographs of Soviet tanks massing against Czechoslovakia in 1968 and Afghanistan in 1979. And detection by Sigint intercept and computer is supposed to have been so sophisti-cated as to enable Washington to overhear conversations of Politburo members. The real penetration of the Soviet Union was made possible by Sigint and satellites, not by agents. The KH 11 satellite was crucial to arms-control implementation; it made possible real-time verification by satellite to back up SALT II.

The crucial thing in war is to understand your opponent's thinking and intention. Towards the end of the Cold War, statesmen came to believe that there were few better ways to do this than to meet and talk to their antagonists. In the most striking rever-sal of all, both the United States and the USSR came to understand that their safety depended on openness and transparency rather than secrecy. Arms-limitation agreements could only be meaningful if verified, and could only be verified if each side laid itself open to the other's inspection.

Aldrich Ames, the ex-middle-rank-ing CIA officer now serving life in prison, spied for money. He was paid $2.7 million, and had $1.9 million coming to him when arrested in 1994. During nearly ten years on the KGB payroll, Ames fingered twenty-five CIA agents in the Soviet Union, of whom ten were shot. One of them was Dmitri Polyakov, the CIA's most productive Russian employee, who had been recruited in 1961. A grand-father, he had retired to his dacha when the KGB came for him in 1986. A long search for the mole who betrayed him led the CIA to Ames.

Markus Wolf, of East Germany's secret service, denies that spying is romantic: "It is dirty; people suffer."

Former CIA officer Aldrich Ames leaves court in Alexandria, Virginia, after pleading guilty to spying for Moscow, April 28, 1994. Ames spied for money, but cost many agents their lives. He was sentenced to life imprisonment.

Markus Wolf, East German spymaster, organized GDR espionage in West Germany. After the Cold War ended, Wolf was bailed, jailed, and released.

Washington, 1987

12 August. President Ronald
Reagan and his wife, Nancy,
escort Mikhail Gorbachev
to a state dinner at the White
House. Both men look as if they
know where they're heading;
in the end they got there.

Gorbachev
1984–1988

Konstantin Chernenko, on top of Lenin's Tomb, waves to the crowd, the last of the three old men to rule the USSR in succession. Appointed general secretary of the Communist Party on 13 February 1984, he died on 10 March 1985.

"Profound Transformations" Are Called For

To everyone inside the Kremlin, it was clear that Konstantin Ustinovich Chernenko was seriously ill; his shortness of breath, a result of emphysema, was impossible to disguise. He had barely got his feet under the table as new general secretary when the jockeying began as to who would succeed him. Those who favoured a return to the stable, good old days of Brezhnev tried to pressure Chernenko into halting Andropov's reforms. Those who favoured reform lost heart; the new leader was spiritless and wavered between factions. Often he was too ill to attend Politburo meetings, and at fifteen minutes' notice the head of the secretariat would be asked to take the chair. This was Mikhail Gorbachev, who more than anyone else represented a new way forward. The old guard resented his position and ganged up against him. As his illness got worse, Chernenko had difficulty in speaking and breathing and ceased to appear in public. He was too ill to deliver his annual election address to the Politburo, but there was no democratic process by which he could be removed. A sick and senile person could still sit at the top of the Soviet pyramid for as long as his closest colleagues chose to put up with him.

On 10 December 1984 Gorbachev gave a major speech on ideology to a party conference. Firmly nailing his colours to the mast of reform, Gorbachev introduced two new concepts to the party lexicon: *perestroika*, reconstruction or restructuring, and *glasnost*, openness or transparency. He declared, "Profound transformations must be carried out in the economy and the entire system of social relations, and a qualitatively higher standard of living must be ensured for the Soviet people.... *Glasnost* is an integral part of a socialist democracy. Frank information is evidence of confidence in the people and respect for their intelligence and feelings, and for their ability to understand events for themselves." Gorbachev was the reformers' man. But within the Politburo, the reformers were in a minority.

On the evening of 10 March 1985, Chernenko died, the third aged party leader to die in three years. The Politburo moved quickly to settle the succession; a meeting was called for 11:00 PM that night. Andrei Gromyko, the first to get to his feet, proposed Gorbachev. The next to speak, Nikolai Tikhonov, the eighty-year-old chairman of the Council of Ministers, was the most conservative opponent of reform, but he too supported Gorbachev's nomination, "without reservation." Gorbachev, age fifty-four, was elected unanimously. This was the Soviet way of doing things. The old men had decided that younger leadership was needed. At a Communist Party plenum the following day, to ratify the succession, there was a barely disguised sense of relief that power was passing to a younger man. Gorbachev's name provoked thunderous applause. After receiving the unanimous acclaim of the party, Gorbachev made a speech outlining his programme. He spoke of the need for the Soviet Union to "move forward" into a system of socialism with more democracy and social consciousness, and of the need for greater openness — glasnost. On foreign policy, Gorbachev announced, "We want to stop and not to continue the arms race, and consequently propose to freeze nuclear arsenals and stop further deployment of missiles." Gorbachev's election marked a new beginning — and the beginning of the end for both the Cold War and the Soviet Union.

Within days, copies of Gorbachev's speech were in circulation. At Chernenko's state funeral, Vice President George Bush and Secretary of State George Shultz represented the United States. They had a brief meeting with Gorbachev and came away knowing they had met a Soviet leader very different from any they had encountered before. When they reported back to President Reagan, all agreed this was a potentially significant moment for US-Soviet relations. Within days, the president, talking more positively, announced, "We're ready to work with the Soviet Union for more constructive relations." Reagan still talked tough, insisting on the importance of space weapons in his SDI initiative, but he also said he thought it was "high time" for a summit with his Soviet counterpart.

New Blood for the Kremlin

Mikhail Gorbachev was from a generation different from that of his predecessors, with attitudes formed not by privations and suffering during the Second World War but by coming of age in a world of co-existence. His formative experiences in the Communist Party came during the thaw of the Khrushchev years and the détente of the Brezhnev era. Within a year of taking charge, Gorbachev removed most of the old guard and brought new blood into the Kremlin. Andrei Gromyko, who had been foreign minister for twenty-eight years, was promoted to chairman of the Supreme Soviet, effectively head of state, or president. To replace him, Gorbachev surprised everyone by appointing as foreign minister a young Georgian, Eduard Shevardnadze, the first non-Russian to take on the role. Boris Yeltsin was brought in too. He would ultimately replace one of Gorbachev's most implacable opponents,

"Don't drink and drive,"
warns this Russian poster.
"It's criminal." Alcoholism was
rampant in the Soviet Union.

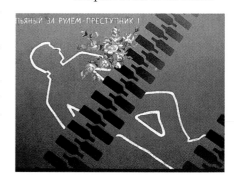

Viktor Grishin, first secretary of the Moscow party committee, known as the "governor" of Moscow. Yeltsin was active, decisive, open to new ideas, and brought sweeping reforms to the stagnant Moscow party administration. Alexander Yakovlev, an old friend of Gorbachev's who had run a think tank that developed many of the ideas behind perestroika, became party secretary with responsibility for news and propaganda. Together, they discussed ways of accelerating the pace of social and economic development.

Many Soviet citizens were excited by the appointment of a young, dynamic new leader; for some he was a messiah coming to save them. "We can't

ABOVE: *The new leader, Mikhail Gorbachev, takes his place at the table. On the far side are Nikolai Ryzhkov, Alexander Yakovlev, and Eduard Shevardnadze, with Anatoli Lukyanov in the foreground.*
ABOVE RIGHT: *Out meeting the people. Gorbachev with his wife, Raisa, in Kuybyshev, 8 April 1986.*

go on living like this" was the phrase that defined everyone's mood. Gorbachev now set about *uskoreniye*, acceleration of reform, with real energy. In a totalitarian state the process of change usually starts at the top, but to awaken Soviet society from its lethargy Gorbachev felt it was essential to inspire working people. He loved to meet people, and from the start regularly visited factories and colleges, even talking with crowds on the street. At first he was treated with the suspicion Soviet people accorded all party bosses. But Gorbachev persisted; he scolded local party officials who had told workers to keep quiet in his presence. People thought that perhaps he would listen, that maybe they could get through to the new leader. In Siberia workers drilling for vital oil and gas asked him, "How is it that we live in slums? There's a shortage of everything. In the Soviet Union and in Europe everyone needs gas, but no one needs us." On his return to Moscow, Gorbachev authorized a speed-up of plans for building houses and providing services in Siberia; new supplies of cement and building materials were soon on their way. At a metal plant in Dnepropetrovsk in the Ukraine, Gorbachev asked workers if reform was going too quickly. Spokesmen came forward and said, "This is right and necessary." Gorbachev asked, "What do we have here, just a few talking or is this everyone's opinion?" The answer was shouted back in unison, "Everyone's." Change could not come fast enough.

Gorbachev's reform was radical, but not revolutionary. He wanted to bring a breath of fresh air to the existing system, not replace it with a new one. He and his supporters longed for new freedoms, but they thought that even with change the Soviet Union would still remain Communist. In this Gorbachev was wrong. Liberal policies loosened party control. Change, particularly economic change, destabilized the system.

Gorbachev and his team of advisers knew that current defence expenditure was crippling the Soviet Union. The Soviet economy could not match the new surge in the arms race that Reagan's administration, now in its second term, was advocating for the United States. The Gorbachev team must champion a lasting détente if the Soviet economy was to grow for the benefit of the Soviet people, as it drastically needed to do. For forty years the absurdities of the system had been disguised, because secrecy surrounded everything official. The state budget was known only in outline form to party leaders. Every year when the budget was presented to the Supreme Soviet, the line "other expenses" comprised more than 100 billion rubles. No deputy ever asked for an itemization of these "other expenses." The huge budget deficit was funded by borrowing from banks, though this was never revealed to the millions who used the banks for their savings. Moreover, anything to do with defence spending was taboo; even members of the Politburo did not dare to ask questions. Without financial monitoring, there were no restraints on inefficiency, and the consequence was immense waste.

Economic Power Poorly Bartered

All foreign trade was treated as a state secret — hiding the fact that the real balance of economic power between the Soviet Union and its empire was heavily weighted *against* the USSR. The vast reserves of oil, gas, and metal ores in Siberia should have made the Soviet Union a wealthy country. But the USSR made energy and raw materials available at low cost to its socialist allies, who had little to offer in return. Valuable resources were bartered at absurdly low prices for manufactured goods of limited industrial use, or for poor-quality consumer products. Cuba received more than $4 billion in aid and oil subsidies between 1981 and 1986; Vietnam got more than $1 billion a year. Iraq received $1.5 billion of trade credits in 1981 alone. The USSR's annual subsidy to its Warsaw Pact allies through discounting of oil prices amounted to about $3 billion. This state of affairs locked both sides into obsolescence and kept the Soviet Union in relative poverty. And the defence budget, hard to quantify because it spread across various ministries, ate up, Shevardnadze once confided, as much as 50 per cent of the Soviet Union's gross national product annually.

Gorbachev knew that no social change was possible without ending the arms race with the West. Only this would free up for other use the gigantic sums spent on the military. On this front, things began to move at speed. Arms-reduction talks, broken off after the shooting down of KAL flight 007, were resumed. Within days of Shevardnadze's becoming foreign minister it was announced that Reagan and Gorbachev would meet in Geneva in November. Preparations for this, the first summit since Carter met Brezhnev, began

If we must compete let it be on the playing fields and not the battlefields. . . . If Soviet youth could attend American schools and universities, they could learn firsthand . . . that we do not wish the Soviet people any harm. . . . They would learn that we're all God's children, with much in common.

— Ronald Reagan,
national television address,
14 November 1985

Preparations for a summit, September 1985. Soviet Foreign Minister Shevardnadze, second from right, and Secretary of State George Shultz, second from left, meet in New York to discuss arms control issues before Geneva. There was a good atmosphere.

When Reagan and Gorbachev met at Geneva in November 1985, they got on famously — even better when alone together.

in earnest. Shultz and Shevardnadze had several meetings, and Reagan too met the Soviet foreign minister, although neither side did much more than lay out its negotiating position. The Soviets were willing to agree to 50 per cent reductions in the numbers of strategic warheads each side possessed, as long as there was agreement not to develop, test, or deploy "space-strike weapons." But the president, urged on by his hawkish national security adviser, Robert McFarlane, insisted that his Star Wars initiative was not a "bargaining chip." He would not consider abandoning it. Prospects for negotiation did not look good.

Reagan prepared for Geneva by speaking with former presidents Ford and Nixon, and by viewing videos of Gorbachev's visits to Britain and France. He even went through a full-dress rehearsal, with US Soviet specialist Jack Matlock playing the part of Gorbachev. Confident of his abilities as the "great communicator," Reagan was sure he could influence the young Soviet leader. Describing his trip as "a mission for peace," Reagan genuinely believed in the need to reduce the nuclear menace and spoke of his "dream" to "escape the prison of mutual terror."

In Moscow, where Gorbachev envisaged not just "cosmetic changes" but a "U-turn" on foreign policy, others took some convincing that renewed dialogue with the United States was worthwhile. Within the Kremlin there was opposition, especially among the military, just as there was opposition to perestroika. Once the agenda for Geneva was set, Gorbachev too prepared thoroughly. Briefed extensively on the US Star Wars programme, he prepared arguments to counter various American positions. Gorbachev is said also to have viewed Reagan's 1942 Hollywood movie *King's Row*.

When the two leaders finally met in Geneva on 19 November 1985, there was intense curiosity around the world whether the seventy-four-year-old American ex-actor could match the fifty-four-year-old youthful Russian. Who would "win" the contest between them? The summit began with a private meeting intended to last only fifteen minutes that went on for more than an hour. Both men outlined their positions in adversarial terms. Reagan attacked the Soviet Union's position on human rights. Gorbachev laid into the power of the military-industrial complex in American politics. They argued about regional conflicts. Each accused the other of dividing the world and of launching a lunatic arms race that had taken civilization to the brink of nuclear catastrophe. Meetings with the full teams of negotiators made little more progress. At lunch with his delegation, Gorbachev described the American president as not just a conservative but a "cave man, a political dinosaur."

Before the Log Fire

In the afternoon the two leaders argued bitterly over the Star Wars programme. Gorbachev opposed extending the arms race into space. Reagan continued to talk about "open labs" and insisted that all the SDI technology would be shared. Gorbachev simply did not believe him; why would the Americans share such sensitive and sophisticated technology when they would not even share the mechanics of milking machines? Reagan suggested

Gorbachev told his aides, after
the leaders' first talk, that
Reagan was a "dinosaur." But
there's nothing like a log fire
and a comfortable armchair to
put men at ease, and they soon
struck up a warm rapport.

Chernobyl

On Saturday, 26 April 1986, at 1:23 AM, an explosion tore apart the no. 4 reactor at the Chernobyl nuclear power plant in the Ukraine, sixty-five miles north of Kiev. The accident occurred while an experiment was being conducted on the reactor, and with the emergency water-cooling system turned off. The force of the explosion was so immense that it blew off the heavy steel lid of the reactor, throwing radioactive debris over a large area. Thirty-one people died almost immediately; five hundred others were taken to hospital. More radioactivity was blown up into the atmosphere than at Hiroshima and Nagasaki.

In Moscow an emergency Politburo meeting was called, but no one then had any real idea of the scale of the disaster. It was two days before Swedish monitoring stations picked up the high levels of radioactivity produced in the atmosphere and forced the Soviet government to admit publicly that an accident had taken place. Slowly the enormity of the event dawned on the Moscow leadership. Even without proper protective clothing available, volunteers began the task of cleaning up radioactive leakage. Most were soon in hospital; many died. Meanwhile, Soviet scientists and engineers tried to minimize further damage to the reactor. One of them told journalists, "No one has ever been in such a difficult position before."

There were several days' delay before the scale of contamination was assessed and evacuation was organized. From a zone of thirty kilometres (nineteen miles) around the plant, 135,000 people were resettled. Chemical defence troops were sent in to try to prevent the radioactive contamination of the Dnieper River.

Strong winds blew the radioactivity, which had risen high into the clouds; it began to fall over the western Soviet Union, and then over Western Europe, as far as Italy, France, Scotland, and Ireland, where steps were taken to protect food supplies.

In July it was finally decided to entomb the damaged reactor in a mountain of concrete. The remaining Chernobyl reactors began to work again, but there was a further series of minor accidents. Eventually, in 1991, the Ukrainian parliament called for a total shutdown.

Although the area was evacuated, emergency work at Chernobyl had been too little and too late. Incidences of thyroid cancer, leukaemia, and other radiation-related diseases in the population affected by the explosion are now much higher than normal. Over the years there have been many instances of livestock being born deformed.

The accident at Chernobyl showed up the obsolete nature of Soviet technology. It also tragically illustrated how incapable the old system was of responding to, or reporting and publishing information about, a disaster of this magnitude. The Soviet nuclear power industry had been closed, secretive, and complacent; this was no longer tolerable. In this sense, the Chernobyl tragedy helped speed reform and glasnost within the Soviet Union. It lent urgency to Gorbachev's drive.

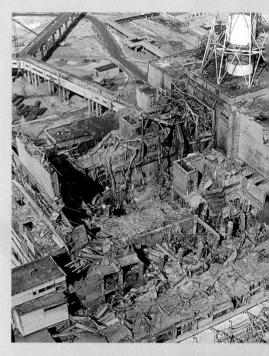

Meltdown. Chernobyl, April 1986, three days after one of four reactors at the nuclear power complex exploded. The photographer, flying over the site in a helicopter, would suffer radiation sickness.

they take a break and go for a walk together. They did, and after a few minutes continued their private dialogue in another room with logs blazing. Here, the atmosphere grew warmer. What happened next was something no one had anticipated: despite ideological differences, the leaders of the two superpowers began to get along. They both realized it was important to just keep talking. The human factor came into play. When they appeared before the cameras later, their body language indicated that they were getting on rather well together.

The second day of meetings was again heated. Despite coming under intense pressure from the Soviets, Reagan and his team refused to yield on Star Wars. Gorbachev made only limited progress with strategic arms reductions. But again, in several private conversations, the two leaders developed their rapport. Whatever problems arose in drafting the final joint communiqué were ironed out by the two men themselves. When they signed it, all appeared positive. Arms talks would continue; in principle they would work towards cutting nuclear arsenals by one-half. New exchanges of various sorts would take place between the peoples of the United States and the Soviet Union. The two leaders agreed that "a nuclear war cannot be won and must never be fought"; war between their countries must be prevented at all costs. Reagan, less strident than in his early days in office, when he wanted to out-gun the Soviets, agreed that the two sides "will not seek to achieve military superiority." None of this amounted to much in direct, practical terms, but successful meetings had taken place. The two leaders had spent more than five hours alone together. Invitations were extended for further summits. A dialogue had been started.

The Reagan team felt the summit had been a success. They had made no concessions over Star Wars and had pressed all the issues they intended to. There was no need for new initiatives from Washington. Gorbachev, however, felt he had only begun work on arms reduction and had no concrete success to report. More needed to be done. So in January 1986 Gorbachev offered to eliminate all nuclear weapons by the year 2000. He also proposed a bilateral US-USSR agreement to remove all intermediate-range nuclear missiles from Europe — SS-20, Pershing, and cruise would all go. Gorbachev's dramatic "peace offensive" envisioned nothing less than a nuclear-free world in a decade and a half. This new policy was given wholehearted support at the Twenty-seventh Party Congress, held in Moscow in February, where Gorbachev's leadership and the whole range of his *novoye myshlenniye*, new thinking, was approved by the party.

In the West the peace offensive was regarded as another propaganda trick by Moscow; Washington denounced it as "lacking seriousness." European politicians said it was a sham; even with SS-20s, Pershings, and cruise missiles withdrawn, the Soviets would still be left with superiority in conventional weapons. The Geneva arms-reduction talks continued but made virtually no progress. Meanwhile, it seemed to Moscow that the United States was again taking a belligerent stance. Two American warships, one of them the electronic-intelligence-gathering destroyer USS *Caron*, deliberately entered Soviet territorial waters and steamed within six miles of the Crimean coast. Washington

The Twenty-seventh Congress of the Soviet Communist Party, February 1986, gave enthusiastic support to Gorbachev's "new thinking."

claimed that the vessels were exercising their right to "innocent passage," but it was obvious they were gathering intelligence. Similar exercises along the Libyan coast were fired on by the Libyans. A month later US planes bombed targets in Tripoli and Benghazi. About one hundred Libyans were killed in the bombings. In Washington the raids on Libya were justified as reprisals for terrorist acts. Then, two days after Gorbachev called for an extension to the ban on nuclear testing, the US exploded another nuclear device. These incidents were seen in Moscow as a revival of US militarism, threatening the Soviet Union and Third World countries.

The Issue of Afghanistan

Ronald Reagan continued to keep up his Cold War hyperbole. In March 1986 he pledged continued support for "freedom fighters" around the world and referred to the "long history of Soviet brutality toward those who are weaker." He called for a record defence budget of $320 billion and privately approved $300 million of covert military assistance to the Afghan Mujahedeen. He authorized efforts to drive Soviet forces from Afghanistan "by all means available." By 1987 Washington was spending $630 million in Afghanistan, the largest covert action funded by the United States since the Second World War. The Saudis matched US increases in funding for the Afghan rebels.

One of the first issues to confront Gorbachev as new Soviet leader was what to do about Afghanistan. He received thousands of letters: "Why are our boys losing their lives there?" "Why did you ruin my son?" Until about 1986 the Soviet media maintained strict censorship on Afghanistan. Soviet newspapers, magazines, and television painted only a positive picture: Soviet sol-

The Red Army in Afghanistan

From the beginning of its Afghanistan campaign, the Soviet army made it a priority to win the hearts and minds of the local people. The soldiers would bring in doctors and medical aid, and food and clothing for the children, and hold discussion sessions with the elders. But alongside this charm offensive, the Soviets resorted to increasingly brutal tactics. Artillery barrages were fired against villages to intimidate them; retaliatory bombing raids were launched against communities that had shown sympathy for the rebels. And many soldiers had a casual attitude towards civilian casualties. All of this helped generate grass-roots hatred of the "occupiers." For frightened Soviet conscripts ordered to search villages, every farmer could be a potential enemy: "You never knew what you might meet behind the next corner. You must shoot always," said one. Massacres of civilians occurred. In September 1982, at Padkhwab-e-Shana village in Logar Province, 105 men and women hiding in an underground irrigation channel were burned to death when Soviet soldiers poured petrol into the tunnel and ignited it.

Among Soviet soldiers, the brutalizing experience of service in Afghanistan hardened their attitudes towards each other. "Old soldiers" tyrannized newly arrived conscripts, taking the best rations and, often, beating up the younger men. Desertion rates were high, as was the incidence of illnesses like heatstroke, dysentery, and typhoid. Along with this came alcohol and drug abuse, with hashish and cocaine the two most common drugs, often available through barter with locals. The Red Army in Afghanistan experienced many of the same problems faced by the US Army in Vietnam.

Afghanistan. OPPOSITE:
A Soviet convoy is ambushed
by Mujahedeen. ABOVE:
A monument to those who died.
Gorbachev wanted to end the
war, but only slowly marshalled
the necessary support. BELOW:
After eight years of war, Soviet
soldiers return home.

diers were seen handing out aid and medical support to impoverished villagers, helping the old, caring for the sick, and so on. But this contrasted with stories brought back by veterans who spoke of horrors and atrocities. The media were seen to be telling a gigantic lie. Slowly, under glasnost, Soviet media began to report Afghanistan accurately and, by 1987, even began to call for withdrawal. Across the Soviet Union, new graves were evident in almost every cemetery. Often the only words permitted on the tombstone, besides the name, were "Died fulfilling his internationalist duty." Mothers would learn nothing of their missing sons until, sometimes long after death was confirmed, they were presented with a sealed, plain zinc coffin. Because the bodies inside were often ghastly, incomplete, unembalmed, and naked, the mothers were not allowed a last look. Their grieving continued.

Throughout 1984 and 1985, the Soviet army deployed an increasing number of assault helicopters in mobile search-and-destroy operations. In March 1986 the United States decided to supply the rebels with the latest generation of hand-held Stinger anti-aircraft missiles; the first of them reached Afghanistan in September. The simple-to-fire Stingers guaranteed accuracy against low-flying aircraft as the guided missile homed in on the heat of their engines. The Soviet response was a change in tactics. They used higher-flying bombers, but this resulted in reduced accuracy in their bombing. Although Soviet pilots sometimes outwitted the anti-aircraft missiles by firing decoy flares, the Stingers further turned the tide of war against the Soviets.

Gorbachev had decided to withdraw from Afghanistan even before the Stinger missiles entered the picture. But his offer of a timetable for withdrawal in exchange for US support for a coalition in Kabul of both Communist and Mujahedeen participants was rejected out of hand in Washington. The United States, committed to winning the Cold War, was not about to let the Soviets off the hook. The bloodletting continued.

Despite renewed tensions Gorbachev and Reagan kept in personal touch through correspondence, the bond between them continuing to grow. When Gorbachev proposed eliminating all nuclear weapons by the year 2000, Reagan replied with a seven-page handwritten letter, in which he wrote: "It would be necessary as we reduce nuclear weapons toward zero, that we concurrently engage in a process of strengthening the stability of the overall East-West security balance." Reagan became convinced that American strength now coincided with Soviet willingness to concede.

"Breathtaking" Progress Cut Short

The next summit was intended to have been in Washington. Reagan initially wanted it for June 1986, but Gorbachev made it clear that unless there were prospects of real progress in arms reductions, there would be no meeting. The summit drifted back to later in the year. Then, while on holiday in the Crimea in August, Gorbachev suddenly felt the need to make a gesture to unblock the talks in Geneva and give renewed impetus to the peace process. At short notice it was agreed to hold a mini-summit in October at Reykjavik, in Iceland, midway between the United States and the USSR.

Gorbachev needed to make progress that would help sustain the policy of perestroika at home. He desperately needed to free up resources to fund domestic reform. Although he had no plans to sign an agreement at Reykjavik, he did intend to map out the path forward for strategic arms reductions, and the Politburo backed his negotiating position. Reagan had made his position clear over the preceding months and had displayed American strength throughout. The Soviets could either come to him or he would sit it out and wait for them to weaken. No one expected much of substance to emerge.

On the first day of the Reykjavik summit, 11 October 1986, Gorbachev took the initiative. He proposed a comprehensive set of reductions for strategic arms, intermediate-range missiles, and space weapons. In an entirely new approach, he broke away from arguments that were going round in circles at Geneva, getting nowhere. Reagan had brought his major points written out on a set of cards. When he accidentally dropped them and could not find the prepared response to Gorbachev's proposals, he became flustered. Shultz came to the rescue and agreed that the Soviet opening position was fundamentally acceptable. Negotiations went on throughout the day and through the night as other delegates eased forward agreements for further reductions.

On the second day, when Gorbachev and Reagan picked up from where their representatives left off, the pace quickened. The two leaders agreed on the "zero option" for intermediate-range missiles in Europe: complete withdrawal. They also agreed on a 50 per cent reduction in ballistic missiles (ICBMs and SLBMs) over a five-year period. During lunch the Americans suggested the elimination of all ballistic missiles over a ten-year period. When the full talks resumed, Gorbachev decided to "see and raise" this hand. He proposed to eliminate all strategic nuclear weapons in the ten-year period. Reagan thought the pace of progress was "breathtaking." He later recalled: "George [Shultz] and I couldn't believe what was happening. We were getting amazing agreements. As the day went on, I felt something momentous was occurring." Reagan agreed to Gorbachev's latest proposal and offered to raise him one higher, saying he would be willing to eliminate *all* nuclear weapons in ten years — effectively abolishing the nuclear deterrent. Shultz was astonished. He later said: "I really felt that he's the president. He got elected twice. He has made no secret of his view on nuclear weapons. So who am I to stop him from saying what he believes, and what he's campaigned on?" Gorbachev agreed to the suggestion at once.

The most dramatic and remarkable agreement in twentieth-century history was within a hairsbreadth of being finalized. But Gorbachev continued to press Reagan on his SDI programme. He told Reagan: "Our meeting cannot produce one winner. We both either win or lose." The Soviets already had toned down their earlier position. They now called for all Star Wars research to be limited to "the laboratory," as under the terms of the ABM Treaty. But still the president would not give up on his cherished dream of a space defence system. Work on it would go on apace. Gorbachev pressed further, saying that it was difficult enough to restrict the arms race on earth; it would be impossible to restrict it in space. Reagan, who had been clear and consistent on Star Wars, hesitated for a moment. He passed a note on a scrap of paper to Shultz saying, "George am I right?" Shultz scribbled, "Absolutely," and passed it back. Reagan broke off the meeting. There would be no agreement.

For both sides the collapse came as a massive anticlimax. But each delegation realized that the discussions had crossed a historic line. Forty minutes after the talks ended, although deeply upset at failing to persuade Reagan to abandon SDI, Gorbachev said at a press conference, "In spite of all its drama, Reykjavik is not a failure; it is a breakthrough which for the first time enabled us to look over the horizon." Two days later Reagan declared: "Believe me, the significance of that meeting in Reykjavik is not that we didn't sign agreements in the end; the significance is that we got as close as we did."

Tension Returns

In the aftermath of Reykjavik there was renewed tension. Gorbachev spoke out against the United States: "It turns out that it not only has no constructive proposals on the key questions of disarmament, but it does not even have the desire to maintain an atmosphere for the normal continuation of a dialogue." Washington responded with new attacks on the Soviet record on human rights. Shultz argued: "A government that will break faith with its own people cannot be trusted to keep faith with foreign powers." Meanwhile, America's European allies were startled that the United States had come so near to completely abandoning nuclear deterrence, on which they believed their safety depended, without even consulting them. In London and Bonn, at least, there was relief at the failure of Reykjavik.

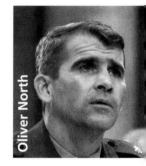

Oliver North

In late 1986 a complex web of intrigue began to emerge that plunged the Reagan administration into scandal. Illegal arms sales to Iran had been used to fund the Contras in Nicaragua. Several senior US officials were involved in it, through a shady network of Israeli and Saudi arms dealers, secret Swiss bank accounts, and intelligence agents from many nations. Vice Admiral John Poindexter, who had succeeded McFarlane as national security adviser, resigned, but most of the blame fell upon the head of National Security Council staff associate Lieutenant Colonel Oliver North, who had directed the illicit operation. The Iran-Contra affair, with its revelations of cover-up, cast bad light on the administration, and Reagan's popularity drooped from 67 per cent to 46 per cent in the polls. Around the world, his credibility plummeted.

In February 1987 Gorbachev announced at a Moscow forum, For a Nuclear-Free World, that the stakes were too high to "waste more time on trying to outplay one another." At risk was the "survival of humanity." Two weeks later he agreed to the elimination of all Soviet and US intermediate-range nuclear forces (INF) in Europe, with no strings attached. Abandoning SDI was not a condition. The British and French nuclear arsenals were excluded. Reagan believed that Gorbachev was caving in to Western strength and, sensing he had the edge, laid down a challenge on a visit to the Berlin Wall later in the year: "If you seek peace, if you seek prosperity for the Soviet Union and Eastern Europe, if you seek liberalization . . . Mr. Gorbachev, tear down this wall."

OPPOSITE: *Reykjavik, October 1986. The summiteers came close to agreement.* BELOW: *Eventually the will drastically to limit armaments came to fruition. Soviet troops crate up missiles for destruction.*

Reykjavik marked a turning point in world history. It tangibly demonstrated that the world could be improved.

— Mikhail Gorbachev, on the October 1986 mini-summit

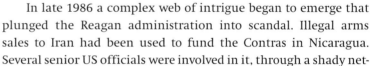

Gorbachev still devoted most of his time to the urgent need for economic and political reform at home. The Central Committee plenum at the beginning of 1987 had launched a renewed campaign for *demokratizatsiya* and glasnost, which was fought all the way by the conservative faction. The entire Communist system was riddled with privileges for the nomenklatura, the elite, who wanted to maintain the status quo from which they benefited. Although Gorbachev made sweeping changes to the party and state bureaucracies, many of his own appointees, embedded in the status quo, began to oppose further reform. His deputy in the party, Yegor Ligachev, led a reactionary clique in criticizing glasnost, predicting that weakening party discipline and the ethnic nationalisms unleashed in the Baltic states and in the southern Soviet republics would prove destructive. Gorbachev continued to deny that perestroika threatened "the values of socialism" and pressed for yet more vigorous reform.

Progress towards agreement with the United States on the INF treaty was at a snail's pace, but real. Shevardnadze and Shultz had regular meetings to settle the agenda for the next summit, but Gorbachev still insisted that there could be no summit without agreement on space weapons. Inside the Kremlin, Gorbachev found it difficult to justify a softer line on arms reductions while Reagan made no concessions to core Soviet concerns.

When the Soviets tacitly dropped their insistence and the summit ultimately did take place in Washington, 7–10 December 1987, its centrepiece was the final signing of the INF treaty. Reagan had first offered the zero option to an ageing Soviet leadership in 1981, but now, with the new thinking of a different leader, he got what he wanted. For his part, Gorbachev was able to display his real commitment to arms reduction. The signing took place in the East Room of the White House and was carried live on both US and Soviet television. The treaty was historic in that it eliminated an entire class of US and Soviet nuclear arms from Eastern and Western Europe; all the SS-20s that had so worried the West would be dismantled along with all the cruise and Pershing missiles that had provoked so much protest. The process of verification was made far more open and extensive. For the first time officials would have the right to inspect missile sites and to visit factories and destruction plants, on both sides. The West realized that the Soviets were willing to apply glasnost to military security. After signing, Gorbachev spoke of his pride in "planting this sapling, which may one day grow into a mighty tree of peace."

On strategic arms, however, the Washington summit failed to bring any dramatic advances like those at Reykjavik. Gorbachev was still disappointed by Reagan's stubbornness over SDI — even though just prior to the summit Congress had cut its budget request by one-third. Talks began on a further ban on nuclear testing, but the general process of disarmament was relegated to an "ultimate objective" in the indefinite future.

The two leaders also discussed regional conflicts, especially Afghanistan and Nicaragua, although they later disagreed on what had been said. The Soviets had made clear to the Americans before the summit their intention to withdraw from Afghanistan, but Reagan now fudged his commitment to end

Glasnost. ABOVE: *General Secretary Gorbachev addresses US business leaders at the Soviet Embassy in Washington, 10 December 1987. Listening at left is CNN chairman Ted Turner.* BELOW: *Soviet youth let it all hang out, as they never dared do before.*

US military assistance to the Mujahedeen when Moscow withdrew. And, on human rights, when Reagan criticized Gorbachev for not allowing more emigration of Soviet Jews, the Soviet leader angrily responded by asking why, if the United States was so keen on the free movement of peoples, it used armed border patrols to keep out Mexicans?

"Man of the Year"

Gorbachev's first visit to the United States was a public relations triumph. "Gorbymania" stormed the American capital; Mikhail and Raisa stopped their motorcade to embrace crowds of well-wishers in the streets. In all, 65 per cent of Americans had a favourable impression of Gorbachev — higher than the president's own approval rating of 58 per cent. *Time* magazine made Gorbachev "Man of the Year." He met hundreds of Americans from the arts and media, science and technology, along with dozens of politicians. Of lasting importance were two brief, private meetings with Vice President George Bush. In one of these, when Bush drove with Gorbachev to the airport, the vice president assured him that whatever would be said during the upcoming presidential campaign, he wanted, if elected, to continue improving US-Soviet relations.

On 14 April 1988 a series of accords on Afghanistan was signed in Geneva. This was the culmination of the long, slow route to peace engineered by UN envoy Diego Cordovez, which had started in 1982. The Soviet Union, Afghanistan, and Pakistan signed the settlement, which George Shultz witnessed for

Glasnost: No Turning Back

Glasnost involved opening up more information to the public and encouraging new forms of expression within the Soviet Union. But granting new freedoms to the Soviet citizenry let the genie out of the bottle; and once out it could not be put back in. Press and television for the first time were allowed to criticize the government.

Films and plays previously banned were now released; books like Boris Pasternak's *Dr. Zhivago* were published. A new critical reinterpretation of much of Soviet history was allowed, including the most hostile treatment yet of Stalin's era and the brutal atrocities committed by him; there were also critical reassessments of Brezhnev and his time. Greater religious freedom was allowed. There

was freer access to Western music, which encouraged a new wave of permissive, anarchic rock and punk bands that would have horrified a previous generation. Most dissidents arrested during Brezhnev's era were now released. Anatoly Sharansky was allowed to emigrate to Israel; Andrei Sakharov was freed from internal exile in Gorky.

Incompetent or corrupt public officials were put on trial, including a former deputy minister of foreign trade, tried for bribery, and Brezhnev's son-in-law, a senior police official, arrested for corruption.

In the Baltic states and in the southern Islamic republics of the Soviet Union, there was a new awakening of nationalist fervour. Protests among

Armenians in the Nagorno-Karabakh province of Azerbaijan in early 1988 were a precursor of a wave of "ethnic nationalism" and of the more fundamental change still to come to the Soviet Union.

All this made for a reaction against the "excesses" unleashed by glasnost. During 1987 and 1988 there were major confrontations at party plenums between progressives and reactionaries, which forced Gorbachev to moderate the pace of reform. And economic reform faltered because no one knew how to put the changeover to a market economy into practice. But there was no going back.

the United States. The Soviet Union agreed to withdraw its troops from Afghanistan over a ten-month period. But none of the parties agreed to end its military support for the different factions inside Afghanistan. The arming of Islamic fundamentalist forces left a legacy of terrorism in the 1990s. A long civil war between rival groups dragged on for years. And although the CIA tried to buy back, at vastly inflated prices, several of the Stinger missiles it had supplied to the Afghan rebels, dozens if not hundreds were left unaccounted for. The United States had spent some $2 billion on its covert operation in Afghanistan. The Soviets had expended unknown billions of rubles and had lost twenty thousand soldiers during the eight-year war. As many as 1 million Afghans had been killed during the fighting; millions more were left wounded or homeless.

The next summit between Reagan and Gorbachev, in Moscow from 29 May to 2 June 1988, was a piece of theatre. Reagan had no real negotiating objectives. But he wanted to meet dissidents, visit the leader of the Russian Orthodox Church, Patriarch Aleksei II, and address the students of Moscow University. During an impromptu walkabout in Red Square a journalist called out, "Do you still think you're in an 'evil empire,' Mr. President?" Reagan replied with a single word, "No." "Why not?" "I was talking about another time and another era." Gorbachev was delighted; the change was since *he* had brought new thinking. Reagan was clearly moved by meeting ordinary Russians, which he had never done before. He told Mikhail and Raisa (since the Washington summit their relationship had been on a first-name basis) that he and his wife, Nancy, thought of them as "friends." He spoke of his "deep feel-

A changing world. Few expected them to go to South Korea, but the Soviets turned up in Seoul for the 1988 Olympic Games. The gymnasts won gold medals.

The Seoul Olympic Games

Gorbachev surprised many in 1988 when he decided that the Soviet Union would attend the Olympic Games in Seoul, South Korea, that summer, even though the Soviet Union had not recognized the Republic of Korea following the Korean War thirty-five years earlier. The North Koreans had demanded that the Games be split North and South, with events shared; failing that, they called for a fraternal boycott of the Olympics by the entire socialist bloc, as in Los Angeles four years before. The International Olympic Committee kept the North Koreans talking, asking how events could be shared across the most heavily militarized border in the world. But Gorbachev summoned

North Korea's elderly Kim Il Sung, leader of one of the last Stalinist regimes, to Moscow for a dressing-down. He told him he had no intention of calling a boycott; the Soviet Olympic team was eager to participate in the Games. For Kim, it was the first realization that the Soviet-led socialist alliance had changed for ever. Most teams from the socialist bloc attended the Seoul Olympics, the first Summer Games not marred by major boycotts for sixteen years. It was another sign of a friendlier world.

ings of friendship" towards the people of the Soviet Union. Over the last three years the relationship had, as Gorbachev observed, "come a long way."

But apart from an exchange of copies of the now-ratified INF Treaty and small-scale bilateral agreements on fishing rights, cultural and student exchanges, and co-operation on space exploration, the summit brought little of substance. Gorbachev still pushed and Reagan still resisted. A sweeping declaration by the Soviet leader renouncing war as a means of resolving disputes

1988. Gorbachev and Reagan in the heart of Moscow. Asked if he now thought he was visiting an "evil empire," Reagan replied, "No."

Quite possibly we're beginning to take down the barriers of the postwar era; quite possibly we are entering a new era in history, a time of lasting change in the Soviet Union. We will have to see.

— Ronald Reagan,
3 June 1988, on the
Moscow summit

was rejected by the US delegation, which feared this might undercut the defence budget in Washington. Despite further talks about disarmament, only limited progress was made. The Soviets agreed to end military support in Angola and Namibia, and had already announced their withdrawal from Afghanistan. Gorbachev did propose reducing conventional forces in Europe by 500,000 men on both sides, but the Americans, suspicious and with no mandate from NATO to negotiate, sidestepped the issue. As before, the central point of dispute was SDI. Reagan refused to give ground. Gorbachev at one point asked, "What is SDI for? What missiles is it supposed to bring down if we eliminate all nuclear weapons?" "It will be there just in case," Reagan replied.

Perestroika Continues Despite Opposition

Within the Soviet Union, the process of restructuring — perestroika — continued despite hardened opposition to reform at a special conference of the Communist Party in late June. Embattled, Gorbachev faced opponents who believed that his concessions to the United States were not based on mutual recognition of shared interests but on capitulation to American demands. By shrewd party management, he was still able to get agreement that elections would be held to appoint most party chiefs. A Congress of People's Deputies was created above the Supreme Soviet. Later in the year Gorbachev was elected president, succeeding Gromyko.

Gorbachev felt that at the Moscow summit "a good opportunity had been missed." Again, it would be up to him to make the next gesture to advance disarmament. He chose the United Nations as the forum. Enjoying the limelight and adulation gained by the radical progress made over the last three years, Gorbachev addressed the General Assembly on 7 December 1988. He spoke not of class struggle in a divided world but of the common interests of all mankind. He urged freedom of choice for all, signalling that the Soviet satel-

lites were free to choose their own paths. He declared: "This new stage [of world history] requires the freeing of international relations from ideology." He then amazed the world by announcing, unilaterally, a cut of 500,000 men in Soviet forces, including the removal of 10,000 tanks, 8,500 artillery pieces, and 800 combat aircraft from Eastern Europe. He also announced large withdrawals from Manchuria and along the border with China. This was more than arms reduction, it was a complete review of the function of military power. The whole Politburo had backed the speech — the Soviet military even suggested larger cuts. The *Washington Post* called it "a speech as remarkable as any ever delivered at the United Nations. . . . Gorbachev invited the world literally to beat its swords into ploughshares."

On that same day Gorbachev had a final meeting with Reagan; also present was President-elect George Bush, although Bush stayed in the background. It would be Ronald Reagan's last major event as president, a meeting intended as more of a courtesy than anything else. Reagan remained convinced that US strength and determination had caused the Soviets to give in and had forced them to the negotiating table. What he never fully recognized in Gorbachev, despite the warm rapport that grew up between the two men, was that here was a Soviet leader with a new line of thinking who no longer fitted the mould of the past. Gorbachev, in countless speeches, stressed his commitment to arms reduction and his unwillingness to play the games of his predecessors; confrontation was simply not a stable basis for peace, he argued. Compromise, mutual trust, and co-operation would be the way forward. Implicit in this new thinking was the realization that, as was said when he took office, the Soviet people "can't go on living like this." Fundamental structural changes were necessary to the Soviet system if it was to survive. The Soviet economy was desperately weak; it could no longer play the superpower role in supporting an ever-spiralling arms race. All this did indeed contrast with American strength. A stop had to be called, and Gorbachev called it. It took an arch-conservative like Reagan to carry this with the American people and the Western alliance. It remained to be seen what impact the Soviet Union's new line would have on its allies in Eastern Europe.

Washington, 8 December 1987. OPPOSITE: *Ronald Reagan and Mikhail Gorbachev sign a historic arms control agreement in the East Room of the White House.* ABOVE: *After the ceremony, the warmest of handshakes. The unlikely couple had pulled it off.*

I . . . know of no one else of a leadership stature in the United States in those days who would have moved forward as Reagan did, to engage Gorbachev, to truly lead the Western alliance, and to take us through what became . . . a very constructive introductory period, to the end of the Cold War. There will be many people who can't stand the notion [that] the credit for this has to go to the man who spoke of the "evil empire," but to my mind it is an inescapable conclusion that Ronald Reagan made the difference.

— Rozanne Ridgway,
US Assistant Secretary
of State for European
and Canadian Affairs,
1985–1989

Hungary, 1989

May. The first chink in the Iron Curtain. Hungarian border guards cut down the barbed-wire fence that marked their boundary with Austria. Through the gap, thousands would flee to the West.

People Power
1989

Seeds of Change

The nations of the Warsaw Pact had been held together by Soviet force: in East Berlin in 1953, in Hungary in 1956, in Czechoslovakia in 1968. When an Eastern European state showed signs of autonomy, the Soviets sent in troops to bring the country back into line. In Poland in 1981, just the threat of force had been enough. The Iron Curtain that Winston Churchill saw descending across Europe soon after the Second World War had remained in place for more than forty years. On the west side were the democracies of the North Atlantic trade and military bloc and the nations of the European Community. To the east were countries run by Communist parties under the thumb of Moscow and kept in power by the threat of Soviet military intervention. Most of the Eastern European Communist leaders were old men who had held power for decades. Mikhail Gorbachev changed all this. His speech at the United Nations in December 1988 was the catalyst for momentous events in Eastern Europe in 1989. His declared commitment to "freedom of choice" for all nations, a principle that "knows no exceptions," sent a signal: Moscow would not again order its tanks and soldiers into Eastern European cities to crush the people's will. Moreover, Gorbachev's promise of huge unilateral troop withdrawals abruptly left the leaders of unpopular regimes to face their own people without the Soviet army to back them up.

But the way 1989 began did not bode well for proponents of reform or of nationalist change. At a demonstration in Prague, eight hundred protesters were arrested — including, in the follow-up, Václav Havel — for inciting protest against the government. The Armenian-populated district of Nagorno-Karabakh in Azerbaijan was brought under direct rule from Moscow. In February fifteen

New York, 7 December 1988. Mikhail Gorbachev addresses the United Nations and promises Soviet troop withdrawals from Europe. The Soviet empire's satellite states could now choose their own way forward.

thousand demonstrated in the Georgian capital of Tbilisi, marking the anniversary of the Soviet "annexation" of Georgia. Throughout the Baltic states of Lithuania, Latvia, and Estonia there were rumblings of protest against Soviet rule. But Gorbachev and the Kremlin leadership were determined that the Soviet Union itself would remain intact. They ignored signs of the gathering storm within the fifteen republics that constituted the Soviet Union.

However, seeds of radical change were planted, first in Hungary, then in Poland. In Hungary, in early January, the parliament voted to allow freedom of association and assembly. It permitted the establishment of political par-

ties, opening the way for multiparty elections, which were scheduled for the following year. In May, in a symbolic gesture, Hungarian soldiers began to pull down the country's barbed-wire border fences with Austria — opening the first chink in the Iron Curtain. Gorbachev expressed support for the reforms, and to encourage them the West German government provided financial credits. In Poland, in the midst of another economic crisis, the Communist leader General Wojciech Jaruzelski reopened "round-table talks" with the Solidarity trade union, which had been banned for seven years. After months of negotiations it was agreed to hold open elections in June. Forces for change were gathering momentum in Eastern Europe.

In Washington 1989 saw a far more cautious administration than that of Reagan's final days. Unlike the previous two presidents, George Bush had a long record of Washington service prior to gaining the White House. He had been a US congressman from Texas, American ambassador to the United Nations, chief of the US diplomatic mission to China, director of the CIA, and for the last eight years, vice president to Ronald Reagan. Unlike his two predecessors, Bush had an exceptional grasp of foreign affairs. But he was no visionary like Reagan; he was suspicious of what he called "the vision thing." Through the last years of Reagan's term, he did not hide his concern about the speed of change. "The Cold War isn't over," he told reporters as he watched the Moscow summit at home on television. "I think the jury is still out on the Soviet experiment," he said during his presidential campaign, in a televised

A change in the air. ABOVE LEFT: *Lech Walesa, leader of Solidarity, meets with Poland's Communist president, General Wojciech Jaruzelski, for the first time in eight years.* ABOVE: *The government and Solidarity hold round-table discussions. The Communists agreed to elections and, if the voters so decided, to share power.*

debate with Democratic presidential candidate Michael Dukakis.

When he took office Bush initiated a full-scale review of Washington's relationship with Moscow. The key foreign policy team in this new administration — Secretary of State James A. Baker III, National Security Adviser Brent Scowcroft, and Secretary of Defense Richard Cheney (not appointed until March 1989) — were all of a mind; his foreign policy advisers were not in continuous competition "for the president's ear." Guided by Bush they presented a cautiously pragmatic approach. There was no sparkling first one hundred days. The policy review, carried out by hundreds of officials, took months to complete. The general sense was that Gorbachev's reforms were "cosmetic." In Afghanistan, although the Soviet army was rapidly withdrawing, the armies of the Soviet-backed Kabul regime were on the offensive against the Mujahedeen at Jalalabad, the nation's second city. In Central America, Soviet and Warsaw Pact weapons continued to pile into the Sandinista arsenal. National Security Council Soviet affairs specialist Condoleezza Rice summed it up for many Bush officials: "We keep telling them to knock it off, but the Soviets are still putting military equipment into every nook and cranny of the Third World." Scowcroft argued that perhaps it would be best to let the Soviets stew in their own juices, allowing reformers and reactionaries to slug it out a bit before the United States became too committed. Western aid to Moscow at this critical time might even reduce the pressure for reform. Others questioned how long Gorbachev could survive; what if the United States conceded too much and Gorbachev was then replaced in a right-wing coup by hard-liners? To many in Washington the future looked highly unpredictable.

Eduard Shevardnadze

In May, James Baker made his first visit to Moscow. He was astonished at how backward and dingy the capital of "the other superpower" actually was. When a reporter asked if it reminded him of certain Third World cities, Baker replied that it was "worse." But Baker began to build a close relationship with Gorbachev's foreign minister, Eduard Shevardnadze; the two men would grow to trust and respect each other. During Baker's visit Gorbachev announced a new unilateral withdrawal of five hundred nuclear warheads from Eastern Europe. Baker, however, had nothing new to offer from Washington.

James Baker

"Status Quo Plus"

The United States's review of its Soviet policy, completed in May, suggested no new initiatives or insights on how to respond to radical change in the Soviet bloc. The policy-makers predicted that Gorbachev had a better than even chance of surviving despite the domestic opposition he faced, but it was recommended that US policy should not attempt either to help or to harm him. The military review concluded that although a real change had occurred inside the Kremlin, it probably would be five to seven years before it took effect. The recommendation was for no new cuts or major changes in US military forces worldwide. A State Department aide summed up the new position as "status quo plus." But given the speed of events in Eastern Europe, the new

Bush administration, which failed to respond, was accused of "sleepwalking through history." Bush himself grew impatient with the lack of new ideas generated by his staff, especially on arms cuts. On this subject he was being openly criticized for inactivity. In a heated exchange in the Oval Office about reducing conventional arms in NATO, Bush burst out, "I want this done. Don't keep telling me why it can't be done. Tell me how it can be done."

Caution in Washington was in marked contrast to the speed with which events were unfolding in Moscow. Gorbachev was a man in a hurry. Talking with Margaret Thatcher in London in April, he expressed impatience with Washington's delay in making up its mind on Soviet policy. "Time has its limits," declared Soviet spokesman Gennadi Gerasimov.

At the end of March the Soviet Union held its first largely free elections in seventy-five years. For the new Congress of People's Deputies, 170 million electors voted. One-third of all seats were reserved for Communist Party members, and overall about 80 per cent of party members won seats. But, significantly, 20 per cent did not, and these included some major figures, even when there was no candidate opposing them. If voters crossed out the name of the only listed candidate this counted as a vote against. Leningrad party chief and Politburo member Yury Solovyev failed to be elected when 130,000 crossed out his name and only 110,000 voted for him. In Moscow dissident Communist Boris Yeltsin demonstrated his growing popularity when 5 million voters swept him back into power as mayor. When the Congress met in late May, its members elected the new Supreme Soviet. They voted Gorbachev president, with 95 per cent of the vote. Debates of the Congress were televised and attracted such interest that workers left their factories to watch daily broadcasts. Productivity plummeted.

Reforms in Moscow sent tremors throughout the Soviet Union. Disturbances in Tbilisi, Georgia, in April were brutally suppressed as Soviet soldiers were sent in; twenty protesters were killed in the crackdown. Eduard Shevardnadze, himself a Georgian, was appalled. Over the next few weeks there were riots in many Central Asian cities. Gorbachev wanted to encourage liberalization in the countries of Eastern Europe, but was deaf to nationalist voices within the Soviet Union. Even when, in Moscow, Gorbachev's colleague Alexander Yakovlev formally condemned Stalin's annexation of the three Baltic republics in 1940, he made it clear that the Kremlin stood firm against calls for independence. In July, however, Lithuania, Latvia, and Estonia declared their "sovereignty." In the following month, to protest the fiftieth anniversary of the Nazi-Soviet Pact, a million demonstrators formed a vast human chain, stretching from Vilnius for 430 miles through Riga to Tallinn, linking the three Baltic capitals.

A Shadow Cast Across Reunion

Meanwhile, Gorbachev made up with one of the Soviet Union's longtime enemies. Three years earlier, in a major speech in Vladivostok, Gorbachev had confirmed that the Soviet Union was prepared to discuss with China measures "to create an atmosphere of good neighbourliness." He spoke of "concrete steps aimed at a balanced reduction of the ground forces" of the two

May 1989. Gorbachev, seen here with Chinese premier Deng Xiaoping in Beijing, was the first Soviet head of state to visit China in thirty years. While he was there, Chinese students confronted police and army. As soon as he left, martial law was imposed.

nations guarding their long, disputed border. Gorbachev had suggested the withdrawal of 200,000 men from Asia at the United Nations, in December 1988. As Soviet troops began to leave Mongolia, the time seemed right to patch up the old quarrel.

On 15 May 1989 Gorbachev arrived in Beijing for the first Sino-Soviet summit since Khrushchev visited the Chinese capital thirty years before. The meetings normalized relations, ending three decades of tension. A host of bilateral agreements to end border disputes, begin troop withdrawals, and increase economic ties were announced. Both sides committed themselves to "restructuring and reform" of their socialist systems and to exchanging "information and

ABOVE: *For days, Chinese students, demanding freedom, demonstrated in the centre of Beijing.* ABOVE LEFT: *Tanks move into Tiananmen Square. When the army opened fire, hundreds were killed.*

experience" from this process. But Gorbachev's historic visit was upstaged by dramatic events on the streets of Beijing. About a million young Chinese of the Democracy Movement were protesting across the city, calling for political reforms. Although the summit was carefully stage-managed to ensure that Gorbachev never actually came into contact with the demonstrators, the great reformer's visit undoubtedly emboldened them. The Chinese politely waited until the day after Gorbachev left to proclaim martial law. A ruthless crackdown on the protesters resulted in a bloody massacre at Tiananmen Square at the beginning of June. Moscow maintained silence on the massacre, not wanting to impede the momentum of relations with Beijing, but Tiananmen Square cast a shadow across the reunion. In Beijing, as the aged leadership followed events in Eastern Europe, they became more convinced that "peaceful evolution" away from socialism was not the path for them. Although economic reform, begun by Deng Xiaoping in the aftermath of the disastrous Cultural Revolution, carried on apace, the Chinese leadership decided to pursue greater self-reliance and tougher political orthodoxy. Deng and the Chinese leadership rejected the way of political reform, and China would remain as the one last Communist world power — politically at least, if not economically.

In June, Gorbachev met with Chancellor Helmut Kohl of West Germany. They agreed to support self-determination and arms reductions and to build a "common European home." Kohl warned Gorbachev that Erich Honecker, the East German Communist Party leader, did not understand perestroika and would pursue his own hard line. Gorbachev made clear that he would not dictate to the East Germans how they should manage their own affairs.

In Poland, in June, Solidarity won the first free elections decisively, gaining 99 of the 100 seats in the senate. The expectation was that the lower house would remain dominated by Communists, but to everyone's astonishment Solidarity won a majority of seats up for election there also. As in the Soviet Union, many Communist Party candidates, although unopposed, were defeated when their names were crossed out by voters. Soon after the elections President Bush paid visits to Poland and Hungary; he praised their first steps towards democracy and was hailed by large crowds. Bush was determined not to inflame the situation, nor to do anything that would make the progress of reform more difficult for Gorbachev. He met with the Polish Solidarity leader Lech Walesa, who asked for $10 billion of US aid to prevent his country from plunging into civil war. Bush had already offered $100 million of aid and was noncommittal as to further support. (Later in the year this sum was increased substantially during congressional hearings on the administration's aid programme.) In Budapest, genuinely moved, Bush was presented with strands of barbed wire from the torn-down border fence with Austria.

From Eastern Europe, Bush went on to Paris to participate in the bicentennial celebrations of the French Revolution. The American superstar soprano Jessye Norman, draped in the French tricolour, sang the "Marseillaise."

The first free elections in Poland brought overwhelming victory for Solidarity in both houses of parliament, and defeat for the Communists.

The Tiananmen Square Massacre

By late May 1989 the situation in Beijing appeared to be moving out of the government's control; 1 million Chinese students and workers, in non-violent protest, occupied large sections of the city and called for more rapid political reforms and a shift towards democracy. In Tiananmen Square, the vast open space at the centre of the city, students erected a monument in the shape of the Statue of Liberty, which they called the Goddess of Democracy.

Behind the scenes a furious power struggle was taking place among party leaders, some of them calling for an accommodation with the pro-democracy movement and for more rapid reform; others wanted to use force to put down dissent. This internal dispute prolonged the protest and allowed it to spread to other cities in China. Doubt also was raised as to whether the People's Liberation Army could be trusted to act against the demonstrators, so at the beginning of June units were called in from distant provinces to deal with protesters in the capital.

On 3 June, Premier Li Peng and the faction demanding the use of force won the argument; army units supported by tanks were sent in to clear the streets of demonstrators. In the massacre that followed, an unknown number of young Chinese were killed, their bodies rapidly gathered up and removed before they could be counted. All estimates suggest that the number of dead ran into hundreds. The massacre took place in full view of the world's media, who captured extraordinary images of heroic, unarmed protesters struggling against tanks. Coverage was carried live on CNN throughout the Western world, immensely discrediting the Chinese leadership. After the bloodbath, thousands more were arrested and imprisoned. The Democracy Movement in China was finished for many years.

Ironically, the Tiananmen Square massacre had a positive effect on events in Eastern Europe later in 1989. It showed that force was no longer an option against large-scale public demonstrations. In a world of instant global communications, no European government gunning down opponents could maintain credibility and survive.

During his stopover in Paris, the president had time to relax and to discuss with Baker and Scowcroft their impressions of Poland and Hungary. His trip there had convinced Bush of the need for a personal meeting with Gorbachev. "Change is so fast, future change is so unpredictable, that I don't want to pass in the night with this guy." Scowcroft was still sceptical of raising expectations by announcing a summit until there was solid progress between the United States and the Soviet Union to build upon. However, Bush, an enthusiast for the personal touch in diplomacy, persuaded the others to begin planning for a "no agenda" informal meeting with Gorbachev with as little summit pomp as possible. "Hell, we're talking about it; let's just do it," he insisted. On *Air Force One* on the flight home, Bush wrote to Gorbachev and suggested a meeting. Gorbachev accepted. Lengthy negotiations about the first Bush-Gorbachev summit began; it proved difficult to agree on a location. Gorbachev did not want to visit the United States again, and Bush did not want the protocol that would accompany a summit in a neutral country. Eventually, it was decided that the two leaders should meet at sea. When the waters off Alaska were ruled out as being too rough, a meeting in the Mediterranean was settled on, near Malta, towards the end of the year. For now, it was decided to keep all plans for the parley top secret.

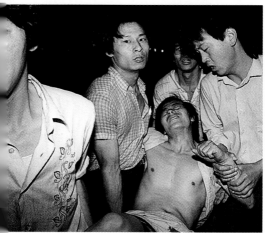

Tanks retire from Tiananmen Square after the killing, while injured demonstrators are carried away. The Chinese government ruthlessly crushed opposition, at heavy cost in lives. Most European Communist regimes, by contrast, gave way to change.

Reform Now Threatened

For Gorbachev there was an essential link between international politics and domestic reform. His international standing, he thought, helped him carry forward the process of reform at home. And perestroika and glasnost in the Soviet Union helped him to argue internationally for his "new thinking" and for an end to the Cold War. Even more crucial, the economic improvement he needed to achieve at home depended on ending the arms race, to save on the vast cost of Soviet defence expenditure. But that could only be wound down with international agreement for disarmament. Throughout the summer of 1989, Gorbachev was preoccupied with restructuring the Soviet Union. However, his reform programme was now threatened; thousands of miners went on strike in Siberia; and the Baltic states and the Asian republics called for greater freedom from Moscow. The pressure on him to relieve the Soviet Union of its international commitments and therefore to advance arms-reduction talks with the United States grew intense.

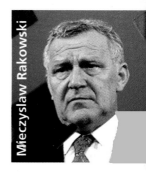

Mieczyslaw Rakowski

During August, Poland reached crisis point; the Communists were negotiating with Solidarity over membership in the new coalition government. At the peak of the crisis, on the evening of 22 August, the secretary-general of the Polish Communist Party, Mieczyslaw Rakowski, telephoned Gorbachev to ask his advice. They talked for forty minutes. The Polish Communists were deeply split; the phone call to Moscow was decisive. Gorbachev told Rakowski bluntly that "the time has come to yield power"; the Communists should join a coalition government with Solidarity as part of a process of "national reconciliation." Two days later the Solidarity leader Tadeusz Mazowiecki was overwhelmingly elected prime minister of a new Solidarity-led coalition. The unthinkable had happened. Communists had given up power — and with Soviet complicity, at the very least, and more probably direct Soviet encouragement. American intelligence officials later said that with Rakowski's phone call to Gorbachev, "the Rubicon was crossed."

Only hours after Gorbachev's telephone intervention in Poland, on 23 August, Hungarian foreign minister Gyula Horn spent a sleepless night worrying about the changes going on around him. Earlier in the year, when the government had dismantled its border fence with Austria, this was of only academic interest to Hungarians, who already had the right to travel to the West. But thousands of disenchanted East Germans had been making their

way into Hungary via Czechoslovakia to escape their own unpopular regime. Hungary had signed a treaty with East Germany in 1968 not to allow East Germans to leave for the West through its territory. Now Horn sounded out Moscow for a reaction if Hungary abandoned this undertaking. The Soviets did not object, so Horn resolved to open to East Germans Hungary's border to the West. "It was quite obvious to me that this would be the first step in a landslide-like series of events," he said later. On 10 September, despite strenuous objections from the East German government, Hungary's border with Austria was opened to East German refugees. Within three days thirteen thousand East Germans, mostly young couples with children, had fled west. This was the biggest exodus since just before the Berlin Wall was built in 1961 — and it was only the beginning.

Meanwhile, Washington still maintained its caution. In a widely reported speech at Georgetown University, Deputy Secretary of State Lawrence Eagleburger expressed concern about possible disorder if confrontation ended between the United States and the Soviet Union, warning that military chaos, political crackdowns, and new dictatorships might arise across Europe. It was better, he argued, to maintain the West's "security consensus" until reforms in Moscow were seen as "irreversible." Congressional critics accused the administration of being "almost nostalgic about the Cold War."

At the end of September, Shevardnadze visited Washington and called on

Eastern Europe in ferment.
ABOVE LEFT: *Demonstrations in Hungary.* ABOVE: *East Germans, to their government's fury, holiday in Hungary and then drive on to the West.* ABOVE RIGHT: *A train conveys East German refugees from Prague to the West, and freedom.*

Bush to adopt "a more energetic and engaged policy" towards the Soviet Union. From Washington, Baker invited Shevardnadze to his ranch at Jackson Hole in Wyoming. On the long, four-and-a-half-hour flight to Wyoming the two men talked continuously. Shevardnadze astounded Baker by his frankness. The Soviet foreign minister had just left Moscow after a two-day Central Committee plenum on the problems of separatism and ethnic conflict within the Soviet Union. Shevardnadze described how the injustices of the Stalin era had generated hostility to Moscow within the Soviet republics; this was now coming home to roost in the unrest sweeping Central Asia and the Baltic. A Georgian, Shevardnadze felt the republics must be given some form of

James Baker and Eduard Shevardnadze held talks at Jackson Hole, Wyoming, in September. Trout fishing was mostly for the cameras. The rapport was real.

autonomy within the Soviet Union. But he insisted on the need to avoid force, telling Baker, "We must not turn protest into riots and riots into bloodshed." Shevardnadze was also candid about Moscow's economic woes. Journalists sitting at the back of the plane could hear nothing of what was said but could see from the intensity of the dialogue that something crucial was going on. Dennis Ross, who translated for Baker, said the two men "crossed a threshold" in candour and confidence as they flew across the continent.

At Jackson Hole, Baker and Shevardnadze, both wearing Stetsons, went trout fishing together — though it was Shevardnadze's first attempt at it. They walked trails through pine and aspen woods and spent an evening dining on ribs and buffalo steaks, listening to a country-and-western band. But the formal talks between the two ministers reverted to conventional form. Shevardnadze made major concessions in the hope of kick-starting the arms-reduction talks. Moscow no longer insisted on limits to the US Star Wars programme before an agreement to sign a START treaty. This was a major climbdown over the single issue that had prevented Gorbachev and Reagan from signing a far-reaching agreement on nuclear disarmament. Second, Shevardnadze agreed to dismantle the giant phased-array early warning radar installation at Krasnoyarsk, in Siberia, that the United States claimed was in violation of the ABM Treaty. The Soviets would do this without any dismantling of corresponding US installations at Thule, Greenland, or Fylingdales

Hungary, 1989

Soviet troops leave Hungary after forty years. Once Gorbachev allowed the satellites of the Soviet empire freedom, armies of occupation had no role.

Moor in England. Despite these concessions, Baker still held firm and rejected Shevardnadze's proposals, perhaps sensing that Moscow's willingness to concede gave the United States the upper hand. The Wyoming talks ended with several bilateral agreements, including a reduction in the stockpiles of chemical weapons. There was also publicly announced agreement on a summit to be held between Bush and Gorbachev the following year (news of the Malta meeting was kept secret for another month). However, the US failure to respond in kind to substantial Soviet concessions was a big disappointment to Shevardnadze and to Gorbachev. Gorbachev now came under increasing pres-

BELOW LEFT: *6 October. Gorbachev exchanges words with Communist leader Erich Honecker as East Germany celebrates forty years of communism. The crowds were not celebrating. They shouted, "Gorby, save us."*
BELOW: *A nighttime demonstration in East Berlin.*

sure from the Soviet military to change tactics. For Baker, however, the Wyoming talks, especially the airborne dialogue en route, marked a watershed. He was now convinced that the new line from Moscow was genuine, that Gorbachev and Shevardnadze "were for real"; now the United States must move to support Moscow, advancing "from understanding to interaction, and wherever possible to partnership." He concluded: "The situation has got the makings of a whole new world."

Transformations Begin

Over the next few months the international situation was transformed. In October the Hungarian Socialist Workers Party officially abandoned Leninism. On the anniversary of the 1956 uprising, it changed the country's name from People's Republic, the term used by Soviet bloc nations, to plain Republic of Hungary. In Budapest, for the first time, a ruling Communist Party rejected its ideological faith and proclaimed a new belief in democracy and democratic socialism. The shift towards capitalism and a market economy in Hungary was well under way.

On 6 October, Gorbachev began a two-day visit to East Germany to celebrate the fortieth anniversary of the German Democratic Republic. The government, led for eighteen years by the seventy-four-year-old Erich Honecker, was one of the most repressive regimes of Eastern Europe. Only four days ear-

The Brezhnev Doctrine is dead. . . . You know the Frank Sinatra song "My Way"? Hungary and Poland are doing it their way. We now have the Sinatra Doctrine.

— Gennadi Gerasimov,
Soviet government
spokesman, October 1989

lier it had sealed its border with Czechoslovakia to prevent people from voting with their feet and flooding to the West through Hungary. In East Berlin, Gorbachev suggested to Honecker that the way to stop public protest engulfing his government could be to introduce a German version of perestroika. Honecker would not listen; during his last visit to Moscow he had looked into shops and been disgusted at the bare shelves. How dare Gorbachev tell the leader of the most prosperous economy in the socialist world how to run things! Gorbachev persisted and told a large rally that East Germany should introduce Soviet-type reforms, adding that East German policy must be decided "not in

In Leipzig, East Germany's second largest city, reformers met weekly, at St. Nicholas Church. ABOVE: *A candlelight procession.* ABOVE RIGHT: *One hundred thousand march, calling for elections, a free press, and new leaders. The authorities considered a violent response, but restrained themselves.*

Moscow but in Berlin." Honecker, standing next to him, glared.

Gorbachev's visit galvanized protests against the deeply unpopular Communist regime. For a torchlight parade down the Unter den Linden in East Berlin, a crowd of thousands of hand-picked party activists was assembled to cheer Gorbachev. To everyone's surprise, they broke into chants of "Gorby, Gorby, Gorby, save us." In an extraordinary turnabout, a Soviet leader was now hailed by Eastern Europeans as a saviour from their own government's tyranny. Gorbachev told his aides he was "disgusted" by Honecker's "inept" handling of the crisis and that "the leadership can't stay in control." Back in Moscow he ordered his general staff to ensure that Soviet soldiers in East Germany stayed in their barracks and did not get embroiled in the chaos that was certain to overwhelm the country.

The day after Gorbachev left, the crunch came in Leipzig. Honecker ordered the security police to open fire on seventy thousand protesters marching through the city streets. Wary of repeating the bloodbath of Tiananmen Square, the local party leaders refused to obey orders. This sparked off a battle within the Politburo; Honecker was ousted and replaced by the youngest member of that body, the chief of internal security, Egon Krenz. Hundreds of demonstrators were released from prison. Rallying the people around a new slogan, "Change and Renewal," Krenz presented himself as the East German Gorbachev.

Berlin, 1989

The night of 9/10 November.
East Germany's frontier to the
West, just before it opened. The
Wall had divided Germany,
and the world. Now, everything
was to change.

This was too little too late to satisfy the sweeping demand for reform. The more conciliatory Krenz appeared to be, the greater was the call for radical change. At the end of October, 300,000 demonstrators in Leipzig and Dresden called for the removal of the Communist regime. Krenz fired his entire cabinet and two-thirds of the Politburo. The border with Czechoslovakia was reopened. Still this was not enough. Krenz called Gorbachev in the Kremlin to ask for advice. Gorbachev suggested that opening the borders would "let off steam" and avoid "an explosion."

On Saturday, 4 November, half a million people jammed East Berlin's streets to hear a concert carried live on East German and West German tele-

People power. Demonstrations in East Berlin at the Wall and in the centre of the city. One more puff and we'll blow the Wall down!

vision. The whole event was intended to rally support for reform while preserving the socialist system. But the protesters had by now grown brave. One by one, poets, musicians, and writers recited or sang satires about East Germany and its failings and demanded full democracy. Stefan Heym, a dissident writer, said he felt "as if the windows had been pushed open and suddenly fresh air was coming in." The huge rally made it clear that the people no longer had any interest in preserving the East German state. In the next few days, another fifty thousand people fled the country. The German Democratic Republic was on the verge of total disintegration.

The Wall Comes Down

Krenz hesitated but finally decided to bow to the inevitable. On 9 November the East German government announced that, effective the next day, exit visas would be granted automatically to all citizens wishing to "visit the West." Crowds gathered that night at the eight crossing points in Berlin. They were still suspicious, not sure what would happen; after all, nearly two hundred people had been shot trying to cross the wall that had divided the city for twenty-eight years. The border guards on duty that night had never seen such crowds and were uncertain what to do. They called their headquarters but received no clear instructions. At first they insisted that everyone must have a valid visa before they could depart the following day. But as numbers grew the situation erupted. People demanded to cross now; why wait for visas? Finally the guards decided to open the gates. At first a few wary individuals passed through. But the trickle soon became an unstoppable flood; hundreds, then thousands, then tens of thousands poured west, across the Berlin Wall, for a taste of freedom. On their side West Berliners came out to welcome and to cheer the Easterners. Families were reunited. Complete strangers embraced each other. With hammers and chisels and anything else that came to hand, people began to chip away at the ugly concrete barrier that snaked through the city. Amidst extraordinary scenes, people power tri-

ABOVE: *Joy unconfined. Hugs and kisses as East Germany opens its borders to the West.*
ABOVE LEFT: *Punk rockers take hammer and chisel to the graffiti-covered concrete of the Berlin Wall.*

umphed. Over the next year, bit by bit, the Berlin Wall, symbol of the Cold War, was almost totally demolished.

Pictures of the Wall coming down were carried live on satellite television and seen around the world. Everywhere people were moved, often to tears, by the emotional scenes unfolding in Berlin. Except, perhaps, in the White House. Reporters and television camera crews were permitted into the Oval Office to record the president's reaction. President Bush sat at his desk, nervously twisting a pen in his hand, and rambled evasively. He said he was "very pleased." Asked why he did not seem more elated, Bush replied, "I am not an emotional kind of guy." He did not want, he said, "to dance on the wall." He feared that might provoke resistance to Gorbachev in Moscow.

Americans were disappointed by their leader's lack of enthusiasm. Every president since Kennedy had called for the dismantling of the Berlin Wall. Polls showed that 90 per cent of the public thought it "exciting and encouraging." Critics accused Bush of failing to rise to the occasion. House majority leader Richard Gephardt said, "Even as the walls of the modern Jericho come tumbling down, we have a president who is inadequate to the moment." Privately Bush was amazed at the developments in Berlin. He told aides, "If the Soviets are going to let the Communists fall in East Germany, they've got to be really serious — more serious than I realized."

Gorbachev in private was far from enthusiastic over the toppling of the Wall. Gerasimov described the event as a "positive and important fact," in line with socialist developments in the Soviet Union. But the prospect of German reunification, of Germany as an economic and political giant at the heart of Europe, filled Gorbachev with anxiety. Moscow did not want to lose East Germany as a "strategic ally" and see it "consolidated" into Western Europe. Gorbachev wrote to Bush and to other Western leaders emphasizing that the Soviet Union had vital interests in the future of Germany, and that events should be handled slowly to prevent their spinning out of control. The president told his staff, "The guy's really upset." When West German foreign min-

Freedom is infectious; the fever spread from East Berlin (BELOW LEFT) to Prague (BELOW). Massive, peaceful demonstrations brought down the Communist government in Czechoslovakia, and no blood was shed. They called it the Velvet Revolution.

ister Hans-Dietrich Genscher visited Moscow in December, Gorbachev told him sharply that Kohl's newly announced plans for a speedy re-unification were premature and threatened to destabilize Europe.

In East Germany the much-hated secret police force, the Stasi, was disbanded. Krenz was replaced as premier by Communist reformer Hans Modrow, and the Volkskammer, the parliament, renounced the "leading role" of the Communist Party and began to expose the corruption and brutality of the Honecker regime. East Germany seemed to be moving steadily towards the West, but for several more months the Soviets continued resolutely to oppose German re-unification.

The gales of change now swept through Bulgaria and Czechoslovakia. The day the Wall came down coincided with a Politburo meeting in Sofia that turned into a showdown between party factions. Todor Zhivkov, the longest-serving leader in Eastern Europe, who had been in power since 1954 and president since 1971, was deposed and replaced by Petar Mladenov, who led the reform group. Under Mladenov, reform communism survived for more than a year in Bulgaria, before finally being swept away by democratic forces.

In Prague on 17 November, a student rally in Wenceslas Square turned into an anti-government protest and was fired on by nervous policemen. Inspired by events in Germany and infuriated by the attempted crackdown, protesters came out onto the streets in greater numbers to demand free elections. An umbrella opposition organization was formed, called Civic Forum.

port of perestroika but only now had seen evidence of this. "I was going to ask you today to go beyond words," he smiled, "but you have done so." To the question of on-site arms verification, Gorbachev said, "You can have as many inspectors as you want." On troop withdrawals from Eastern Europe, Gorbachev agreed, admitting, "We're aware that our troops are unwelcome there anyway." To Robert Blackwill, one of the few American aides at the table with Bush, this sense of genuine rapport seemed to be the transforming moment of the post–Second World War era.

The one divisive issue was still Central America, which Bush described to Gorbachev as "like a gigantic thorn in your shoe." He provided evidence of Cuban arms being shipped to the Sandinistas and Nicaraguan support for the rebels in El Salvador. Gorbachev broke in and said, "I've told Castro he's out of step with us and should be doing what the East Europeans are doing. But he's his own man." Gorbachev made it clear that the Soviets "cannot dictate to him." In their private conversations later, this again became an issue. Gorbachev countered Bush by accusing him of intervening in the Philippines, sending jets to support the regime of President Corazon Aquino, as well as in Panama and Colombia, and told him not to be so self-righteous about Central America. With the United States apparently interfering in the affairs of other states, Gorbachev asked if the Brezhnev Doctrine was about to be replaced by the Bush Doctrine. The president was not amused.

The full delegations met again for lunch, and as waiters served them silver bowls of the best Russian caviar, they discussed the Soviet Union's economic problems. The intention then was to adjourn for three hours of "private time" before another session aboard the *Gorky,* to be followed by a working dinner on the *Belknap.* As the storm raged about them, Gorbachev suggested that Bush remain on the *Gorky,* but the president insisted on returning to his ship. As the storms closed in there would be no further talks that day.

By Sunday morning the storm had abated a little, but the meetings intended for the *Belknap* were transferred to the more stable *Maxim Gorky.* Gorbachev told Bush that the changes in Europe opened up an important role for the United States on the continent. "We want you in Europe. You need to be in Europe," affirmed Gorbachev. Then decisively he went on to say, "We don't consider you as an enemy anymore. Things have changed." He assured Bush that the Soviet Union would never start a war against the United States. For some present, this was the determining sentence that ended an era.

Gorbachev urged Bush not to use one-sided expressions about the changes in Eastern Europe, such as describing them as the "triumph of Western values." "Why do you have to say Western? We have these values too," said Gorbachev. Baker suggested calling them "democratic values," and Gorbachev agreed. Bush saw Western values as the same as democratic values, but he would be careful in future to avoid triumphalist language offensive to the Soviets and would refer only to "universal" values.

After the morning session it was decided to hold a joint press conference — another first for this historic meeting. In front of the world's media in the hastily prepared discotheque of the *Gorky,* Bush and Gorbachev exemplified

In shipboard meetings at Malta, Gorbachev and Bush declare that their countries are no longer enemies. Ahead, co-operation. The Cold War had lasted from Yalta to Malta.

the new spirit of co-operation and partnership between two nations that had opposed each other for forty-four years. "We stand at the threshold of a brand new era of US-Soviet relations," claimed Bush. "This is just the beginning," said Gorbachev. "We're just at the very beginning of our long road to long-lasting peace." No agreements were signed at Malta, but in many ways the meeting marked a symbolic end to the Cold War. It offered a glimpse ahead to a new relationship between East and West. Soviet Foreign Ministry spokesman Gerasimov quipped to journalists, "We buried the Cold War at the bottom of the Mediterranean Sea."

In Romania, a grim coda to Eastern Europe's transformation. ABOVE: *Nicolae Ceausescu and his wife, Elena, after their capture. Court-martialled for crimes against their own people, they were sentenced to death and shot.* ABOVE RIGHT: *Romanians express grief, and the will to resist, as the bodies of countrymen killed in the uprising are borne by.*

The Last Stalinist

To the extraordinary events of 1989, there was one grim postscript. The only Eastern European nation still ruled by its old-school Communist leader was Romania. The tyrant Nicolae Ceausescu had run the country with a rod of iron since 1965, turning it into a police state. The Securitate, the secret police, terrorized people into submission while Ceausescu imposed his Stalinist will over the nation and its economy. At a meeting of Warsaw Pact leaders in Moscow the day after Gorbachev returned from Malta, Ceausescu was the sole Eastern European Communist Party boss still in office since the last Warsaw Pact summit, only five months before. Gorbachev spoke of eliminating the Cold War; Ceausescu said the West was "out to liquidate socialism." He called for building up the Warsaw Pact against the common danger of NATO. The other Eastern European heads ignored him. They went on to support a Czech resolution condemning the Soviet invasion of 1968. Ceausescu refused to sign. After a "frank exchange of opinions" with Gorbachev, the Romanian leader flew home in a bad temper.

Two weeks later Ceausescu's secret police opened fire on protesters who had gathered in the traditionally dissident Transylvanian city of Timisoara, in the west of Romania. For several days the shootings continued, but still people came out onto the streets in ever growing numbers. On 22 December, Ceausescu gave a prepared speech from the balcony of his presidential palace in Bucharest to a huge, specially assembled crowd. He intended to show he still had supporters and to use the speech to restore order, and it was carried live on television. But Romanians had had enough. There were catcalls, boo-ing, and whistling. A dazed Ceausescu broke off his speech and retired from the balcony. He decided to flee. Next day he was carried away in a helicopter as the unarmed crowd stormed the Communist Party headquarters. A National Salvation Front was declared, consisting of former Ceausescu aides and a few prominent dissidents, and the army transferred its allegiance to the new government. There was sporadic street fighting between soldiers and the remaining secret policemen loyal to the old regime. The United States informed the Soviets that if they decided to intervene militarily against Ceausescu's supporters, Washington would not object. No intervention was needed. The day they fled, Ceausescu and his equally unpopular wife, Elena, who was a Politburo member and the country's de facto vice president, were caught by forces of the new regime. They were put before a military tribunal, whose legality they refused to accept. After a hasty trial, they were taken out and shot on Christmas Day. Their bodies were shown on Romanian television, and throughout the world.

At the beginning of 1989 the Iron Curtain still divided Europe, as it had done for more than forty years. By the end of the year, the leaders of every Eastern European nation except Bulgaria, which soon followed suit, had been ousted by popular uprisings; in every case the will of the people had prevailed and, except in Romania, hardly a drop of blood was spilt. With dizzying speed, the Soviet Union's European empire, the buffer zone ruthlessly built up by Stalin and maintained with brutal force when necessary by his successors, had imploded. Truly, 1989 was an annus mirabilis.

Romanian revolutionaries joy-ride through Bucharest in a commandeered truck. At first chaos followed the ending of dictatorship.

It was Gorbachev who gave Russians the freedom to demonstrate. Now they demonstrated for an end to the power monopoly of the Communists and for the radical democrat Boris Yeltsin.

Endings
1990–1991

January 1990. Walking the streets of Vilnius, Lithuania's capital, Gorbachev argues that Lithuania must stay a part of the Soviet Union. The Lithuanians persisted in their demand for independence.

Ring In the New

On New Year's Day 1990, the ancient bells of St. Basil's Cathedral in Red Square rang out for the first time in many years. The changes they rang reverberated throughout the Soviet Union — ringing out the old, ringing in the new.

From 11 to 13 January 1990, Mikhail Gorbachev was in Vilnius, capital of Lithuania, where, the previous month, the Communist Party had voted to declare the country independent from Moscow. Lithuania, Estonia, and Latvia, the Baltic republics, were comparatively recent additions to the Soviet Union. They had been ceded to Stalin, without their knowledge or consent, by a secret codicil to the infamous Nazi-Soviet Pact of 1939, which cleared the way for Hitler to invade Poland through an agreement to divide that country with the USSR. Stalin's determination to have a buffer zone of client states on his western border ensured also that the three Baltic republics would be swallowed up in the Soviet maw.

But their peoples, independent since the First World War, had never willingly accepted this fate. And the United States had never recognized Soviet rule over the Baltics or formally withdrawn recognition of their independence. Now the Baltic states claimed that independence again. Yet if Gorbachev gave in to Lithuania's declaration, where would it end? In the breakup, perhaps, of the USSR? Gorbachev began to grasp at formulas for compromise, while insisting that the Union must be preserved.

No sooner was he back in Moscow than, on 15 January, ethnic rioting and civil war broke out elsewhere in his domain, in Azerbaijan. The Muslim Azerbaijanis, concerned that the largely Armenian Christian population of Nagorno-Karabakh was rebelling against their rule and manoeuvring for independence from Moscow, rioted near the Iranian border and mobilized. Gorbachev sent troops; in the subsequent fighting, hundreds of Azerbaijanis, perhaps a thousand, were killed. Then in early February, the East German government proposed a re-united and neutral Germany; Gorbachev accepted the concept, although to live with a re-united Germany would further test hard-line Soviet tolerance.

A massive demonstration in Moscow called for an end to the Communist Party's monopoly on power, and on 5 February, Gorbachev, hurrying now to keep abreast of pressure for change, proposed that the Soviet Union,

ABOVE LEFT: *Soviet tanks and troops in the streets of Baku crush an Azerbaijani revolt. A thousand died.* ABOVE: *Victims of the crackdown. People wondered if scenes like these would be repeated throughout the Soviet Union as member states claimed independence.*

for more than seventy years a Communist state autocracy, should end one-party rule, accept a multiparty system, and adopt "humane, democratic socialism." Specifically, he put forward economic reforms, proposed a reduction in the membership of the Central Committee, and called for a new executive office of president of the USSR. After a stormy debate, in which voices of reaction from the Communist right clashed with reformers on the left, these proposals were accepted. Gorbachev, riding the troika of right, left, and centre, had to find a way forward without losing control. The ride could only get bumpier.

US secretary of state James Baker met Gorbachev in Moscow on 9 February to propose what he called a "Two-plus-Four" solution to the problem of German re-unification: the two Germanys and the four wartime Allied occupying powers, the United States, the United Kingdom, France, and the Soviet Union, would determine the conditions under which re-unification would be countenanced. The next day Chancellor Kohl and Foreign Minister Genscher were in Moscow. Gorbachev signalled that he would not oppose German re-unification, and the Two-plus-Four stratagem was approved by the Four in Ottawa on 13 February. During these amazing weeks — Nelson Mandela was released from his prison in South Africa on 11 February, presaging the transition to democracy there — the pace for Gorbachev never slackened. Soviet public opinion, as street demonstrations showed, was impatient but divided; the right complained that he was going too fast, the left that he was not moving fast enough. The Supreme Soviet voted him sweeping presidential powers.

On 11 March, Lithuania formally declared its independence. Vytautas Landsbergis, a musicologist, was elected president. Gorbachev attacked the action as "illegitimate and invalid," but was reluctant to use force to reverse it. At Malta he had agreed with Bush not to do so; Bush in return had promised to try not to make Gorbachev's task more difficult. The president kept his public remarks on the situation low-key. The United States wanted to see the Baltic republics gain their freedom, but relied at this point for world stability on a lasting relationship with a strong Soviet Union. It did not welcome chaos.

As the crisis deepened in March, Soviet paratroopers occupied party buildings in Vilnius. On 25 March, Estonian Communists voted for independence; Latvia would follow in May. On 28 March independent Hungary held its first free elections since 1945.

Struggling to regain control, Gorbachev imposed an economic embargo on Lithuania. He cut off oil supplies and 84 per cent of the flow of natural gas by pipeline, letting through just enough to keep essential services, such as hospitals, going. And he prohibited the supplying of other goods. The United States considered, but rejected, sanctions against Moscow, though US citizens from Lithuania, Latvia, and Estonia lobbied Washington. The Americans threatened instead to withhold the signing of a projected trade agreement with the Soviets.

Yeltsin Becomes Parliamentary Leader of Russia

On 24 May, Nikolai Ryzhkov, the prime minister appointed by Gorbachev, announced the latest programme of economic reforms, on whose successful implementation future US economic aid depended. Ryzhkov's plan, perhaps to sabotage Gorbachev, threatened a three-fold increase in the price of bread. The predictable result was a rush on bread shops. Popular distrust of Gorbachev intensified. On 29 May, Boris Yeltsin, who had resigned his membership in the Soviet Union's Politburo and the Communist Party, was chosen leader of the Russian Republic by its parliament, which declared that its laws took precedence over Soviet laws. This was in effect a declaration of Russian sovereignty and, very nearly, of independence from the Soviet Union. A fork in the road had come clearly into view: one branch pointed towards Gorbachev and a restructured Soviet Union; the other towards Yeltsin and Russia, and the dissolution of the Soviet Union.

Boris Yeltsin

From 30 May to 2 June, Gorbachev met with President Bush at a summit in Washington and at Camp David. Gorbachev now abandoned the Soviet requirement that a united Germany remain neutral, and faced the fact that the German people would decide whether they were to be in NATO.

Over the next few weeks the conditions to be attached to German reunification were hammered out. The Soviet Union failed to secure a transitional period in which the military forces in East Germany retained "associated membership" in the Warsaw Pact — an obvious nonsense — or agreement on a hard-line plan whereby for three to five years the other powers would oversee

Moscow. In the Congress of People's Deputies, Gorbachev argues that, even after perestroika, the Soviet Union must remain intact. But he could not hold back the nationalist tide.

Germany's conduct. In London in early July, a NATO summit made a declaration of non-aggression with the Warsaw Pact nations. That helped. Germany, meanwhile, vowed to confirm its borders with Poland, promised to limit the future size of a German army, agreed not to station nuclear weapons in East Germany, and said it would pay the costs for moving Soviet troops — half a million of them — from East Germany and resettling them in Russia. Kohl and Genscher came to Moscow. At a press conference on 16 July, Gorbachev declared, "Whether we like it or not, the time will come when a united Germany will be in NATO, if that is its choice. Then, if that is its choice, to some degree and in some form, Germany can work together with the Soviet Union."

ABOVE LEFT: *West German chancellor Helmut Kohl (second from right), with Mikhail Gorbachev in Moscow. Kohl pledged to curb German military strength and offered substantial financial aid. Eventually Gorbachev agreed that Germany could be re-united, within NATO.*

This extraordinary utterance was, as Chancellor Kohl put it, "a breakthrough, a fantastic result." A fortnight earlier, at the Twenty-eighth Party Congress, Gorbachev had been ferociously attacked by party hard-liners for letting the Baltics go, for weakening the Warsaw Pact, and for undermining the ideological foundations of the Soviet Union and the party. He was, nevertheless, re-elected general secretary. Now Gorbachev was publicly committing the Soviet Union to uprooting the cornerstone of its security policy since the end of the Second World War.

Some say the Cold War ended when the Berlin Wall came down; others say it was when Gorbachev, at Malta, told Bush, "We don't consider you as an enemy any more." Now the Soviet Union had reconciled itself to seeing Germany, which had cost it more than 20 million dead, in military alliance with the West. Since Germany had always been at the epicentre of the Cold War in Europe, this has a strong claim to be considered the decisive moment of the Cold War's ending.

Superpower Co-operation

Within weeks, the superpowers' commitment to peaceful collaboration was tested by events in the Persian Gulf region. On 2 August the army of Saddam Hussein, Iraq's brutal dictator, overran neighbouring Kuwait, a tiny but oil-rich nation. Iraq was a Soviet ally, and several thousand Russians worked there. James Baker and Eduard Shevardnadze, who were meeting in Irkutsk, flew to Moscow. Baker was anxious to ensure that the Soviet Union would stand with the United States in its condemnation of the invasion and support whatever action it eventually would take against it. In spite of Iraq's ties to the Soviet Union, and the initial reactions of Gorbachev and some of his colleagues against an alliance, Shevardnadze stood with Baker at Vnukovo Airport the next day. Together they told the press that the two great powers were "jointly calling upon the rest of the international community to join with us in an international cut-off of all arms supplies to Iraq." Superpower confrontation had become co-operation. For James Baker, this was the Cold War's ending; for others it was the first joint act of security policy in the post–Cold War world.

ABOVE: *August 1990. The Iraqi army, on orders from Saddam Hussein, invades and annexes Kuwait. Although Iraq was a Soviet ally, the USSR joined in condemning the invasion.*
ABOVE RIGHT: *Ukrainians protest at continued Soviet domination. The Ukraine was one of several Soviet republics to assert a claim to independence in 1990.*

But if the contest was over, the combatants had not yet left the ring. The Soviet Union was still in being, though beset with problems. Gorbachev had to cope with two desperately difficult tasks at home. He was trying, as fast as he could, to reform an economy and a system of government that had become a way of life. And he was trying, against the odds, to hold the Soviet Union together when every single member state sought, or would seek, independence. On 16 July the Ukraine declared its sovereignty, followed by Armenia, Turkmenistan, and Tadzhikistan in August, and Kazakhstan and Kirghizia in October. In October too, ominously, both Russia and the Ukraine declared their state laws sovereign over Union laws. The Supreme Soviet declared this invalid in November. Gorbachev proposed to set up a new central government that would have in it representatives from the fifteen Soviet republics. Yeltsin, leader of the Russian Republic, made clear that he did not want to see power concentrated at the centre, in Gorbachev's hands. By the end of November, Gorbachev had shifted again; now he proposed a new Union Treaty: a Union of Sovereign Soviet Republics, but with loosened ties between each republic and the central Soviet government.

In other crucial matters the USSR Supreme Soviet had taken giant strides; on 1 October it passed a law guaranteeing freedom of worship and on 9 October legislation to bring into being a multiparty system. Constitutional issues, even of this fundamental sort, could be settled by a vote and a stroke of the pen.

Berlin, 1990

*Berlin's Brandenburg Gate,
3 October 1990. Crowds celebrate as Germany is re-united.*

Media too were freed from state control. But the economy was a harder nut to crack; just the prospect of economic change threatened social chaos and caused immediate fear and distress. To go from a command economy, where everyone did what they were told by the centre, to one that operated without central planning and left prices to market forces was to travel a pathless route into unknown territory. Not many wanted to go that way; few knew how to arrive at the destination.

On 20 July a "500-day" economic programme to move the Soviet Union to a market economy was published. It proposed the sale of large numbers of state enterprises, the dissolution of state collective farms, currency reform, and a new banking system. But Gorbachev's nerve failed him. The reforms were not introduced. Things were bad; uncertainty made them worse. Appealed to for urgent financial and economic aid, the Bush administration steadfastly refused; any aid given would be a reward for implementing reform, not an inducement. The United States, concerned that Gorbachev might be deposed, also maintained a full state of military readiness.

Dramatic changes outside the USSR continued to make the headlines. In August the United States had begun to despatch land, sea, and air forces to Saudi Arabia in Operation Desert Shield, to discourage Iraq from a further invasion. The UN Security Council voted the first of a dozen resolutions demanding Iraq's withdrawal from Kuwait. On 3 October, East and West Germany were joined; Germany was re-united. In November, NATO and Warsaw Pact leaders, meeting in Paris, signed a historic treaty to set reduced levels for conventional forces in the whole of Europe (CFE), from the Atlantic to the Urals. Gorbachev reassured Bush of his good faith: "We've been with you since Day One in the Gulf, and we'll continue to be with you." Already, in Helsinki in September, Bush had secretly agreed to an international conference on the Middle East when the crisis in the Persian Gulf was over, giving the Soviet Union what Kissinger had worked to deny it: a role in that region. On 29 November, the United Nations passed Security Council Resolution 678, authorizing the use of force in the Gulf if Iraq was not out of Kuwait by 15 January 1991.

TOP: *Berlin; the crowds and the flags say that Germany is re-united within the European Community.* BOTTOM: *Chancellor Kohl and his wife celebrate his finest hour. The economic cost of re-unification would come later.*

As 1990 ended Gorbachev, under persistent conservative criticism, moved to the right. The USSR Supreme Soviet, which could not agree on an economic programme, had granted Gorbachev special powers to rule by decree during the transition to a market economy. Gorbachev fired a moderate interior minister and replaced him with a former KGB chief, Boris Pugo. "The country," said Gorbachev on 17 December, "needed firm executive rule to overcome the threat posed by the dark forces of nationalism." Television announced that the army, if attacked in the streets, would open fire. On 20 December, Shevardnadze resigned his post as foreign minister, warning that a hard-line dictatorship was near.

Shevardnadze had played a key role in advancing perestroika, glasnost, and the policies that were ending the Cold War. But he felt that Gorbachev had let him carry the blame alone for what they had done together that was most criticized, concessions in Eastern Europe and on Germany, and support for the

Boris Pugo

United States in the Persian Gulf. He had been a scapegoat. Now, knowing that Gorbachev intended to kick him upstairs as vice president, he resigned and returned to his native Georgia. He was replaced as foreign minister by Alexander Bessmertnykh. On 26 December 1990 the Congress of People's Deputies approved new executive powers for the president of the USSR, Gorbachev. He now chose as his vice president a conservative, Gennady Yanayev, who assured the Congress he was a Communist "to the depths of my soul."

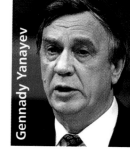

Gennady Yanayev

George Bush telephoned Mikhail Gorbachev on New Year's Day 1991. He was grateful to the ally who had stood by him in opposing Saddam Hussein's invasion of Kuwait. It was the greatest challenge of his presidency, putting together the international coalition to liberate Kuwait without imperilling Gorbachev's reforms. He understood what difficulties Gorbachev faced and did not, this time, warn against precipitate action in the Baltic republics, feeling that the United States had said enough. He did not want US objections to destroy the US-USSR alliance on the Gulf. Within weeks Bush would launch the air war against Iraq and shatter its military capability.

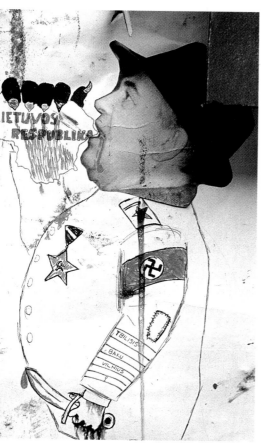

The unkindest cut of all. Lithuanians portray Gorbachev, who would deny them national freedom, as a Nazi occupier with blood dripping from his knife blade.

A Return to Cold War Rhetoric

On 2 January tensions in the Baltics escalated, as Moscow sent riot police to seize the state-owned buildings in Vilnius, Lithuania, and Riga, Latvia; on 7 January elite paratroopers were ordered to round up draft dodgers and deserters. The United States now cautioned against the use of force. The Soviet Union, slipping back into Cold War rhetoric, warned the United States not to interfere in its internal affairs. On Sunday, 13 January, in Vilnius, "Bloody Sunday," Soviet troops stormed the television tower and other public buildings. Fourteen Lithuanians, men and women, were killed. On 20 January in Riga, "Black Beret" Soviet troops stormed the Interior Ministry, killing five Latvians. The United States and world opinion were outraged; if these methods — the tactics of Tiananmen Square — were used against every republic seeking independence, bloodbath would succeed bloodbath.

The orders for the crackdown in Vilnius were said to come "from the very top," but Gorbachev, after the first killings, got cold feet and ordered a stop to the operation. Urged to go to Vilnius, Gorbachev was told his security there could not be guaranteed. He stayed in Moscow. Speaking to the Supreme Soviet, he defended what was done and refused to condemn the use of force. On 21 January, Gorbachev did condemn brutality, and promised to punish those responsible. He was walking a tightrope between hard-liners who wanted a nationwide crackdown on all forces opposed to the centre and reformists who were for change at whatever cost to the unity of the Soviet state. Meanwhile, Boris Yeltsin, as parliamentary leader of Russia, signed a mutual security pact with the Baltic states.

A summit meeting between Gorbachev and Bush, planned for February, was abandoned as East-West relations deteriorated. Gorbachev, conscious of Soviet ties to Iraq and of hard-line opposition to US gunboat diplomacy, even if the Soviet Union had voted with the United Nations to support the use of

Vilnius, 1991

January. Crack Soviet troops move into Vilnius to seize back public buildings. Lithuanians flock to defend their parliament, as well as the radio and television stations. In the confrontation, fourteen are killed.

ABOVE: *Gulf War: US marines at Khabji, Saudi Arabia, reinforce the front line. The marines suffered casualties here.* BELOW: *Boris Yeltsin, elected president of the Russian Republic, speaks to his people, July 1991.*

force against Iraq, tried to persuade the United States to stay its hand and allow him time to work on Iraq. On 18 February, Gorbachev met with Iraq's foreign minister, Tariq Aziz, in Moscow in a last attempt at mediation. But the timetable for the ground war against the Iraqis was set. Operation Desert Storm began on 24 February. On 27 February, President Bush announced that Kuwait was "liberated."

In Moscow, Gorbachev fought on. He held a referendum and won approval of his proposed Union Treaty; the Soviet Union was to be preserved as a renewed federation of equal sovereign republics in which human rights and the freedoms of all nationalities would be guaranteed. Several republics boycotted the vote, and Yeltsin made clear that he sided with the boycotters. In March a coal miners strike began in Donbass, in the Ukraine, and mass demonstrations were held in Moscow — for Yeltsin and against Gorbachev. The demonstration on 28 March proceeded in spite of a ban and the presence of fifty thousand police and soldiers in the capital. The marches went off peacefully, but the ban and the massing of armed forces caused tremendous offence. Gorbachev's new, more hard-line stance was losing him respect among reformers.

Georgia declared its independence from the USSR in April. Gorbachev's conservative prime minister, Valentin Pavlov, presented an "anti-crisis" programme designed to restore power to the central government. Retail prices went up. Gorbachev, shifting away from hard-line policies, held talks with the leaders of nine Soviet republics to formulate a political and economic reform package and a modified relationship between Moscow and the republics. The leaders reached a new understanding on a treaty, the Nine-plus-One agreement. On 12 June, Boris Yeltsin was elected to the newly created post of president of Russia, in a landslide. Yeltsin received 57 per cent of 80 million votes. He was the first democratically elected leader in Russian history.

The Soviet Union was desperate for American economic aid; it was no longer Soviet military strength that posed a threat to world peace but Soviet economic weakness. Would the United States recognize this and, in a "Grand Bargain," offer massive dollar aid — say, $20 billion a year over five years — to do for the Soviet Union what the Marshall Plan had done for Western Europe forty-odd years earlier? This was the question posed jointly by a group of Soviet and American academics, who then tried to sell their plan to the two governments. Some of Gorbachev's colleagues denounced the Grand Bargain as a Western conspiracy, but in any case the United States was not interested — the Soviet Union was a poor credit risk. And President Bush had no political support in Washington for bailing out the rival system.

The climax of Gorbachev's attempts to get American aid in propping up the ruble and in stocking Soviet shelves with consumer goods came in London on 17 July at the Group of Seven (G7) meeting, the world's financial top table. His problem all along had been in convincing the United States that he was serious about moving directly to a free market economy, as serious as Boris Yeltsin had been when in Washington he proclaimed himself an avid free marketeer. At the G7 meeting, with everything at stake, Gorbachev was unconvincing and left empty-handed.

*Anti-Gorbachev demonstration.
The president of the USSR faces
opposition from both sides,
from those for reform and those
against it. The move to oust
him would come from hard-line
Communists.*

CFE and START

While confrontation between the superpowers continued, arms control and arms reduction were seen by both as the best route to a safer world. In 1990 sweeping initiatives had drastically altered the political landscape; the Soviets no longer controlled Eastern Europe. Yet arms control remained a key issue between the United States and the USSR — the last one to be resolved.

To make a final result stick, each side needed not just a political rationale; every provision of the text had to be acceptable to the military — to the Pentagon and to the Soviet Ministry of Defence — as well as to the State Department and the Kremlin. The devil was in the details.

Two sets of arms negotiations remained as unfinished business between Bush and Gorbachev: START (Strategic Arms Reduction Talks) and CFE (Conventional Forces in Europe). Soviet troops would withdraw from Europe; and most US troops, in Western Europe to defend against Soviet incursion, would withdraw also. The Soviets had far higher numbers deployed and agreed to send home many more men. The CFE agreement set limits to the numbers of conventional arms — tanks, artillery, aircraft — allowed between the Atlantic and the Urals. It ended the military division of the continent.

The historic CFE agreement was signed by twenty-two nations in Paris in November 1990, at a meeting of the Council for Security and Co-operation in Europe (CSCE). The member states of the Warsaw Pact and NATO "welcomed the end of an era of division and confrontation." As friends they declared that "security is indivisible." Bush and Gorbachev, both present, could take pride in what was done.

Some CFE details and points of interpretation still gave trouble. The Soviets sought to exclude naval units from the count, arguing that they might need them for internal purposes in the Baltic and the Black Sea. The United States insisted that everything be counted. It was not till June 1991 in Vienna that the final text was initialled.

START's broad objective was also clear enough: to reduce the numbers of long-range strategic weapons. Achieving this was complicated. Should the two sides reduce nuclear warheads or missile types carrying the warheads? The Soviets, with two new missile types in development, wanted to download warheads and protect their missile types. The United States was against this. The Soviets were negotiating against a clock that was ticking away the continued existence of the USSR. In Washington, Secretary of State Baker was readier to reach agreement than was Brent Scowcroft, national security adviser.

Eventually, just minutes before Bush and Gorbachev were due to meet in London, on 17 July 1991, minor concessions produced a text acceptable to both. In Moscow, on 31 July, Bush and Gorbachev signed START I. The two superpowers reduced their nuclear arsenals below 9,000 countable warheads and bombs, and 1,500 delivery vehicles.

START II, signed in 1993 by Bush and Yeltsin and ratified by the US Senate in 1996, will, when implemented, require further deep cuts, to some 3,500 warheads and bombs. The nuclear powers are committed, under Article VI of the Non-Proliferation Treaty signed by 175 nations at the UN in 1995, to "the ultimate goal of complete elimination of nuclear weapons."

Cold War relics. Thousands of Soviet tanks are up for sale, as arms-reduction treaties come into force. Armaments kept the peace, but at the end, the junkyard awaited.

"If Perestroika Fails . . ."

Gorbachev, who had been awarded the Nobel Peace Prize in 1990, had given his acceptance speech in Oslo on 5 June. In it he warned, "If perestroika fails, the prospect of entering a new peaceful period of history will vanish, at least for the foreseeable future." The message was received, but not acted upon. Gorbachev had embarked on perestroika; it was up to him, and the Soviet Union, to see that it did not fail. But Gorbachev's Peace Prize was acclaimed, and the consequences of his actions were apparent everywhere. In June 1991 Soviet troops completed their withdrawal from Hungary and from Czechoslovakia. The Czechs and Hungarians had longed for this moment for decades and cheered as the Soviets left. More matter-of-factly, both Comecon, the Council for Mutual Economic Assistance, and the Warsaw Pact were formally dissolved. In Vienna, also in June, the United States and the Soviet Union signed an agreement that refined the previous text on conventional forces in Europe (CFE), which had been in negotiation since 1989. On 31 July, at a summit in Moscow, Bush and Gorbachev signed START I, beginning a new sequence of strategic arms reduction agreements.

George Bush had undertaken to visit Ukraine, and went on to Kiev after Moscow. The Ukrainians hoped for US support in their move to independence from Moscow. Bush perceived clearly how perilous was Gorbachev's position; the CIA already had warned of a possible hard-line coup against him. The warning was passed on to Gorbachev, who ignored it. Bush did not want to do anything to make matters worse. In Kiev he denounced the grim consequences of "suicidal nationalism." (Croatia, having left the Yugoslav Federation with Slovenia, was already at war.) The Ukrainians were disappointed. The speech went down even less well in the United States, where the president's own hard-line, right-wing critics picked up a journalist's verdict and damned it as Bush's "Chicken Kiev" speech.

At a Villa by the Sea

In August, holiday-time, Gorbachev went to his villa at Foros on the Black Sea. In June the old-guard Communists had been foiled in an attempt to unseat him by passing resolutions in the Congress of People's Deputies (the so-called constitutional coup); now they moved again to dislodge him from power, this time by force. In Moscow, early in the morning of Monday, 19 August, as Gorbachev's holiday was ending, radio and television started broadcasting an announcement by the "State Committee for the State of Emergency": President Gorbachev was ill and could not perform his duties; Vice President Yanayev had assumed the powers of the presidency; an emergency had been declared. It was a coup, but to the ordinary citizen in Moscow or Leningrad, matters were unclear. Where was Gorbachev? Perhaps he really was ill? Information was hard to come by. The television programme schedule kept changing; Moscow's children missed their favourite nightly puppet show. Later that evening television showed the ballet *Swan Lake*.

On Sunday afternoon, 18 August, a delegation from Moscow had arrived at the seaside villa to see Gorbachev. Before they were permitted inside, Gorbachev tried to telephone out, but the phones had been cut off. At sea naval

Moscow, 19 August 1991. Plotters against Gorbachev give a televised press conference. From left, Boris Pugo, Gennady Yanayev, and Oleg Baklanov. When the coup failed, Pugo, a former KGB chief, shot his wife and then himself.

craft manoeuvred menacingly near the shore. The conspirators pushed their way in: Oleg Baklanov, Gorbachev's deputy at the Defence Council; Party Secretary Oleg Shenin; Deputy Defence Minister General Valentin Varennikov; Gorbachev's chief of staff, Valery Boldin. They told Gorbachev that he should approve a declaration of a national state of emergency and sign it, or else resign and hand over his authority to Yanayev. Gorbachev flatly refused; to have agreed would have legitimized the plot. They left, putting Gorbachev under house arrest, cut off from communication with the outside world.

The plotters included several other members of the government: Prime Minister Pavlov; KGB Chairman Vladimir Kryuchkov; Interior Minister Pugo; Minister of Defence Marshal Dmitry Yazov. Most of them had been urging Gorbachev for months to impose emergency rule. Now they imposed it themselves, and hoped he would go along with it. He had underestimated their strength; they had underestimated his determination to resist. Gorbachev's refusal to give in was brave. But the real struggle was in Moscow.

In every Moscow ministry and in the republics, every civil servant had to make up his or her mind what to do. Most temporized and watched to see how things would turn out. But enough men and women in government, the army, and the KGB refused to obey orders from the Emergency Committee to ensure that the coup went off at half-cock. Gorbachev's insistence on moving to democracy was paying off. Resistance was led from the White House, the seat of the Russian parliament, by Boris Yeltsin. Yeltsin, usually at odds with Gorbachev, on this occasion stood firm. He denounced the coup and those behind it, rallying support for legitimate government and a liberal future rather than a return to the dark ages of totalitarian tyranny. He called for a general strike. Those who agreed with Yeltsin, and had the courage to say so, went to the White House, ringed by troops and tanks, to declare their support. Shevardnadze was one of the first.

On holiday in Kennebunkport in Maine, President Bush had gone to bed on the night of Sunday, 18 August, looking forward to a round of golf in the morning, when the telephone rang with the news from Moscow. He faced a classic diplomatic dilemma when it came to deciding what statement to make early next day: condemn the coup out of hand? But suppose it prevailed, and the plotters held on to power? The United States would have to do business with them. Or should he fudge, and risk encouraging the conspirators? It was agreed that Bush would talk to the press early, but not on the golf course; it was raining hard in any case.

At eight in the morning, Bush met the press. He praised Gorbachev as "a historic figure," hedged on Yanayev, and stopped short of outright denunciation when he called the seizure of power "extraconstitutional." He insisted that US reaction would aim not to "overexcite the American people or the world. . . . We will conduct our diplomacy in a prudent fashion, not driven by excess." It was not much more than "wait and see."

At Foros the Gorbachevs, on a transistor radio no one knew they had, learned what was happening in Moscow from the BBC World Service. Raisa

George Bush ponders the news from Moscow. Whatever the coup's outcome, the United States would have to deal with the government holding power.

Gorbachev, in her diary, expressed indignation at the news on state television: Kazakhstan's president, Nursultan Nazarbayev, appealed to the people of his republic "to remain calm and cool and maintain public order." "Not a word," she noted, "about the ousting of the President of the USSR." Gorbachev sent a message to Yanayev: Cancel what you've done and convene the Congress of People's Deputies or the USSR Supreme Soviet.

On the night of 20 August, the first blood was spilt. Three young men were killed by armoured personnel carriers moving towards the White House

ABOVE: *Tanks in the streets; attempted coup in Moscow. But the army was halfhearted in obeying the Emergency Committee's orders. The plotters failed to seize power outright.*
ABOVE RIGHT: *Crowds surround the Russian parliament building, where Boris Yeltsin leads the resistance against the unconstitutional coup.*

in support of the coup. Had the Emergency Committee been more resolute, many more lives would certainly have been lost. But they were hesitant, unsure of themselves, and of their support, perhaps even of their cause. The coup had failed.

It was announced the following day that a delegation would be permitted to leave for the Crimea to see for themselves that Gorbachev was gravely ill. At Foros this caused alarm. They were already boiling their food against poison. Would the plotters now try to make their statements good and, somehow, have Gorbachev killed? The delegation, which actually wanted to make up, reached Foros at 5:00 PM that day, and asked to see Gorbachev; Kryuchkov, Yazov, Baklanov, and Anatoli Lukyanov, chairman of the Supreme Soviet, were among them. Gorbachev declined to receive them. "Tell them I refuse to see anyone until communications are restored." At 5:45 PM, the telephones came back into use. Gorbachev rang Yeltsin, who said: "Mikhail Sergeyevich, my dear man, are you alive? We have been holding firm here for forty-eight hours." Shortly afterwards, a Russian delegation arrived, led by Alexander Rutskoi, Yeltsin's vice president, to bring Gorbachev and his family party back to Moscow. Without packing, they prepared to leave.

Later, Kryuchkov wrote to Gorbachev, expressing remorse; Yazov, with his excellent military record, knew he had made an ass of himself; Lukyanov had no good answer to Gorbachev's question: "Why did you not exercise your own constitutional powers?"

In Moscow, Yanayev had taken to the bottle; Pugo shot his wife and then himself when loyalists came to arrest him. Marshal Sergei Akhromeyev, Gorbachev's military adviser, also committed suicide. He left a note: "Everything I have worked for is being destroyed." Bessmertnykh, who had been careful not to commit himself either way, had to resign.

22 and 23 August 1991. Exiting the plane that Yeltsin sent for him, Gorbachev returns to a changed Moscow. Yeltsin was now in charge, and next day, in the Russian parliament, he forced Gorbachev to read out documents implicating his own Communist colleagues in the coup against him.

A Different Man, a Different Country

All was changed utterly. Gorbachev when he returned to Moscow did not seem to recognize it. He made a spontaneous statement: "I have come back from Foros to another country, and I myself am a different man now." But he gave the impression that he thought things could go on as before, even reaffirming his belief in the Communist Party and the need to renew it.

This was not what many wanted to hear. Gorbachev was jeered in the Russian parliament and humiliated by Yeltsin who, without warning, put into his hand a set of minutes he had not seen before and forced him to read the documents out loud on live television. They showed that his Communist allies, members of his government, had been behind the coup. US diplomats watching these pictures knew, as did Russian viewers, that Gorbachev was finished, destroyed by a coup that failed, and that Yeltsin, who had led the resistance, was now the master. On 24 August, Gorbachev resigned as leader of the Soviet Communist Party, disbanding the Central Committee. It was too late to do him any good. On 29 August, the Soviet Communist Party effectively dissolved itself. An era was — almost — over.

All that now remained was to establish the precise relationship between the Soviet Union and the individual republics. On 20 and 21 August, Estonia and Latvia declared for independence, and Lithuania reaffirmed its declaration of 1990. The republics of Ukraine, Belarus, Moldavia, Azerbaijan, Uzbekistan, Kirghizia, Tadzhikistan, and Armenia all followed soon after.

On 2 September, doing Gorbachev no favour, President Bush announced that the United States recognized the independence of the Baltic states. The Soviet State Council did so on 6 September. On the same day, Georgia broke all ties with the USSR. Gorbachev still hoped for a federation, like the United States, with residual powers held in the centre. But the others were against it. At most, a loose confederation of independent states now looked likely.

The Americans could tolerate this, provided they had assurances on security and the control of nuclear weapons. Who would in future carry the small suitcase with the computer in it that could launch a nuclear strike? The US Congress meanwhile voted $500 million of the defence budget to help dismantle Soviet nuclear warheads.

The Soviet republics voted to reject Gorbachev's Union Treaty; the new state would be a confederation. On 30 November, Yeltsin's Russia, the leading power in the new association, took control of the Soviet Foreign Ministry and of all its embassies abroad. On 8 December, in Minsk, Yeltsin for Russia, Leonid Kravchuk for Ukraine, and Stanislav Shushkevich for Belarus, the three Slav states, without bothering to take the other republics with them, signed a pact ending the USSR and creating instead the Commonwealth of Independent States (CIS). By telephone they told first George Bush, then Mikhail Gorbachev, what they had done. Gorbachev, humiliated, next day denied their right to have done it; but the Russian parliament ratified the commonwealth agreement, and within days all but one of the other republics joined.

James Baker, in Moscow a week later, saw both Yeltsin and Gorbachev and had it brought pointedly to his attention that the Soviet military was now backing Yeltsin and the CIS. Gorbachev, accepting a fait accompli, announced that all Soviet central structures would cease to exist at the end of the year. The four republics that possessed nuclear weapons — Russia, Ukraine, Belarus, and Kazakhstan — announced that they would abide by and implement the cuts in arms and nuclear weapons agreed to by Bush and Gorbachev.

On 25 December 1991 the Union of Soviet Socialist Republics ceased to exist. The Red flag, with its gold hammer and sickle, prophesying a worldwide workers' revolution that never came, was lowered over the Kremlin for the last time. Gorbachev had never intended this result. He resigned his now non-existent office.

State of the union? Pretty good. George Bush reports victory in the Cold War, 28 January 1992.

A Common Victory

Gorbachev telephoned his farewells to Bush at Camp David. He wished Bush and his wife, Barbara, a merry Christmas. He was, he said, still convinced that keeping the independent republics within the Soviet Union would have been the better way forward, but he hoped that the United States would co-operate instead with the CIS and would help Russia economically. The "little suitcase" carrying the nuclear button had been transferred, constitutionally, to the Russian president, Boris Yeltsin. "You may therefore feel at ease as you celebrate Christmas, and sleep quietly tonight."

Two hours later Gorbachev delivered a long, self-justifying television

I do not regard the end of the Cold War as a victory for one side. . . . The end of the Cold War is our common victory.

— Mikhail Gorbachev, January 1992

address to the citizens of the fifteen former Soviet republics. Again, he insisted that the Soviet Union could not have gone on as it was when he took office in 1985. "We had to change everything." He did.

Bush left Camp David for Washington to make his Christmas broadcast. He praised Gorbachev, announced formal diplomatic recognition of the new republics, and called on God to bless their peoples. For over forty years, he said, the United States had led the West "in the struggle against communism and the threat it posed to our most precious values. That confrontation is over."

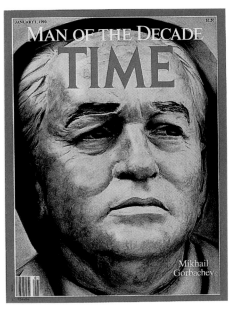

January 1990, Time's Man of the Decade; December 1991, out of a job. Mikhail Gorbachev, hailed worldwide for his role in ending the Cold War, was rejected in his native Russia.

In his State of the Union address for 1992, an election year, George Bush claimed triumphantly that the United States had "won the Cold War." Others claim the same. Gorbachev preferred to believe it was "our common victory." Certainly at the Cold War's end the United States remained the world's one great power and the Soviet Union had ceased to exist. But the United States did not achieve this end simply by facing down its enemy. Bush moved cautiously towards great power co-operation, and skilfully avoided giving the Soviet right a pretext to reverse perestroika. It was Gorbachev who made the moves in ending the arms race. He surrendered Communist rule in Eastern Europe and, however gradually, he introduced multiparty rule in the USSR itself. He failed in economic reform; Moscow shops were still empty. He could not prevent the breakup of the USSR; he could not save his own office. But he played a major role in ending the Cold War and particularly in the manner of its ending. The verdict of former State Department analyst Raymond L. Garthoff will stand: "He may not have done so alone, but what happened would not have happened without him; that cannot be said of anyone else."

What It Cost

The Cold War was a confrontation between military giants. A balance of terror preserved the world's peace. But the balance was struck at a ludicrously high and costly level; both the United States and the Soviet Union equipped themselves with thousands more nuclear missiles than were needed for self-defence, or to deter the other. Those weapons, added to conventional armaments, cost the superpowers trillions of dollars; much of this money was wasted, and could have been diverted to other social needs, though we do not know that it would have been. Each side could regard some crucial part of the cost as essential to containing the other.

In 1955 President Eisenhower, the only professional soldier among America's postwar presidents, warned, "The problem in defense spending is to figure how far you should go without destroying from within what you are

trying to defend from without." One estimate shows that some $8 trillion ($8,000,000,000,000) was spent, worldwide, on nuclear and other weapons between 1945 and 1996. At their peak, the world's nuclear stockpiles held 18 billion metric tons of explosive energy: 18 megatons. Today, they still hold 8 megatons. Compare these totals with the entire explosive energy released by all bombs dropped in the Second World War (6 megatons); in the Korean War (0.8 megaton); in Vietnam (4.1 megatons).

Total Soviet expenditure during the Cold War is hard to quantify; records are inadequate. But Eduard Shevardnadze reckoned that perhaps as much as 50 per cent of Soviet national product was spent on defence, on arms and the armed forces, depriving the Soviet people of a better life.

In the United States, according to government figures, expenditure on national defence, which had peaked as a proportion of gross domestic product during the Second World War at nearly 40 per cent, ran at over 10 per cent in the 1950s, 9 per cent in the 1960s, and declined to around 5 per cent in the 1970s, the years of détente. It rose steeply again, however, in the 1980s to over 6 per cent. And in real terms it ran at $400 billion annually, in 1996 dollars, during Korea, Vietnam, and the second half of the 1980s, when it contributed to overall budget deficits.

The United States ended the Cold War a superpower still, with a booming economy. But the poor of the United States, and of the world, could certainly have used some of the resources committed to Cold War armaments, if gov-

If walls could speak. ABOVE: *A memorial to Ida Siekmann, who was killed at the Berlin Wall, 22 August 1961. Windows overlooking West Berlin were bricked up to prevent escapes to the West.* ABOVE LEFT: *The most touching war memorial — the names of more than fifty-eight thousand US servicemen and women who died in Vietnam. No wall would have been big enough to commemorate the victims of a nuclear holocaust.*

ernment had so willed it. Martin Luther King, Jr., complained that Lyndon Johnson's promise of a Great Society was lost on the battlefields of Vietnam.

A continuing cost will be that for cleaning up weapons-related nuclear pollution. Estimates of what this will cost in the United States range from $100 billion to $400 billion. In Russia and the old USSR, the problem is intractable; they simply will not be able to deal with it.

Above and beyond the dollar cost is the cost in human lives. Though a nuclear catastrophe was averted by the balance of terror, the Cold War's shoot-

Moscow, August 1991.
Parading the Russian tricolour
in mourning for those who
died during the failed coup.

ing wars did take their toll in death: millions in Korea, in Vietnam, and in Afghanistan; hundreds of thousands in Angola; tens of thousands in Nicaragua, El Salvador, and Ethiopia; thousands in Hungary and Romania. Civilians accounted for more deaths than soldiers in uniform. Men and women died attempting to cross the Berlin Wall; strikers were shot in Poland; protesters were crushed by Soviet tanks in Prague; rebels were killed in Budapest; worshippers were gunned down on cathedral steps in San Salvador. Some of the wars people perished in, post-colonial struggles, would have happened anyway. But the Cold War made each local conflict it touched even more deadly. Covert actions by intelligence services killed tens of thousands more.

The Cold War stifled thought; for decades the peoples of Eastern Europe, living under a tyranny, were, someone said, "buried alive" — cut off from and, as they felt, abandoned by the West. When the chance came, Germans, Czechs and Slovaks, Poles, Hungarians, Romanians, and Bulgarians all rejected communism. So too did the peoples of the Americas; in Nicaragua the Sandinistas held free elections and lost them. Given the choice, people chose democracy. Only Fidel Castro in Cuba, the great Cold War survivor, kept the Red flag flying and the cause of socialist revolution alive.

China is the great question mark of the twenty-first century: what will China do? The world's most populous nation is still ruled by a Communist autocracy, though no longer along Marxist-Leninist lines. Will China succeed in reconciling Communist ideology with a free market? Will the Communist Party monopoly of power be broken there also?

A Safer World

Although no new world order is in place, the world is far safer for the Cold War's ending, despite continual outbreaks of ethnic slaughter. It is hard now to realize or recall it, but whole generations in our time lived with the fear that one crisis or another — in Korea, Vietnam, Berlin, Cuba, the Middle East — might trigger a nuclear holocaust, as the two great power blocs clumsily breathed defiance, dug their heels in, took stances, refused to yield. The world too often went to the brink.

And always, more omnipresent than we ever realized, was the chance of nuclear accident. More than once, as we know now, we came close. Fear was routine, endemic. Children who grew up in the fifties and sixties remember the air-raid shelter and the precautionary drills — "Duck and Cover." Chernobyl revealed how inadequate such precautions would have been. Parents in many countries remember that when the world news grew grimmer, they looked at their children and at each other and hoped they would all live to see another day. That fear has been lifted from us.

The balance of terror worked because, when it counted, those in command, on both sides, put humanity's interests higher than short-term national, political, or strategic advantage. But although they might have known what they were doing in any crisis, we, at the time, were unsure of the outcome.

For forty-five years the peoples of the world held their breath, and survived.

It's all over; happy faces at the Berlin Wall mark the Cold War's ending. Humanity has survived.

General

Cold War, A Television History, Essays. John Lewis Gaddis; Vladislav Zubok; Lawrence Freedman; John Lloyd; Neal Ascherson. JIP: Unpublished, 1995.

John Lewis Gaddis, *We Now Know: Rethinking Cold War History.* Oxford University Press, 1997.

James G. Hershberg (ed.), *Bulletins of the Cold War International History Project,* 1991–present.

Martin Walker, *The Cold War.* Fourth Estate, 1993.

Vladislav Zubok and Constantine Pleshakov, *Inside the Kremlin's Cold War: From Stalin to Khrushchev.* Harvard University Press, 1996.

Comrades

John Lewis Gaddis, *The United States and the Origins of the Cold War, 1941–47.* Columbia University Press, 1972.

Alonzo L. Hamby, *Man of the People: A Life of Harry S. Truman.* Oxford University Press, 1995.

Melvyn P. Leffler, *A Preponderance of Power: National Security, the Truman Administration, and the Cold War.* Stanford University Press, 1992.

Charles L. Mee, *Meeting at Potsdam.* Deutsch, 1975.

Richard Rhodes, *The Making of the Atom Bomb.* Simon and Schuster, 1986.

Dmitri Volkogonov, *Stalin: Triumph and Tragedy* (ed. and trans. Harold Shukman). Free Press, 1994.

Daniel Yergin, *Shattered Peace: The Origins of the Cold War.* Penguin, 1990.

Iron Curtain

Dean Acheson, *Present at the Creation: My Years at the State Department.* Norton, 1969.

Noel Annan, *Changing Enemies: The Defeat and Regeneration of Germany.* HarperCollins, 1995.

Neal Ascherson, *The Struggles for Poland.* Random House, 1987.

John Lewis Gaddis, *Strategies of Containment: A Critical Appraisal of Postwar American Security Policy.* Oxford University Press, 1982.

George F. Kennan, *Memoirs: 1925–50.* Little, Brown, 1967.

Melvyn P. Leffler and David S. Painter (eds.), *Origins of the Cold War: An International History.* Routledge, 1994.

David Reynolds (ed.), *The Origins of the Cold War in Europe: International Perspectives.* Yale University Press, 1994.

Hugh Thomas, *Armed Truce: The Beginnings of the Cold War, 1945–46.* Sceptre, 1988.

Marshall Plan

Alec Cairncross, *Economic Ideas and Government Policy.* Routledge, 1996.

David Ellwood, *Rebuilding Europe: Western Europe, America, and Postwar Reconstruction.* Longman, 1992.

Michael J. Hogan, *The Marshall Plan: America, Britain, and the Reconstruction of Europe, 1947–52.* Cambridge University Press, 1947.

Alan Milward, *The Reconstruction of Western Europe, 1945–51.* University of California Press, 1984.

Berlin

Beatrice Heuser, *Western "Containment" Policies in the Cold War: The Yugoslav Case, 1948–53.* Routledge, 1989.

Avi Shlaim, *The United States and the Berlin Blockade.* University of California Press, 1983.

Ann and John Tusa, *The Berlin Blockade.* Hodder and Stoughton, 1988.

Korea

Rosemary Foot, *The Wrong War: American Policy and the Dimensions of the Korean Conflict, 1950–53.* Cornell University Press, 1985.

Max Hastings, *The Korean War.* Michael Joseph, 1987.

Chen Jian, *China's Road to the Korean War: The Making of the Sino-American Confrontation.* Columbia University Press, 1994.

David Rees, *Korea, the Limited War.* Macmillan, 1964.

Shu Guang Zhang, *Mao's Military Romanticism: China and the Korean War, 1950–53.* University Press of Kansas, 1995.

Reds

Jonathan Aitken, *Nixon: A Life.* Weidenfeld and Nicolson, 1993.

Piers Brendon, *Ike: His Life and Times.* Harper Row, 1986.

David Caute, *The Great Fear.* Secker and Warburg, 1978.

Anthony Summers, *Official and Confidential: The Secret Life of J. Edgar Hoover*. Victor Gollancz, 1993.

Evan Thomas, *The Very Best Men: Four Who Dared*. Simon and Schuster, 1995.

After Stalin

Stephen E. Ambrose, *Eisenhower: The President*. Simon and Schuster, 1984.

Sergei Khrushchev, *Khrushchev on Khrushchev* (ed. and trans. William Taubman). Little, Brown, 1990.

Sputnik and the Bomb

Robert A. Divine, *The Sputnik Challenge: Eisenhower's Response to the Soviet Satellite*. Oxford University Press, 1993.

David Holloway, *Stalin and the Bomb*. Yale University Press, 1994.

Chris Pocock, *Dragon Lady: The History of the U-2 Spy Plane*. Airlife, 1989.

The Wall

Henrik Bering, *Outpost Berlin: The History of the American Military Forces in Berlin, 1945–1994*. Edition Q, 1995.

Michael R. Beschloss, *The Crisis Years: Kennedy and Khrushchev, 1960–63*. HarperCollins, 1991.

Norman Gelb, *The Berlin Wall: Kennedy, Khrushchev and a Showdown in the Heart of Europe*. Simon and Schuster, 1986.

Ann Tusa, *The Last Division: Berlin and the Wall*. Hodder and Stoughton, 1996.

Peter Wyden, *Wall: The Inside Story of Divided Berlin*. Simon and Schuster, 1989.

Back Yard: Guatemala and Cuba

Anatoly Dobrynin, *In Confidence*. Times Books, 1995.

Aleksandr Fursenko and Timothy Naftali, *"One Hell of a Gamble": Khrushchev, Castro, and Kennedy, 1958–64*. Norton, 1997.

Piero Gleijeses, *Shattered Hope: The Guatemalan Revolution and the United States, 1944–54*. Princeton University Press, 1991.

Richard Ned Lebow and Janice Gross Stein, *We All Lost the Cold War*. Princeton University Press, 1994.

Robert Smith Thompson, *The Missiles of October*. Simon and Schuster, 1992.

Vietnam

Philip Caputo, *A Rumor of War*. Random House, 1977.

Stanley Karnow, *Vietnam: A History*. Viking Press, 1983.

Robert S. McNamara, *In Retrospect: The Tragedy and Lessons of Vietnam*. Random House, 1995.

The Pentagon Papers. Bantam, 1971.

Neil Sheehan, *A Bright Shining Lie*. Jonathan Cape, 1989.

MAD

Zhores A. Medvedev, *Nuclear Disaster in the Urals* (trans. George Saunders). Angus and Robertson, 1979.

Richard Rhodes, *Dark Sun: The Making of the Hydrogen Bomb*. Simon and Schuster, 1995.

Scott D. Sagan, *The Limits of Safety: Organizations, Accidents, and Nuclear Weapons*. Princeton University Press, 1993.

Culture Wars

Stephen Ambrose and James Alden Barber, Jr. (eds.), *The Military and American Society*. Free Press, 1972.

Terry H. Anderson, *The Movement and the Sixties: Protest in America from Greensboro to Wounded Knee*. Oxford University Press, 1995.

David Caute, *Sixty-Eight*. Hamish Hamilton, 1980.

Karen Dawisha, *The Kremlin and the Prague Spring*. University of California, 1984.

Lloyd C. Gardner, *Pay Any Price: Lyndon Johnson and the Wars of Vietnam*. Ivan R. Dee, 1995.

Doris Kearns, *Lyndon Johnson and the American Dream*. Andre Deutsch 1976.

Nikita Khrushchev, *Khrushchev Remembers* (ed. and trans. Strobe Talbott). Little, Brown, 1970.

Norman Mailer, *Miami and the Siege of Chicago*. Weidenfeld and Nicolson, 1968.

R. Remington (ed.), *Winter in Prague*. MIT Press, 1969.

Détente

Raymond L. Garthoff, *Détente and Confrontation: American-Soviet Relations from Nixon to Reagan* (rev. ed.). Brookings Institution, 1994.

Seymour Hersh, *The Price of Power: Kissinger in the Nixon White House.* Simon and Schuster, 1983.

Walter Isaacson, *Kissinger: A Biography.* Faber and Faber, 1992.

Henry Kissinger, *White House Years.* Little, Brown, 1979.

Harrison Salisbury, *The New Emperors: China in the Era of Mao and Deng.* Little, Brown, 1992.

Frank Snepp, *Decent Interval.* Random House, 1977.

Surrogates

Georgi Arbatov, *The System: An Insider's Life in Soviet Politics.* Times Books, 1992.

Mike Bowker and Paul Williams, *Superpower Détente: A Reappraisal.* Royal Institute of International Affairs, 1988.

Richard Crockatt, *The Fifty-Years' War: The United States and the Soviet Union in World Politics, 1941–1991.* Routledge, 1995.

Paul B. Henze, *The Horn of Africa: From War to Peace.* St. Martin's, 1991.

Kissinger, Henry, *Years of Upheaval.* Little, Brown, 1982.

Anthony Mockler, *The New Mercenaries: The History of the Mercenary from the Congo to the Seychelles.* Sidgwick and Jackson, 1985.

Howard M. Sachar, *A History of Israel: From the Rise of Zionism to Our Time.* Knopf, 1979.

Avi Shlaim, *War and Peace in the Middle East.* Penguin, 1995.

John Stockwell, *In Search of Enemies: A CIA Story.* Norton, 1978.

T. E. Vadney, *The World Since 1945* (2nd ed.). Penguin, 1992.

Freeze

Christopher Andrew and Oleg Gordievsky, *KGB: The Inside Story of Its Foreign Operations from Lenin to Gorbachev.* HarperCollins, 1990.

Timothy Garton Ash, *The Polish Revolution.* Granta, 1991.

Peter G. Bourne, *Jimmy Carter: A Comprehensive Biography from Plains to Postpresidency.* Scribner's, 1997.

Diego Cordovez and Selig S. Harrison, *Out of Afghanistan: The Inside Story of the Soviet Withdrawal.* Oxford University Press, 1995.

Jonathan Steele, *The Limits of Soviet Power: The Kremlin's Foreign Policy, Brezhnev to Chernenko.* Simon and Schuster, 1984.

Reagan

Lou Cannon, *President Reagan: The Role of a Lifetime.* Simon and Schuster, 1991.

Raymond L. Garthoff, *The Great Transition: American-Soviet Relations and the End of the Cold War.* Brookings Institution, 1994.

Seymour Hersh, *"The Target Is Destroyed": What Really Happened to Flight 007.* Faber and Faber, 1986.

R. W. Johnson, *Shootdown: The Verdict on KAL 007.* Chatto and Windus, 1986.

Anthony Lake, *Somoza Falling: A Case Study of Washington at Work.* University of Massachusetts Press, 1989.

Gorbachev

Archie Brown, *The Gorbachev Factor.* Oxford University Press, 1996.

Mikhail Gorbachev, *Memoirs.* Doubleday, 1996.

Angus Roxburgh, *The Second Russian Revolution.* BBC Books, 1991.

People Power

Timothy Garton Ash, *The Magic Lantern: The Revolution of '89 Witnessed in Warsaw, Budapest, Berlin, and Prague.* Random House, 1990.

John Lewis Gaddis, *The United States and the End of the Cold War: Implications, Reconsiderations, Provocations.* Oxford University Press, 1992.

Endings

Michael R. Beschloss and Strobe Talbott, *At the Highest Levels: The Inside Story of the End of the Cold War.* Little, Brown, 1993.

Raisa Gorbachev, *I Hope* (trans. David Floyd). HarperCollins, 1991.

Pavel Palazchenko, *My Years with Gorbachev and Shevardnadze: The Memoirs of a Soviet Interpreter.* Pennsylvania State University Press, 1997.

David Remnick, *Lenin's Tomb: The Last Days of the Soviet Empire.* Random House, 1993.

Picture Credits

The publishers have made every effort to contact the owners of illustrations used in this book. If they have been unsuccessful, they invite the copyright holders to contact them direct.

ABBREVIATIONS

T	= Top	C	= Centre
B	= Bottom	R	= Right
L	= Left		

SSEES = School of Slavonic and Eastern European Studies, London University

Front Matter
Camera Press, London.

Comrades
2: Hulton Getty. 3: Camera Press, London. 4: Novosti. 5: Hulton Getty. 6: Novosti. 7L: Corbis-Bettmann/UPI; R: Popperfoto. 8L: Peter Newark's Military Pictures; R: Corbis-Bettmann/UPI. 9L: Peter Newark's Military Pictures; R: David Low, *Evening Standard*/Centre for the Study of Cartoons and Caricature, University of Kent, Canterbury. 10L: Camera Press, London; R: Novosti. 11L: David King Collection; TR: Camera Press, London; BR: Imperial War Museum, London. 12: Master and Fellows of Churchill College, Cambridge. 13: E.T. Archive/Imperial War Museum, London. 14–15: Yevegnny Khaldei/Camera Press, London. 16L: Corbis-Bettmann/UPI; R: Popperfoto. 17: Popperfoto. 18T: Popperfoto; B: Hulton Getty. 19: Harry S. Truman Library. 20L: Popperfoto; R: Corbis-Bettmann. 21L: Hulton Getty; R: E.T. Archive.

Iron Curtain
22: Corbis-Bettmann/UPI. 23: Hulton Getty. 24T: Peter Newark's Military Pictures; B: Corbis-Bettmann/UPI. 25L: Novosti; R: Popperfoto. 26L: Hulton Getty; R: Popperfoto. 27: Corbis-Bettmann/UPI. 28L: Popperfoto; R: Robert Capa/Magnum Photos. 30L: Corbis-Bettmann/UPI. R: Harry S. Truman Library. 31L: David King Collection; R: Popperfoto. 32–33: Popperfoto. 34L: Corbis-Bettmann/UPI; 34–35: Camera Press, London; 35R: Hulton Getty/Frederick Gamage. 36L: Popperfoto. 37: Corbis-Bettmann. 38TL, BL: Corbis-Bettmann/UPI; 38–39: Lustige Blatter; 39R: Popperfoto. 40L: Popperfoto; R: Imperial War Museum, London. 41L: Imperial War Museum, London; R: Corbis-Bettmann/UPI.

Marshall Plan
42: Corbis-Bettmann/UPI. 43: Popperfoto. 44L: *Krokodil*, SSEES; R: Corbis-Bettmann/UPI. 45L: Fitzpatrick/Colliers Magazine; R: Hulton Getty. 46: George C. Marshall Research Library. 47: Popperfoto. 48–49: Corbis-Bettmann/UPI. 50: Corbis-Bettmann/UPI. 51: Hulton Getty. 52L: Hulton/Haywood Magee; R: Fitzpatrick/*St. Louis Post-Dispatch*/Peter Newark's Military Pictures. 53L: *Krokodil*, SSEES; R: Popperfoto. 54: Agence France Press. 55: *Krokodil*, SSEES. 56L: Popperfoto; R: Camera Press, London. 57: AKG. 58: Private Collection. 59: Popperfoto. 61T: Popperfoto; B: National Archives, Washington.

Berlin
62–63: Popperfoto. 64: Corbis-Bettmann/UPI; 64–65: Hulton Getty; 65: Corbis-Bettmann/UPI.

66T: Popperfoto; B: Corbis-Bettmann/UPI; 66–67: Popperfoto. 68L: Private Collection; R: Imperial War Museum, London. 69: Fitzpatrick/*St. Louis Post-Dispatch*/Peter Newark's Military Pictures. 70L: Corbis-Bettmann/UPI; R: Popperfoto; B: AKG. 71: Hulton Getty. 72: Popperfoto. 73L: Hulton Getty; R: Corbis-Bettmann/UPI. 74: Popperfoto. 75T: Popperfoto; B: *Krokodil*, SSEES. 76–77: AKG. 78L: Private Collection; R: Landesbildstelle. 79L: Popperfoto; R: Private Collection. 80L: Corbis-Bettmann/UPI; R: NATO. 81: Popperfoto.

Korea
82: Sovfoto. 83: Hulton Getty. 84: Corbis-Bettmann/UPI. 85: Camera Press, London. 86: *Krokodil*, SSEES. 87L: David King Collection; R: Sovfoto. 88L: Corbis-Bettmann/UPI; R: *Krokodil*, SSEES. 89: E.T. Archive. 90: Popperfoto. 91: Yonhap/Camera Press, London. 92–93: Hulton Getty. 94: Camera Press, London. 95L: *Krokodil*, SSEES; R: Popperfoto. 96: Xinhua/Eastfoto. 97L: Camera Press, London; R: Popperfoto. 98–99: Corbis-Bettmann/UPI. 100L: Corbis-Bettmann/UPI; R: Hulton Getty. 102–103: Popperfoto. 104T: New China Pictures/Eastfoto; B: Sovfoto. 105L: Camera Press, London; R: Hulton Getty.

Reds
106: Elliott Erwitt/Magnum Photos. 107: Corbis-Bettmann/UPI. 108: Popperfoto. 110–111: Corbis-Bettmann/UPI. 112T: Hoover Institution Archives/International News Soundphoto; B: Corbis-Bettmann. 114: 20th Century Fox/Kobal Collection. 115L: Camera Press, London; R: Popperfoto. 116–117: David King Collection; 116B: Advertising Archives; 117R: Popperfoto. 118T: Associated Press; B: Kratky Films. 119L: David King Collection; B: Popperfoto. 120: Popperfoto. 121T: *Krokodil*, SSEES; B: Hulton Getty. 122: United Artists/Ronald Grant Collection. 123T: United Artists/British Film Institute; C: Universal/British Film Institute; B: MGM/British Film Institute.

After Stalin
124: Hulton Getty. 125: Novosti. 127L: Popperfoto; TR: Corbis-Bettmann/UPI; BR: Popperfoto. 128: Archiv der Sozialen Demokratie. 129T: Herblock Cartoons; B: Hulton Getty. 130–131: Popperfoto. 132T: Popperfoto; C: David King Collection; B: Associated Press. 133: Popperfoto. 134–135: Popperfoto. 136L: Popperfoto; 136–137: Hulton Getty; 137R: Hungarian Press Agency. 138–139: Popperfoto; 139R: John Frost Historical Newspapers. 140–141: Hulton Getty. 142: Hulton Getty. 143: Corbis-Bettmann/UPI.

Sputnik and the Bomb
144: Collection Jamie Doran. 145: Hulton Getty. 146: Novosti; 146–147: John Frost Historical Newspapers; 147: Corbis-Bettmann. 148T, B: Corbis-Bettmann/UPI; 148–149: Popperfoto. 150–151: Corbis-Bettmann/UPI. 152–153: Popperfoto. 154L: Camera Press, London; TR: *Krokodil*, SSEES; BR: Novosti. 155L: Novosti; R: Corbis-Bettmann/UPI. 156L: MGN Ltd; R: Corbis-Bettmann/UPI. 157: Salamander Picture Library. 158TL: Corbis-Bettmann; TR: David King Collection; CL: Edward Santalone; CR: Popperfoto.

159: Popperfoto. 160L: Novosti; 160-161: Corbis-Bettmann/UPI; 161T: Carl Mydans/Life Magazine © Time Inc./Katz; B: Novosti. 162: Novosti. 163L: Camera Press; R: Novosti.

The Wall

164: Camera Press, London. 165: Popperfoto. 166TL, TR: Popperfoto; B: Camera Press, London. 166-167: Camera Press, London. 168-169: Popperfoto. 170: Popperfoto. 171L: Corbis-Bettmann; R: Carl Purcell/Camera Press, London. 172: Popperfoto. 173TL, TR: Camera Press, London; B: Joseph Parrish/*Chicago Tribune*. 174: Novosti. 175L: Popperfoto; R: Camera Press, London. 176-177: AKG. 178T: AKG; B: Camera Press, London. 179L: Wolfgang Bera; R: AKG. 180: Popperfoto. 181L: Hulton Getty; R: AKG. 182: Popperfoto. 183: AKG.

Back Yard: Guatemala and Cuba

184: Popperfoto. 185: Popperfoto. 186L: Popperfoto; TR: Corbis-Bettmann/UPI; BR: Associated Press. 187L: Richter Library, University of Miami; R: Corbis-Bettmann. 188L: Hulton Getty; R: Popperfoto. 189L: Kukryniksky/Pravda; R: Popperfoto. 190-191: Corbis-Bettmann/UPI. 191TL: Corbis-Bettmann/UPI; TR: National Archives. 192: AP Newsfeatures. 193: Corbis-Bettmann/UPI. 195L: John Frost Historical Newspapers; R: Hulton Getty. 196-197: Hulton Getty. 198T: Popperfoto; B: Hulton Getty. 199: Corbis-Bettmann/UPI. 200L: Popperfoto; 200-201: Corbis-Bettmann/UPI. 202: John Frost Historical Newspapers. 203T: Hulton Getty; B: Novosti.

Vietnam

204: Corbis-Bettmann/UPI. 205: Camera Press, London. 206: Camera Press, London. 207: Popperfoto. 208: Hulton Getty. 209: Hulton Getty. 210: Cornell Capa/Magnum Photos. 211: Corbis-Bettmann/UPI. 212T: Corbis-Bettmann/UPI; B: Hulton Getty. 213T: Hulton Getty; B: Corbis-Bettmann/UPI. 214-215: Carl Mydans/Life Magazine © Time Inc./Katz. 216: Hulton Getty. 217: David King Collection. 218T: Corbis-Bettmann/UPI; B: James Pickerell/Camera Press, London. 219TL: Novosti; TR: Richard Gott/Camera Press, London; B: Philip Jones-Griffiths/Magnum Photos. 220-221: Yoichi R. Okamoto/LBJ Library Collection. 222: Max Sheler/Camera Press, London. 223T: Bruno Barbey/Magnum Photos; B: Tim Page. 224-225: Corbis-Bettmann/UPI; 225: Larry Burrows/Life Magazine © Time Inc./Katz. 226L: Popperfoto; R: Philip Jones-Griffiths/Magnum Photos. 227: Corbis-Bettmann/UPI. 228: *Krokodil*, SSEES. 229L: Hulton Getty; R: Corbis-Bettmann/UPI.

MAD

230: Popperfoto. 231: Corbis-Bettmann/UPI. 232L: Corbis-Bettmann/UPI; R: Ron Cobb/*Los Angeles Free Press*. 233: Novosti. 234-235: Popperfoto; 236-237: Popperfoto; 237T: British Museum. 238: Camera Press, London. 239L: Corbis-Bettmann/UPI; R: Popperfoto. 240: Popperfoto. 241: Camera Press, London. 242: Hawk Films/Columbia/Kobal Collection. 243T: AKG; B: Hulton Getty. 244: *Krokodil*/SSEES. 245: Rex Features.

Culture Wars

246: Associated Press. 247: Cornell Capa/Magnum Photos. 248: Camera Press, London. 249TL: Advertising Archives; BL, R: Corbis-Bettmann/UPI. 250L: Hulton Getty; R: Corbis-Bettmann/UPI. 251: Corbis-Bettmann/UPI. 252-253: Popperfoto. 254T: David King Collection; B: British Museum. 255T: Paul Conklin/Time Magazine © Time Inc./Katz; B: Corbis-Bettmann/UPI. 256TL: Hulton Getty; BL: Popperfoto; R: Corbis-Bettmann/UPI. 257L: Popperfoto; TR: Corbis-Bettmann/UPI; BR: Rex Features. 258: Taylor Downing. 259: Hulton Getty. 260-261: Novosti; 261B: Popperfoto. 262L: Popperfoto; 262-263: Novosti. 264L: Czech News Agency; R: Hulton Getty. 265: Czech News Agency. 267: Czech News Agency. 268T, C, B: Image Diggers. 269T: Associated Press; C: Camera Press, London; BL: Associated Press; BR: Image Diggers.

Détente

270: Corbis-Bettmann/UPI. 271: Hulton Getty. 272: Novosti. 273L: Hulton Getty; R: Nixon Presidential Archives. 274T: Corbis-Bettmann/UPI; B: Howard Ruffner/Life Magazine © Time Inc./Katz. 275L: Corbis-Bettmann/UPI; R: David King Collection. 276-277: Corbis-Bettmann/UPI. 278-279: Popperfoto. 280: Hulton Getty; 280-281: Rex Features; 281: Camera Press, London. 282: Popperfoto. 283: Popperfoto. 284-285: AKG. 286T: Hulton Getty; B: Corbis-Bettmann/UPI. 287: Nixon Presidential Archives. 288: Corbis-Bettmann/UPI. 289L, R: AKG.

Surrogates

290: Gamma/Frank Spooner Pictures. 291: Camera Press, London. 292: Popperfoto; 292-293: Corbis-Bettmann/UPI. 294-295: Popperfoto. 296: Corbis-Bettmann; 296-297: Corbis-Bettmann/UPI; 297B: Philip Jones-Griffiths/Magnum Photos. 298: Micha Bar-Am/Magnum Photos. 299: Corbis-Bettmann/UPI. 300: Contact Press/Colorific. 300-301: Christian Belpaire/Camera Press, London; 301T: Lynn Pelham/Camera Press, London; B: Corbis-Bettmann/UPI. 302-303: M. Piquemal/France Match/Camera Press; 303L, R: Corbis-Bettmann/UPI. 304: Salamander Picture Library. 305: Gamma/Frank Spooner Pictures. 306L: Gamma/Frank Spooner Pictures; R: Y. G. Berges/Sygma. 307: Gamma/Frank Spooner Pictures. 308: Rene Lefort/Gamma/Frank Spooner Pictures; 308-309: Gamma/Frank Spooner Pictures; 309: Gamma/Frank Spooner Pictures.

Freeze

310: Sichov/Sipa Press/Rex Features. 311: David Burnett/Colorific. 312: Corbis-Bettmann/UPI. 313L: Marc Boulet/Sipa Press/Rex Features; R: Georgi Mikhailov/Sipa Press/Rex Features. 314-315: Corbis-Bettmann/UPI. 316-317: Corbis-Bettmann/UPI; 316B: Salamander Picture Library; 317R: Rex Features. 318L: General Dynamics/TRH Pictures; 318-319: Sipa Press/Rex Features; 319B: Gilbert Uzan/Gamma/Frank Spooner Pictures. 320: Corbis-Bettmann/UPI. 321: Frank Spooner Pictures. 322-323: Gianfranco Gorgoni/Contact/Colorific; 323T: Reza/Sipa Press/Rex Features. 324L: Sipa Press/Rex Features; R: Gamma/Frank Spooner Pictures. 325L: Gianfranco Gorgoni/Contact/Colorific; TR: Corbis-Bettmann/UPI; BR: Dilip Mehta/Contact/Colorific. 326L: Gamma/Frank Spooner Pictures; 326-327: Gamma/Frank Spooner Pictures; 327R: Borrel/Sipa Press/Rex Features. 329T: Gianfranco Gorgoni/Contact/Colorific. B: Society for Co-operation in Russian and Soviet Studies. 330L: Apesteguy-Bulka/Gamma/Frank Spooner Pictures; R: Flochon/Gamma/Frank Spooner Pictures. 351: Czar/Gamma/Frank Spooner Pictures.

Reagan

322: Corbis-Bettmann/UPI. 333: Corbis-Bettmann/UPI. 334: Gamma/Frank Spooner Pictures. 335TL: Popperfoto; BL: Emilio Rodrigues/Gamma/Frank Spooner Pictures; R: Jacques Goffinon/Gamma/Frank Spooner Pictures. 336: Gamma/Frank Spooner Pictures. 337: Gamma/Frank Spooner Pictures. 338-339: Roland Neveu/Gamma/Frank Spooner Pictures. 340: Chip Hires/Gamma/Frank Spooner Pictures. 341TL: Shamin Ur Rahman/Frank Spooner Pictures; TR: Corbis-Bettmann/UPI; B: Paul Conklin/Colorific. 342: Paul Conrad/*Los Angeles Times*. 343: Novosti. 344: Corbis-Bettmann/UPI. 345T: K. Edmondson/Frank Spooner Pictures; B: Corbis-Bettmann/UPI. 346L, R: Yonhap/Camera Press, London. 347L, R: TRH Pictures. 348: Salamander Picture Library. 349: Deville/Frank Spooner Pictures; R: Alain Morvan/Frank Spooner Pictures. 350: Novosti. 351: Colorific. 352T, B: Associated Press. 353T: Popperfoto; B: Associated Press.

Gorbachev

354: Corbis-Bettmann/UPI. 355: Novosti. 356-357: Novosti. 358-359: Ferry/Liaison/Frank Spooner Pictures; 359: Contact/Colorific. 360-361: Fackelman/Camera Press, London. 362: Shone/Zoufarov/Gamma/Frank Spooner Pictures. 363: Lehtikuva/Colorific. 364: Chris Gregory/Frank Spooner Pictures. 365: Novosti. 366: Corbis-Bettmann/UPI; 366-367: Novosti; 367: Brad Markel/Gamma/Frank Spooner Pictures. 368: Ricki Rosen/Colorific; 368-369: Corbis-Bettmann/UPI. 370: Du Clos/Guichard/Gduyer/Gamma/Frank Spooner Pictures. 371: Corbis-Bettmann/UPI. 372-373: Corbis-Bettmann/UPI.

People Power

374: Eric Bouvet/Gamma/Frank Spooner Pictures. 375: Corbis-Bettmann/UPI. 376L: Gamma/Frank Spooner Pictures; 376-377: Gamma/Frank Spooner Pictures; 377 TR, BR: Shone/Gamma/Frank Spooner Pictures. 378: Xinhua/Gamma/Frank Spooner Pictures. 379L: Chip Hires/Gamma/Frank Spooner Pictures. R: Eric Bouvet/Gamma/Frank Spooner Pictures. 380: O'Driscoll/Gamma/Frank Spooner Pictures. 381TL: Chip Hires/Gamma/Frank Spooner Pictures; BL: David Turnley/*Detroit Free Press*/Black Star/Colorific; R: KOK/Gamma/Frank Spooner Pictures. 382L: David Turnley/*Detroit Free Press*/Black Star/Colorific; R: Contrast/Gamma/Frank Spooner Pictures. 383L: Piel/Gamma/Frank Spooner Pictures; R: Gamma/Frank Spooner Pictures. 384-385: P. Guerrini/Liaison/Gamma/Frank Spooner Pictures. 386L: Gamma/Frank Spooner Pictures; R: Peter Turnley/

Black Star/Colorific. 387L: *Detroit Free Press*/ Black Star/Colorific; R: Merillon/Gamma/Frank Spooner Pictures. 388–389: Eric Bouvet/ Merillon/Gamma/Frank Spooner Pictures. 390L: Piel/Gamma/Frank Spooner Pictures; R: Merillon/ Gamma/Frank Spooner Pictures. 391L: David Turnley/*Detroit Free Press*/Colorific; R: Camera Press. 392L: Eric Bouvet/Merillon/Gamma/Frank Spooner Pictures; 392–393: David Turnley/*Detroit Free Press*/Colorific. 395T: Chip Hires/Gamma/ Frank Spooner Pictures; B: Chip Hires/V. Shone/ Gamma/Frank Spooner Pictures. 396L: Gamma/ Frank Spooner Pictures; R: Peter Turnley/Black Star/Colorific. 397: David Turnley/Black Star/Colorific.

Endings

398: Shone/Blanche/Gamma/Frank Spooner Pictures. 399: Contrast/Katz. 400L: Osvald/Gamma/ Frank Spooner Pictures; R: Azer/Gamma/Frank Spooner Pictures. 401L: Heikki Saukkoma/Katz; R: Novosti. 402: Erma/Camera Press, London; 402–403: Gamma/Frank Spooner Pictures; 403: Grytsyuk/Soja/Gamma/Frank Spooner Pictures. 404–405: DPA/Camera Press, London. 406L: Tass/ Camera Press, London; TR: Van der Stockt/ Gamma/Frank Spooner Pictures; BR: Gilles Saussier/Gamma/Frank Spooner Pictures. 407L: Stephen Ferry/Gamma/Frank Spooner Pictures; R: Novosti. 408–409: Stephen Ferry/Gamma/Frank Spooner Pictures. 410T: Corbis-Bettmann/Reuter; B: Blanche/Gamma/Frank Spooner Pictures. 411: Shone/Gamma/Frank Spooner Pictures. 412: Tom Stoddart/Katz. 413: Gamma/Frank Spooner Pictures. 414L: Roberta Koch/Contrast/Katz; R: Markel/Liaison/Gamma/Frank Spooner Pictures; 414–415: Gamma/Frank Spooner Pictures; 415: URSS/Gamma/Frank Spooner Pictures. 416L: Tass/ Camera Press, London; R: Shone/Gamma/Frank Spooner Pictures. 417: Markel/Liaison/Gamma/ Frank Spooner Pictures. 418L: Peter Turnley/Black Star/Colorific; R: © Time Inc./Katz. 419L: Bresse/ Liaison/Gamma/Frank Spooner Pictures; R: Gert Schütz/AKG. 420: Klaus Reisinger/Black Star/ Colorific. 421: Erma/Camera Press, London. 422: Camera Press, London.

Television Acknowledgements

The authors thank the television series production team:

Nini Aldridge, Neal Ascherson, Laurence Aston, Rosalind Bain, Martina Balazova, Olivia Baldwin, James Barker, Robin Barnwell, Steve Bergson, Thomas Blanton, Shelagh Brady, Lee Brooks Rivera, William Burr, David Boardman, Milica Budimir, Ian Buruma, Neil Cameron, Kate Clark, Tessa Coombs, Mary Currie, Carl Davis, Andrew Denny, Alexander Dunlop, Peter Eason, Mark Frankland, Lawrence Freedman, Marilyn Freeman, John Lewis Gaddis, Jody Gottlieb, Germaine Greer, Stephen Hallett, Cate Haste, Max Hastings, Jim Hershberg, Beatrice Heuser, Isobel Hinshelwood, Cathy Houlihan, Ann Howard, Jim Howlett, Crystal Hutton, Margaret Kelly, Ken Kirby, Jerome Kuehl, Deuk-Sung Lee, Jonathan Lewis, John Lloyd, Gerald Lorenz, Alison McAllan, Aileen McAllister, Richard Melman, Pat Mitchell, Abi Moore, Brian Moser, Dunja Noack, Andrew Page, Mike Pavett, Svetlana Palmer, Ana Ransom, Hugh O'Shaughnessy, Hella Pick, Lynda Regnier, Simon Reid, Gina Sanchez, Vivian Schiller, William Shawcross, Martin Smith, Janina Stamps, Roy Stamps, Catherine Stedman, Ben Steele, Jonathan Steele, Karin Steininger, Maggie Still, Alexander Tchoubarian, David Thaxton, Mike Thomas, John Veal, Miriam Walsh, Nicola Wicks, Gillian Widdicombe, Beryl Wilkins, Trevor Wilkinson, Joe Zak, Vladislav Zubok.

Heym, Stefan, 269, 390
High Treason, 122
Hillenkoetter, Roscoe, 58
Hilsman, Roger, 210
hippies, 251–54, 256
Hirohito, emperor of Japan, 21, 84
Hiroshima bombing (1945), 20, 21, 146
Hiss, Alger, 107–12
Hitler, Adolf, 9–11, 17, 19, 31, 108, 114, 166, 292, 399
Hoare, "Mad Mike," 307
Ho Chi Minh, 205–8, 217, 225
Ho Chi Minh Trail, 207, 208, 213, 225
Hodge, John, 84
Hoffman, Paul G., 57
Hofmann, Albert, 254
Holloway, David, 147
Hollywood, 171
    allegations of Communist influence in, 108, 110–14, 122, 333
Hollywood Ten, 108, 113, 114
Holocaust, 23, 292
Honduras, 186, 335, 345
Honecker, Erich, 165, 174, 175, 283, 379–80, 386–87, 392
Hoover, J. Edgar, 109, 112, 114–15, 255
Horn, Gyula, 382
House Un-American Activities Committee (HUAC), 113–16, 269
    Hiss affair and, 107–12
    Hollywood targeted by, 108, 110–14, 122
    universities investigated by, 114–15
Houston, Lawrence, 58
human rights, 288, 289, 308, 310, 313–16, 323, 335, 359, 367, 369
Humphrey, Hubert, 219, 228, 229, 256–57
Hungarian Communist Party, 117, 137, 142
Hungarian Socialist Workers Party, 142, 386
Hungary, 43, 128, 135, 387, 420
    fall of Communist regime in, 374, 376, 380–82, 384–86, 401, 413
    Great Terror in, 116–17
    Marshall Plan and, 51
    postwar fate of, 13, 20, 26
    uprising in (1956), 124, 136–43, 266, 352, 375
Husák, Gustav, 267, 393
Hussein, Saddam, 402–3
hydrogen (H) bomb, 86, 128–29, 148–51
    accidents with, 238, 239–43
    Chinese development of, 238, 272

I

I Married a Communist, 122
imperialism, 189, 251, 300, 302
Inchon invasion (1950), 91–94
India, 40, 133, 206, 324
Indochina:
    French colonial rule in, 205–7
    see also Vietnam; Vietnam War
Indonesia, 133, 209
Institute of World Economy, 47
intercontinental ballistic missiles (ICBMs), 159, 160, 162, 230, 232–33, 236, 240, 241, 245, 316, 322, 342, 366
intermediate-range ballistic missiles (IRBMs), 159, 245
    SS-20s, 316–18, 342, 363, 368

Intermediate-Range Nuclear Forces (INF) Treaty (1987), 342, 349, 363, 366–68, 371
International Olympic Committee (IOC), 328, 329, 370
Ipcress File, The, 123
Iran, 44–45, 292, 327, 345
    hostage crisis in, 322–24, 330
    Islamic revolution in, 320, 321, 324
    Soviet troops in, 28, 30–34
Iran-Contra scandal, 345, 367
Iraq, 292, 296, 320, 358
    Persian Gulf War and, 88, 402–3, 406–10
Iron Curtain, 29
    Churchill's proclamation of, 30–31, 375
    fall of, 376
Iron Curtain, The, 114, 122
Islamic fundamentalism, 293, 320, 321, 324, 337, 370
Israel, 118, 292, 293, 316–17, 352
    Camp David agreements and, 316–17
    Lebanon invaded by (1982), 336
    October War and, 283–86, 296–99
    Six-Day War and, 243, 292–97
    Suez Crisis and, 137–39
Italian Communist Party, 25, 46, 53, 57–60
Italy, 34, 317, 329, 336, 393
    election of 1948 in, 57–60
    Marshall Plan and, 52, 53, 55, 59–61
    nuclear weapons based in, 190
    postwar fate of, 20
It Can't Happen Here, 122
ITT, 300, 302, 303
I Was a Communist for the FBI, 114

J

Jackson, Henry, 286, 289
Jackson State incident (1970), 274
James Bond movies, 123, 269
Japan, 5, 86, 255, 328, 329
    atom bombs dropped on, 20, 21, 146, 147
    Korean War and, 104–5
    occupation of, 90
    Second World War and, 11, 13, 19–21, 83, 146, 147, 150, 205, 206
Jaruzelski, Wojciech, 300, 331, 376
Jewish Anti-Fascist Committee, 120
Jews, 9, 23, 40
    Soviet, 286, 314–16, 369
    Stalinist purges and, 117–18, 120–21
Jiang Qing, 258, 319
John Paul II, Pope, 329, 393
Johnson, Lyndon B., 156, 181, 311
    arms race and, 243
    Great Society and, 213, 219, 224, 226, 249, 250, 420
    Latin America and, 300, 301
    presidency assumed by, 212
    racial discrimination and, 249, 250
    re-election bid declined by, 227, 228, 256–59
    Vietnam and, 212–29, 251, 255–59
Jordan, 292–93, 296
Justice Department, US, 109, 202

K

Kádár, János, 117, 137, 142
Kaganovich, Lazar, 143

Kahn, Herman, 242
Kalandra, Zavis, 117
Kalashnikov, Mikhail, 304
Kane, James, 4
Karmal, Babrak, 327
Kaufman, Irving R., 113
Kazakhstan, 146, 155, 260, 403
Kazan, Elia, 113
Kennan, George F., 8, 30, 58, 66, 127
    Marshall Plan and, 46, 52
Kennedy, Edward, 203
Kennedy, John F., 172–83, 249, 301, 311, 353
    arms race and, 231, 232, 237–38, 241, 248
    assassination of, 212, 214–15
    Berlin and, 173–83, 203, 209
    Cuba and, 188–203, 208, 209, 212, 232, 238
    Khrushchev's summit with, 172–74, 189
    presidential campaign of, 160–62, 172
    space program and, 163, 255
    Vietnam and, 208–12
Kennedy, Robert, 209, 227, 249
    assassination of, 256
    Cuban missile crisis and, 192, 193, 195, 199–202
Kent State incident (1970), 274
KGB, 244, 262–64, 268, 325–26, 340, 342, 346, 349–50, 352, 353, 414
Khmer Rouge, 282, 345
Khomeini, Ayatollah Ruhollah, 320, 323, 324
Khrushchev, Nikita, 132–43, 356
    agricultural initiatives of, 260, 263
    arms race and, 160, 162, 190, 217, 231, 233, 238
    Berlin and, 165–66, 170–75, 181, 182, 233
    China and, 171–72, 217, 238, 271
    coup attempt against (1957), 142–43
    Cuba and, 186, 187, 190–203, 217, 238, 263
    Hungarian uprising and, 136–42
    Kennedy's summit with, 172–74, 189
    liberal period of, 261–63
    Middle East and, 291, 292, 294–95
    ouster of, 217, 263
    Polish unrest and, 135–36, 138
    rise to power of, 125, 129
    space program and, 155, 162
    Stalin denounced by, 134–36, 142, 172, 217, 261, 262, 269, 352
    Third World and, 133–34
    U-2 incident and, 161
    US visited by, 171, 172
Killian, James, 155
Kim Il Sung, 84–89, 91, 94, 95, 102, 104, 370
King, Martin Luther, Jr., 228, 249, 250, 256, 420
Kinoy, Arthur, 113
Kirghizia, 403, 417
Kissinger, Henry, 288, 406
    Angola and, 306–8
    Chile and, 301–3
    détente and, 278, 279, 283
    Middle East and, 286, 296–99
    SALT and, 245, 311, 313
    US-China rapprochement and, 273, 275, 278
    Vietnam and, 280–81, 286
Kohl, Helmut, 341, 379–80, 392, 400, 402, 406
Komsomol, 259, 262
Korea, 83–85, 89, 127
    division of, 83–85
    postwar fate of, 21

N

Nagasaki bombing (1945), 20, 146, 147
Nagorno-Karabakh, 399–401
Nagy, Imre, 137–39, 142
Namibia, 371
napalm, 219
Nasser, Gamal Abdel, 138, 291–96
National Aeronautics and Space Administration (NASA), 159, 247
National Defense Education Act (1958), 156
National Guard, 249, 251, 255
National Lawyers Guild, 112
National Peasant Party (Hungary), 137
National Security Act, 58
National Security Agency (NSA), 352
National Security Council, 58, 75, 86, 139, 174, 209, 299, 335–37
National Union for the Total Independence of Angola (UNITA), 290, 304–7
Navy, US, 149, 189, 195, 198, 337
Nazarbayev, Nursultan, 415
Nazism, 9, 64
Nazi-Soviet Pact (1939), 10, 378, 399
Netherlands, 23, 65–67, 317
Neto, Agostinho, 304
New Deal, 8, 107
Nhu, Ngo Dinh, 208, 210, 212
Nicaragua, 188, 334–37, 340, 345, 367, 395, 420
Nicholas I, tsar of Russia, 25
Nicholas II, tsar of Russia, 4
Nicolson, Harold, 36
Nitze, Paul, 29, 86, 192
Nixon, Richard M., 162, 189, 203, 273–88, 296, 359
    arms race and, 244, 245, 273, 278–80
    Chile and, 301–2
    détente and, 270, 278–80, 283, 296, 323
    HUAC and, 108–12
    Middle East and, 283–86, 296–99
    1960 presidential campaign of, 248
    1968 presidential campaign of, 228–29, 257
    US-China rapprochement and, 273–78, 283, 319
    as vice president, 109, 157
    Vietnam and, 228, 257, 273–74, 278–82
    Watergate and, 274, 280, 282, 286–88, 297–99, 308, 311
Nobel Prize, 162, 268, 286, 308, 413
Non-Proliferation Treaty (1995), 412
Normandy landing (1944), 3, 12
North, Oliver, 367
North American Air Defense Command (NORAD), 232, 242
North Atlantic Treaty (1949), 80
North Atlantic Treaty Organization (NATO), 120, 159, 166, 182, 282, 283, 318, 323, 326, 329, 340–42, 344, 371, 375, 401, 402, 406, 412
    establishment of, 66, 80
    Germany admitted to, 129–33
    1983 exercises of, 349–50
    SS-20 missiles as threat to, 316–17
    Turkish missile sites and, 190, 191, 200–203
Norway, 23
Novotný, Antonín, 263
NSC-30, 75
NSC-48/2, 86
NSC-68, 86, 88, 91
NSC-5814, 159

nuclear energy, 340
    Chernobyl accident and, 362, 369, 421
Nuclear Non-Proliferation Treaty (1968), 244
Nuclear Test Ban Treaty (1963), 237–38, 271
nuclear weapons, 166
    ABMs, 243–44, 344, 366, 383
    Afghanistan invasion and, 327
    Berlin and, 73, 75, 170, 173, 174
    Cuban missile crisis and, 190–203, 212, 217, 231–33, 237, 238, 241–43, 263, 271, 300, 352, 353
    deployed in Eastern Europe, 264–66, 316
    and dissolution of USSR, 417
    ICBMs. See intercontinental ballistic missiles
    IRBMs, 159, 245
    Korean War and, 90, 97, 104, 105
    manufacture of, banned in Germany, 133
    massive retaliation and, 150
    Middle East conflicts and, 286, 299
    MIRVs, 244, 245, 288, 316, 322
    MRBMs, 191, 245, 272
    NSC-30 and, 75
    Sino-Soviet border clashes and, 272–73
    SLBMs, 233, 236, 237, 245, 322, 366
    Vietnam and, 213
    see also arms control; arms race; atom bomb; hydrogen bomb

O

October Revolution, 4–6, 258
October War (1973), 283–86, 296–99
Ogaden, 308–9
oil, 30, 31, 34, 286, 320–24, 330, 358
Olympic Games, 318, 328, 329, 350–51, 370
One, Two, Three, 122–23
On the Beach, 122, 123, 269
OPEC (Organization of Petroleum Exporting Countries), 286, 320, 330
Open Skies, 133
Operation Able Archer 83, 349
Operation Barbarossa, 10
Operation Desert Shield, 406
Operation Desert Storm, 410
Operation Mongoose, 189–90, 300
Operation Plainfare, 72
Operation Vittles, 72
opium, 223
Oppenheimer, J. Robert, 18, 46, 148
Organization for European Economic Cooperation (OEEC), 57
Organization of African Unity (OAU), 305, 307
Organization of American States (OAS), 186, 303
Orlov, Yuri, 318
Ortega Saavedra, Daniel, 335
Orwell, George, 268
Ostmark, 68–69
Ostpolitik, 282–83, 288
Oxford Committee, 237

P

Pace, Frank, 88
Pacific, military buildup in, 347, 348
Pakistan, 154, 273, 275, 292, 326–28, 345, 369
Palestine, 40, 292
Palestine Liberation Organization (PLO), 336
Palestinian Arabs, 40, 118, 286, 292, 296, 336

Palomares incident (1966), 238, 239
Panama, 395
Paris Accords (1973), 281
Parish, Joseph, 173
Paris Peace Conference (1946), 36, 45
Paris peace talks (1968–1973), 228–29, 280, 281
Paris summit (1960), 161, 171, 172
Parker, Dorothy, 269
Pasternak, Boris, 268, 369
Pavlov, Valentin, 410, 414
peaceful co-existence, 171, 217, 271, 280, 289, 323, 347, 356
peace movements, 236–37, 317–19, 340, 341
Pearl Harbor attack (1941), 11
Peasant Party (Poland), 26, 28
Peng De-Huai, 97
Penkovsky, Oleg, 352–53
Pentagon, anti-war protest at (1967), 255
perestroika, 355, 357, 359, 366, 368, 371, 380, 381, 387, 393–95, 406, 413, 418
Pérez de Cuéllar, Javier, 340
Permissive Action Link, 150, 236
Pershing missiles, 317–18, 323, 326, 340, 341, 349, 363, 368
Persian Gulf War (1991), 88, 402–3, 406–10
Philby, Harold "Kim," 50–51, 352
Philippines, 209, 395
Pickup on South Street, 122
Ping-Pong diplomacy, 275
Pinochet Ugarte, Augusto, 303
Pius XII, Pope, 59, 113
Podgorny, Nikolai, 263, 280
Poindexter, John, 367
Poland, 4, 5, 120, 126, 166, 225, 269, 283, 375, 399, 402, 420
    crises of 1968 in, 263, 264
    fall of Communist regime in, 376–77, 380–82
    Marshall Plan and, 50–52
    in Nazi era, 9, 10
    postwar fate of, 12, 13, 16, 19, 20, 26, 28, 36
    protests in (1956), 135–36, 138, 142, 352
    resistance crushed in, 12–13
    Solidarity movement in, 329–31, 344, 376–77, 380–82
    wartime devastation of, 22, 23, 26, 28
Polaris missiles, 160, 162, 233, 237
Polish Workers (Communist) Party, 28, 135–36, 331, 380–82
Politburo, 47
Pol Pot, 282
Polyakov, Dmitri, 353
Popular Fronts, 53, 57
Popular Movement for the Liberation of Angola (MPLA), 290, 304–7
Portugal, 304
Potsdam Conference (1945), 17, 19, 20, 28, 34, 35, 38, 39, 63, 65, 68, 83
pound, British, 24, 52
Power, Thomas, 231–36
Powers, Francis Gary, 154, 161, 172, 352
Prague Spring (1968), 263–67
Pravda, 31, 121, 133, 189, 243, 262, 263, 272
Prevention of Nuclear War (1973), 283
Pugo, Boris, 406, 413, 414, 416
purges, 120
    of McCarthy era, 113–16
    of 1930s, 6, 8, 120, 126, 132, 134
    of 1940s–1950s, 116–21